Namibia
Handbook

Sebastian Ballard & Nick Santcross

Footprint Handbooks

*We stared down in fascination ... Barren cliffs fell away
steeply into deep ravines all around the canyon like a
wild and gigantic maze. They had a name, the* gramadoelas *and as someone had aptly said, they looked as
though the devil had created them in an idle hour.*

Henno Martin, *The Sheltering Desert*

2

Footprint Handbooks

6 Riverside Court, Lower Bristol Road
Bath BA2 3DZ England
T 01225 469141 F 01225 469461
E mail handbooks@footprint.cix.co.uk
www.footprint-handbooks.co.uk

ISBN 0 900751 92 4   ISSN 1363-7495
CIP DATA: A catalogue record for this book is
available from the British Library

In North America, published by

🛂 **PASSPORT BOOKS**
a division of *NTC/Contemporary Publishing Company*
Lincolnwood, Illinois USA

4255 West Touhy Avenue, Lincolnwood
(Chicago), Illinois 60646-1975, USA
T 847 679 5500 F 847 679 24941
E mail NTCPUB2@AOL.COM

ISBN 0-8442-4905-X
Library of Congress Catalog Card
Number: 96-72517
Passport Books and colophon are registered
trademarks of NTC Publishing group

©Footprint Handbooks Limited
April 1997

**Every effort has been made to ensure that
the facts in this Handbook are accurate.
However travellers should still obtain
advice from consulates, airlines etc about
current travel and visa requirements and
conditions before travelling. The authors
and publishers cannot accept responsibility
for any loss, injury or inconvenience,
however caused.**

**The maps are not intended to have any
political significance.**

Cover design by Newell and Sorrell; cover
photography by TRIP/M Pepperell; and TRIP/S
Kaye

Production: Design by Mytton Williams;
Typesetting by Jo Morgan, Ann Griffiths and
Melanie Mason-Fayon; Maps by Sebastian
Ballard; Charts by Ann Griffiths; Original line
drawings by Andrew Newton; Proofread by
Rod Gray.

Printed and bound in Great Britain by
Clays Ltd., Bungay, Suffolk

Contents

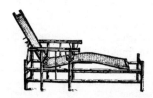

Authors

Sebastian Ballard

After living in Africa for 11 years Sebastian went on to take a degree in African and Asian Geography at the London School of Oriental and African Studies. He has visited Africa 37 times and travelled in all the countries between Nairobi and Cape Town. He has also worked in Mali and visited many of the Francophone countries. Hitchhiking back across the Sahara and visiting Djenne and Tombouctou added to his understanding and enjoyment of all things African.

Sebastian is co-author of the *South African Handbook* and has also contributed to our *India* and *Indonesia Handbooks*. He has been our cartographer since 1990. His holidays tend to be spent in Asia where he can pursue his interests in hiking, ornithology, scuba diving, following the English cricket team wherever they are playing and watching Chelsea in Europe.

Nick Santcross

After a childhood trip to Hong Kong in the early 1970s, Nick was hooked on foreign travel. Following graduation and a spell working in London he finally made it back to the Far East where he worked for 3 years. Here, in addition to learning to speak mandarin, Nick developed an abiding passion for all culinary matters Chinese, a hobby he still pursues.

In Africa, work has taken Nick first to Ghana and then on to Namibia where he now works as an advisor with the Ministry of Education. Nick's long friendship with Sebastian finally caught up with him when he was persuaded to help with the compilation of the *Namibia Handbook*. He is currently reconsidering their status as friends.

Acknowledgements

Many people have contributed to this book. These have been tremendously helpful and are acknowledged on page 297. In particular, special acknowledgements are due to Shirley Palframan for all the research on the Owamboland section and Lucy Wells for her work on the Caprivi. Sally and friend tested early notes and made some very useful suggestions. Thanks.

Our wildlife section has been based on Margaret Carswell's text published by Footprint Handbooks in the *East Africa Handbook* and we are indebted to her. The drawings of the animals are reproduced from Steele, David (1972) *Game sanctuaries of Southern Africa*, Howard Timmins: Cape Town. Illustrated by John Perry.

Special thanks

To Kate for the use of the landrover, to Andrew and Fatu who always had a welcome home and knew how to set up the perfect campsite. Margo O'Sullivan for help and advice in compiling the section on Kaokoland and in the same breath thanks to the Himba tribesmen for helping to dig out the Land Rover! In Windhoek, Dia Strauss deserves a medal for her tolerance, patience and support in humouring procrastinating editors. Her cocktails were the perfect tonic at the end of each day. Back in the UK: Dave, Claudia and Lynn continued to remind us of a good life away from the keyboard – many thanks. Finally thanks to the folks, it was a little easier this time.

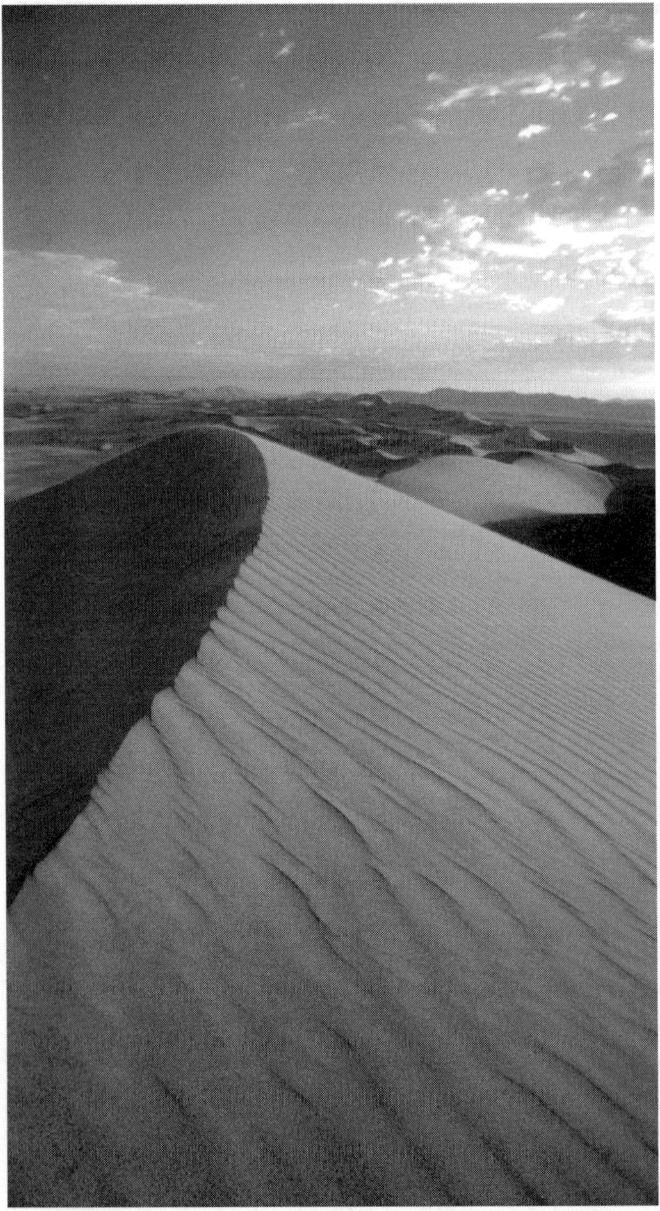

Introduction and hints

SINCE emerging from the dark ages of apartheid at Independence in 1990, Namibia has slowly been growing in popularity as a tourist destination. Without any doubt, Namibia is a land of superlatives; the oldest desert in the world, the highest sand dunes and the second largest canyon in Africa.

As a land of contrasts it is also hard to beat Namibia; from the moonscape stone desert of the south through the sand dunes of the 80 million-year-old Namib desert, the eerie Skeleton Coast where wrecked vessels lie on sand dunes washed by the ice cold waters of the South Atlantic Ocean to the endless white salt pans of Etosha and the dense forest of the Caprivi Strip, Namibia offers visitors a startling vision of Africa.

Conservation started early in Namibia – in 1907 – with the proclamation of Africa's first national park, Etosha. Since then more than 20 national parks, game reserves and resorts have been established in the country, and a total of 13% of Namibia's land area is given over to these conservation areas. There is wildlife in abundance, from Africa's "Big Five" to the most unusual species of insects specifically adapted to the arid conditions of the Namib desert. Namibia has the world's largest cheetah population – around 3,000, of which 90% live outside of proclaimed conservation areas. In the remote mountainous desert of the northwest, roam the last free-ranging desert rhino in the world and with them the uniquely adapted desert elephant follow ancient migration routes.

For visitors interested in history and culture, Namibia's history spans thousands of years, recorded first by the nomadic bushmen in the numerous sites of rock art to be seen around the country. Later migrations have brought many other peoples to the vast plains of Namibia, each with their own unique customs and lifestyles. The period of German colonial occupation has left many parts of the country with a distinctly European feel and the uniquely preserved turn-of-the-century German towns of Swakopmund and Lüderitz give visitors a taste of those colonial days.

During the 20th century, Namibia's history has been dominated by her giant neighbour, South Africa, with the philosophy of apartheid dominating the lives of all her inhabitants. During this dark period of the country's history, Namibia's peoples united to fight a heroic struggle against South Africa's illegal occupation of the country. Finally after a 23 year bush war, in 1990 Namibia became the last African country to gain Independence. Since then the country, lead by President Sam Nujoma, has pursued a policy of national reconciliation which has maintained peace and allowed democracy to flourish, setting a shining example to other African nations.

A unique blend of African and European, Namibia offer visitors the choice of exploring the African bush either in luxurious game lodges or by simply camping in the bush at one of the well-run government rest camps. With an excellent infrastructure of well-marked roads, modern telecommunications, and a genuine commitment to developing sustainable eco-friendly tourism, Namibia is an ideal place to come and experience the beauty of southern Africa.

Visitors can either organize the tour of their choice through one of the numerous safari companies or travel independently by hiring a vehicle and heading off. In both cases, though, it is worth doing some research on the flora and fauna of the country, as well as at least reading up on the country's recent history, in order to make the most of one's visit.

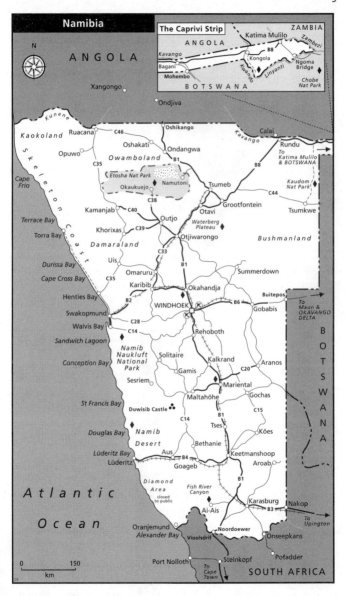

Where to go

NAMIBIA is a vast country with the attractions spread out; this means that a full visit to the country will require at least a month with a car, which can be prohibitively expensive for many people. On the other hand, careful research beforehand can help to narrow down the options of what to see and make for an enjoyable trip.

Depending on how much driving you are prepared to do, you may wish to focus more on the N or S of the country. On the other hand if you are driving through Namibia en route between Zimbabwe and South Africa you will have the chance to sample a bit of all the country, including the Kavango and Caprivi Strip regions. These are not included in the main itineraries purely for reasons of time and distance.

Below are three suggested routes of 10, 14 and 21 days respectively, which seek to take in the main places of interest for those pressed for time. They do not include special interest activities such as the Fish River Canyon Hike, a Canoe Trip down the Orange River or a safari in Kaokoland, all of which require 4 or 5 days in themselves. Depending also on whether you are more interested in a general cultural visit or a more wildlife oriented trip you may prefer to skip places such as Swakopmund or Lüderitz, and focus more on Etosha, Sossusvlei, the Naukluft Mountains and a private game lodge.

The fourth tour is for lottery winners and anyone else wishing to see Namibia at its best. Much of this tour could be arranged in advance with a specialist Namibia travel agent such as Olympia Reisen or Sunvil Discovery UK.

ROUTE 1: 10 DAYS

Day	Activity	Overnight
1& 2	Sightseeing, preparing for trip in Windhoek – short visit Daan Viljoen Game Park	Windhoek
3	Drive to Etosha	Okakuejo
4	Game drive visit Namutoni fort	Namutoni Camp (Etosha)
5	Drive through northern Damarland	Omaruru
6	Drive through Damaraland	Swakopmund
7	Welwitschia Drive/Desert Tour	Swakopmund
8	Drive through desert to Sessriem/ Sossusvlei	Camp at Sessriem
9	am early visit dunes at Sossusvlei, pm drive towards Windhoek	Naukluft Park, Zebra River Lodge, Büllsport Guestfarm
10	Drive to Windhoek	Windhoek

Suggested Tours

ANGOLA

Etosha Namutoni

Okakuejo Grootfontein

Khorixas

Waterberg

Omaruru

Swakopmund Windhoek

Rehoboth BOTSWANA

Sesriem Büllsport Intu Afrika

Duwisib

Aus Keetmanshoop

Lüderitz

Atlantic Ocean Ai-Ais

10 Day -------
21 Day - - - -

ROUTE 2: 14 DAYS

Day	Activity	Overnight
1& 2	Sightseeing, preparing for trip, visit Daan Viljoen Game Park	Windhoek
3	Drive to Etosha	Okakuejo
4	Game drive, visit Namutoni fort	Namutoni Camp (Etosha)
5	Game drive	Okakuejo
6	Drive through Damaraland to Swakopmund	Swakopmund
7	Welwitschia Drive/Desert Tour	Swakopmund
8	Drive through desert to Sessriem/ Sossusvlei	Camp at Sessriem or stay at nearby Lodge
9	am early visit dunes at Sossusvlei, p.m drive to Duwisib Castle	Duwisib Rest Camp or guestfarm in the area
10	Drive to Lüderitz via Helmeringhausen & Aus	Lüderitz
11	Kolmanskop tour Coast Tour	Lüderitz
12	Drive to Fish River Canyon	Ai-Ais Hot Springs Resort or Hobas Campsite
13	Drive Keetmanshoop: visit Quiver Tree Forest & Giant's Playground	Keetmanshoop
14	Drive Windhoek	Windhoek

ROUTE 3: 21 DAYS

Day	Activity	Overnight
1& 2	Sightseeing, Preparing for trip, visit Daan Viljoen Game Park	Windhoek

3	Drive to Waterberg (3 hrs) am, relax – short walks pm	Waterberg
4	Drive to Etosha, visit Hobas Meteorite, short stop in Tsumeb or Grootfontein	Namutoni Camp (Etosha)
5	Game drive	Halali
6	Game drive	Okakuejo Camp (Etosha)
7	Drive to Damaraland, visit Rock art at Twyfelfontein, Organ Pipes, Burnt Mountain	Aba-Huab Campsite; Damaraland Camp; Khorixas Rest Camp; Vingerklip Lodge
8	Drive via Brandberg to see White Lady to Game Farm in Omaruru Area	Ovita Game Lodge; Epako Game Lodge; Mount Etjo Safari Lodge
9	Game drive	As above
10	Drive to Swakopmund	Swakopmund
11	Sightseeing in Swakopmund, Welwitschia drive, Desert tour	Swakopmund
12	Drive through Namib Desert via Kuiseb Canyon to Sessriem/Sossusvlei	Sessriem Campsite; Lodge in area
13	am visit dunes at Sossusvlei, pm drive to Duwisib Castle	camp or bungalows at Duwisib
14	Drive to Lüderitz via Helmeringhausen & Aus	Lüderitz
15	Kolmanskop tour, Coast tour	Lüderitz
16	Drive to Fish River Canyon	Ai-Ais Hot Springs or Hobas Campsite
17	Relax at Hot Springs or 1-day hike in Canyon	Ai-Ais Hot Springs or Hobas Campsite
18	Drive to Keetmanshoop, sunset visit to Quiver Tree Forest/Giant's Playground	Keetmanshoop or Quiver Tree Forest
19 & 20	Either: drive to Intu Afrika for stay Or: drive and relax at Reho Spa/Lake Oanob Resort Or: return Windhoek and relax at Gros Barmen Hot Springs	Intu Afrika Kalahari Game Reserve, Rehoboth, Gros Barmen
21	Return to Windhoek	Windhoek

DREAM TOUR

Day	Activity	Overnight
1& 2	preparing for trip; visit Daan Viljoen Game Park	Hotel Henitzburg
3	fly to the Skeleton Coast on private safari	Khumib River base camp

4	explore the Skeleton Coast with guides on foot	base camp
5	fly up to the Kunene river for the day	base camp
6	fly down to Swakopmund	town walkabout
7	explore the town or join a tour to Walvis Bay	Swakopmund Hotel & Entertainment Centre
8	join a day tour to the Namib Desert (Afro Ventures)	Swakopmund Hotel & Entertainment Centre
9	am to yourself; pm transfer to railway station board train	Desert Express luxury train
10	arrive Windhoek 1000; pm explore town	Kalahari Sands Hotel
11	fly to Etosha National Park; pm game drive	Mokuti Lodge
12	game viewing in Etosha Park	lunch at Okaukuejo
13	fly to Victoria Falls; pm visit the falls	Victoria Falls Hotel
14	explore the town; fly over the falls; pm sundowner cruise on Zambezi	Victoria Falls Hotel
15	fly to Mpacha (Katima Mulilo), transfer by minibus to Mudumu Nat Park	Lianshulu Lodge
16	early morning bush walk; pm peaceful boat trip on Kwando	Lianshulu Lodge
17	am game drive; pm transfer to airport, fly to Windhoek	Windhoek Country Club
18	am fly to Sossusvlei; pm drive into the desert to view dunes	Sossusvlei Karos Lodge
19	am early morning balloon trip above the dunes; pm visit Sesriem Canyon	Sossusvlei Karos Lodge
20	fly back to Windhoek and catch flight back home	

ADVENTURE SPORTS

BALLOONING

With virtually all year round clear blue skies and warm sunshine, Namibia is an ideal place to go ballooning. A 1-hr trip over the desert at Sossusvlei is a favourite with many people, and there are a number of guestfarms which also offer balloon safaris. The only drawback is the expense – currently a 1-hr trip costs around N$900, champagne breakfast included. (See page 242 for a description of a balloon trip over Sossusvlei.)

CANOEING

Whether it's a casual 30 mins paddle on the Zambezi or a fully-fledged expedition down the Kunene or Orange rivers, a canoe trip down one of Namibia's perennial rivers is great fun. For wildlife enthusiasts, gliding down the river in a canoe is an excellent way of getting a close look at birds and game without frightening them away. For the brave at heart there are a number of organizations (see below) which offer the chance to shoot the rapids along the Kunene and Orange rivers (see page 267, Orange River Canoe Adventure). Prices are reasonable, with a 4 or 5-day trip starting at around N\$750 all inclusive.

Orange River Canoe Safaris: *Felix Unite*, T 00 27 21 6836433 (Cape Town); *River Rafters*, T 00 27 21 725094; *Which Way Adventures*, T 00 27 21 8522367.

GAME FISHING

Extremely popular with Namibians, fishing trips can be organized either from Walvis Bay or Swakopmund. The cold, clean waters of the South Atlantic provide rich feeding grounds for a wide range of species; contact *Mola-Mola Safaris* (see page 98).

GLIDING

Namibia is reputed to be one of the best places in the world for gliding, due to near perfect atmospheric conditions. The *Bitterwasser Flying Centre* in the Mariental District is the place to contact on T 06672 3802.

HORSE RIDING

For riding enthusiasts the best will be found on the privately-owned guest-farms, where the only limits will be the boundaries of the farms – or ranches. At guestfarms stocked with game, horse-back can be an excellent way of getting close-up to game. When booking a guest-farm check up whether riding is on offer and whether or not an accompanied game ride is possible.

HUNTING

Although, certainly not to everyone's taste, hunting is a part of Namibian life and the season runs during the winter months – June and July. Increasingly, hunting is seen as an integral part of the whole nature conservation process, allowing for the sustainable use of natural resources. There are a number of registered guestfarms specializing in guided hunting trips for visitors, and for those with the cash and the inclination, these are the places to head for. For more details, contact *Namibia Hunting & Photo Safaris*, T 061 232572.

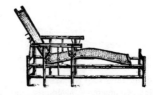

How to go

If you travelling from Europe there are two peak periods, around Christmas and between July and September. During these periods air tickets are more expensive and it is advisable to book your flight at least 3 months in advance to guarantee you can travel on the days of your choice. You can visit Namibia at anytime of the year and find good weather, but if you are interested in hiking, game viewing or birding then there are certain periods which are more suitable than others.

The climatic seasons in Namibia are in reverse to those in Europe and the United States. The peak domestic holiday season is at Christmas. During this holiday two of Namibia's most popular holiday destinations will be fully booked, Swakopmund and Etosha National Park. To help plan your trip local school holiday dates are included in the information at the back of this book.

From a weather point of view the 'best time' rather depends on what conditions you prefer. In the summer the central highlands experience temperatures in the mid-40°C. This is too hot for most people, and it is not safe to walk or play any sport in these conditions. When it rains there can be some very heavy storms. If you are driving in these conditions slow down and pull-over if the rains gets too heavy. During such weather you must always be on the look out for flash floods, especially if you are camping. Check the climatic charts within the text for the rainy seasons, but as a general rule it gets progressively more wet the further NE you travel from the coast. The best time to visit the game parks, including Etosha, is between August and September. It will not be too hot and because of the dry conditions the wild animals will be found closer to the waterholes.

A final point to take note of, and an important one of you are planning on tackling some of Namibia's hikes, is that the major trails are closed for part of the year because of extreme heat and lack of drinking water. The Fish River Canyon hike is **open** from May to the end of September; the Naukluft Mountains hike is **open** between 1 March and the third Friday in October. Advance booking is required for both of these hikes, we would recommend you plan at least a year in advance and remember that medical certificates of physical fitness need to be shown to the local ranger before starting.

You will only come across good medical facilities in Windhoek and Swakopmund. Visitors to Namibia are responsible for their own medical needs. A medical practitioner will generally arrange hospitalisation. In an emergency visitors can telephone or go directly to a hospital. The most important point to remember is the size of the country and the relative isolation of most tourist destinations. If you fall sick away from Windhoek there is a strong possibility that you will have to rely upon the air ambulance service. Make sure your health insurance will cover you for such a service. In areas such as Caprivi, Damaraland, Kaokoland and the Namib desert this is the only way of getting a patient to a hospital quickly.

WHAT TO TAKE

Pack your bags once, lift them up, and then pack them again. One advantage of visiting Namibia is that everything is available in the shops if you happen to forget something vital. If you know in advance you are going to travel by car or fly everywhere then a small suitcase is suitable. However if you plan on going on some long hikes, or camping quite a lot, then a rucksack is a more appropriate means of carrying your possessions.

It is always advisable to dress in clean smart clothes, dressing down and looking scruffy is not appreciated by anyone in Namibia. At formal functions a jacket is only necessary in the smartest of restaurants and hotels. During the day shorts are accepted everywhere, but many restaurants do not like jeans or flipflops in the evenings. It would be very unusual for an overseas visitor to be turned away because they did not have the right clothes. You will need to bring one item of warm clothing, but it is more important to bring cotton clothes which are comfortable in hot conditions.

Checklists
Air tickets
Cash
Cheque-book
Credit cards
Passport including visa
Passport photographs
Photocopies of main documents (keep separate)
Travellers' cheques

Toiletries
Comb
Concentrated detergent
Contact lens cleaner
Deodorant
Elastoplasts
Insect repellent
Nailbrush
Razor and blades
Shampoo
Sleeping tablets
Soap
Sun protection cream
Talcum powder
Tissues and toilet paper
Toothbrush
Toothpaste
Vaseline/moisturizer

Other
Ear plugs
Electric plug adaptor
Eye mask
Folding umbrella
Inflatable cushion
Lock and chain (securing luggage at night)
Multiple outlet adaptor
Short-wave radio and batteries
Small torch plus batteries
Sun glasses
Swiss army knife
Water bottle

Those intending to stay in budget accommodation might also include:
Cotton sheet sleeping bag
Money belt
Padlock (for hotel room and pack)
Soap
Student card
Towel
Toilet paper
Universal bath plug

Health kit
Anti-acid tablets
Anti-diarrhoea tablets
Anti-malaria tablets
Anti-infective ointment
Condoms
Contraceptives
Dusting powder for feet
First aid kit and disposable needles
Flea powder
Sachets of rehydration salts
Tampons
Travel sickness pills
Water sterilizing tablets

MONEY

Travellers' cheques can be exchanged with ease at high street banks in most provincial centres. Many visitors are starting to make use the Automatic Tellar Machines (ATM's) to obtain cash. There are several advantages when using these machines; they are open 24 hours a day, the commission charged works out less than the cost of buying travellers cheques and the charge levied by each bank when you cash the cheque and finally it is a much quicker way of obtaining money. If you are planning on spending a lot of time in Damaraland and Kaokoland make sure you have sufficient cash, there are no foreign exchange facilities in these regions.

ISIC

Anyone in full-time education is entitled to an International Student Identity Card (ISIC). These are issued by student travel offices and travel agencies across the world and offer special rates on all forms of transport and other concessions and services. The ISIC head office is: ISIC Association, Box 9048, 1000 Copenhagen, Denmark, T (45) 33 93 93 00.

GETTING THERE

AIR

There are direct flights to Windhoek from London (Heathrow) and Frankfurt. Visitors from the United States will have to fly to Europe first or look into a direct flight to South Africa. For many visitors it may be easier to fly to Cape Town or Johannesburg and then transfer to a daily flight to Windhoek. Check with your local travel agent for the exact timings if you do not wish to overnight in South Africa. If you are in a neighbouring country there is a flight once a week from Harare or Lusaka to Windhoek.

ROAD

It is possible to enter Namibia by road from Angola, South Africa, Botswana and Zambia. There are long distance bus services, overland trucks and private cars using these routes. If you are crossing in a private car you must be in possession of a blue book, insurance and a driver's licence with a photograph. At quieter border crossings officials can be very inconsistent in their interpretation of the laws. Border times are listed on page 284.

DISABLED TRAVEL

South Africa is not an impossible destination for the disabled visitor. There are a couple of organizations to contact in advance, but in general this is a very sympathetic destination.

SAFETY

Since independence Namibia has enjoyed a remarkably crime free existence as far as the tourist is concerned. In Windhoek it would be sensible to observe the usual precautions when on holiday. This is not a city where you are continually being warned about where you can and cannot go, however it is never advisable to flaunt your wealth in the poorer suburbs. Elsewhere in the country visitors will find most of Namibia friendly and safe. However always remove or hide valuables in a car when left unattended.

WHERE TO STAY

The quality of hotels in Namibia has improved markedly during the last few years, but there are still no 5-star hotels. On the otherhand the country is blessed with some superb private Guestfarms which cater for small groups. By their nature these establishments are all located in the bush away from urban centres. The South African influence is very strong, campsites have good clean facilities and the national parks camps are efficient and good value. For many local residents the hotels are too expensive for their holidays, consequently the service is sometimes substandard since visitors are less likely to return. This is an area which is currently improving. Close to all the major tourist attractions you will either find a hotel or several guestfarms. Windhoek and Swakopmund have a few Bed & Breakfast style houses. For the budget traveller Namibia used to be very limiting, but once again the situation has changed over the last year or so and several new backpacker establishments have sprung up. But the budget visitor may well have to camp in Namibia more often than not.

Camping

If you are used to camping and have all the equipment this is the cheapest and most flexible way of seeing Namibia. Make sure you hire a car which has sufficient space to carry everything. Just about every town has a municipal campsite, many have chalets. The sites tend to be well grassed and shady. The wash blocks are kept very clean and there is always plenty of hot water. For most of the year the weather is ideal for camping. The only problem at campsites is petty theft in built up areas.

FOOD AND DRINK

Food

Namibia is not a good destination for vegetarians. This is a great meat and fish eating country. Taken as a whole the food is very bland and the visitor will not enjoy too many exotic meals. There are plenty of cheap fast food outlets close to bus stations and long distance taxi stands.

With the current exchange rate eating out is good value, but the more expensive restaurants are now charging prices which are on a par with restaurants in Europe. Outside of the major tourist centres people tend to eat early and many kitchens will close around 2100, except at the weekend. Many private restaurants are closed on Sunday evenings when a hotel dining room may well be the only choice for eating out.

Water

Tap water in Namibian towns is chemically treated and safe to drink. Bottled mineral water is available from most shops. There is also a good range of fruit juices available at most outlets including petrol stations.

GETTING AROUND

AIR

There is a far reaching, safe and efficient domestic service run by Air Namibia from Eros Airport. All the major towns can be reached within a couple of hours flying time of each other. If you make your reservations from overseas there are some good value deals available. When you consider the time saved, taking an internal flight can be a very attractive proposition.

TRAIN

The train network has been cut back in recent years and is a very slow means of getting about. Seats can be reserved in advance, but few visitors use the service. For example it takes all night to travel between Windhoek and Swakopmund; by bus the journey is a little over 4 hours, and you get to see the desert enroute.

DRIVING IN NAMIBIA

For most visitors to Namibia the easiest and most practical way of seeing the country is to hire a car. Whilst generally speaking most of the roads in Namibia are well-maintained the numbers of accidents that occur on Namibian roads, involving both residents and visitors, is alarmingly high. The majority of accidents involving visitors to Namibia are unnecessary and are caused by speeding, fatigue and over-confidence in unfamiliar conditions. Visitors are therefore strongly recommended to exercise caution when driving in Namibia and to follow these tips and guidelines.

Hire cars

There are a large number of car hire companies to choose from, and between them they offer a wide range of on and off-road vehicles. However, car hire is not cheap, and even if you take out collision damage waiver insurance (which you are strongly advised to do), you will still be liable for excess payments in the event that you overturn a car, hit an animal, or damage the car by driving through rough terrain. **Check what you are liable for when renting the car**.

Local conditions

Roads in Namibia tend to be long and straight and the temptation is to put one's foot down. However, for most of the year the weather is very hot and the combination of the heat and the glare from the sun make driving tiring for those not accustomed to the heat. **Drink lots of water, stop or change drivers regularly and try to avoid driving during the hottest part of the day whenever possible**.

Animals

All over Namibia, but particularly in the N, wild animals and cattle are liable to wander across the road at any time, and many accidents are the result of collisions between cars and animals. **You are strongly advised never to drive at night when the risk of hitting animals is greatest**.

Other vehicles

It is unfortunately the case that a proportion of the vehicles on Namibian roads are overloaded and/or poorly maintained. On weekends the main routes around the country can be very busy, as people return to their villages, go to the farm or visit friends. Drinking and driving is not uncommon at these times, and caution should always be exercised when passing other vehicles.

Fuel and water

Although there is an extensive network of modern, efficient service stations around the country, in some of the more remote areas, such as Damaraland, the Kaokoland, the Caprivi and parts of the S, garages can be far apart. Keep a spare canister with a minimum of 20 litres of fuel in the boot at all times. Likewise, once you are off the main roads you are unlikely to see many other vehicles, so make sure you have plenty of water with you in the event that you break down.

Driving on gravel roads

Even if you intend only to visit the main attractions in Namibia such as the Fish River Canyon and Sossusvlei, you will end up driving on gravel roads. These vary in quality between very good and very poor. However, appearances can be deceptive and even a flat, well maintained gravel surface needs to be approached with caution. A very high number of accidents in Namibia involve drivers overturning their vehicles on the gravel, many of whom end up dead. The following guidelines should be observed:

● keep your speed down to between 80 and 100 km per hour

● observe all road signs

● follow the tracks other cars have left

● slow down before curves by easing your foot off the accelerator

● avoid sudden braking as this will cause the vehicle to career across the road

● when overtaking other vehicles put on your headlights so that on-coming vehicles can more easily see you

● on corrugated surfaces accelerate gently until you find the right speed so that you hardly feel the corrugations

● tyre pressures should be slightly lower on gravel, check regularly

● ensure that you wrap up cameras, walkmans etc when driving on gravel, as within a few minutes everything will be covered in dust; if you intend to do a lot of driving on gravel, you may wish to hire a car with a/c, thereby allowing you to keep the windows closed.

Driving on sand

If you intend to visit Bushmanland or the

Kaokoland you may well end up driving on sand. The following points are worth remembering:

● ensure you have suitable tyres on your vehicle and that the tyre pressure is correct (lower than normal)
● remember that sand is firmest when cool, ie early morning and late afternoon
● keep the vehicle moving at all times and stick to low gears
● carry a spade and a tow rope

If stuck:

● do not over-rev the engine
● deflate the tyres by pressing on the valve and counting to 10 in the first instance and repeat if necessary
● rock the vehicle backwards and forwards to free the wheels from sand

HITCHHIKING

Hitchhiking (hiking) is extremely common in Namibia, and for many Namibians it is the only way they can travel around the country. It is however not uncommon for drivers to charge a fee for picking up hikers, and visitors planning to hike should expect to pay for lifts, especially on longer journeys. At the same time you may wish to think twice about accepting lifts on the back of open pick-up trucks (*bakkies*), as your chances of survival in the event of the vehicle overturning are not good. Apart from anything else, riding on an open bakkie means you are exposed to the elements and is an extremely uncomfortable way of travelling.

Women can and do hitchhike, either alone or in pairs, but bearing in mind the alarming increase in rape in the country, it may not be a good idea for women unfamiliar with the country to hitchhike on their own.

LANGUAGE

English is widely spoken and understood. There are a few pockets where German is only spoken, but people should understand enough English to meet your needs. Many of the white people will speak Afrikaans is in the S and Windhoek.

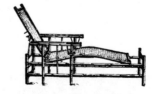

Writing to us

Many people write to us - with corrections, new information, or simply comments. If you want to let us know something, we would be delighted to hear from you. Please give us as precise information as possible, quoting the edition and page number of the Handbook you are using and send as early in the year as you can. Your help will be greatly appreciated, especially by other travellers. In return we will send you details about our special guidebook offer.

For hotels and restaurants, please let us know:

- each establishment's name, address, phone and fax number
- number of rooms, whether a/c or air-cooled, attached (clean?) bathroom
- location - how far from the station or bus stand, or distance (walking time) from a prominent landmark
- if it's not already on one of our maps, can you place it?
- your comments - either good or bad - as to why it is distinctive
- tariff cards
- local transport used

For places of interest:

- location
- entry, camera charge
- access - by whatever means of transport is most approriate, eg time of main buses or trains to and from the site, journey time, fare
- facilities - nearby drinks stalls, restaurants, for the disabled
- any problems, eg steep climb, wildlife, unofficial guides
- opening hours
- site guides

Horizons

It is a reasonable assumption that anyone interested enough in wildlife to be travelling on safari in Africa is also able to identify the more well known and spectacular African animals. For example an **Elephant** (*Loxodonta africana*) or a **Lion** (*Panthera leo*) can hardly be confused with anything else, so they have not been described in great detail here. It is indeed fortunate that many of the large and spectacular animals are also on the whole fairly common, so you will have a very good chance of seeing them on even a fairly short safari. They are often known as the Big Five. Unfortunately, no one agrees on quite which species constitute the Big Five! The term was originally coined by hunters who wanted to take home trophies of their safari. Thus it was, that, in hunting parlance, the Big Five were **Elephant**, **Black Rhino**, **Buffalo**, **Lion** and **Leopard**. Nowadays the **Hippopotamus** (*Hippopotamus amphibius*) is usually considered one of the Big Five for those who shoot with their cameras, whereas the Buffalo is far less of a 'trophy'. Equally photogenic and worthy to be included are the **Zebra**, **Giraffe** and **Cheetah**.

But whether they are the Big Five or the Big Nine these are the animals that most people come to Namibia to see, and, with the possible exception of the Leopard, and the White Rhino, you have an excellent chance of seeing all of the animals in Etosha National Park. Namibia also has a number of privately owned Guestfarms and Game Ranches which offer good game viewing opportunities, but perhaps not the variety of wildlife that you will find in the larger national parks. Some of the private concessions represent the luxury top end of the game viewing safari market; it is worth bearing in mind that when you pay top dollar there is far greater pressure on the operator to guarantee his guests see the Big Five or Big Nine. This takes something out of the thrill of game viewing when you know you are just as likely to see a Rhino or a Leopard as you are a family of Impala. Yes you have the pleasure of seeing all these magnificent animals, but a lot of the thrill in looking for them at dawn or dusk has gone.

Of the more well known animals the only two that could possibly be confused are the **Leopard** and the **Cheetah**. The **Leopard** (*Panthera pardus*) is less likely to be seen as it is more nocturnal and more secretive in its habits compared with the Cheetah. It frequently rests during the heat of the day on the lower branches of trees. A good place for viewing leopard is *Tsaobis Leopard Nature Park* close to Otjimbingwe.

The **Cheetah** (*Acinonyx jubatus*) is well known for its running speed. In short bursts it has been recorded at over 90 km per hour. But they are not as successful at hunting as you might expect with such a speed advantage. They have a very specialized build which is

Cheetah
Source: Steele, David (1972) *Game sanctuaries of Southern Africa* Howard Timmins: Cape Town. Illustrated by John Perry

long and thin with a deep chest, long legs and a small head. But the fore-limbs are restricted to a forward and backward motion which makes it very difficult for the cheetah to turn suddenly when in hot pursuit of a small antelope. They are often seen in family groups walking across the plains or resting in the shade. The black 'tear' mark on the face is usually obvious through binoculars. Any visit to a private game farm in Namibia should be rewarded with a sighting of cheetah, Namibia has the largest population in southern Africa of cheetah not contained within national parks. The excellent *Okonjima Guestfarm*, 50 km from Otjiwarongo, is home to the Africat-Foundation, here guests are guaranteed to see cheetah and leopard in natural and artificial surroundings.

Elephants are awe-inspiring by their very size and it is wonderful to watch a herd at a waterhole. Although they have suffered terribly from the activities of war and poachers in recent decades they are still readily seen in many of the game areas, and you will not be disappointed by the sight of them. Everyone has their elephant tale. But it is the Rhinoceros which has suffered the most from poaching. Both species are on the verge of extinction, if there had been no moves to save them during the last 20 years they probably would have gone from the wild by now. The **White Rhino** (*Ceratotherium simum*) and the **Black Rhino**

(*Diceros bicornis*) occurred naturally in Namibia. Although today you will find that in many of the reserves where you find them they have in fact been reintroduced. Their names have no bearing on the colour of the animals as they are both a rather nondescript dark grey. The name White Rhino is derived from the Dutch word 'weit' which means wide and refers to the shape of the animal's mouth. The White Rhino has a large square muzzle and this reflects the fact that it is a grazer and feeds by cropping grass. The Black Rhino on the other hand, is a browser, usually feeding on shrubs and bushes. It achieves this by using its long, prehensile upper lip which is well adapted to the purpose.

The horn of the rhino is not a true horn, but is made of a material called keratin, which is essentially the same as hair. If you are fortunate enough to see Rhino with their young you will notice that the White Rhino tends to herd its young in front of it, whereas the Black Rhino usually leads its young from the front. The White Rhino is a more sociable animal, they are likely to be seen in family groups of 5 or more. Their preferred habitat is grasslands and open savanna with mixed scrub vegetation. The Black Rhino lives in drier bush country and usually alone. They will browse on twigs, leaves and tree bark. Visitors to Etosha National Park have a good chance of seeing Rhino with their young at one of the three floodlit water holes in the evening. It is worth staying up late one night to see these magnificent ancient creatures.

The **Buffalo** (*Syncerus caffer*), once revered by the hunter as the greatest challenge for a trophy. But more hunters have lost their lives to this animal than to any other. This is an immensely strong animal with particularly acute senses. Left alone as a herd they pose no more of a threat than a herd of domestic cattle. The danger lies in the unpredictable behaviour of the lone bull.

These animals, cut off from the herd, become bad-tempered and easily provoked. While you are more likely to see them on open plains they are equally at home in dense forest. To see a large herd peacefully grazing is a great privilege and one to remember as you continue your safari. Mahango Game Reserve in the Caprivi strip has a good record for sightings of herds of buffalo.

The most conspicuous animal of inland waters is the **Hippopotamus** (*Hippopotamus amphibius*). A large beast with short stubby legs, but nevertheless quite agile on land. They can weigh up to 4 tonnes. During the day it rests in the water, rising every few minutes to snort and blow at the surface. At night they leave the water and to graze. A single adult animal needs up to 60 kilos of grass every day, and to manage this obviously has to forage far. They do not eat aquatic vegetation. The nearby banks of the waterhole with a resident Hippo population will be very bare and denuded of grass. Should you meet a Hippo on land by day or night keep well away. If you get between it and its escape route to the water, it may well attack. They are restricted to water not only because its skin would dry up if not kept damp but because the body temperature is regulated closely to 96.8°F. It is essentially an aquatic animal and needs to live in a medium where the temperature changes relatively slowly. Mudumu, Mamili and Mahango Game Parks all have family groups of Hippo, if you are lucky you may also see them in the vicinity of Popa Falls restcamp.

The **Giraffe** (*Giraffa camelopardalis*) may not be as magnificent as a full grown Lion, nor as awe-inspiring as an Elephant buts its elegance is unsurpassed. To see a small party of Giraffe strolling across the plains is seeing Africa as it has been for hundreds of years. You should note that in the giraffe both male and female animals have horns, though in the female they may be smaller. A mature male can be over 5m high to the top of its head. The lolloping gait of the giraffe is very distinctive and it produces this effect by the way it moves its legs at the gallop. A horse will move its diagonally opposite legs together when galloping, but the giraffe moves both hind legs together and both fore legs together. It achieves this by swinging both hind legs forward and outside the fore legs. They have excellent sight and acute hearing. They are browsers, and can eat the leaves and twigs of a large variety of tall trees, thorns presenting no problem. Their only natural threat are lions who will attack young animals when they are drinking.

The **Zebra** is the last of the easily recognized animals. There are two common types in Namibia, **Burchell's Zebra** (*Equus burchelli*) and **Hartmann's Mountain Zebra** (*Equus zebra hartmannae*). Generally Hartmann's mountain zebra only occurs in mountainous areas close to the Namib desert. They are found in three isolated pockets. In Kaokoland and as far S as the Brandberg, along the escarpment to the S of the Swakop River and in the Huns Mountains close to the Fish River Canyon. Burchell's Zebra will often be seen in large herds, sometimes with antelope. You are most likely to see them in Etosha National Park. It stands 145-150 cm at the shoulder. Hartmann's mountain zebra is larger than Burchell's zebra, it stands 160 cm at the shoulder. As the name suggests it lives in hills and stony mountains. They are good climbers and can tolerate arid conditions, going without water for up to three days. During the heat of the day they seek shade and keep very still, making spotting them more difficult. They are closely related to the Cape Mountain Zebra, but stand about 25 cm taller than the southern sub-species.

THE LARGER ANTELOPE

The first animals that you will see on safari will almost certainly be antelope. These occur on the open plains. Although there are many different species, it is not difficult to distinguish between them. For presentation purposes they have been divided into the larger antelopes which stand about 120 cm or more at the shoulder; and the smaller ones about 90 cm or less. They are all ruminant plains animals, they are herbivores like Giraffe and the Zebra, but they have keratin covered horns which makes them members of the family *Bovidae*. They vary greatly in appearance from the small Dik-diks to the large Eland, once you have learnt to recognize the different sets of horns, identification of species should not be too difficult.

The largest of all the antelopes is the **Eland** (*Taurotragus oryx*) it stands at 175-183 cm at the shoulder. It is cow-like in appearance, with a noticeable dewlap and shortish spiral horns, present in both sexes. The general colour varies from greyish to fawn, sometimes with a rufous tinge, with narrow white stripes on the sides of the body. It occurs in herds of up to 30 in a wide variety of grassy and mountainous habitats. Even during the driest periods of the year the animals appear in excellent condition.

Eland
Source: Steele, David (1972) *Game sanctuaries of Southern Africa* Howard Timmins: Cape Town.
Illustrated by John Perry

Research has shown that they travel large distances in search of food and that they will eat all sorts of tough woody bushes and thorny plants.

Not quite as big, but still reaching 140-153 cm at the shoulder, is the **Greater Kudu** (*Tragelaphus strepsiceros*) which prefers fairly thick bush, sometimes in quite dry areas. You are most likely to see them in the northern areas of Etosha National Park and in the much smaller Mahango Game Park. Although nearly as tall as the Eland it is a much more slender and elegant animal altogether. Its general colour also varies from greyish to fawn and it has several white stripes running down the sides of the body. Only the male carries horns, which are very long and spreading, with only two or three twists along the length of the horn. A noticeable and distinctive feature is a thick fringe of hair which runs from the chin down the neck. Greater Kudu usually live in family groups of not more than half a dozen individuals, but occasionally larger herds up to about 30 can be seen.

The **Roan Antelope** (*Hippotragus equinus*) and **Sable Antelope** (*Hippotragus niger*) are similar in general shape, though the Roan is somewhat bigger, being 140-145 cm at the shoulder, compared to the 127-137 cm of the Sable. In both species, both sexes carry ringed horns which curve backwards, and these are particularly long in the Sable. There is a horse-like mane present in both animals. The Sable is usually glossy black with white markings on the face and a white belly. The female is often a reddish brown in colour. The Roan can vary from dark rufous to a reddish fawn and also has white markings on the face. The black males of the Sable are easily identified, but the brownish individuals can be mistaken for the Roan. Look for the tufts of hair at the tips of the rather long ears of the Roan (absent in the Sable). The Roan generally is found in open grassland. Both the Roan and the

Sable live in herds. Kaudom Game Park is home to the largest Roan population in Namibia, there are also small herds in Etosha which were originally transported from Kaudom. Sable can be seen in the Waterberg Plateau Park as well as Kaudom and the Caprivi region; attempts to introduce them to Etosha have failed.

Another antelope with a black and white face is the **Gemsbok** (*Oryx gazella*), which stands at 122 cm at the shoulder. They are large creatures with a striking black line down the spine and a black stripe between the coloured body and the white underparts. The head is white with further black markings. This is not an animal you would confuse with another. Their horns are long, straight and sweep back behind their ears, from face on they look V-shaped. The female also has horns but overall the animal is of a slightly lighter build. One of the lasting images of Namibia is a picture of a single gemsbok with the sand dunes of Sossusvlei as a backdrop. Visitors to Etosha will see large herds close to the waterholes, you will also see gemsbok in the Namib-Naukluft desert, western Damaraland and the Unaib Delta in the Skeleton Coast National Park.

The **Wildebeest** or **Gnu** (*Connochaetes taurinus*) is a large animal about 132 cm high at the shoulder, looking rather like an American bison in the distance. The impression is strengthened by its buffalo-like horns (in both sexes) and humped appearance. The general colour is blue grey with a few darker stripes down the side. It has a noticeable beard and long mane. They are often found grazing with herds of Zebra. Blue Wildebeest migrate into Etosha during the summer months in search of fresh grasslands, their numbers have been greatly reduced by the construction of game fences and attacks from predators around artificial water points.

The **Common Waterbuck** (*Kobus ellipsiprymnus*) stands at about 122-137 cm at the shoulder, it has a shaggy grey-

Gemsbok
Source: Steele, David (1972) *Game sanctuaries of Southern Africa* Howard Timmins: Cape Town.
Illustrated by John Perry

brown skin which is very distinctive. The males have long, gently curving horns which are heavily ringed. There are two species which can be distinguished by the white mark on their buttocks. In the Common Waterbuck there is a clear half ring on the rump and round the tail. In the other species, the Defassa Waterbuck, the ring is a filled-in white patch on the rump. Although they no longer occur in Mudumu National Park, due to hunting, herds of waterbuck can be seen in the remote marshlands and flood plains of Mamili National Park.

There are three other species of antelope that you can expect to see in the wetlands of Caprivi; red lechwe, sitatunga and puku. **Red Lechwe** (*Kobus leche leche*), is a medium sized antelope standing at about 100 cm at the shoulder. They are bright chestnut in colour, with black markings on the legs. Only the males have horns. The horns are relatively thin, they rise upwards before curving outwards and backwards forming a double curve. Only the sitatunga is known to favour the aquatic environment more than the lechwe. In the past herds of over a thousand were recorded, but hunting and the destruction of habitat has seen their numbers fall to less than a tenth of the numbers 50 years ago. In Namibia you can still be sure of seeing Lechwe along the Kavango or Kwando rivers in the Caprivi region. They tend to feed on grass and water plants, favouring water-meadows. As the river levels rise and fall so the herds migrate to the greenest pastures. All of the large cats as well as wild dog and hyaena prey upon the lechwe. They are unable to move fast on dry land, so when they feel threatened they will take refuge in shallow pools, if needs be they are very good swimmers. **Puku** (*Kobus adenota vardoni*) favour a similar habitat to the red lechwe, but you are only likely to see them in small numbers in Mamili National Park. They have a golden yellow long hair coat and stand at about 100 cm at the shoulder. Their underparts are white and there are no black markings on the legs. The horns are thick and short with heavy rings, only the males have horns. They usually live in small groups of 5-10 animals, but during the mating season the males gather in groups and will strongly defend their respective territories. The chances of spotting the **Sitatunga** (*Tragelaphus sekei*) are rare since this species of antelope favours swampy areas where there are thick reed beds to hide in. It is the largest of the aquatic antelope standing at 115 cm at the shoulder. If you only catch a glimpse of the animal you can be sure it was a sitatunga if the hindquarters were higher than the forequarters. Their coat is long and shaggy with a grey brown colour, they have thin white stripes similar to those of the bushbuck. The horns are long, twisted and swept back. They have long hooves which are highly adapted to soft, marshy soils. When frightened they will enter the water and submerge entirely, with just their snout breaking the surface. This is a very shy antelope which few visitors will see, but if you spend some time at a quiet location by the river you may be rewarded with a sighting as they quietly move through the reedbeds. Mamili and Mahango are the best locations for viewing the sitatunga.

The **Red Hartebeest** (*Alcephalus caama*) stands about 127-132 cm at the shoulder. It has an overall rufous appearance with a conspicuous broad light patch on the lower rump. The back of their neck, chin, and limbs have traces of black. Small herds can be seen at Hardap Dam, Kaudom and Etosha National Park. The hartebeest has the habit of posting sentinels, which are solitary animals who stand on the top of termite mounds keeping a watch out for predators. If you see an animal on its 'knees' digging the earth with its horns then it is marking its territory, they are very territorial in behaviour. Their slightly odd appearance is caused by its sloping withers and a very long face. They have short horns which differ from any other animal, they are situated on a bony pedicel, a backward extension of the skull which forms a base.

Finally, you have a good chance of seeing the Nyala on your travels. The **Nyala** (*Tragelaphus angasi*) stands about 110 cm at the shoulder. Although large in appearance it is slenderly built and has a narrow frame. This is disguised, in part, by a long shaggy coat, dark brown in colour with a mauve tinge. The lower legs are a completely different colour, light sandy brown. When fully grown the horns have a single open curve sweeping backwards. Look out for a conspicuous white streak of hair along the

Nyala
Source: Steele, David (1972) *Game sanctuaries of Southern Africa* Howard Timmins: Cape Town.
Illustrated by John Perry

back. Another feature which helps identification is a white chevron between the eyes and a couple of white spots on the cheek. The female is very different, firstly they are significantly smaller and they do not have horns. Their coat is more orange than brown in colour, the white stripes on the body are very clear.

Their numbers have been threatened in the past and their status has been one of endangered. You should consider yourself fortunate if you enjoy a clear sighting on safari. They like to live in dense bush and the 'savanna veld'. You will always find them close to water, which makes the task of finding them a little easier once you have located the water holes. They are known to gather in herds of up to 30, but a small family group is more likely. One interesting aspect of their life is that they are almost exclusively browsers. Research has shown their diet to consist of wild fruits, pods, twigs and leaves. They will eat fresh young tender grass shoots after the first rains.

THE SMALLER ANTELOPES

The most well known of the antelope species in Namibia is the **Springbuck** (*Antidorcas marsupialis*), or Springbok, as it is called in Afrikaans. It stands 76-84 cm to the shoulder. It is the only gazelle found S of the Zambezi River. The upper part of the body is fawn, it is separated from the white underparts by a dark brown lateral stripe. A distinguishing feature is a reddish brown stripe which runs between the base of the horns and the mouth, passing through the eye. When startled they start to 'pronk'. The head is lowered almost to the feet, the legs are fully extended with hoofs bunched together. Then the animal takes off, shooting straight up into the air for some 2 to 3m, before dropping down and shooting up again as though it were on coiled springs.

The remaining common antelopes are a good deal smaller than those described above. The largest and most frequently seen of these is the **Impala** (*Aepyceros melampus*). The Impala stands 92-107 cm at the shoulder and is bright rufous in colour with a white abdomen. From behind the white rump, with black lines on each side, is characteristic. Only the male carries the long lyre shaped horns. Just above the heels of the hind legs is a tuft of thick black bristles, which are surprisingly easy to see as the animal runs. This is unique to the Impala. Also easy to see is the black mark on the side of the abdomen, just in front of the back leg. They are noted for their graceful leaps which they make as they are running after being startled. You are most likely to see them in herds in the grasslands but they also live in light woodlands. They are the most numerous of the smaller antelope and no matter what the state of the veld they always appear to be in immaculate condition. During the breeding season male animals fight to protect, or gather their own harem. It is great fun to come across such a herd and pause to watch the male trying to keep an eye on all of the group. Young males may be seen in small groups until they are able to form their own harem. In parts of Etosha National Park you will see a distinct sub-species, the **Black-**

Springbuck
Source: Steele, David (1972) *Game sanctuaries of Southern Africa* Howard Timmins: Cape Town.
Illustrated by John Perry

Faced Impala, which as its name implies as a black streak on the face, aside from this it is identical in appearance to the common impala.

The **Bohor Reedbuck** (*Redunca redunca*) is often seen in the Caprivi game parks, it stands 68-89 cm at the shoulder. The horns are sharply hooked forwards at the tip. Their general colour is described as reddish fawn, they have white underparts and a short bushy tail. It lives in pairs or small family groups. During the hottest time of day they will seek out shelter in reed beds or long grasses and are never far from water.

Another tiny antelope is the **Oribi** (*Ourebia ourebi*), which stands around 61 cm at the shoulder. Like the Reedbuck it has a patch of bare skin just below each ear, but that's where the similarities end. The Oribi is slender and delicate looking. Its colour tends to be sandy to brownish fawn. Their ears are oval-shaped. Horns are short and straight with a few rings at their base. They live in small groups or as a pair. As the day-time temperatures rise, so the Oribi seeks out its 'hide' in long grass or the bush. Like the Reedbuck they never like to venture far from water. Mudumu National Park has a few family groups.

The last two of the common smaller antelopes are the Bushbuck and the Dik-dik. The **Bushbuck** (*Tragelaphus scriptus*) is about 76-92 cm at the shoulder. The coat has a shaggy appearance and a variable pattern of white spots and stripes on the side and back. There are in addition two white crescent shaped marks on the front of the neck. The horns, present in the male only, are short, almost straight and slightly spiral. The animal has a curious high rump which gives it a characteristic crouching appearance. The white underside of the tail is noticeable when it is running. The Bushbuck tends to occur in areas of thick bush especially near water. They lie up during the day in thickets, but are often seen bounding away when disturbed. They are usually seen either in pairs or singly. **Damara Dik-dik** (*Rhynchotragus kirki*) is so small it can hardly be mistaken for any other antelope, it only stands 36-41 cm high and weighs only 5 kg. In colour it is a greyish brown, often washed with rufous. The legs are noticeably thin and stick-like, giving the animal a very fragile appearance. The snout is slightly elongated which it wriggles from side to side, it has a conspicuous tuft of hair on the top of the head. Only the male carries the very small straight horns. The Damara Dik-dik is considered to be the same species as Kirk's Dik-dik which occurs in East Africa, what is so unusual is that there are no recorded sightings in between these two regions.

OTHER MAMMALS

Although the antelope are undoubtedly the most numerous animals to be seen on the plains, there are others worth keeping an eye open for. Some of these are scavengers which thrive on the kills of other animals. They include the dog-like **Jackals**, you are likely to come across two species in Etosha National Park, both are about 41-46 cm at the shoulder. The **Side-striped Jackal** (*Canis adustus*) is greyish fawn and it has a rather variable and sometimes ill-defined stripe along the side. The **Black-backed Jackal** (*Canis mesomelas*) is more common and will often be seen near a Lion kill. It is a rather foxy reddish fawn in colour with a noticeable black area on its back. This black part is sprinkled with a silvery white which can make the back look silver in some lights. They are timid creatures which can be seen by day or night.

The other well known plains scavenger is the **Spotted Hyaena** (*Crocuta crocuta*). It is a fairly large animal being about 69-91 cm at the shoulder. Its high shoulders and low back give it a characteristic appearance. It is brownish with dark spots and has a large head. Usually occurs singly or in pairs, but occasionally in small packs. Few people talk of the Hyaena in a complimentary manner. This is as much to do with their gait as their scavenging habits. But they play an important role in keeping the countryside clean. When hungry they are aggressive creatures, they have been known to attack live animals and will occasionally try to steel a kill from lions. They always look dirty because of their habit of lying in muddy pools which may be to keep cool or alleviate the irritation of parasites. Both jackal and hyaena are occasionally spotted along the coast of the Skeleton Coast National Park where they scavenge for carrion.

Another aggressive scavenger is the **African Wild Dog** or **Hunting Dog** (*Lycaon pictus*). These creatures are easy to identify since they have all the features of a large mongrel dog. They have a large head and a slender body. Their coat is a mixed pattern of dark shapes and white and yellow patches, no two dogs are quite alike. The question is not what do they look like, but whether you will be fortunate and see one. They are seriously threatened by extinction. In many areas of Namibia they have already been wiped out. The problem it seems is a conflict between the farmer and conservation. The dogs live and hunt in packs. They are particularly vicious when hunting their prey, they will chase the animal until it is exhausted and then start taking bites out of it while it is still alive. Their favourites are Reedbuck and Impala.

A favourite and common plains animal is the comical **Warthog** (*Phacochoerus aethiopicus*). They are unmistakable being almost hairless and grey in general colour with a very large head with tusks and wart-like growths on the face. These are thought to protect the eyes as it makes sweeps sideways into the earth with its tusks, digging up roots and tubers. Often they kneel on their forelegs when eating. They frequently occur in family parties.

Warthog
Source: Steele, David (1972) *Game sanctuaries of Southern Africa* Howard Timmins: Cape Town.
Illustrated by John Perry

When startled the adults will run at speed with their tails held straight up in the air followed by the young. Look out for them around the edges of waterholes, they love to cake themselves in the thick mud. This helps to keep them both cool and free of ticks and flies.

In rocky areas, such as the Waterberg Plateau, look out for an animal that looks a bit like a large grey-brown guinea pig. This is the **Dassie** or **Rock Hyrax** (*Heterohyrax brucei*), an engaging and fairly common animal. During the morning and afternoon you will see them sunning themselves on the rocks. They have the habit of always defecating in the same place, and where the urine runs down the rock face the latter can have a glazed appearance. Perhaps their strangest characteristic is their place in the evolution of mammals. Ancestors of the hyraxes have been found in the deposits of Upper Egypt of about 50 million years ago. The structure of the ear is similar to that found in Whales, their molar teeth look like those of a Rhinoceros. Two pouches in the stomach resemble a condition found in birds, and the arrangement of the bones of the forelimb are like those of the Elephant. In spite of all these features it is regarded as being allied to the Elephant!

You are likely to see two types of monkey on your travels, the **Vervet Monkey** and the **Chacma Baboon**. Both occur widespread and you are just as likely to see them outside a Game Reserve than in one.

The **Vervet Monkey** (*Cercopithecus pygerythrus*), is of slim build and light in colour. Their feet are conspicuously black, so to is the tip of the tail. They live in savanna and woodlands but have proved to be highly adaptable. On your first visit you might think the Vervet Monkey cute, it is not, it is vermin and in many places treated as such. They can do widespread damage to orchards and other crops. On no account encourage these creatures, they can make off with your whole picnic, including the beers, in a matter of seconds.

Chacma Baboon (*Papio ursinus*) The adult male is slender and can weigh up to 40 kg. General colour is a dark olive green, with lighter undersides. They never roam far from a safe refuge, usually a tree, but rocks can provide sufficient protection from predators. They occur in large family groups, known as a troop, and have a reputation for being aggressive where they have become used to man's presence.

SAFARIS

GAME VIEWING

Game viewing in Namibia's game reserves is left to the individual to a much greater extent than in East Africa. Most of the reserves are rarely crowded and visitors have the opportunity to drive on an extensive network of surfaced gravel roads which are laid out to visit waterholes, hides and the various different ecosystems within a park.

As visitors are left to their own devices to such a great extent it is a good idea to buy some of the wildlife identification books which are available in camp shops. The best times to go viewing game are early in the morning and late in the afternoon. The midday heat is usually too intense for the animals who will rest up in thickets for most of the day. The best season for game viewing is during the winter months from Jul to Sep when the dry weather forces animals to congregate around rivers and waterholes. The height and thickness of the vegetation is much less at this time of year making it easier to spot wildlife. The disadvantage of game viewing at this time of year is that the animals are not in such good condition and the winter landscape looks harsh and barren. Summer weather, from Nov to Jan, with the high rainfall is the best time of year for the animals. They will be in good condition after feeding on the new shoots and there are chances of seeing breeding displays and young foals. The landscape is green and lush at this time of year and is particularly beautiful but the thick vegetation and the wide availability of water will mean that the wildlife is far more widespread and difficult to spot.

Driving around endlessly searching for animals is not the best way to spot many of these creatures. The optimum speed for game viewing by car is around 15 km per hour. The drives can be broken up by stops at waterholes, picnic sites and hides. Time spent around a waterhole out of your car gives you an opportunity to listen to the sounds of the bush and experience the rhythms of nature as game moves to and from the water. The areas where you are allowed out of your car are quite specifically designated, game reserves are not just large parks and the animals are wild and should not be approached on foot. Never get out of the car unless it is at a designated area, not only are you liable to be prosecuted and thrown out of the park, but you may well be seriously injured or killed.

Namibia's game reserves are very well organized and following the few simple park rules will ensure an enjoyable stay. The parks are only open to visitors during daylight hours, the camp leaflets will give you the details of seasonal changes, so it is important to plan your game viewing drive so that you can start at first light and return before the camp gates shut just before dark.

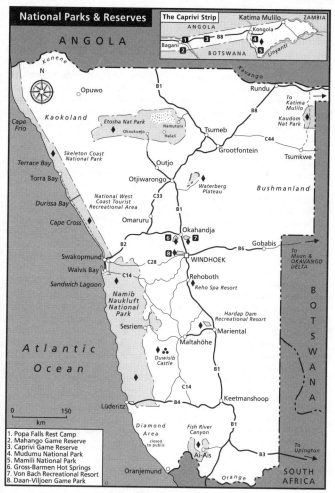

National Parks & Reserves

ANGOLA

Kunene

N

Opuwo

Kaokoland

Etosha Nat Park

Okaukuejo · Namutoni
· Halali

Tsumeb

Cape
Frío

Skeleton Coast
National Park

Terrace Bay

Torra Bay

Outjo

Grootfontein

C44

Tsumkwe

To
Katima
Mulilo

Kaudom
Nat Park

Rundu

B8

Otjiwarongo

C33

Waterberg
Plateau

Bushmanland

*National West
Coast Tourist
Recreational Area*

Omaruru

B1

Durissa Bay

Cape Cross

B2

6 · Okahandja 7

8 · WINDHOEK

Gobabis

B6

To
Maun &
OKAVANGO
DELTA

Swakopmund

Walvis Bay

C14

C28

Rehoboth

· Reho Spa Resort

Sandwich Lagoon

*Namib
Naukluft
National
Park*

Sesriem

Hardap Dam
Recreational Resort

Mariental

B
O
T
S
W
A
N
A

*Atlantic

Ocean*

Duwisib
Castle

Maltahöhe

0   150
km

Lüderitz

B1

C14

B4

Keetmanshoop

B1

*Diamond
Area*
closed
to public

Fish River
Canyon

Ai-Ais

B3

To
Upington

Oranjemund

Orange

SOUTH
AFRICA

The Caprivi Strip — Katima Mulilo — ZAMBIA

ANGOLA

1 · 3 · B8 · Kongola 4

Bagani 2 · BOTSWANA · 5 Linyanti

1. Popa Falls Rest Camp
2. Mahango Game Reserve
3. Caprivi Game Reserve
4. Mudumu National Park
5. Mamili National Park
6. Gross-Barmen Hot Springs
7. Von Bach Recreational Resort
8. Daan-Viljoen Game Park

Whilst you are in the park it is always forbidden to feed the animals as they will develop a dependency on humans as a source of food. Once animals such as elephants learn that food is available from humans they can become aggressive and dangerous when looking for more and will eventually have to be shot. Litter is not a serious problem within the parks but throwing rubbish out of your car will spoil other people's enjoyment of nature. Keep your litter inside the car and dispose of it when you reach a camp.

If your car does break down whilst you are in the park don't leave the car in search of help. Stay inside your car until a park ranger comes to your rescue.

Other visitors will be using the same roads as you and you will be able to pass a message on to the park authorities. If the worst happens and night falls before you are rescued remember that the park keeps a record of all the cars that have entered each day. If your car has not returned before dark the park rangers will know you are missing and send out a search party.

Whilst game viewing in some of the larger parks the weather can be hot and dusty and it is a good idea to take water bottles and fruit juice with you.

Travelling around on dusty roads will also mean that the car and passengers inside will be covered in dust before the end of the trip. The only sure way of avoiding this is to travel with the windows rolled up and the a/c unit on full. Otherwise wear comfortable old clothes, preferably in dull greens or khakis.

One piece of invaluable equipment for game viewing are a good pair of binoculars. The wildlife is not always conveniently close to the car and a pair of binoculars will enhance your enjoyment of the game reserve. It is a good idea to buy your binoculars before you reach Namibia as they are imported here and will be more expensive. When you are buying a pair of binoculars don't just consider the strength of magnification, much of the best game viewing is done when light levels are low so a large aperture letting in more light can be as useful as high magnification.

Game Reserve Camps

Once you have reserved accommodation in a game reserve (see page 289), you will be able to move in anytime after midday until the camp gates shut at nightfall. The most organized camps in Etosha have shops, laundrettes and car hire facilities but most camps in game reserves are rather more basic. Camp reception will be located with the shop and the office. The shops sell a good range of books for identifying game as well as

maps, leaflets and food. It is at the camp office where you will be able to reserve guided walks and game drives (see below). Most accommodation is self-catering so there will often not be a restaurant to eat at. The camp shops do sell some food but this tends to be just basic provisions which are not enough for a balanced meal. Road conditions between camps on game viewing trips are good. There are well maintained surfaced gravel roads which are quite adequate for a saloon car, a 4WD is not necessary. When you make your reservation you will receive a leaflet detailing all the available facilities at your camp.

SAFARI COMPANIES

There are numerous safari companies operating out of Windhoek who can arrange accommodation and game viewing trips as part of a tour. The cost of tours varies, there are good budget options as well as more expensive luxury safaris. Visitors must balance the advantages of going on an organized tour where all your needs are taken care of with the option of hiring a car and staying in self-catering accommodation.

HIKING

For those visitors interested in experiencing the bush at first hand, there are ample opportunities for bush hiking in Namibia, whatever your experience and level of fitness. For the uninitiated, walking in the bush is an excellent way of getting a close look at Namibia's diverse flora and fauna, and whether you walk for an hour or a day, you are sure to see something new and interesting.

Many of the game parks have trails suitable for both experienced and inexperienced walkers, furthermore most guestfarms in the country have well marked hiking trails. In many cases an experienced guide, who will be able to fill in a great deal of detail on the plants, birds and game in the area, will accompany you, and this can be a particularly rewarding way to enjoy what might be a new and unfamiliar environment.

For the experienced hiker there is the challenge of the Fish River Canyon (see page 262), Ugab River (page 215) and Naukluft Hiking Trails (page 237), all of which require high levels of fitness, and a willingness to carry everything necessary with you on your back. At an intermediate level there are fantastic hikes in the Naukluft Mountain Park (see page 240) and at the Waterberg Plateau Park (page 116). Finally, for those people not wishing to get too serious, there are rewarding but manageable hikes at Daan Viljoen Game Park near Windhoek (see page 90) and numerous easy trails at the Waterberg Plateau.

As experienced walkers will already know, good preparation is the key to a successful and enjoyable hike. It is also important to remember that however short or easy a walk may appear to be, walking in the bush is not like going for a stroll in the park, and a few basic steps should be followed. Below is a checklist of equipment and guidelines to hiking in the bush:

Basic equipment for day hikes

Good walking boots or shoes
Sunhat
Minimum of 2 litres of water per person on all walks
Basic first aid kit
Penknife
Trail snacks, eg peanuts, biltong, dried fruit
Binoculars and birdbook/gamebook
Toilet paper and matches to burn paper
Additional overnight gear
Sleeping bag
Sweatshirt/tracksuit for nights in the mountains – even in summer
Torch
Lightweight camping stove (it is not always permitted to collect firewood)
Matches/lighter/firelighters
Dehydrated food, eg pasta, instant soups etc.

General tips

Don't leave litter or throw away cigarette butts
Leave everything as you find it – don't pick plants or remove fossils or rocks
Stick to marked trails especially in the bush – it's easy to lose your way!
Camp away from waterholes so as not to frighten game away
Never feed baboons
Remember in the southern hemisphere the sun goes via the N not the S

The Land

NAMIBIA is located on the W coast of Africa between the 17th and 29th latitudes. The territory stretches from Angola and Zambia in the N to South Africa in the S, most of the eastern border is with Botswana. The total surface area is 824,269 sq km, nearly four times the size of the UK, or twice the size of California.

As you travel around the country you are likely to form the impression that the countryside is harsh and forbidding and that most of the country is either desert or semi-desert in appearance. If you do not like hot, dry and dusty countries then Namibia is not for you. There are only five perennial rivers, the Cuando, Kunene, Kavango and Zambezi in the N and the Orange River which forms the border with South Africa.

There are four distinct regions, although only the far N can be truly described as being green in appearance. The dominant feature is the Namib-Naukluft desert which occupies almost a fifth of the total area. The desert varies between 80 and 120 km in width and stretches along the entire Atlantic coastline, a distance of approximately 1,600 km. This whole region receives less than 100 mm of rain per year. The central portion of the desert is an impassable mass of giant sand dunes which are one of the major tourist attractions.

The centre of the country is a semi-arid mountainous plateau, the capital Windhoek is located on this plateau.

Most of the annual rains fall during the summer months when the plateau is covered with green grasslands and the occasional flowering acacia tree. The average elevation is 1,100m, the highest mountains are the Brandberg (2,573m) and the Moltkeblick (2,446m) in the Aus range. Throughout the plateau are numerous dry, seasonal river courses, most will only flow for a few days each year, and few drain into the ocean, much of the drainage disappears into the Kalahari. The dramatic Fish River canyon in the S of the country is evidence of a time when the rivers must have flowed with large volumes of water for long periods.

The southeastern area of the country is characterized by low lying plains covered with scrub vegetation, typical of the Kalahari and Karoo regions of Botswana and South Africa.

The far north of the country is the only region which receives sufficient rainfall each year to sustain agriculture and a wooded environment. As you travel N of Etosha National Park the vegetation cover gradually increases and the overall landscape is more green than brown. The Caprivi Strip has some magnificent woodlands and lush riverine vegetation along with a wide variety of wild animals.

CLIMATE

Namibia, like so many countries in Africa, eagerly waits for the first rains to fall every year. The country lies within the dry latitudes and depends upon the unpredictable movements of the climatic zones for its rainfall. These zones are known as the Inter-Tropical Convergence Zone (ITCZ), the Mid-Latitude High Pressure Zone (MLHPZ) and the Temperate Zone. Generally rains can be expected in areas dominated by the ITCZ or the Temperate zone, whereas the MLHPZ is associated with little or no rainfall. The weather in the N of the country depends upon the southerly movement of the ITCZ, while in the extreme S the rains can be expected if the Temperate zone pushes N into the MLHPZ. Predicting the movement of these climatic zones is the key to understanding Namibia's weather.

Namibia is blessed with a climate in which the sun shines for more than 300 days per year, an important consideration for many holiday makers. Most visitors will enjoy clear blue skies during their visit, it is only during the height of the rainy season that you might encounter

Droughts & famine – the life of an old man

"I am Tate Mwafangeyo, the oldest man in this village of Okalondo, Ongenga. I was born on the 4 April 1914, and I have lived here all my life. My wife died 4 years ago, and now I am living with my children and relatives.

I can remember my parents telling me of a very bad drought, during the time of King Naketo, who was king at the same time as Mandume. I was not yet born at this time. There was a very serious dry year which killed thousands of people. During this time people were forced to eat *ombadwa*, which is cattle leather. When this food ran out, they turned to the insects, which also became scarce soon. There was no food and no water. Many people died, and their bodies were pulled to an *oshana*, far away in the bush. People were very weak, and there was not enough space or energy for digging graves. This period is called *Ondjala yo kapuka*, and many of our people and nearly all of our livestock died. Just before I was born came *Oshipuluka* (good rain). Those who survived the bad drought were very happy because the rain season brought frogs, birds, *ombidi, eembe, omwungo*, and so on. The people were on their feet again.

Since I was born there have been several droughts, but none so bad as the one I have told you about. During this time people used to sacrifice their cattle for rain. When there was no rain they would go to King Nehale who lived in Angola. Thy went to him because rain came from N. They would take him women of the Omulamba group and black cattle as a rain offering. If you took him these two offerings he would send you rain.

We also used to sing rain songs, but I cannot remember any of them now. What I can tell you are some words to use to promise rain: "Xekulu yo mapongo, Ina yo mawila ndjila, Omapongo aha ka kwa te sha sho munhu" – "Father of the refugees, mother of the starving, the refugees will not touch anybody's belongings". This means that whenever there is rain there will be no stealing, because everybody will have something to eat.

In Oshiwambo we even have special names for those people born during rain. "*Ondula*" means rain, and men who were born during the rain can be called *Haidula*, while women born during the rain are called *Nadula*".

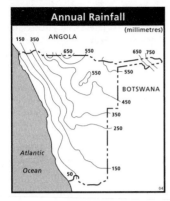

Annual Rainfall
(millimetres)

150 350 ANGOLA
650 550
650 750
550
550
BOTSWANA
450
350
250
Atlantic
Ocean
150
50

cloudy days. While these warm clear days are what most visitors are looking for it is important that you protect your skin from sunburn. The combined effect of latitude and altitude means that if you are fair skinned you will quickly burn without some form of protection – always wear a hat, sunglasses, apply sunblock on a regular basis and drink plenty of liquid throughout the day, preferably water. The warmest months are January and February, when the daytime temperature in the interior can reach 40°C, this will be far warmer than most visitors from the temperate latitudes will have experienced. This is not the weather to walk about in, especially without a hat or protection.

In general the rain season lasts from November to March, during this period it might not rain for several weeks, but by February most parts of the country should have received a significant proportion of their annual rainfall. Visitors to Namibia in April and May will see a country far greener than most would imagine or expect. The Caprivi region receives the most rainfall each year, the annual average for Katima Mulilo is over 700 mm. The isohyets run NW to SE, with total rainfall decreasing as you travel from the Caprivi towards the Karas region in the S. In a good year

Lüderitz may receive 20 mm, which is insignificant when you take into account the high evapotranspiration rates. In a good year the first rain in the N may fall as early as October, this can cause havoc with the agricultural system if farmers plant their seed expecting the rains to continue. There is always the danger of planting too early, the young shoots of millet and maize emerge only to die from lack of water because the next rains don't fall until mid-November.

A quick glance at any map of Namibia will clearly show all of the coast to be desert. The three major coastal settlements all depend upon water piped from the interior for their survival. During the height of the summer, December, there is a mass exodus from the interior (especially Windhoek) to the coast. This is the peak tourist season for Swakopmund. The reason is quite simple, local residents are looking to escape the heat. The cold Benguela ocean current has a modifying influence on the weather. One negative aspect of the coastal climate are the frequent sea fogs which form when the cool ocean air mixes with the hot Namib desert air. It really can get very gloomy, but this fog is vital to the survival of plants and animals in the Namib desert. Do not be fooled into thinking the sun cannot harm you when there is a fog, the uv rays will still penetrate the mist and burn your skin.

The most pleasant weather in the interior is experienced during the autumn (April/May) and spring (August/September), when it tends to be neither too hot, nor too cold. Here the altitude has a modifying influence on temperatures.

A final point to remember when visiting Namibia is that more often than not the country may be suffering from a period of drought. Do not be wasteful with water, it is a valuable commodity which many people have to walk miles for each day. When you are camping or travelling in remote areas make sure you carry extra water with you – there are no guarantees of a clean source in the middle of the bush. By chance the rains were exceptionally good during January and February of 1997.

VEGETATION

While much of the Namibian landscape is characterised by deserts and mountains, the country extends far enough north into the tropical latitudes to have a varied range of plant life. The most interesting ecological area is the Namib desert where the diverse flora and fauna have had to adapt to a unique set of climatic conditions. Botanists from all over the world have visited the Namib to study some of the more unusual plants and the ways in which they cope with the hot and dry conditions. A good tour of the desert should include an introduction to some of these plants. This is the only desert in the world where you can see elephant, lion and rhino.

Although a large proportion of the country is desert there are four distinct vegetation zones which together support more than 4,000 seed-bearing vascular plants, 120 different species of tree, over 200 endemic plant species and a 100 varieties of lichen. These zones are loosely defined as follows: the tropical forests and wetlands along the banks of the perennial rivers in Kavango and Caprivi; the savanna plains with occasional trees in the Kalahari; the mountainous escarpment regions such as Kaokoland and Damaraland, which support a mixture of succulent and semi-succulent plants; and the low altitude coastlands and Namib desert.

Along the mountainous escarpment most of the plants are either arborescent, succulents or semi-succulents. The most common species are the quiver tree, or kokerboom (*Aloë dichotoma*), the spiky tall cactus like plants known as *Euphorbia* and the paper bark tree or *Commiphora* which can be seen along the road between Sesfontein and Opuwo in Kaokoland. The vegetation mix in the Kaokoland is largely determined by physical and climatic factors. In the extreme north the Marienfluß and Hartmann valleys are covered with open grasslands with very few trees and shrubs, further to the south a few more trees start to appear in the savanna, notably the mopane (*Colophospermum mopane*) and purple-pod terminalia (*Terminalia prunioides*). Along the Kunene river the dominant trees are leadwood (*Combretum imberbe*), jakkalsbessie (*Diospyros mespiliformis*) and sycamore fig (*Ficus sycamorus*). After the rains look out for the magnificent pink flowers of the Boesmangif (*Andanium boehmianum*), a creeper which is found on many of the larger trees. The palm trees along the river are Makalani palms (*Hyphaene petersana*), they are a common sight further east in Owaboland. In areas where there is slightly more rainfall there are a variety of flowering annuals which will cover the land with a carpet of colour for a couple of months, most of these annuals are of the *Brasicaceae* and *Asteraceae* families.

The Kavango and Caprivi regions are the only areas where you will see large stands of forest, most of the trees are deciduous so like the rest of the country the area looks at its best after the rains. Along the river beds you can expect to see mopane (*Colophospermum mopane*), the palm (*Hyphaene ventricosa*) and a couple of reed species on the flood plains; *Phragmites australis* and *Typha latifolia*. The woodland areas of the game reserves are dominated by *Terminalia* shrubs, *Boscia albitrunca*, *Bauhinia macrantha* and *Grewia*.

Along the edge of the Kalahari desert the sands gradually give way to trees and tall shrubs, although most of the vegetation is restricted to grasslands; *Stipagrotis* is the dominant grass. The most common flower is the driedoring (*Rhigozum trichotomum*).

As noted above the Namib desert has

the most interesting mix of plants in Namibia, many of which have been subjected to intensive studies. One of the most unusual of all plants is the *Welwitschia mirabilis*, a plant first seen by the white man in 1859. These plants are found in small groups inland from the coast at Swakopmund. Each plant has two long leaves which are often torn and discoloured. Using carbon dating they have been shown to live for over a thousand years in the harshest of conditions. One of the oldest plants in the Namib is now protected by a fence, however you can still get close to smaller plants. After the welwitschia it is the lichens which attract the greatest attention in the desert. The lichens are found on west facing slopes and surfaces where they are able to draw moisture from the sea fogs. If it were not for the fog the plants would have no source of water. They are now recognised as a vital component of the Namib environment and most areas are protected. Many of the animals rely upon the lichen as an important source of water after the fog has condensed on the plants. While they can survive long periods of drought they will quickly die when disturbed.

Visitors with a keen interested in the plants of Namibia will find the following publications helpful for background and identification purposes. *Namib Flora (86)*, P Craven & C Marais; *National List of Indigenous Trees (86)*, Von Breitenbach; *Trees of Southern Africa (77)*, KC Palgrave; *Waterberg Flora (89)*, P Craven & C Marais.

PRECIOUS STONES, ROCKS & MINERALS

Every visitor to Namibia will at some point have read or perhaps been told something about the country that sparked their imagination and desire to see the place for themselves. For many holiday makers it is the beauty and variety of the flora and fauna that initially tempts them to visit southern Africa – few return home disappointed. But Namibia can also prove to be an exciting and interesting destination for a much smaller interest group, it is a country that has an outstanding assembly of precious and semi-precious stones as well as grand and spectacular rock formations. Throughout the Namib desert and the surrounding countryside there is a superb record of the events that took place millions of years ago as the landscape was formed and sculptured. The magnificent Fish River Canyon, the isolated Waterberg Plateau, the Spitzkoppe, Etosha Pan, the Naukluft Mountains, the Hob Meteorite are just a few of the more popular sites. Namibia is often described as a geologists paradise, and rightly so.

The few notes below are intended for the visitor who has never really taken an interest in rocks and gemstones, someone whose knowledge of semi-precious stones is confined to the jewellery which has been in the family for generations. One stone you are unlikely to be picking off the ground and carrying back home in the suitcase, is a diamond. Most of the diamonds are found in the S of the country around Lüderitz, in the Atlantic as well as on land (see page 269). When you look at a map of the Lüderitz district the National Diamond Areas can clearly be seen. This area is closed to the public and well patrolled, many of the diamonds are literally on the surface waiting to be picked up, the diamond industry is an important component of the Namibian economy. Where there are diamonds you will also usually fine garnets, a dark maroon semi-precious stone. Along the Skeleton Coast the fine garnet sand can be sometimes seen on the dunes forming dark patterns.

If you set your sights on something a little less valuable then you may well stumble across a few small samples to take back home. As has already been mentioned the area around the northern town of Tsumeb has long been a popular mining region. Here you will find a wide variety of copper ores. One of the most beautiful semi-precious stones is amethyst, the deeper the violet in colour, the better the gem quality, it is a versatile stone which can be turned into rings, necklaces and broaches with great effect. Many stone are found around Omaruru and Otjiwarongo. Further S is the small town of Usakos, here you may come across tourmaline both blue and green varieties, elsewhere it occurs in red, pink, yellow and black. The uranium mine at Rössing had found aquamarine; in the desert just inland from Swakopmund you are bound to come across outcrops of rose quartz, as well as some ancient rock formations which date back to the time when Africa and the Americas were one.

Where there is a town museum you are likely to come across a small display of locally found rocks and minerals. If you wish to collect pieces for your own collection ask around until you find who the local specialist is, there is always someone. Always check with the local police station about access to the land, and once in the bush don't forget about the other more popular attraction – wild animals. Leopards tend to live in rocky regions. In Windhoek you can buy a geological map of the country which shows farm boundaries and mines as well as the major rock types. One final point to note is that to remove or possess meteorites or fossils a permit is needed from the government. Semi-precious stones can be picked off the land as long as you are not trespassing and have a good eye for small glinting stones; happy hunting.

History

PRE-COLONIAL NAMIBIA

Archaeological finds from southern Namibia suggest that humans have been wandering the vast plains, dense bush and harsh deserts of the country for around 45,000 years. Ancient cave paintings at the Apollo 11 shelter in the southern Huns Mountains have been estimated to be 27,000 years old and similar rock art of the same period has also been found at a number of sites around Damaraland in NW Namibia. These are believed to have been the work of the San or Bushmen as they are most commonly known, descendants of pre-historic people who had migrated from southern Africa into East and North Africa before subsequently returning to the tip of the continent.

The San were traditionally hunter gatherers, extraordinarily successful at surviving in the bush and desert despite their limited technology and weapons. They lived in small bands of up to 50 people roaming across the veld in a continuous search for food and water, rarely coming into contact with other San groups. Rock art all around Namibia, clearly seen at sites such as Twyfelfontein and Brandberg, provides vivid evidence of the widespread distribution of San communities all over the country.

Around 2,000 years ago the San were joined by groups of Khoi-khoin (Nama) who had migrated from Botswana to the middle stretches of the Orange River. From here, it is believed that the group split into two, one group heading N and W into present day Namibia, the other

group moving S into the Cape Province area of South Africa. Unlike the San, the Khoikhoi were both hunter-gatherers and livestock herders, living a semi-nomadic existence moving around the country with their herds of animals. Despite the differences in lifestyle, it appears as if Khoi and San people co-existed peacefully with each other.

By the 9th century AD a third group were settled in Namibia living alongside the Khoisan; these were the Damara people. Sharing common cultural and linguistic ties with the Nama people, rather than the Owambo, Herero or other Bantu-speaking tribes in Namibia, the exact origin and migration route of the Damara into Namibia remains a mystery. Some anthropologists argue that the Damara must have originated in West Africa whilst others maintain that they developed alongside the Khoi-khoin in Botswana and merely migrated later to Namibia.

By the early 19th century the Damara were living all over Namibia both alongside Nama and Herero communities as well as in their own settlements which were reported to be more permanent than those of the Nama. They had also evolved a number of distinct characteristics; they practised communal hunting techniques, the cultivation of tobacco and *dagga* (marijuana), mined and smelted copper and manufactured soapstone pipes.

Bantu-speaking tribes started arriving in Namibia during the 16th and 17th centuries, having migrated S and W

Namibia - Historical

ANGOLA

N

Kunene River

Owamboland

Kaokoland

Caprivi

Ongulumbashe
26 Aug 1966

✕ 28 Jan 1904

Fort
Sesfontein

Fort
Namutoni

OMEG Mine
(Tsumeb)

Terrace Bay

Waterberg
Plateau

Omaheke
Sandveld

Twyfelfontein

Hamakari
11 Aug 1904

White Lady
Brandberg

Okahandja
Dec 1880

Cape Cross
1486

Omaruru
Mission

Herero Graves

Swakopmund

Von
Francois
Fort

Klein Windhoek

B
O
T
S
W
A
N
A

Walvis Bay

Otjimbingwe

Otjonguere
✕ 22 Jun 1864

Sandwich Bay

Rhenish
Church

Hoornkrans

Rehoboth
Mission

Conception Bay

Naukluft Mts
Aug/Sept 1894

War
Memorial
1905

St Francis Bay

Duwisib
Castle

Gibeon

Atlantic

Bethanie

Ocean

Lüderitz &
Kolmanskop

Keetmanshoop

Aus

Angra
Pequena
1486

Rock
engravings

Huns
Mts

Fish River
Canyon

Warmbad

Orange River

SOUTH AFRICA

0   150
km

from the Great Lakes area of East and Central Africa. These tribes settled in the northern parts of the country alongside or close to the perennial Kunene, Kavango and Zambezi rivers which more or less correspond to their distribution in present-day Namibia.

These peoples brought with them a variety of skills such as pottery and met-al working, and lived by a mixture of farming, fishing and hunting. This influx of people looking for land to establish semi-permanent settlements inevitably put pressure on existing groups, and the San and Damara in particular were forced to move further S or into less hospitable parts of the country on the fringes of the Namib and

Alain Mallet's 1683 map
Monomotapa et la Cafrerie
Source: Tooley, T.V. (1969) *Collector's guide to maps of the African Continent and Southern Africa*, Carta Press: London

Kalahari deserts.

The Herero people had arrived in Namibia from East and Central Africa during the 16th century and had originally settled in the Kaokoland area in the extreme NW of the country. As cattle herders they required increasingly large areas of land to feed their growing herds and by the middle of the 18th century the marginal veld of the Kaokoland had become overgrazed, and suffering severe drought, was no longer able to support the Herero.

Gradually the majority of the Herero migrated southwards, and by around 1750 the first groups of Herero came into contact with groups of Khoi-khoin in the Swakop River area. Pressure from the Herero pushing southward more or less coincided with the northwards migration of Oorlam groups from the Cape Province. These two opposing movements created enormous pressure which was to erupt into almost a century of upheaval and at times open warfare in Central Namibia. It was against this backdrop that the first European missionaries and traders came into the country, and their presence contributed significantly to the eventual establishment of the German colony of Southwest Africa.

OORLAM MIGRATION

The emergence of industrial capitalism in England during the second half of the 18th century drastically changed the economy of the satellite Cape Colony. Urban centres grew and Boer farmers moved progressively inland, claiming land and resources further and further away from the reach of the English authorities in the Cape Colony. The Boer farmers' freedoms were won largely at the expense of the local Khoisan (Nama and San) population who lost their land, their hunting grounds and livestock, and even their liberty, as many became servants or even slaves of these European farmers.

In the wake of these developments a new group of frontiers people emerged. These were the Oorlams, a mixed bunch of Khoi-khoin, runaway slaves, and people of mixed race descent who worked for the Boer farmers and traders as hunters and guides. They were baptized, had access to guns and horses and had shed the traditional lifestyles of other Nama groups. Some of these formed themselves into commandos, autonomous groups living separate from the European farmers and traders, surviving by hunting, trading and raiding the cattle of the Nama tribes living over the Orange River into southern Namibia.

Early missionary reports at the time described the Nama tribes of southern Namibia to be living in highly organized communities numbering in some cases over a thousand individuals. They had large herds of cattle, sheep and goats, and were completely self-sufficient, producing all their own food and manufacturing the reed mats for their huts, as well as growing tobacco and *dagga*. The

Jonker Afrikaner

One of the key figures in Namibia during the first half of the 19th century was Jonker Afrikaner, an Oorlam from the Cape Province who established his authority over the central and southern part of Namibia, and who established the settlement at Windhoek which was to eventually become Namibia's capital.

Jonker Afrikaner belonged to an Oorlam group, who around the turn of the century crossed the Orange River and established a fortified village in the Karasburg District. The leader of the clan at the time was Jager Afrikaner, Jonker's father, who had killed his white employer, a farmer named Pienaar, in a dispute over wages, and had subsequently fled over the Orange River beyond the reach of the Cape Province authorities. After his father's death in 1823, Jonker Afrikaner trekked N with a group of his followers, and by the 1830s had established himself as leader of central and southern Namibia.

Due to the lack of accurate historical records during this period, there are differing accounts of how Jonker established himself as the senior Nama/Oorlam leader. One explanation is that by force of arms and constant cattle raids upon neighbouring Nama tribes, Jonker was able to establish his predominance. Other theories suggest that Nama leaders, fearing the steady encroachment of the Herero on their grazing lands, called in Jonker to force the Herero back. The English explorer Sir James Alexander met Jonker in 1836 in the Rehoboth area and reported that the Afrikaners had defeated the Hereros in three decisive battles in 1835, allowing the Afrikaners to steal the Herero cattle and establish themselves as the dominant power in the area.

By the 1840s an informal but definite alliance between Jonker Afrikaner and other Nama Chiefs, such as Oaseb and Swartbooi existed. The basis of the alliance recognized Jonker Afrikaner as an equal of the Nama leaders, gave the Afrikaners sovereignty of the land between the Swakop and Kuiseb rivers and made Jonker Afrikaner overlord of the Herero lands N of the Swakop River. In this way the Afrikaners effectively acted as a buffer between the Hereros to the N and the Nama tribes of the S, ensuring greater security for the Nama lands to the S. This informal alliance was officially confirmed in 1858 in an agreement between Chief Oaseb and Jonker Afrikaner.

During the 1840s and 1850s, Jonker established relations with various Herero leaders, in particular Chief Tjamuaha and his son Kamaherero and Chief Kahitjene. The basis of these relations obliged the Herero to look after Afrikaner cattle and to pay regular tributes in the form of cattle, and in return the Herero leaders was generally spared cattle raids and were able to enrich themselves at the expense of their fellow Herero.

In 1840, Jonker had established the settlement of Windhoek in the Klein Windhoek valley. In 1842, invited by Jonker, the first two missionaries Hahn and Kleinschmidt arrived to find a flourishing community, boasting a whitewashed stone church capable of seating up to 500 people. There were also well established gardens where corn, tobacco and dagga (marijuana) were being cultivated in irrigated fields. For the next 20 years Windhoek was to flourish as a centre of commerce between the Hereros and the Oorlam/Namas.

Jonker Afrikaner died in 1861 and the years immediately following his death were to see the gradual erosion of Afrikaner hegemony over central and southern Namibia, and the abandonment of the settlement at Windhoek.

Charles John Andersson

Charles Andersson was born in Sweden in 1827 of a Swedish mother and English father. After a short spell at the University of Lund in 1847 he abandoned his studies in order to hunt and trade with his father. In 1849 he left for England with the intention of pursuing a career of hunting and exploration in Iceland, however sailed for South Africa instead upon the invitation of an Englishman named Galton.

During the 1850s Andersson travelled and hunted for ivory all over south-western Africa, visiting King Nangolo in Ondongo, exploring Lake Ngami and reaching the Okavango River. By 1860 he was in a position to buy up the assets of the defunct Walvis Bay Trading Company in Otjimbingwe and set up a trading company there. Andersson was interested in ivory and cattle for the Cape trade and was able to set up other hunters and traders to work for him. The fact that Andersson's trading post was permanent made it the first of its kind in Namibia. He and his traders were able to set up the best possible deals and if required, Andersson was able to travel to the Cape himself, leaving his partners to look after the business in Otjimbingwe.

However, the opening of the trading post at Otjimbingwe coincided with the outbreak of lung sickness in cattle in the region. This posed a serious threat to all the groups raising cattle, Nama, Herero and European alike. Determined to protect their herds and pastures from the deadly disease, Jonker Afrikaner and his allies were extremely reluctant to let Andersson drive his cattle S through their lands. Furthermore, by opening up Hereroland to trade, Andersson posed a threat to the hegemony of the Afrikaner clan.

In 1861 whilst Jonker Afrikaner was in Owamboland, Andersson set off with 1,400 head of infected cattle for the Cape. Between Otjimbingwe and Rehoboth he was attacked by Hendrik Zes, a close ally of Jonker Afrikaner, who made off with 500 of the animals. Although Andersson and his traders were able to force Zes to return the cattle, the incident served as a serious warning to him. Thereafter, Andersson started to recruit and train mercenaries, mainly from the Cape, to protect his trading interests.

different Nama tribes co-existed peacefully, sharing and respecting each other's water and grazing rights.

Initial contact between the first Oorlams groups to cross the Orange River and the local Nama tribes was relatively peaceful, but as more and more Oorlams poured over the river, demanding watering and grazing rights, the level of conflict increased to open warfare. Although the Nama were superior in numbers to the Oorlams, they had far fewer guns and horses and with their large herds of livestock were less mobile than the Oorlams. Consequently the Oorlams were soon able to establish footholds in the region from where they continued to harry and raid the Nama tribes.

Over a 40 year period up until the 1840s, southern Namibia – or Namaland as it became to be known – was in a virtually constant state of turmoil. Traditional patterns of living were disrupted, a new economy emerged and previously pastoral people started to settle in more permanent settlements.

In the 1840s Chief Oaseb, a paramount Nama chief and Joker Afrikaner, the foremost Oorlam leader, struck a deal that allowed Nama and Oorlam groups to live in peace. This deal was struck against the increasing realization that there was now little difference between the Oorlam and the Nama. The

By January 1862, 5 months after Jonker Afrikaner's death, Andersson was established as a successful trader, organizing expeditions N into Hereroland, gradually changing the focus of his interest towards ivory and ostrich feathers. However, his position was not secure, as he noted in his diary on 26 January 1862. "The Hottentots (Namas) are fearfully jealous of me: they got a notion that I am the only person who benefits by my presence. I am not afraid of any Hottentot individually or collectively, but I may have to leave the country unless I resort to bloodshed."

The scene was then set for an escalation of the conflict between Andersson and his traders on the one hand and the Afrikaners and their allies on the other. A series of cattle raids and skirmishes took place during 1863, culminating with an attack on Otjimbingwe by the Afrikaners in June of that year. Andersson, his traders and mercenaries, the "Otjimbingwe volunteers" as they had come to be known, routed the attackers killing about a third of them including their commander Christian Afrikaner. However, the power of the Afrikaners was not broken, and guerrilla attacks on Andersson's cattle trains continued.

In 1864 Andersson decided to seek an alliance with the Herero chiefs in an attempt to muster a big enough army to settle the conflict in one decisive battle. The Hereros had a long series of grievances going back many years against the Afrikaners, and after a series of negotiations and the election of Kamaherero as chief of all Herero speakers, a joint army of about 2,500 men was put together. On 22 June 1864 the two armies met near Rehoboth in a battle that proved to be anything but conclusive. The Afrikaners retreated after a day's battle, neither having been defeated nor emerging victorious. Andersson's shin was shattered by a bullet, a wound he never fully recovered from. He sold his business interests to the Rhenish Mission and retired to the Cape to put together his bird book on Namibia.

He returned to Namibia in 1865 leaving his wife and two young children in Cape Town. However, he was never to return, and died in Owamboland in 1867 of a combination of diphtheria, dysentery and exhaustion.

intense struggle for land and water had brought the two groups close together, inter-marriage had become commonplace so that making distinctions between the two groups was increasingly difficult. Furthermore, Herero-speaking groups who had been migrating southwards for almost a hundred years were threatening the common interests of both Oorlam and Nama.

Oaseb and Afrikaner divided the land S of Windhoek amongst themselves and Afrikaner was declared overlord of the Herero lands N of the Swakop River up as far as the Waterberg Plateau. By force of arms, Afrikaner was able to maintain his hegemony over these Herero groups with their large herds of cattle, and in so doing was able to control loosely most of Central and Southern Namibia. Until his death in 1861, Jonker Afrikaner was probably the single most influential leader in this part of Namibia.

MISSIONARIES AND TRADERS

The first Europeans had appeared off the coast of Africa in the 15th century. In 1486, the Portuguese explorer Diego Cao erected a cross at Cape Cross and Bartholomew Diaz planted another at Angra Pequena near Luderitz in 1486. However, the coast was barren and inhospitable, and the interior of the country at this time would have only been accessible to these explorers by crossing the Namib Desert. No other Europeans are believed to have visited Namibia until the late 18th century when a small number of Dutch settlers trekked N from the Cape Colony and established themselves as farmers. Following them a small number of traders also came to Namibia but without initially having any significant impact.

The earliest missionaries, from the London Mission Society, began to operate in southern Namibia at the beginning of the 19th century and were soon joined later by the German Rhenish and Finnish Lutheran Mission Societies. The appearance of the earliest missionaries coincided with increasing numbers of Oorlams crossing the Orange River, and the presence of these missionaries was crucial to the success of the Oorlam commando groups in establishing themselves in Namibia.

Missionaries were important in 19th century Namibia as they fulfilled a number of different roles, in addition to their primary aim of preaching the gospel. Indeed one early missionary, Ebner, regretting that he was unable to provide the Nama leader Titus Afrikaner with a supply of gunpowder as earlier preachers had done, was driven to write that "it seems to me that he is more interested in powder, lead and tobacco than in the teachings of the gospel".

Until the arrival of the missionaries, the Nama communities in the S of Namibia were semi-nomadic, however, the building of churches and the development of agriculture saw the establishment of the first stable settlements. The stone-walled churches fulfilled the role of mini-fortresses, and the brass bells that the missionaries provided were an effective warning system during raids! Many missionaries also introduced agriculture to the communities in which they lived, and the more stable food supply that followed allowed larger numbers of people to settle in an area. In turn, these larger settlements allowed

for improved defence against raids through better organization.

Second, the missionaries acted as focal points for traders from the Cape, who were able to supply the missionaries and their families with the goods they needed. In this way the trade routes to the Cape were established and kept open, thus guaranteeing the Oorlam leaders continued supplies of the guns and ammunition upon which they depended for their supremacy. In the early years of the 19th century it seems as if some missionaries even supplied the guns themselves. Schmelen, who established a mission at Bethanie in southern Namibia, found it necessary to "furnish some of my people with arms". Even in later years when the export of guns and gunpowder from the Cape was prohibited, Kleinschmidt, who operated the mission at Rehoboth, provided Chief Swartbooi with gunpowder.

The almost constant conflict brought about the breaking down of social structures, however, the missionaries armed with their Christian rules proved effective control mechanisms for tribal leaders. In 1815, referring to the Afrikaner clan, Ebner noted that "it is only the baptised who are allowed ... to use the gun." Blameless Christian behaviour was also a prerequisite to political positions in communities such as Bethanie, Rehoboth, and Warmbad, behaviour defined, of course, by the missionaries. Missionaries also performed the roles of social worker and doctor, and Jonker Afrikaner once explained to Schonberg why he wanted a missionary at Otjimbingwe "... traders come and go, but the missionary stays, and consequently we know where to get our medicines from."

By the 1860s an extensive network of trading posts existed in Namibia, the most important being Otjimbingwe NW of present-day Windhoek. Set up by the Anglo-Swede Charles John Andersson, Otjimbingwe was also a key mission station for the Herero-speaking peoples.

Under Andersson's influence the European community of missionaries, traders and hunters were gradually sucked into the escalating Herero-Nama conflict (see box).

Following the death of Jonker Afrikaner in 1861 and the defeat of the Afrikaners and their allies at Otjonguere S of Windhoek in 1864, the years leading up to 1870 saw a virtual constant jockeying for position amongst the various Nama and Oorlam leaders. Once again the southern and central parts of Namibia were the scene of skirmishes and cattle raids. This in-fighting amongst the Oorlam/Namas effectively allowed the Herero-speaking people under the leadership of Kamaherero to break free of Afrikaner dominance.

THE 1870 PEACE ACCORD

In 1870 Jan Jonker Afrikaner arrived at Okahandja with a large group of armed men with the intention of renewing the old alliance between Kamaherero and the Afrikaners. However, missionary Hahn intervened and when the treaty was concluded in September of that year the Afrikaners had lost their old rights over the Herero-speaking peoples. Furthermore, Hahn obtained permission for the Cape Basters to settle at Rehoboth. The Basters were a farming community of mixed Khoi-European descent who, having been forced from their lands in the Cape Province, had been looking for a place to settle. The Baster settlement at Rehoboth acted as an effective buffer between the Herero-speaking peoples and the Oorlam-Namas.

Peace was preserved between the Nama and Herero-speaking peoples throughout the 1870s, and it was not until the beginning of the 1880s that conflict broke out once more. However, this period of relative peace amongst indigenous Namibians also saw the consolidation of the position of the missionaries and traders – particularly the latter. As the Nama leaders developed a taste

for manufactured goods and alcohol, the economy of Namaland – virtually all the land S of Windhoek as far as the Orange River – became inextricably linked with that of the Cape. As a result the numbers of hunters, traders and explorers entering Namibia grew uncontrollably, and this in turn saw the over-exploitation of animal and natural resources in the central-southern part of Namibia.

The hunters and traders were chiefly interested in obtaining ivory and ostrich feathers to export to the Cape, at the same time they were selling guns, coffee, sugar, soap, gin and brandy to the Namibians. The only way the Nama chiefs could support their habit for western manufactured goods and alcohol was by granting licenses to the hunters and traders, leading one explorer, A Anderson, to complain to the Cape government that "every petty kaptein claims a license fee" for hunting, passing through and trading.

However, whilst the Oorlam/Namas of southern Namibia became caught up in this trading network, the Herero-speaking peoples living N of Windhoek remained largely aloof from this burgeoning trade. True, they were the main purchasers of guns, for they had learned during the middle part of the century of the importance of modern weapons, but for the rest, trade with Hereroland was tightly controlled.

Given the vast numbers of cattle which the Herero were breeding, it seems strange that the European traders were not more active in their contact with the Herero. The main reason for this it seems, was a lack of interest on the part of the Herero in exchanging their cattle for western goods.

Unlike the inhabitants of Namaland who were experiencing a spiralling circle of dependency on imported manufactured goods together with the virtual invasion of their territory by Europeans of one description or another, the Herero-speaking peoples retained their traditional kinship-oriented pastoral way of life. In other words the Herero valued their cattle far more highly than any manufactured goods, and rather than exchanging cattle for goods, they actually increased the size of their herds.

Despite renewed cattle raids during the early part of the 1880s by Oor-

lam/Namas who succeeded in stealing thousands of head of cattle, ex-missionary Hahn – now a full-time trader – remarked that the Herero ".... will in a few years make up for these losses. There is, perhaps, no people in the world who equals the Damaras (Hereros) as cattle breeders ...".

Hendrik Witbooi

Hendrik Witbooi was born in 1830 and died in 1905 and was unique both as a Namibian and African leader. He was the first to realize that conflict between Namibians was of far less consequence than German attempts to colonize the country. Furthermore, he kept detailed written records of his thoughts and of contemporary events, including detailed minutes of meetings with other Namibian leaders and German officers.

Witbooi came from an Oorlam group brought over the Orange River by his grandfather Kido Witbooi sometime in the late 1820s. The group eventually settled in present-day Gibeon in 1863 and with missionary Knauer established their church and community. By 1871 missionary Olpp calculated that the Witboois numbered around 3,000 people living in about 30 villages around the Gibeon area. By 1893, Olpp calculated that this number had doubled and were settled over an area stretching as far away as Gobabis in the E. In effect the Witboois became a nation of affiliated Oorlam commando groups and Nama tribes which Hendrik Witbooi came to be leader of in 1884.

Up until 1880 Witbooi and his wife and children lived in Gibeon and missionary Olpp noted that Witbooi was a "quiet" man, living more by hard work than by raiding. Baptised in 1868, Witbooi and his eldest son made the church the centre of their lives. In 1875 he became an elder of the church and from 1880 onwards, by his own record, his public actions were guided by divine revelation. However, in early January 1883 Witbooi resigned from his position as elder of the mission church, apparently to devote his time to his growing political responsibilities and also in recognition of his role as leader-to-be of the Witbooi community.

In June 1884, Witbooi had negotiated the right to trek through Herero lands in order to settle further N. It seems that this proposed move was quite in line with Witbooi tradition, as Witbooi's grandfather, Kido, had declared Gibeon to be merely a temporary home. In his papers, Witbooi himself informed the missionaries and his father that the move was the will of God. The following year however when Witbooi attempted to make the move, despite two written assurances from Maherero that the previous year's treaty still applied, his followers were attacked and routed, cattle, horses and wagons stolen, and two of his sons killed. This event sewed the seeds of future conflict between Witbooi and Maherero.

The rest of the 1880s saw a series of battles between the different Namaland leaders that catapulted Hendrik Witbooi and his followers into the forefront of Namaland politics. At the same time Witbooi was administering to the needs of his own community as well as dealing with both the Herero and Germans who were moving towards an alliance intended to control Witbooi. It was the energy and vision of Witbooi that allowed him by 1891 to have established his authority

NAMIBIA BECOMES A COLONIAL POSSESSION

In 1880, after 10 years of relative peace, fierce fighting broke out once more in Central Namibia. Once again the disputes were over cattle and grazing rights and they involved all the key players in Central Namibia at the time. There were the Herero – lead by (Ka)Maherero as he came to be known, the Nama Swartboois, the Afrikaners under Jan Jonker, and the Rehoboth Basters – relative newcomers to the scene. All through 1880 and 1881 the fighting continued with a number of important leaders falling in battle – in particular Maherero's eldest son Willem

over the other Namaland chiefs, and to have established a fortified stronghold at Hoornkrans in the Gamsberg Mountains W of Rehoboth.

In 1890 the German Commissioner to Namibia, Heinrich Göring, wrote to Witbooi ordering him to return to Gibeon and to desist from any plans to attack the Herero, as they were now under German protection. In an extraordinary letter to Maherero at the end of May of that year, Witbooi warned Maherero that he would bitterly regret making a treaty with the Germans for " ... I doubt that you and your Herero nation will understand the rules and laws and methods of that government ..... for he (Göring) will not act according to your will, or traditional law or customs." Witbooi understood what the Herero had so far clearly failed to grasp, namely that the Germans intended taking absolute control over Namibia as part of their imperial designs.

Witbooi's warnings fell on deaf ears and between 1890 and 1892 he waged a campaign of cattle raids on the Herero, succeeding in carrying off thousands of animals. At the same time, anticipating war with the Germans, he secured a steady supply of weapons and ammunition from the Cape, using European traders and even a lawyer to assist him secure these supply lines.

In 1890, the Germans had established their headquarters in Windhoek, and had gradually been increasing their military strength. In April 1893, the German forces, led by Captain Curt von François, attacked Witbooi's stronghold at Hoornkrans, forcing Witbooi to abandon his stronghold. Thereafter a guerrilla war ensued, with the Germans constantly attempting to locate and subdue the Witboois, who with their superior knowledge of the country, were able to harass and evade the Germans. The decisive battles took place between 27 August and 5 September 1894 in the Naukluft Mountains, to where Witbooi had retreated. Although superior in numbers, arms and ammunition, the Germans were not able to defeat Witbooi, on the other hand Witbooi was not able to successfully break out of this siege, and the two sides eventually fought each other to a standstill. A visit and hike in the Naukluft Park gives a vivid idea of how impossible it must have been for both sides to have fought under such conditions (see page 236).

On 15 September Witbooi signed a conditional surrender which required him and his supporters to return to Gibeon, to accept the paramountcy of the German empire and the stationing of a German garrison at Gibeon. In return Witbooi retained jurisdiction over his land and people, and the right to keep guns and ammunition. This treaty was largely respected by both sides until 1904, when the Herero declared war on the Germans. Witbooi also took up arms against the colonizers, but died in the saddle in 1905 from a bullet wound. Thereafter the Witboois largely withdrew from the war.

in the fight for Okahandja in December 1880. Up until 1884 and the rise of Hendrik Witbooi, a bewildering series of shifting alliances, cattle raids and skirmishes characterized the scene in S and Central Namibia.

However, it was the arrival of German representatives in 1884, the subsequent treaties with the Herero and the effective subduing of Hendrik Witbooi 10 years later that fundamentally changed the way in which Namibia was governed. Power steadily shifted away from traditional leaders, such as Witbooi and Maherero, into the hands of the German colonial administrators. Furthermore, over the next 25 years vast tracts of Namaland and Hereroland passed into the hands of the colonial government and individual settlers. This fundamental change culminated with the 1904-1907 German-Namibian war which saw the final consolidation of colonial authority over the country, and the subjugation of the Namibian peoples by Europeans.

Between 1883 and 1885, the German trader and businessman Adolf Lüderitz negotiated a series of agreements which saw him buy practically the entire coastal strip of Namibia between the Orange and Kunene rivers, extending as far as 150 km inland. A settlement was established at Angra Pequena, soon renamed as Lüderitzbucht, which helped to open the country up to German political and economic interests. German policy in Namibia was that private initiative and capital would 'develop' the country, secured by German government protection.

In order to bring 'order' to Namibia, the German authorities pursued a policy of persuading local leaders to sign so-called protection treaties (Shuzverträge) with them. This they achieved by exploiting local conflicts to serve their own ends, and in the face of continuing conflict between Maherero and Hendrik Witbooi, were able to persuade Maherero to sign a protection treaty with the German authorities in 1885. In the same year Commissioner Göring wrote to Hendrik Witbooi ordering him to desist from continuing with his cattle raids against the Herero and threatening him with unspecified consequences.

However, these threats were empty gestures, as during the period from 1884-1889, the official German presence in Namibia consisted of three officials based in a classroom at the mission school in Otjimbingwe, plus a small number of business representatives who effected the protection treaties. It was not until 1889 that the first force of 21 soldiers (Schutztruppe) landed in Namibia, to be followed by another 40 the following year, and only after 1894, following the subduing of Hendrik Witbooi, that significant numbers of settlers were able to enter the country.

Between 1894 and 1904 the Witboois sold a third of their land to European settlers, and the treaties that Samuel Herero signed with the German colonial government in 1894 and 1895, ceded Herero land to them. Meanwhile, following the death of old Maherero in 1890, the German administration established its headquarters in Windhoek, and during the confusion over the succession of the Herero leader, was able to consolidate its position there. However, the greatest sale of Herero land took place in the years after 1896, and was the result of the trade on credit systems in operation at the time, the rinderpest epidemic of 1897 and the fever epidemic of 1898.

With the further opening of Hereroland to trade following the treaties signed with the German colonial administration, there was a dramatic increase in the number of traders operating in the country. For Europeans without their own capital but prepared to put up with the hardships of living in the veld, this was a perfect opportunity to make money and acquire cattle and land. Large firms employed these traders to go out to Herero settlements in the

Schutztruppe on patrol at the turn of the century

veld and sell their goods there. Due to the risks involved, all parties attempted to maximise profit, often adding 70-100% on the value of goods to achieve this. There were also quite happy to give the Hereros credit in order to encourage them to buy more and more, until the situation arrived whereby an individual or community's debt was greater than their assets.

In addition, following the rinderpest epidemic of 1897 in which up to 97% of unvaccinated cattle died, the only way in which the Hereros could pay for the goods they wanted or settle their debts was to sell land. An addiction to alcohol amongst many Hereros, not least their leader Samuel Maherero, also caused large debts which had to be settled through land sales. Although the colonial government attempted to put all business dealings between Europeans and Namibians on a cash basis, the protests of the traders brought about a suspension of this regulation almost immediately after its introduction.

Inevitably tension grew amongst the Herero as they saw their traditional lands gradually disappearing. The Rhenish Missionary Society petitioned the colonial government to consider creating reserves for the Herero where the land could not be sold, and despite initial resistance both within Namibia and from Germany, so-called paper reserves (because initially they only existed on paper) were created around Otjimbingwe at the end of 1902 and around Okahandja and Waterberg in 1903. However, there were many Herero leaders who were deeply dissatisfied with the land issue, and pressure was growing on Herero leader Samuel Maherero to take some action to recover lost lands – although he himself had been responsible for the sale of much of it.

THE 1904-1907 GERMAN-NAMIBIAN WAR

The 3 years of fighting between the German colonial forces and various Namibian tribes ended with victory for the Germans and the consolidation of their colonial rule of Namibia. Thousands of

Namibians died either as a result of the fighting or in the aftermath and the effect that this had was to put a stop to organized resistance to outside rule. The trauma of defeat and dislocation meant that 50 odd years were to pass before the emergence of the independence movements in the late 1950s.

The war began following a revolt of the Bondelswarts Namas in the extreme S of the country at the end of 1903. The majority of German soldiers were sent to the S to quell the uprising and in January 1904 Samuel Maherero, under intense pressure from other Herero leaders and fearing for his own position as paramount Herero leader, gave the order to the Herero nation to rise up against the German presence in Namibia. At the same time he also appealed to Hendrik Witbooi and other Namibian leaders to follow suite.

During the first months of the uprising the Herero were successful in capturing or isolating German fortified positions, however, following the appointment of Lothar von Trotha as German military commander, the Herero were gradually forced to retreat from around Okahandja and other strongholds in Central Namibia. They made a final stand at the waterholes at Hamakari by the Waterberg Plateau S of Otjiwarongo in August of 1904. The German plan was to encircle the assembled Herero, defeat them, capture their leaders and pursue any splinter groups which might have escaped. The Herero objective was to hold onto the water holes, for without these they and their cattle would either die or be obliged to surrender.

The German troops attacked the Herero forces on 11 August with the battle continuing on a number of fronts all day. By nightfall no clear picture had yet emerged, however, the following day it became apparent that although the Herero had not been defeated, their resistance was broken and Samuel Maherero and the entire Herero nation fled into the Omaheke sandveld in eastern Namibia en route for Botswana. Stories from those who eventually arrived in Betchuanaland (Botswana) tell horrific stories of men, women and children struggling through the desert, gradually dying of thirst.

A section of the German forces initially gave chase but by 14 August they had returned to the original battle site, both soldiers and horses suffering from exhaustion, hunger and thirst. The chase was once again taken up on 16 August but finally abandoned at the end of September as it was impossible to provision both troops and horses in the Omaheke sandveld, into which a large number of Hereros had fled.

On 2 October Von Trotha issued a proclamation ordering all Herero-speaking people to leave German South-West Africa or face extermination, and then turned his attention to subduing uprisings in the S of the country. Just over a month later, Von Trotha received orders from Berlin to spare all Herero except the leaders and those "guilty". Following the retreat of the Herero, 3 more years of sporadic resistance to German rule took place in the centre and S of Namibia as the Nama-speaking people continued the revolt.

Much has been written on the German-Namibian War, specifically of the deliberate intention of the German colonial administration to "exterminate" the Herero nation. Until recently it was widely accepted that the Herero nation was reduced from a population of 60,000-80,000 people before the war, to between 16,000-18,000 people after the war. Similarly, the generally accepted view is that the population of the Nama-speaking peoples was also reduced by 35-50% to around 10,000 people.

It is impossible to obtain accurate figures to either confirm or refute the allegations of genocide, however, some recent research, especially by the late Brigitte Lau, former Head of the National Archives, challenges a number of popular conceptions of the war. In particular questions have now been raised on how the numbers were calculated and on the capacity of the German forces to actually set about the deliberate process of genocide.

The only figures available were based on missionary reports in the 1870s, but the missionaries only worked in a relatively small area of Hereroland. Furthermore, any accurate estimate of the numbers of Herero would have been near impossible, as the Herero were scattered across the veld. In addition, the effects of the rinderpest epidemic of 1897 and the fever epidemic of 1898 were also not taken into account. The suggestion is therefore that there were far fewer Herero than was originally believed.

As far as the capacity of German military to wipe out the Herero is concerned, medical records of the time show that the average military presence during the war was 11,000 men. Of these an average of 57% per year were sick from the effects of a lack of water and sanitation, typhoid fever, malaria, jaundice, suicide and chronic dysentery. This information suggests that the German military presence was simply not capable of a concerted attempt to commit genocide – even if that had been the intention.

There is no question, however, that following the war both Herero and Nama prisoners of war died in concentration camps, there were executions of captured leaders and many survivors were forced into labour – working on the railroads and in the mines. By the end of the war, the German colonial administration was firmly in control of Namibia from the Tsumeb-Grootfontein area in the N down to the Orange River in the south.

ECONOMIC DEVELOPMENT

With the consolidation of German control of Central and Southern Namibia came rapid economic growth and infrastructural development. Land in the most productive areas in the country was parcelled up and given to settler families, forming the basis of much of the existing white agricultural wealth in the country today. The railway network, already in place between Lüderitz and Aus in the S and Swakopmund, Okahandja and Windhoek in the centre of the country, was expanded to reach the central-northern towns of Tsumeb and Otavi and Grootfontein, Gobabis in the E and Keetmanshoop in the south.

The discovery of diamonds at Kolmanskop near Lüderitz in the S in 1908 financed the economic boom in that part of the country – between 1908 and 1914, German mining companies cut a total of 5,145,000 carats of diamonds. The introduction of the karakul sheep to the S saw the start of the highly successful karakul wool and leather industry, which brought tremendous prosperity to white farmers in the ranchlands S of Windhoek. Finally, the development of the Tsumeb mines producing copper, zinc and lead brought wealth and development to the Tsumeb-Grootfontein-Otavi triangle in the central-northern areas.

Whilst the wealth that accrued from this flurry of economic activity was concentrated in the hands of white settlers, the labour which built the railroads and worked the farms and mines was predominantly black. A vivid example of this was the estimated 10,000 Oshiwambo-speaking workers who came down from Owamboland in the far north (an area still outside of German colonial control, although technically part of German South-West Africa) to work on the railroads and in the mines. This was the start of migratory work patterns upon which the apartheid era contract labour system was built.

Self-government for the white population was granted by Germany in January 1909 and the following month the main towns including Windhoek, Swakopmund, Keetmanshoop, Lüderitz,

Okahandja and Tsumeb were granted the status of municipalities. In Windhoek this period up to the beginning of WW1 in 1914 saw the building of many landmarks – in particular the Christuskirche (German Lutheran Church) and the Tintenpalast – now the seat of the Namibian Parliament. Self-government in German South-West Africa lasted until the peaceful surrender of the territory to South African troops fighting on the side of the British in July 1915. This brought to an end the brief period of German colonial rule and ushered in the beginning of 75 years of South African rule.

THE LEAGUE OF NATIONS MANDATE

Following the end of WW1 and the signing of the Treaty of Versailles in 1919, the newly formed League of Nations gave the mandate for governing Namibia to Britain. The mandate, which was to be managed by South Africa on behalf of Britain, came into effect at the beginning of 1921 and was the beginning of South African control of Namibia, which was to end only with Independence in 1990.

The pattern of South African rule over Namibia was established from the start with the relentless expropriation of good farm land for white farmers and the removal of the black population, first to native reserves and later to the so-called homelands. When South Africa took over control of Namibia about 12 million ha of land were in the hands of white (mainly German) farmers, however, by 1925 a further 11.8 million ha had been given to white settlers.

A great number of these new settlers were poor, illiterate Afrikaners which the Union government in South Africa did not want within their own borders. In this way Namibia effectively became a dumping ground for these unwanted farmers, who were given the most generous of terms. New farmers were not only given land for free, but also received credit in the form of cash, wire fences

and government-built boreholes to help them get started.

In contrast, in 1923 the Native Reserves Commission proclaimed a mere 2 million ha for the black population of the country, making up 90% of the total population. At the same time a series of laws and regulations governed where the black population was entitled to live and work, severely restricting their freedom of movement in the white controlled areas. The most obvious consequences of these laws was the creation of a pool of readily available, cheap labour – the nascence of the contract labour system.

The bulk of the population of Namibia was forced to live in a narrow strip of land N of Etosha and S of the Angolan border, marked by the Kunene and Okavango rivers. The Red Line, a veterinary fence established by the Germans to prevent the spread of rinderpest and foot and mouth disease, effectively separated the communal grazing lands of the N from the commercial white-owned land of the centre and S of the country. This strip of land was far too small to support the number of people living there, obliging many to put themselves into the hands of the contract labour system by seeking work further south.

In 1925 two recruitment agencies were established to find workers for the mines in the centre and S of the country and in 1943 these two original agencies were amalgamated into the South West Africa Native Labour Association (SWANLA). Potential workers were sorted into three categories – those fit and able to work underground, those suitable for work above ground at the mines, and the rest only suitable for farm work. Workers themselves had no choice in this and "...Only the servant is required to render to the master his service at all fit and reasonable times."

The period following WW2 saw further land give-aways, mainly as rewards to Union soldiers who had served in the war. By the mid 1950s a further 7 million ha of farmland had been put into white hands and the number of whites in Namibia had increased by 50% to around 75,000. The last viable farmland was given away in the 1960s to white conservatives who supported the South African regime's hardline apartheid policies.

At the same time the Odendaal Commission of Inquiry formulated a plan for the creation of bantustans or black homelands around the country, involving the forced removal of black population from all areas designated for whites. The Commission also called for the even closer integration of Namibia into South Africa and stated explicitly that "... the government of South Africa no longer regards the original (League of Nations) mandate as still existing as such.

THE ROAD TO INDEPENDENCE

Following the end of WW2, the newly formed United Nations Organization assumed responsibility for the administration of the former German colonies, such as the Cameroons, Togo and Namibia. The UN set up a trusteeship system intended to lead to independence for these territories and in response the South African government sought to in-corporate Namibia into South Africa. A series of 'consultations' with Namibian leaders during 1946 were intended to convince the UN that Namibians themselves sought to become part of South Africa. Although these efforts were unsuccessful, it was not until 1971 that the South African presence was deemed to be 'illegal'.

Organized resistance to South African rule took off in the 1950s and was initially led by Herero Chief Hosea Kutako, who initiated a long series of petitions to the UN. In 1957 the Owamboland's People's Congress was founded in Cape Town by Namibian contract workers lead by Andimba Toivo Ja Toivo, its prime objective being to achieve the abolition of the hated contract labour system. In 1958 Toivo succeeded in smuggling a tape to the UN giving oral evidence of South African suppression and for his pains was immediately deported to Namibia. The same year the name of the organization was changed to the Owamboland People's Organization and in 1959 Sam Nujoma and Jacob Kuhangu launched the organization in Windhoek.

1959 also saw the founding of South West Africa National Union (SWANU), initially an alliance between urban

Early leaders of Namibia's independence movement

Shooting at the Old Location

In order to comply with apartheid policy regulations that a 5 km buffer zone should exist between white and black residential areas, Windhoek Municipality formulated plans to remove the black and coloured communities from the so-called *Old Location* close to the city centre. Two new townships – Khomasdal and Katutura were intended to be the new homes for these communities, however the residents of the Old Location were not inclined to move. For a start their homes, businesses and lives were based in and around the Old Location, furthermore the proposed new townships were far out of town, had none of the necessary amenities, and the rents on the municipality-built houses were expensive.

Resistance to removal started as early as 1956 and was well established by the time matters came to a head in the second half of 1959 when the community of the Old Location took a decision to boycott all municipal services, including the buses and the beer hall, an important source of municipal profit. On 9 December a procession of women succeeded in leading a demonstration from the Old Location to demonstrate in front of the house of the South African administrator. The following evening South African Police and military units with armoured cars were sent into the Location, only to be met by gathering crowds and stone road blocks.

At around 2230 on the night of 10 December tear gas cannisters were fired into the crowd followed by gunshots, killing 13 protestors and wounding dozens more. The repercussions of the shootings were to be felt for many years, as the resistance of the inhabitants of the Old Location became a symbol of the wider Namibian resistance to apartheid policies and South African rule itself.

youth, intellectuals and the Herero Chief's Council. In September of that year the executive of the organization was broadened to include members of the OPO and other organizations, thereby widening the base of the organization to make it more representative of the Namibian population as a whole.

These new organizations were soon in conflict with the South African authorities and the December 1959 shootings at the Old Location (see box) effectively marked the start of concerted resistance to South African rule. In 1960 the OPO was formally reconstituted into the South West Africa People's Organization (SWAPO), with the central objective of liberating the Namibian people from colonial oppression and exploitation. SWAPO leader Sam Nujoma had managed to leave Namibia and was to lead the organization in exile until his return to the country in 1989.

In 1966, SWAPO appealed to the International Court of Justice to declare South Africa's control of Namibia illegal, however, the court failed to deliver – even though the UN General Assembly voted to terminate South Africa's Mandate. SWAPO's response was to launch the guerrilla war at Ongulumbashe in Owamboland on 26 August, with the declaration that the court's ruling ..."would relieve Namibians once and for all from any illusions which they might have harboured about the United Nations as some kind of saviour in their plight ..."

In the early stages, the bush war was by necessity a small scale affair. SWAPO's bases were in Zambia, close only to the Eastern Caprivi region, and and it was only after the Portuguese withdrawal from Angola in 1975 that it became possible to wage a larger scale campaign. In response to the launching of the guerrilla war, the South African government established military bases all across Namibia's northern borders, and as the scale of the fighting escalated during the 1980s, life became increasingly intolerable for the inhabitants of these areas.

On the political scene, SWAPO activists in Namibia were arrested, tried and sentenced to long prison terms. Amongst the first group to be sentenced in 1968 was Toivo Ja Toivo, at that time Regional Secretary for Owamboland. He was sentenced to 20 years imprisonment on Robben Island where he was to remain until 1984. Following the International Court of Justice ruling in 1971 that "... the continued presence of South Africa in Namibia being illegal ..."a wave of strikes lead by contract workers broke out around the country, precipitating a further round of arrests of strike leaders.

Although the South African government succeeded in quelling the strikes of late 1971 and early 1972, the rest of the decade saw growing resistance to South African rule of Namibia. Ordinary Namibians everywhere, but especially in the densely populated N, buoyed by the International Court of Justice ruling, became politicized, resisting South African attempts to push forward apartheid policies to create separate bantustans around the country.

In response to pressure from Western countries South Africa struggled to find an 'internal solution' to the deadlock in Namibia, which would both satisfy the outside world and at the same time defend white minority interests in the country. In 1977 the Turnhalle Conference (see page 87, Windhoek section) produced a draft constitution for an independent Namibia based on a three tier system of government which would change little. Needless to say, no one was fooled and the war continued.

During the 1980s South Africa's position in Namibia became increasingly untenable. The bush war was expensive and never-ending and was seriously affecting the South African economy; at the same time attempts to find a political solution within Namibia which excluded SWAPO were proving impossible. Furthermore opinion amongst the influential Western nations was swinging away from South Africa, making it inevitable that sooner or later Namibia would have to be granted independence with black majority rule.

The key to the solution was the withdrawal of Cuban troops from Angola in return for the withdrawal of South African soldiers from Namibia. At the same time a United National Transitional Government (UNTAG) was to oversee the transition to independence, with elections taking place in November 1989. The final months leading up to the elections saw the return of SWAPO President Sam Nujoma from 30 years in exile along with thousands of ordinary Namibians who had fled into exile during the long years of the bush war.

The main political parties were SWAPO and the DTA, formed in the wake of the unsuccessful Turnhalle Conference. Support for SWAPO was almost universal in Owamboland where the majority of the population live, whilst the DTA looked to the S and much of the white community for its support. Although SWAPO won the elections it did not gain the two thirds majority required to draw up a new constitution for the country.

Following the successful elections a new constitution was drafted by the various political parties with the help of international advisers from a number of countries including the USA, France, Germany and the former Soviet Union. Widely viewed as a model of its kind, the new constitution guaranteed wide-ranging human rights and freedom of speech, as well as establishing a multiparty democracy governed by the rule of law. The final date for independence was set for 21 March 1990.

Culture

NAMIBIA is a blend of many different peoples and cultures, similar in some respects to the 'rainbow' nation next door. Home to the Bushmen, the oldest inhabitants of southern Africa as well as to the more recently arrived Europeans, Namibia's culture has absorbed both African and European elements and fused them into a blend of the two. The choral tradition brought from Germany has been adopted and modified and is one of Namibia's most vibrant art forms, whilst cooking in a *potjie*, a traditional three legged iron pot over an open fire is a favourite pastime of many Namibians.

Namibia's population of 1.6 million has doubled in the past 30 years and is currently growing at an exponential 3.5% per year. Whilst most Namibians still live in the rural areas, practising subsistence farming of one form or another, increasing mobility and a lack of employment opportunities in the rural areas are causing a rapid migration to the towns. As people lose touch with their homes and traditional ways of life and adopt a more urban, western lifestyle, the levels of crime and unemployment experienced in many western cities are unfortunately also becoming a fact of life in Namibia.

In a predominantly rural country where many aspects of culture are closely linked with land ownership, unresolved land issues dating back to pre-colonial, colonial and apartheid days are still live issues for many communities.

One recent example saw the blockade of the Etosha Game Park entrance by groups of Bushmen calling for the return of their traditional lands. Other communities, such as the Rehoboth Basters, have been involved in a series of court cases with the government over the issue of ownership of traditional lands.

As in neighbouring Zimbabwe and South Africa, the majority of quality commercial farmland is still in the hands of white farmers. The problem of how to satisfy the demands of landless peasants whilst not alienating an important revenue generating section of the community is yet another unresolved issue facing the government.

PEOPLE

Namibia's people consist of 11 major ethnic groups scattered around the country. From semi-nomadic cattle herders and hunters to the sophisticated urban elite both black and white, ethnicity is an important unifying force in this sparsely inhabited country. Since independence in 1990 there has been a resurgence of support for traditional leaders who the government has recently banned from becoming political leaders. At the same time there are tensions between different ethnic groups, in part for historical reasons and in part due to the overwhelming numerical superiority of the Owambo and their strong support for and involvement with SWAPO – the governing party.

Nevertheless, for the time being, unlike some other African countries, Namibia is largely free of tribal conflict, however, the potential for conflict does exist. The government's stance on the issue was summarized by Prime Minister Hage Geingob at a 1993 conference on tribalism. "For too long we have thought of ourselves as Hereros, Namas, Afrikaners, Germans, Owambos. We must now start to think of ourselves as Namibians."

OWAMBO

Made up of 12 tribes in all of whom 8 live in Namibia and 4 in Angola, the Owambo are the single largest ethnic group in Namibia with an estimated population in 1994 of 670,000. Traditionally the Owambo live in round, pallisaded homesteads built on raised ground between the *oshanas*, seasonal lakes which flood during the rainy season.

The few hectares of land surrounding each homestead is farmed with livestock such as cattle, goats and sheep for which the men are traditionally responsible. Crops are also grown, in particular finger millet, *omuhango* which is used to make porridge and brew beer; other crops grown are sorghum, maize, beans and pumpkins, and this is traditionally the work of the women.

During the apartheid era tens of thousands of Owambos migrated to the central and southern parts of the country in search of work. In recent years the lack of availability of land and water have forced many more people to abandon subsistence farming as a way of life

A chief and his family photographed in 1905

and instead enter the labour market. This in turn has caused the growth of villages and larger urban centres such as Oshakati, Ongwediva and Ombalantu which function as part of the wider urban cash economy.

Namibia's governing party SWAPO emerged from the Owamboland People's Organization which was constituted in 1957, and originally dedicated to fighting the hated contract labour system. A breakdown of the traditional leadership system amongst four of the tribes left a political void which SWAPO stepped in to fill. Offering itself initially as the voice of the Owambo nation, the party eventually took the moral, political and military initiative for the whole country in launching the independence struggle against the South African government. Today SWAPO enjoys overwhelming support in the country as a whole and within the Owambo-speaking areas of the N draws over 90% of the vote.

KAVANGO

The Kavango region stretching from Owamboland to the W as far as the Caprivi strip in the E and bordered to the N by the Kavango River is home to five distinct tribal groups totalling around 140,000 people. Traditionally the five Okavango tribes the *Geiriku*, *Shambiu*, *Mbunzu*, *Kwangai* and *Mbukushu* followed a matrilineal system of leadership and inheritance, however, the growth of livestock farming by men has increased their economic and social status and stimulated a system of patrilineal ties of inheritance.

All of the five tribes live along the banks of the Kavango River and predominantly practise a subsistence economy made up of pastoralism, fishing and hunting. Fishing is a prime source of protein to the Kavango peoples and is practised by both men and women, who specialize in using funnel-shaped baskets to make their catch. Thanks to a rich store of wildlife, hunting has played an

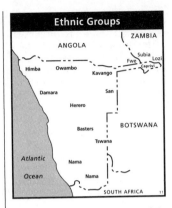

Ethnic Groups

important part in the economy of the Kavango communities. However, today no game remains in the inhabited areas of the region and strict control is enforced over hunting in less densely populated areas.

Most Namibian wood carving originates in the Kavango area and objects such as masks, drums, stools are available in Windhoek curio shops. It is also not uncommon to see the carvers working and selling their products by the side of the road outside towns in the central and southern parts of the country.

As the population grows and more young people become educated, a gradual migration to the urban areas is taking place, although not on the same scale as with the Owambo. At the same time, stimulated by cross-border trade with Angola, the economy of the region is becoming more commodity and cash-based, most visible in the regional capital Rundu.

CAPRIVI

Stretching from the Kavango Region in the W to the Zambezi in the E, the narrow strip of land that constitutes the Caprivi Region is home to the Subia and Fwe tribes, the latter including a number of Yeyi, Totela and Lozi communities. An estimated 92,000 people in all live in this well-watered, subtropical region which forms part of the northern Kalahari basin.

Historically the area has been dominated by the Lozi tribe from Zambia and the Kololo from South Africa. The more recent intervention of Europeans followed the agreement between Britain and Germany in 1890 which gave colonial authority over the land to the Germans, who only arrived, however in 1909.

The Lozi first conquered the area in the late 17th and early 18th century only to be ousted following the migration of southern Sotho tribes from South Africa in the wake of the Zulu wars in Natal. The existing Lozi customs were adapted to suit Sotho institutions in a so-called Kololo Empire – until a Lozi revolt in 1864 restored their control over the area.

During the consecutive periods of Lozi and Kololo rule, Lozi was established as the *lingua franca* of the area and subsequently as medium of instruction in schools. Both Lozi and Kololo empires promoted patrilineal institutions making the patrilineal extended family the basic social unit.

Both Fwe and Subia practise a mixed economy including hunting, gathering, fishing, hoe-farming and pastoralism, with agriculture forming the backbone of the traditional economy. There are few urban centres asides from the regional capital Katima Mulilo and job opportunities outside of subsistence farming are few and far between. Inevitably this is leading to many young people moving away from the land to look for work in urban areas in other parts of the country.

In recent years the population of the Caprivi has been hit very hard by the spread of HIV and AIDS and there is considerable concern over how this will effect the community as a whole.

HERERO

Like the other Bantu-speaking tribes in Namibia, it is believed that the Herero originated in the great lakes region of East Africa, before migrating W and S. Initially settled in Kaokoland in the NW of Namibia, the majority of Herero started a southward migration from the middle of the 18th century onward. By the time the first Europeans arrived in Namibia in the early part of the 19th century, the Herero were well established in the central areas of the country.

The second half of the 19th century saw virtual constant low-level warfare between the Herero and the Nama over the question of land and grazing rights for their cattle. Following the German occupation of Namibia late in the 19th century, more and more Herero land passed into the hands of the colonizers, leading to increasing discontent amongst the people.

Finally in 1904 the Herero rose up against the Germans in an attempt to claim back their tribal land. The final battle was fought at the Waterberg Plateau in August 1904 and in itself was not decisive. However, the subsequent retreat of the Herero into the *Omaheke* sandveld, in the E of the country, saw the deaths of thousands due to hunger and starvation. Defeat also brought about the further loss of traditional grazing lands and the displacement of the survivors into so-called homelands.

Traditionally, the Herero followed a semi-nomadic pastoral way of life, keeping large herds of cattle and following their cattle around in search of good grazing. However, unlike commercial farmers, the Herero have traditionally seen their cattle as an indication of wealth and status, not to be sold or slaughtered arbitrarily for food. Until relatively recently in fact, the Herero have largely remained outside of the formal labour market, preferring to focus on their livestock.

During the 20th century there has been a resurgence of Herero culture and former paramount Chief Hosea Kutako was a key figure in carrying the case for

Namibian independence to the United Nations. One important expression of Herero identity is the annual 26 August Hero's Day parade in Okahandja, when the people march to the grave of their former leaders in order to pay respect to those fallen in battle. Some Herero women are also easily identified by the huge, colourful dresses and hats which they wear. These Victorian remnants of the influence of the 19th century German missionaries' wives are nevertheless a symbol of pride to their wearers.

HIMBA

During the Herero-Nama conflict of the second half of the 19th century, the Herero still living in Kaokoland lost much of their cattle to marauding Nama bands. Those dispossessed of their cattle were forced into a hunter-gatherer way of life, considered an inferior way of existence to the pastoral Herero. This led to the branding of such people as *Tjimba* derived from *ondjimba-ndjimba* meaning an *aardvark* or digger of roots.

During the early years of this century groups of Tjimba-Herero who had fled into Angola, and other Hereros who had joined them there following the defeat at the hands of the Germans, united behind a Herero leader, Vita. Under his leadership, an effective fighting force operated in southern Angola, building up substantial herds of cattle. Following the German withdrawal from South-West Africa after WW1, Vita and many of his followers crossed back over the Kunene River into Namibia. Today their descendants form the bulk of the Himba and Herero population in Kaokoland.

Elevated to almost legendary status in Namibia, the Himba still live a more or less traditional existence, with their cattle as the centre of their lives. Largely eschewing westernization, the Himba have managed to successfully live in balance with nature in the fragile Kaokoland, pursuing their old customs such as ancestor worship and the keeping of the sacred fire at the homestead.

Today, however, the Himba's independent way of life is being seriously challenged on a number of fronts. Like many traditional peoples the Himba are susceptible to the effects of strong alcohol; unscrupulous traders from both Namibia and Angola are currently spreading this curse to even the remotest Himba communities, whilst enriching themselves with Himba livestock in exchange for the alcohol. But perhaps even more serious than this is the proposed Epupa Dam scheme (see page 180, Kaokoland section) which is likely to finally break the Himba's geographic isolation from the rest of the country and introduce whole-scale modernization and westernization to that part of Kaokoland.

DAMARA

Widely believed to be the oldest inhabitants of Namibia after the Bushmen and the Nama, and sharing a similar language and customs with the Nama, the precise origins of the Damara remain something of a mystery. Two conflicting theories suggest first that the Damara migrated from West Africa to Namibia, where they were subjected by the Nama people, and in this way acquired similar language and customs. An alternative theory suggests that the Damara evolved alongside the Nama in Botswana thousands of years ago, thereby explaining the similarities in language and culture, and simply migrated at a later date into Namibia.

By the beginning of the 19th century Damara communities were established throughout the central parts of Namibia, living by a mixture of hunting, livestock farming and limited crop cultivation. The Damara are also known to have been skilled smelters and workers of copper and it seems likely that they were engaged in trade with the Owambo to the N and the Nama to the S.

However, as tension over land issues grew during the 19th century, in particular between the Nama and the Herero, the Damara were squeezed out of many of the areas in which they were settled. Some became servants to the Herero and the Nama, others fled to the remote mountainous areas, earning them the name *Berg* or 'mountain' Damara.

Following the establishment of German colonial rule over Namibia, the first Damara 'reserve' was created in 1906 around the Okombahe area. This original area was enlarged upon the recommendations of the Odendaal Commission of Inquiry in the 1960s, when so-called tribal homelands were created for the different ethnic groups in Namibia. The Damara 'homeland' was established in the NW of the country, from Uis in the S to Sesfontein in the N, and this remains a predominantly Damara area today.

Today the majority of the estimated 132,000 Damara community actually lives outside of this area, working in the towns of the central part of the country, such as Windhoek, Okahandja, Swakopmund, Walvis Bay, Otavi and Tsumeb. Many Damara are today active in public life, notably the Prime Minister Hage Geingob and Labour Minister Moses Garoeb.

NAMA

Ethnically the Nama living in Namibia are descendants of Khoisan groups who have been living in southern Africa for many thousands of years. It is believed that the first Nama groups to arrive in Namibia did so about 2,000 years ago, having migrated first from Botswana.

Traditionally the Nama were semi-nomadic pastoralists who also continued to hunt and gather food from the veld. The various different clans shared the available grazing and water in Southern and Central Namibia, moving with their animals as need dictated. Although little is known of the precise relations between Nama and Bushmen, it is assumed that there must have been contact between the two groups, and even some social movement between them.

At the turn of the 19th century the first groups of Oorlam Namas started to cross the Orange River in search of land. These mixed race newcomers were generally Christians, having had extensive contact with white settlers in the Cape, and in most cases having lost their land to them. The Oorlams' contact with Europeans meant that they had acquired guns and horses and were consequently able to establish themselves in southern Namibia alongside existing Nama groups.

Although the first half of the 19th century saw significant conflict between the Nama and the Oorlams, by the end of the century the old differences had largely disappeared. Inter-marriage and common enemies in the form first of the Herero and then the Germans had united the two groups so that today no differentiation is made between them.

In the 1890s, the famous Nama leader Hendrik Witbooi, was the first Namibian leader to see that differences between the various ethnic groups in the country were far less important than the struggle against the Germans. Together with other Nama leaders he led resistance to German rule in the S of Namibia during the 1904-07 war.

Like the Herero, the Nama suffered heavy losses during this period as a result of war and famine and their numbers declined significantly. In addition the loss of traditional land, a process which had begun during the 19th century, continued under German and then South African rule. During the apartheid era, the majority of the Nama-speaking population was confined to a tribal homeland SW of Mariental and NW of Keetmanshoop.

Today the majority of the Nama still live in the S of the country, although small groups, such as the Topnaars who live in the Kuiseb Canyon area, live in other parts of the country. Their main source of income is derived from livestock farming, especially cattle and goats, but the struggle for survival in the harsh environment of the semi-desert of the S of Namibia means that most Namas today still live a subsistence existence.

The estimated 80,000 Nama are famous for their poetry and singing, in the form of traditional praise poems and their church choirs, and these are an important form of modern-day Nama cultural expression.

SAN

The San or Bushmen as they are often called are generally accepted to be the oldest indigenous inhabitants of southern Africa, and numerous examples of their rock art, dating back thousands of years, is to be found all over the sub-region.

Traditionally the San were skilled hunter-gatherers living in small independent bands with the family as the basic unit. Different bands had limited contact with each other, although individuals were free to come and go as they pleased, unhampered by possessions or fixed work responsibilities.

Although successful and well-adapted to their environment, about 300 years ago the San started to come under pressure both from migrating Bantu tribes and early European settlers. Regarded as cattle thieves and considered as more or less sub-human by these groups, the San were hunted down and forced off their traditional lands, the majority seeking the relative safety of the Kalahari Desert in Botswana and Namibia.

Today, the estimated 45,000 San living in Namibia live a marginalized existence on the fringes of mainstream society. Like other aboriginal peoples in Australia and North America, the loss of their land and traditional way of life has seriously undermined the San people's culture. Human rights groups in Namibia maintain that the San are seriously exploited and discriminated against by other ethnic groups in the country.

However, the San have not given up hope and there are groups who since independence in 1990 have been campaigning for the return of traditional hunting lands. The most recent protest in January 1997 saw a group of around 70 Hai/Om San demonstrate at the gates of Etosha National Park. The response of the authorities was to teargas and arrest these peaceful protestors, for which they were condemned by human rights groups and various opposition parties.

However, the future for the San in Namibia does not look good. They are unlikely to be granted significant tracts of land on which to return to their former way of life, and unless educational and employment opportunities can be provided for them, they will remain a poor and marginalized community.

WHITES

The majority of the estimated 100,000 Whites living in Namibia are of German and Afrikaner descent, with a small group of English speakers. The first Europeans to arrive in Namibia were missionaries travelling with Oorlam groups over the Orange River from Namaqualand. These were followed during the first half of the 19th century by traders and hunters who opened up the interior of the country for further European exploration.

Following the consolidation of German colonial rule towards the end of the 19th century, Europeans started to settle in larger numbers, most earning a living through trading and livestock farming. The discovery of diamonds and other minerals early this century attracted outside investment and led to further European control of the economy of the country.

The period of South African rule from 1917 until independence in 1990 saw the bulk of the viable farmland transferred into the hands of white farmers. Mineral rights were controlled by

Two baster women pose outside of their hut at Rehoboth

the multi-national European and American conglomerates and apartheid legislation ensured that all significant commercial activities were firmly placed in white hands.

Following independence, although political power has passed into the hands of the black majority, the bulk of viable commercial farmland is still in white hands. Likewise, most businesses in the towns of central and southern Namibia belong to Whites and the majority of the private sector of the burgeoning tourist industry is also in white hands.

Whilst many white people are making an effort to adapt to the realities of living in independent Namibia, an equal number still live as in the past, sticking exclusively to their own communities. Inevitably the barriers of the past will take time to be overcome, but with the integration of the education system, there is hope that the next generation of white Namibians, who have nowhere else to go, will participate fully in the wider society in their country.

BASTERS

The 39,000 strong Rehoboth Basters are the descendants of a group of Khoi-European mixed race settlers who arrived in Namibia in 1869. After negotiations with the Herero and the Swartbooi Namas, the Basters bought and settled land in the Rehoboth area, where the majority earned a living through livestock farming.

During the apartheid era, the Basters managed to hold on to their land, enabling the community to retain a strong sense of its own identity; at independence a section of the Basters even called for the creation of a separate Baster homeland. The traditional leadership under *Kaptein* or leader Hans Diergaardt have also been engaged in a series of court cases against the government concerning the rights to administer communal land in and around the town of Rehoboth. The matter was finally settled in 1996 with a Supreme Court ruling in favour of the government.

Recurrent drought over recent years has forced many Basters off land to seek employment in Rehoboth and Windhoek. Today, despite the isolationism of some, the majority of Basters have entered the mainstream of Namibian society working in a wide range of trades and professions.

COLOUREDS

Around 60,000 people in Namibia today regard themselves as "Coloureds". These people were originally of mixed European and African descent, but the vast majority today are born from Coloured parents. The apartheid reality of Coloured townships, Coloured schools and Coloured churches means that there is a strong sense of shared community and culture.

Afrikaans-speaking and urban-dwelling, the Coloured community is predominantly Christian and western oriented. Most Coloureds live in the central and southern parts of the country.

TSWANA

The Tswana make up the smallest ethnic group in Namibia, numbering around 9,000. Related to the Tswana in South Africa and Botswana, they are the descendants of a group who migrated to Namibia from South Africa during the 19th century. These people eventually settled in the E of the country between Aminuis and the Botswana border where they live predominantly as livestock farmers.

Modern Namibia

SINCE independence the SWAPO government lead by Sam Nujoma has pursued a policy of national reconciliation designed to heal the wounds of 25 years of civil war and over a century of colonial rule. Strongly supported by the various UN agencies and major donors, the Namibian government has set about to redress the injustices of the past and rebuild the economy, so badly damaged by the war. The mining sector, which is by far the largest sector of the economy, has been further developed and significant growth has also occurred in both the fishing and tourist industries. However, Namibia is still largely dependent on South Africa for foodstuffs and manufactured products, and this is one of the weak links in the economy.

The provision of educational and health care facilities to previously neglected sections of the community has also been a priority for the government, however this has placed a heavy burden on the country's finances. Education alone has been consuming around 30% of the national budget since independence, whilst the combined effects of rapid population growth (around 3.5%) and an inflation rate hovering around the 10% mark, have made it difficult for the country to address the problem of massive unemployment.

Elections in 1994 saw SWAPO win with a massive 68% of the vote, effectively giving the party the right to change the constitution if it so wishes.

With the next elections due in 1998 there is currently talk of the President possibly standing for a third term in office. Whilst Sam Nujoma is immensely popular and respected by the vast majority of Namibians, the constitution restricts the number of terms a person can be president to two. Some people fear that if the constitution is amended to allow Nujoma to stand for a third term Namibia might start to slide towards becoming a one party state, with all the negative connotations that go with this.

However, for the time being the country remains calm and peaceful, the economy is more or less on track and key industries, such as tourism, are growing steadily. Human rights and freedom of speech are both respected and Namibia is an active member of the Southern African Development Community (SADC). There is therefore a generally optimistic air, that despite the many challenges and problems to be faced by this developing nation, Namibia can look forward to a bright future in the 21st century.

ECONOMICS

Since independence Namibia has enjoyed a steady economic growth, but this has been checked by periods of drought and low world commodity prices. Income per head was estimated at US$1,820 in 1994, which is significantly higher than Zimbabwe or Moçambique. However, this figure disguises the great inequality in income distribution, the white minority enjoy a much higher income than most of the black population.

Since 1990 the economy has grown at an average rate of 4.5%, but a 3.2% population growth has eroded many of the economic gains. In 1982 mining contributed to 26.9% of GDP, by 1995 this figure had fallen to 11%, tourism and the fisheries sector have made significant contributions to recent growth. However, these sectors have been unable to absorb the increase in the number of Namibians looking for work.

In 1995, 66% of the adult population were literate, primary school enrolment was 83% (1993), while secondary school enrolment was 42% (1991). Namibia has placed a high priority on education, since independence the system has been rationalized and the quality and relevance of the education for all Namibian children has been improved. Over 10% of GDP is devoted to education, a proportion exceeded by few countries in the world. In the long run the government is hoping to reap the dividends, assuming sufficient jobs can be created.

The Namibian health care system is one of the government's four priority sectors. Before independence the system concentrated on curative care for the urban elite, while neglecting the majority of the poor. The system was racially based with inequitable quality and access to care. The government has embarked upon a programme to redistribute resources from curative to primary care. Investment in health care has been 14% of government spending, a high proportion by regional and international standards. Improvements have been made but many of the remote rural areas are still without access to clinics and community health workers. In the future Namibia is going to have to cope with a serious AIDS epidemic which will have a significant impact on future economic development. The country still fails to record accurately the number of deaths due to AIDS, in 1995 tuberculosis and diarrhoea were recorded ahead of AIDS as the cause of death. These are primary symptoms of AIDS among adults, and it is likely that many of these deaths were also due to AIDS.

Namibia is in a unique position due to its dualistic economy and the legacy of apartheid. Resources have been concentrated in the hands of a small minority. Despite a high per capita income the living standards for the majority of the population are very low. Namibia is one of the worst performers in the world in terms of human development levels relative to national income. Despite great improvements in human development the country still faces a great challenge before the economic benefits and wealth can be enjoyed by the majority of the population and not the minority.

Economic performance

Mining In simple statistical terms Namibia is mineral rich. The country has the world's largest uranium mine, Namibia is Africa's second largest producer of zinc, its third largest producer of lead and fourth largest supplier of copper. The diamond mines around Lüderitz are the leading producers of

Regional Boundaries

OMUSATI
OSHANA
OHANGWENA
Opuwo
OTJIKOTO
KUNENE
Tsumeb
Grootfontein
OTJOZONDJUPA
ERONGO
OMAHEKE
Swakopmund
Windhoek
Gobabis
KHOMAS
HARDAP
Mariental
Keetmanshoop
KARAS

Katima Mulilo
CAPRIVI
Rundu
OKAVANGO

002

page 133). While the sector may be an important source of employment it does not employ that many people. In 1983 the sector employed 16,600 people, by 1992 this figure had fallen to 11,400. This was mainly due to job losses at Rössing Uranium and Namdeb Diamond Corporation and the closure of the Namib Lead Mine. After the most recent dispute at TCL it is hoped that the industry is now in a position to consolidate and hopefully take advantage of an anticipated world economic recovery. In April 1994 the Minerals Act was promulgated to govern all future prospecting. It is the government's intention to diversify the sector and promote small-scale mining. It will take some time before the sector is not dominated by large-scale foreign owned companies, which employ a limited number of Namibians, and repatriate a large proportion of their profits overseas. At present many of the locally owned small mines suffer from a lack of financial assistance, technical expertise and administrative skills.

gem-quality diamonds in the world; and then there are significant reserves of silver, gold, tin, cadmium, zinc, vanadium, tungsten and germanium. There are over 40 different operating mines and quarries in the sector, producing a wide range of precious metals and minerals.

Overall the sector is the largest private sector employer and the largest source of corporate tax. But since 1989 the industry has had to undergo major structural readjustments and retrenchment, during this period the contribution to GDP has fallen from 28% to 11% (1995), while the absolute value has not varied a great deal in constant prices since 1988. Mining is always vulnerable to demand and worldwide price fluctuations, during the recent industrial dispute at TCL it was claimed that the company had had to cope with a 30-35% drop in world copper prices (see box

Diamonds In recent years the diamond industry in Namibia has undergone some major changes, both in means of production and ownership. At the end of 1994 a new operating company, Namdeb Diamond Corporation, acquired the diamond assets of the Consolidated Diamond Mine based in Oranjemund. The new company is equally owned by the Namibian government and De Beers Centenary AG. While the importance of income from diamonds has declined they remain an important source of income for the government. In 1980 diamonds contributed to 40% of the state revenue, but this figure quickly fell to just 9% in 1983. More recently trade in diamonds has accounted for N\$818mn in 1992, 22.7% of Namibia's total exports. A recovery in prices has lead to several operations being reopened but overall the trend around Lüderitz and Oranjemund is to increase the exploitation of offshore diamond fields. The Namibian Minerals Corporation, NAMCO, hold the concession rights to over 1,000 sq km offshore, an area estimated to contain 73 million carats of gem diamonds. In 1994 total production of diamonds was 1.3 million carats.

Uranium 50 km inland from Swakopmund is the Rössing uranium mine, the world's largest single producer of a low-grade uranium. The mine has been developed by the Rio Tinto-Zinc group, the first oxide was extracted in 1976, since when the mine's fortunes have fluctuated along with world prices. Most of the uranium is sold to Europe, Japan and Taiwan on long term contracts. In 1994 a deal was struck with Electricité de France which should ensure the mine remains profitable until at least 2000. Once the reserves have been exhausted the mine is committed to a major environmental cleanup project, while it will not be difficult to dismantle machinery and housing how best to deal with the giant hole in the ground is another matter.

Oil and gas Prior to independence there was no investment in the exploration for hydrocarbon potential because of political uncertainty. Since 1990 offshore geological investigations have revealed conditions to be similar to the N, off the coast of Angola where oil has already been discovered. A World Bank study has indicated that there may be up to 14 years worth of natural gas reserves in the Kudu fields offshore from Lüderitz. In 1993 the exploration rights were awarded to a consortium of Shell and Engen. While exploration continues no plans have yet been announced as to whether or when the proven reserves may be extracted.

Agriculture Agriculture is a very important sector in terms of the employment it provides, but the environment and continued threat of drought mean that its overall contribution to the economy is limited. The most important component is livestock, beef and mutton production account for almost 75% of the gross agricultural income. The sector directly or indirectly supports over 70% of the total population. Of all the economic sectors agriculture is the most emotive, under successive colonial governments much of the land was expropriated from the black majority to a few white settlers. This led to a dualistic agricultural sector; just over 4,000 white farmers owned 43% of agricultural land under freehold title, with approximately 150,000 households on 42% of the land. Since independence the government has been very cautious in its approach to the land question. In 1991 a national conference on land reform was held, the conference rejected radical land expropriation, but recommended that the government place a ban on foreign ownership of agricultural land and called for redistribution of commercial land within the provisions of the Constitution. In 1995 the government drafted the Commercial Land Reform Act which prescribed the procedure for land acquisition and distribution. Small scale farmers have been helped with low-interest loans but the issue of tenure remains unresolved. While the government remains undecided on how to deal with the issue of land redistribution a new worrying trend has emerged where the wealthy new black elite are enclosing communal land for private use; this has been made possible by the gradual breakdown of traditional forms of land administration, once again it is the smallest and most poor farmers who suffer.

Namibia's low and erratic rainfall pattern places severe limits on potential rainfed agriculture. It is only possible to grow a single rainfed crop each year, and this has to be in areas where the annual summer rainfall is more than 450 mm. The yields for rainfed crops are affected by the uneven distribution of rains during the wet season and by poor soils. Many of the soils in the N suffer from deficiencies of zinc, phosphorus and organic matter. In order to obtain high yields the government is forced to use expensive imported fertilizers and other chemicals. Namibia remains a net importer of basic food crops, drought has forced the country to appeal for emergency food aid on several occasions in recent years. In 1994 Namibia produced 76,000 tonnes of cereals, in 1995 this figure was only 41,000 tonnes – in 1993 32,000 tonnes were harvested, but during the 1991/92 drought the figure was as low as 13,000 tonnes. Faced with such variations it is very difficult for the government to plan a reliable cereals policy.

The centre of the beef industry is the eastern central part of the country where a variety of breeds freely roam the nutritious grasslands. White farmers have developed Bonsmara and Afrikaner breeds as well as Brahman and Simmentaler to suit local conditions. Most beef products are chilled and vacuum packed before being exported frozen to South Africa and the EEC. The export market demands lean beef from cattle of between 20 and 36 months old. When Namibia signed the Lomé convention it agreed to supply the EEC with 10,500 tonnes of beef in 1991 and 1992, rising to 13,000 tonnes in 1993. But like the arable sector livestock ranching remains vulnerable to drought, and these figures have had to be revised in response to losses through drought.

Fishing Namibia ranks amongst the top 10 in the world in terms of the value of its catch. The fishing industry is in the same league as Norway and Canada and bigger than the UK or Australia. The cold waters of the Benguela current produce a nutrient-rich system which is very productive and typified by a low number of species being present but with large numbers of individuals per species. While these waters are ideal for industrial scale exploitation the careful management of the resources is vital (see below).

The recently revived Namibian industry is subdivided into two sectors, white fish and pelagic. The white fish species, kingklip, hake, sole, monk and snoek, occur along the continental shelf which stretches from the Kunene River in the N to the Orange River in the S. The total exploitable area is some 60,000 sq nautical miles. The pelagic species, pilchard and horse mackerel, are found in more shallow waters which stretch from just S of Walvis Bay to Cape Frio in the N. The industry has yet to start exploiting the waters beyond the edge of the continental shelf.

The fishing industry is an excellent example of how conditions have changed to the benefit of Namibia since independence. Prior to independence Namibia had no control over the illegal fishing which took place within the internationally recognized fishing zone of 200 nautical miles (370 km), the exclusive economic zone, EEZ. As Namibia did not exist as an independent nation no foreign fishing fleet was obliged to pay any of the taxes or licence fees that would normally be due when fishing within another nation's EEZ. Without any controls in place this nearly resulted in the total destruction of some of the richest fishing waters in the world. Overfishing during the 1980s resulted in the closure of five out of nine processing factories and the loss of jobs for four-fifths of the work force. It was estimated that foreign fleets were catching over

80% of the fish within Namibian waters, and that this catch was worth at least 1,500 million rand.

Immediately after independence the new government proclaimed the existence of Namibia's EEZ and instructed foreign vessels to respect the zone and cease fishing within it. The government has been quick to introduce legislation which promotes the conservation of the marine environment and the managed exploitation of marine resources. The National Fisheries Act was passed at the end of 1992. By introducing new quotas and awarding long term concessions the government has managed to facilitate the recovery of stocks while at the same time seeing its revenue grow each year. In 1992 a government-owned National Fishing Corporation was set up.

The fisheries sector contributed to 70% of the growth in real GDP in the 2-year period from 1990 to 1992. In 1990 fishing contributed 1.5% to GDP, by 1994 this figure had risen to 3%. In 1992 the value of the landings was N$800mn, in 1994 the combination of higher prices for hake and pilchards meant the value of the landings had increased to N$1,200mn. A further examination of the figures shows that the fishing sector accounted for close to 22% of all exports in 1994 (Bank of Namibia). This tremendous growth has only been made possible by a considerable amount of investment both by local and foreign private sector firms. Over N$400mn has been invested in upgrading the Namibian fishing fleet and the construction of new onshore processing plants. A new factory has been built in Lüderitz and a processing plant in Walvis Bay. The number of people employed by the sector has increased from 6,000 to over 9,000, making the fishing sector the second largest source of private-sector employment behind mining.

It is estimated that fish stocks have more than doubled since independence, but the government has been wary not to increase the catch limits too quickly, despite pressure from within the industry, it is very easy to over-judge the extent of any recovery. A good example of how effective the recovery has been is to look at figures for hake, one of the most important species. Before the Namibian government was able to introduce controls hake was being heavily overfished. As much as 600,000 tonnes had been caught in a single year. In 1991 the catch was limited to 60,000 tonnes, for 1992 the limit was set at 90,000 tonnes and in

Namibia: Fact File	
Geographic	
Land area	824,292 sq km
Demographic	
Population (1995)	1,610,000
annual growth rate (1980-95)	3.16%
urban	32.0%
rural	68.0%
density	1.9 per sq km
Birth rate per 1,000 (1992)	37.0
Death rate per 1,000 (1992)	10.5
Life expectancy at birth (1992)	
male	55 years
female	57 years
Ethnic composition (1991)	
Black	89%
of which	
Ovambo	50%
Kavango	9%
Damara	7%
Herero	7%
Nama	5%
Caprivian	4%
Bushmen	3%
Baster	3%
Tswana	1%
White	6%
Coloured	4%
Others	1%
Economic	
Total GDP (1995)	US$2,682 m
GDP/person (1995)	US$1,666
Real GDP growth (1995)	2.6%
GDP growth rate, 1990-1995	4.5%
Govt Expenditure as % of GDP	38.6%

Source: *UNDP Human Development Report, 1996.*

1993 the permitted catch was raised to 120,000 tonnes. Throughout this period research showed that the stocks were continuing to recover. In 1994 a joint report published by the FAO and the Namibian Sea Fisheries Research Institute in Swakopmund noted that it could take at least a decade for all the severely depleted fish stocks to recover to former levels. A worrying trend was the considerable year-to-year variation in some stocks, the government must plan carefully for the future, despite the unexpected level of recovery for some fish species.

As long as Namibia is careful in its management of its marine resources the sector will continue to be a valuable source of income. Further investment is required but this will lead to a more efficient industry and greater profits in the long term. But while stocks of white fish, anchovies and pilchards have all shown signs of growing, the tale of the rock lobster is not so good, the 1995 allowable catch was set at 230 tonnes, in 1990 the figure had been 1,800 tonnes. A reminder that not all the components in a damaged ecosystem can recover at the same rate. A final positive point that will help ensure the future success of the industry is that all the fish come from one of the least polluted coastal seas in the world. There are no perennial rivers polluted by industry, and virtually no sewage, either raw or treated flows into the ocean. With expert quality control the industry should be able to expect premium prices for most of its products.

Other sectors The tourist sector is rightly regarded as having a tremendous potential for growth. Namibia has a wild and varied landscape which is ideal for up-market, high-value, low-volume tourism. Since independence the country has enjoyed a peaceful existence, an important factor for the tourist industry. Many tourists from overseas are attracted to remote areas which are essentially 'unspoilt', Namibia has an abundance of such areas. These are also the areas where the local community have no employment opportunities and have suffered the most during periods of drought. If the right training can be provided for these people they will be able to directly benefit from tourism. Since independence there has been a 50% growth in the hotel and restaurant sector. New hotels and guestfarms have opened across the country, this has meant that room occupancy rates have remained around 50%. In 1993 an independent study reported 255,000 visitors with 60% from South Africa. Since 1990 tourism receipts have increased from N$300mn to over N$1bn, the sector now contributes 6% to GDP and is the third largest foreign exchange earner. For future developments the government is looking closely at Community-based tourism. Rural communities must enjoy the benefits of conservation policies, especially if such tourist projects are based in communal areas. Once people start to derive significant benefits from wildlife and conservation policies they are more likely to work with the government and private sector to preserve the environment. Rural households must enjoy a cash income as well as job opportunities.

The manufacturing sector provides less than 8% of annual GDP, it remains a small sector based around processing meat, fish and minerals for export. The sector has a high cost structure and operates with a low competitiveness. Many of the businesses were established under an apartheid government where wages were not linked to productivity. Most goods have in the past been produced in South Africa thus the sector remains underdeveloped within Namibia. Small-scale and informal sector industries have limited access to credit and markets, poor management skills and outdated technologies. Future success and growth will depend in part upon these issues being fully addressed in the long term.

Windhoek

WINDHOEK, Namibia's capital city, is located at an altitude of 1,646m in the country's central highlands, with the Auas Mountains to the southeast, the Eros Mountains to the northeast and the hills of the Khomas Hochland rolling away to the west. Lying more or less in the geographical centre of the country, the city and surrounding suburbs are spread out over a series of picturesque valleys which lie at the crossroads of all Namibia's major road and rail routes. Although relatively small for a capital city by international standards, and despite recent talk about decentralization, Windhoek remains the political, judicial, economic and cultural centre of the country. As such it is a place worth spending a few days looking around before setting off to view the game of Etosha or the sand dunes of the Namib.

(*STD code* 061) Windhoek's history reflects the movements of different peoples through the country, and in particular offers the visitor an insight into the past hundred years of colonial conquest, apartheid and struggle for independence. Originally Windhoek was known by the Khoikhoi or Nama people as *Ai-gams* (steam or fire-water) and by the Herero people as *Otjomuise* (place of smoke) due to the hot water springs found in what is now the Klein Windhoek district. These springs had been used for centuries as watering holes by the Bushmen (San) and Khoikhoi (Nama), nomadic and semi-nomadic peoples who trekked through the area with their animals.

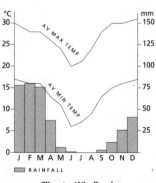

Climate: Windhoek

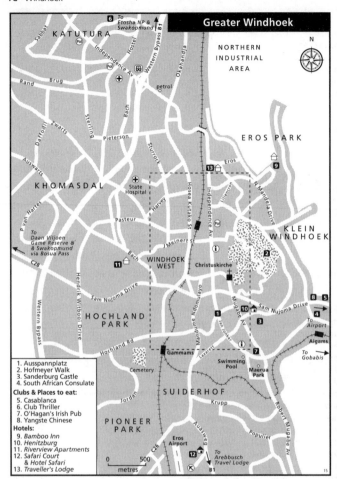

Greater Windhoek

KATUTURA

To Etosha NP & Swakopmund

NORTHERN INDUSTRIAL AREA

KHOMASDAL

EROS PARK

State Hospital

KLEIN WINDHOEK

To Daan Viljoen Game Reserve & Swakopmund via Bosua Pass

WINDHOEK WEST

Christuskirche

HOCHLAND PARK

To Airport

Aigams

To Gobabis

Gammams

Swimming Pool

Maerua Park

Cemetery

SUIDERHOF

Krupp

PIONEER PARK

Eros Airport

To Arebbusch Travel Lodge

1. Ausspannplatz
2. Hofmeyer Walk
3. Sanderburg Castle
4. South African Consulate

Clubs & Places to eat:
5. Casablanca
6. Club Thriller
7. O'Hagan's Irish Pub
8. Yangste Chinese

Hotels:
9. Bamboo Inn
10. Heintzburg
11. Riverview Apartments
12. Safari Court & Hotel Safari
13. Traveller's Lodge

0   500
metres

The roots of today's city, however, lie in the settlement established by the Oorlam leader Jonker Afrikaner in the 1840s and 1850s at *Ai-gams*, stretching along the ridge of the Klein Windhoek valley. In 1836 Jonker urged the British explorer Sir James Alexander, who called the settlement Queen Adelaide's Bath, to organize a missionary for him. In 1842 the Rhenish missionary Hahn arrived to find a well-established settlement, which he called Elberfeld after a centre of the Rhenish mission in Germany. He was so impressed by the settlement that he was drawn to comment, "The location of Elberfeld is superbly beautiful ... seeing the extensive thorntree forest with its delicious green and curious forms, the lovely gardens, and the beautiful greensward ...".

Jonker himself, in an 1844 letter to the Wesleyan Mission Station, referred to the settlement as *Wind Hoock*, and despite much speculation that he named the settlement after *Winterhoek*, his ancestral home in the Cape, there is no solid evidence to suggest this. However, it is certain that Windhoek was the original name given by Jonker and his followers when they settled here around 1840.

Under Jonker, the settlement flourished and served both as a trading station between the Oorlam/Namas and Herero, as well as a headquarters from which Jonker and his commandos launched cattle raids on the Herero living N of the Swakop River. Following Jonker's death at Okahandja in 1861, Windhoek was temporarily abandoned until the missionary Schröder installed himself in the remains of the original buildings in the 1870s.

In 1890 the Germans, under Curt von François, were still not well established in Namibia, and having been effectively driven out of Otjimbingwe and Tsaobis by the Nama leader Hendrik Witbooi, made a strategic retreat to Windhoek. This move neatly coincided with the death of Herero leader Maherero, and by the time his successor Samuel Herero sent envoys to Windhoek a few weeks later, the Germans were already halfway through the completion of the original fort. This served as the headquarters for the **Schutztruppe** (colonial troops) and is known as the **Alte Feste** (Old Fort). It now houses the historical section of the State Museum and is the oldest surviving building in Windhoek.

The German colonial settlement of Windhoek emerged around the Alte Feste and the springs surrounding it. The settler John Ludwig established substantial vineyards and fruit and vegetable gardens which fed the small settlement; the modern suburb, Ludwigsdorf, is named after him. The Klein Windhoek valley continued to be agriculturally productive until the beginning of the 1960s with the hot springs below the Alte Feste 'smoking away'.

With the completion in 1902 of the railway to Swakopmund on the coast, the settlement was able to expand and develop as the economic and cultural centre of the colony. In 1909 Windhoek became a municipality and this period saw the construction of a number of fine buildings, including the **Tintenpalast**, the present site of Namibia's Parliament, and the **Christuskirch** with its stained glass windows donated by Kaiser Wilhelm II.

During the 1960s the South African government pursued a policy designed to incorporate Namibia into South Africa as the fifth province, and this period saw a further era of rapid development and growth, not just in Windhoek but in the country as a whole. In Windhoek, the government started forcible movements of people from the 'Old Location' in 1959, and as the black population was gradually obliged to settle in Katutura, the white suburbs of Hochland Park and Pioneer's Park were developed on the western side of the city.

The period since independence has seen further growth characterized by some distinctly post-modern buildings in the city centre. The still very much low level skyline is dominated by the Kalahari Sands Hotel and the Namdet (formerly CDM) building, but new office blocks, the new Supreme Court Building and other Ministry buildings currently under construction are quickly changing the face of the city. The most recent major project to be proposed is a 5-star hotel and casino, to be built next to the Zoo Park on Independence Ave. The scheme is to be financed with Malaysian money, and the sales pitch is that the complex will cater for an influx of Asian visitors to the country.

On a more modest scale, the last 2-3 years have seen a rapid explosion of

Townships

👈 Most people with a rudimentary knowledge of South Africa have heard about the Johannesburg township Soweto, usually in the context of violent crimes like 'necklacing' or civil unrest between rival ANC and Inkatha Freedom Movement urban guerrillas. What is perhaps less well-known is that all towns in South Africa and Namibia, from the smallest *dorp* to the largest city, have their own townships. Usually far from the town centre and well hidden from the white suburbs, the townships are home to the vast majority of black and coloured Namibians in the central and southern regions.

In keeping with the apartheid policy of separateness, it was not sufficient to merely reserve the most desirable parts of town for whites, a policy of divide and rule required that the black and coloured communities also be separated. On the apartheid scale of civil rights, the coloured community enjoyed better educational and employment opportunities than the black community. The construction of separate townships for the two groups in the late 1950s and 1960s was a further expression of the divide and rule strategy of apartheid.

Towards the end of the 1950s the white community in Windhoek decided that the 'non-whites' were living too close for comfort, and so the black and coloured communities were evicted from the 'Old Location' on the western side of the city centre, and relocated further away to the W and NW. Resistance to the forced removals was mobilized by the then two recently formed liberation movements, Swanu and Swapo, and culminated in the Dec 1959 uprising when police shot dead 13 protestors and wounded many others. In the Namibian context this massacre signalled a landmark in the liberation struggle comparable to the events that were to take place in Sharpeville, South Africa a few months later.

Two new townships were built, Khomasdal for the coloured community, and Katutura (variously translated as 'we have no dwelling place' or 'the place where we don't want to stay') for the black community. The black township was itself divided along tribal lines with different sections for the Damara, Herero, Owambo and so on. Whilst no expense was spared when it came to providing facilities for the white community, the opposite applied to the creation of Katutura. Thousands of uniform shoe-box houses were built, lining the dirt and dust roads of the township, and until the late 1970s black people were not even entitled to own property and businesses in their own communities!

After the scrapping of this legislation and of the **Group Areas Act** restricting freedom of movement, Katutura saw both an influx of newcomers from rural areas and an upsurge in black-owned businesses. This emergent class of business people were soon profiting enough to build themselves some fancy houses in areas such as Soweto and Wanaheda.

Although nowadays, in theory, anyone can live where they want, the fact remains that the overwhelming majority of black Windhoekers live in Katutura in cramped, poor quality accommodation, little changed since independence. Furthermore, Namibia has a rapidly expanding population, 70% of whom are under 25 years old, and an estimated adult unemployment rate of over 40%. This has resulted in a continuing influx of people from the regions to the capital placing further pressure on the limited housing stock. Contrast the average street in one of the former white-only suburbs with Katutura and you have a vivid picture of the combined legacies of apartheid and colonialism.

medium to low cost housing developments around the western and south-eastern outskirts of the city. These new developments, many of them built in the no-man's land that once separated the white suburbs from the black and coloured townships, are intended to meet the housing needs of upwardly mobile young black and coloured Namibians no longer confined to living in the township ghettos, as well as young white Namibians not able to afford property in the expensive 'white' suburbs.

First impressions

The drive into town from the International Airport 42 km away, takes you through a typically empty Namibian landscape of rolling hills of dry scrub savannah, until almost without warning you're in a distinctly Western-feeling city. It's easy to be disoriented by the turn-of-the-century German architecture, the well maintained roads, the continental style street cafés and the surrounding mountains into thinking that you're in a medium-sized Bavarian or Austrian town. If you're expecting a bustling, chaotic West African-type city then you're likely to be disappointed.

The most obvious feature of the city is its size – or lack of it. The central district consists of Independence Ave running from S to N, and a series of well-ordered streets laid out on a grid around it. The main shops, banks, Post Office, tourism offices and larger hotels are all found along Independence Ave, so it doesn't take long for the visitor to feel comfortable getting around. **Zoo Park**, with its lawns and palm trees, lies on Independence Ave right at the heart of the city, and offers a green and shady place used for some Windhoekers to relax at lunchtimes. Adjacent to the park there is a small open-air rural crafts market. **Post Street Mall**, the main shopping area, is close by with its traditional arts and crafts street market, and at its far end lies the main Werne Hill Shopping Mall with its department stores.

The numerous street cafés and outdoor restaurants lining the side streets running into Independence Ave, are pleasant places to sit, eat and drink and watch people going about their business. The streets themselves are generally busy without being intolerably crowded, even at the end of the month when long queues of Windhoekers form at the banks waiting to cash their pay cheques before going off on the monthly spending spree. Traffic pollution has yet to become a serious issue, and gridlock is, for the time-being, unheard of.

If you venture into the suburbs close to the centre of the city, you'll get a good idea of the very pleasant lifestyle that white Namibians created for themselves before independence. In areas such as Klein Windhoek or Eros Park, most houses are spacious bungalows with attractive gardens, many with their own swimming pools. Here, wealthy Windhoekers relax and barbecue as they enjoy the average 300 days of sunshine a year. The high barbed wire fences, alarm systems and guard dogs are the other side of the coin.

PLACES OF INTEREST

As virtually all the sites of interest are in the city centre, the most obvious way to see them is on foot. One full day will allow the visitor with limited time the opportunity to see the more than dozen old German colonial buildings sprinkled around the city, and visit a couple of the museums. For people with 2 or 3 days to spare, a fairly thorough exploration of the city will be possible.

A good place to start a walk around the city is by the **clock tower** on the corner of Independence Ave and Post St. The tower itself is modelled on that of the old Deutsch-Afrika bank built in 1908, but now long-since gone. Cross the road, turn right and walk along Independence Ave as far as **Zoo Park**. Before walking into the park itself, look back across the road and you will see three buildings designed by Willi Sander, a German architect responsible for the design of a number of Windhoek's original colonial buildings.

The **Erkrathus Building**, the furthest right of the three, was constructed in 1910 and is typical of buildings of the period, incorporating business premises downstairs and living quarters upstairs. Two buildings to the left is **Gathemann House**, commissioned by the then Mayor of Klein Windhoek, Heinrich Gathemann, and now home to Gathemann's restaurant. The stepped roof was of European design intended to prevent the roof from collapsing under the weight of a build-up of snow! The third building bears the inscription **Kronprinz**, the name of the hotel which occupied the building until 1920, and the date of its completion in 1902 can also be seen carved in the stone. The photo shop here has a fine collection of turn-of-the-century photographs of Windhoek, which can be bought as souvenirs.

Walk into the park about 20m and you will see a **sculptured column** depicting scenes of a prehistoric elephant kill believed to have taken place some 5,000 years ago on this site. The fossilized remains of two elephants and a variety of Stone Age weapons were found when the park was reconstructed in 1962, evidence that the hot springs were already attracting game to the area in pre-historic times. A message to that effect is carved into the side of the column. On top of the column is part of a fossilized elephant skull, however the rest of the bones and tools were removed to the State Museum's research collection in 1990. Also in the park is the **Kriegerdenkmal**, unveiled in 1907, a memorial to the German soldiers killed between 1893-94 whilst fighting the Namas led by Hendrik Witbooi.

Continuing up Independence Ave the first road on the left is Peter Müller St. On the opposite corner by the taxi rank there is a small **craft market** selling carvings and baskets. At the top of this steep hill on the corner of Lüderitz St is the **Hauptkasse**, the former home of the German colonial government's finance section. The building now serves the Ministry of Agriculture's Directorate of Extension Services. Directly opposite is **Ludwig Van Estorff House**, named after the former Schutztruppe commander who, between campaigns, lived here from 1902-10. Over the century it has housed senior officers, a hostel and a trade school until the **National Reference Library**, usually referred to as the Van Estorff library, moved here in 1984. On the far side of the library the new Supreme Court Building is currently under construction, and when com-

Early view of Kaiser Wilhelm Strasse, now Independence Avenue

pleted will look down over the parking area and over to the Kalahari Sands Hotel.

The Christuskirche At the top of the hill on an island in the middle of the road is one of Windhoek's striking landmarks, the Christuskirche often called the fairycake church. Designed by Gottlieb Reddecker, the church's foundation stone was laid in 1907 and the building itself finally consecrated in 1910. The church was built by the Germans to commemorate the 'peace' between the Germans and the Nama, Herero and Owambo peoples, and inside there are seven plaques bearing the names of German soldiers killed during the wars. Of the Nama, Herero and Owambo dead there is no record.

This Lutheran church was constructed from local sandstone and its design is an interesting mix of neo-Gothic and Art Nouveau styles. As the sun moves across the sky, the colours on the church walls also change to reflect the colours on the mountains of the Khomas Hochland to the SW. The church looks most striking at sunrise and sunset which are probably the best times to take photographs. The stained glass windows were donated by Kaiser Wilhelm II and the altar bible by his wife Augusta, and although not particularly impressive looking from outside, are well worth climbing up the steps to the balcony to get a better look

at. The **key** to the church is available to visitors during working hours from the **church offices**, at 12 Peter Müller St just down the hill.

The walk along Robert Mugabe Ave, running S from the church, takes you towards the whitewashed walls of the **Alte Feste**, the Old Fort which has looked over central Windhoek for the past century. Before reaching the steps leading up to the fort's entrance one can't fail to notice the enormous Reder Denkmal, **The Rider Memorial**. The statue of a mounted soldier depicts General von Trotha, the German Commander who succeeded in 'pacifying' the rebellious Herero and Nama peoples during the 1904-1907 uprising. These victories allowed the colonizers to consolidate their control over Namibia and in turn subjugate the indigenous Namibians.

The Alte Feste The Old Fort itself was built as the headquarters of the first Schutztruppe to arrive in Namibia in 1889 and is Windhoek's oldest surviving building, an impressive sight shimmering in the sunlight on top of the hill. The plaque on the wall outside the entrance states that the fort was built as a 'stronghold to preserve peace and order between the rivalling Namas and Hereros'. This statement was a convenient justification for the colonization and subjugation of Namibia, and typical of the

Post Street at the turn of the century; note Christuskirche on the hill top

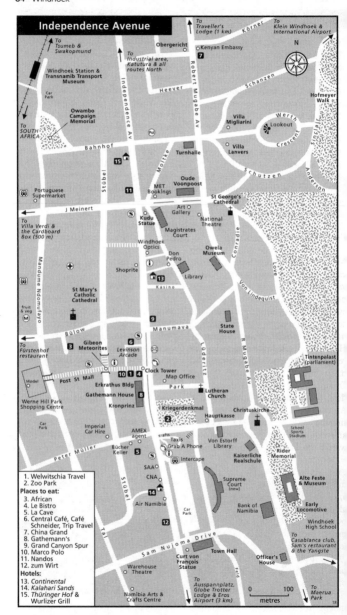

Independence Avenue

To Tsumeb & Swakopmund

To Traveller's Lodge (1 km)

To Klein Windhoek & International Airport

Obergericht

Kenyan Embassy

To Industrial area, Katutura & all routes North

Windhoek Station & Transnamib Transport Museum

Car Park

Owambo Campaign Memorial

Villa Migliarini

Hofmeyer Walk

Lookout

To SOUTH AFRICA

Villa Lanvers

Turnhalle

Heever

Bahnhof

Independence Av

Robert Mugabe Av

Moltke

Schanzen

Werth Crescent

Anderson

Schutzen

Stübel

15

11

MET Bookings

Oude Voonpoost

St George's Cathedral

Portuguese Supermarket

J Meinert

Kudu Statue

Art Gallery

National Theatre

To Villa Verdi & the Cardboard Box (500 m)

Magistrates Court

Windhoek Optics

Owela Museum

Conradie

Mandume Ndemufayo

St Mary's Catholic Cathedral

Shoprite

Don Pedro

13

Library

Kasino

Love

fruit & veg

Bülow

Manumava

State House

Von Lindequist

To Fürstenhof restaurant

Gibeon Meteorites

6

Levinson Arcade

9

Löderitz

R Mugabe Av

Tintenpalast (parliament)

Model

Post St Mall

10

4

Clock Tower

Map Office

Erkrathus Bldg

Gathemann House

8

Park

Lutheran Church

Christuskirche

School Sports Stadium

Werne Hill Park Shopping Centre

Car Park

Kronprinz

Kriegerdenkmal

2

Hauptkasse

Rider Memorial

Alte Feste & Museum

Imperial Car Hire

AMEX agent

Peter Müller

Bücher Keller

5

crafts

Taxis

Grab A Phone

Von Estorff Library

Kaiserliche Realschule

Early Locomotive

Windhoek High School

Intercape

SAA

CNA

14

Air Namibia

Supreme Court (new)

Bank of Namibia

To Casablanca club, Sam's restaurant & the Yangste

Stübel

Tal

12

Sam Nujoma Drive

Car Park

Warehouse Theatre

Curt von François Statue

Town Hall

Erid

Officer's House

To Ausspannplatz, Globe Trotter Lodge & Eros Airport (3 km)

Namibia Arts & Crafts Centre

0   100
metres

To Maerua Park

1. Welwitschia Travel
2. Zoo Park

Places to eat:
3. African
4. Le Bistro
5. La Cave
6. Central Café, Café Schneider, Trip Travel
7. China Grand
8. Gathemann's
9. Grand Canyon Spur
10. Marco Polo
11. Nandos
12. zum Wirt

Hotels:
13. Continental
14. Kalahari Sands
15. Thüringer Hof & Wurlizer Grill

War memorials

All over Windhoek there are memorials, dating back to the early German colonial occupation, which remember German losses during wars with the different Namibian peoples. Among these are the Kriegerdenkmal in Zoo Park, the plaques on the walls in the Christuskirche, the Rider Memorial outside the Alte Feste and the Owambo Campaign Memorial next to the railway station. As with all such memorials the victors have commemorated their own dead without any acknowledgment of those conquered or defeated. Since independence a debate has raged about what should be done with these relics of the country's colonial past, and in particular with the war memorials. Some argue that these symbols of oppression and occupation have no place in a free, independent Namibia and should be removed. Others maintain that these statues and memorials are part of history and therefore should remain. Inevitably these conflicting opinions reflect the different emotions and views of the descendants of those involved in the wars. Nevertheless, whilst wandering around Windhoek it is worth keeping in mind what the monuments represent to the majority of Namibian citizens.

European rhetoric of the time.

The Alte Feste now houses the **State Museum's Alte Feste Display and Education Centre** which is well worth a visit. The first room has an exhibition of photographs depicting significant events in Namibia over the whole of this century, and includes photographs of important Namibian leaders such as Hendrik Wittbooi, Maherero, and current President Sam Nujoma. One of the most powerful photographs is of Owambo King Mandume Ndemufayo's dead body being recovered by South African troops in 1917. One story has it that the South Africans cut off his head and took it to Windhoek to serve as a warning to other 'rebellious' leaders.

In other rooms there are displays of the early household implements, tools and musical instruments of the first missionaries and European settlers. Arranged alongside these are similar objects used by the different ethnic Namibian peoples, making for an unorthodox, but nevertheless interesting, display.

The Independence Exhibition contains photographs, flags, uniforms and other memorabilia of the transition period from South African colonial rule to independence, monitored by the United Nations Transitional Assistance Group (UNTAG). In addition there are interesting sections looking at the various sectors of the economy and their respective roles in Namibia's future development. One prominent section focuses on SWAPO, Namibia's governing party since independence. Climb the turret before leaving and you'll be rewarded by a splendid view of Windhoek and the hills of the Khomas Hochland to the W.

Windhoek High School is next to the fort and across the road opposite the school is the old **Officer's House** built in 1906-1907, now serving as the Office of The Ombudsman. The highly decorative and rather attractive brickwork is a recreation of Putz architecture which was fashionable in Germany at the time. The architect, Gottlieb Redecker, designed the building after returning from a year's visit to Germany, and this was the first building of its style in Namibia. Walking back in the direction of the Christuskirche one passes the former **Kaiserliche Realschule**, which opened in 1909 as the first German high school in Windhoek. After WW2 the building became an English-medium school and now functions as the administrative part of the National Museum.

Walk back in the direction of the Christuskirche and down Robert Mugabe Ave until you see some gardens on your right. These gardens were laid out in the 1930s and contain an olive grove consisting of 100 trees and a bowling green. More significantly, they surround the home of Namibia's Parliament, the **Tintenpalast**, an impressive yellow and white double-storied building with a verandah running around it. This building was also designed by Gottlieb Redecker, and first opened for business in 1914 as the German colonial government headquarters. It reputedly acquired its name, The Ink Palace, from the amount of paper work that went on here. Over the course of the century the Palace has housed successive governments, before being renovated at independence, in preparation for its role as the home of an independent Namibian **Parliament**.

Further down Robert Mugabe Ave you will find **State House** on your left hand side. Currently home to President Nujoma this grandiose building was formally the official residence of the South African Administrator-General.

The Owela Display This section of the state museum is located just below State House and houses the ethnology hall. The exhibition consists of a series of diaromas intended to give the visitor a picture of the life-styles of the inhabitants of the country within their various environments. They include depictions of the cultivation of omahangu (millet), fishing in the Kavango, the Kalahari Bushmen (San) and the Owambo oshanas (water pans). The foyer of the museum has an informative and poignant display on the management of water in this drought-stricken desert country. An interesting booklet entitled 'Man In His Environment', giving more information on the diaromas, is available free of charge at the entrance.

In contrast to the plethora of German inspired architecture, **St George's Cathedral** in Love St offers a taste of rural England with its solid brown brickwork and exposed beams inside. It is the smallest functional cathedral in southern Africa and is the spiritual home of the Anglican community in Namibia. Designed by GHS Bradford and dedicated in 1925 the bell tower houses a bell cast in 1670, one of a set made for St Mary's Church in Northwall, Canterbury. Love St starts opposite the Owela Display next to the Engen garage. On Werth and Sinclair streets round the corner from the Cathedral are a pair of fine houses, **Villa Migliarini** and **Villa Lanvers**, both dating back to 1907.

The **National Theatre of Namibia (NTN)** building lies at the bottom of Robert Mugabe Ave on the corner of John Meinnert St. Turn left at the corner onto John Meinnert St and walk past the **Art Gallery**, and cross over Luderitz St where the Magistrate's Courts are located until you find yourself back at Independence Ave. The bronze statue of a kudu on the corner is a familiar Windhoek landmark, commemorating the kudu which died during the 1896 rinderpest epidemic. Opposite the kudu is the **Oude Voonpoost**, formerly the survey offices and now home to the National Theatre's offices, with a fire-proof archives room. Next to this building are the offices of Nature Conservation, a classic piece of colonial architecture dating from 1902.

The **Owambo Campaign Memorial**, a stone obelisk in the garden next to the railway station in Bahnhof St, is reputed to have the head of King Mandume buried beneath it. Another war memorial is the **Cross of Sacrifice** on Robert Mugabe Ave.

OTHER PLACES OF INTEREST

You can't miss the **Gibeon Meteorites** or **Meteor Fountain**, claimed to be the largest collection of meteorites anywhere in the world. Fashioned into a series of

The Turnhalle Conference

In 1973, South African Prime Minister Vorster made a gesture of granting civil rights to the black population in Namibia by creating a 'native council'. Remarkably, this event happened to coincide with SWAPO being granted observer status at the UN. A constitutional conference was summoned, from which all political parties were banned, and charged with the task of writing a constitution for an independent Namibia.

Delegates were strictly divided along ethnic lines into 11 groups, and the agenda was still fundamentally racist; the first draft which appeared in Mar 1977 was a model for an ethnically segregated country and unsurprisingly was condemned by the group of five western members of the Security Council. However, the meeting was significant, since it was the first time that members of all the different ethnic groups in Namibia had sat down together to talk about their country's future. Although in the end the conference failed to bring Namibia closer to independence, it did inspire the creation of a new political party – the Democratic Turnhalle Alliance or DTA – which today is Namibia's main opposition party.

sculptures sitting on top a series of steel columns set around a fountain, they dominate the middle of **Post Street** right in the heart of Windhoek. The meteorites get their name from the area in which they were found, SW of Mariental, and are believed to have belonged to the world's largest ever meteor shower which took place some 600 million years ago. Although they look like fairly ordinary rocks, the meteorites are in fact made from solid metal, mostly iron, with nickel and some smaller amounts of cobalt, phosphorus and other trace elements. The average weight of the meteorites is an impressive 348.5 kg and in total 77 rocks were originally recovered of which a total of 33 are on display here.

The **Crafts Market**, running most of the way down Post St is an enjoyable place to wander around, whether you're planning on buying any souvenirs or not. If you **do** decide to buy be prepared to bargain over the price. You should be able to pick up some objects at considerably lower prices than in the boutiques around town. If you're planning on going to Zimbabwe you can buy everything, apart from the wicker baskets, a lot cheaper there.

The **Crafts Centre**, Tal St, open Mon-

Fri 0900-1700, Sat 0900-1300 is located in the old breweries building next to the Warehouse Theatre. This is a small indoor market on 2 floors, selling a variety of Namibian carvings, pottery, basket, leatherwork and jewellery.

If you're interested in African arts and crafts **Bushman Art**, a trendy boutique on Independence Ave opposite the park is worth a visit as it has probably the best selection of anywhere in Windhoek. In the back of the store there's an interesting display of carvings, metalwork, jewellery and pottery from all over the continent.

Other buildings of interest around Windhoek are the **Roman Catholic Cathedral** on the corner of Stübel and Bülow Streets, the **Turnhalle Building** on Bahnhof St which played a role in the process of Namibian independence, and the **Railway Station** itself.

The Windhoek Conservatoire on the corner of Peter Müller and Stübel sts, built in 1911-12, was formerly the Regierungsschule (Governement School), and has an impressive ornamental weather vane perched on top of its pyramidal tower.

The **statue** of **Curt von François** stands outside the Windhoek Municipality on Independence Ave, and was unveiled in 1965 on the 75th anniversary of the 'founding' of the city.

A short distance from the city centre sitting atop a series of hills to the E are Windhoek's three elegant castles, **Schwerinburg**, **Heinitzburg** and **Sanderburg**. All three were designed by the architect Willi Sander, the first for Graf Schwerin in 1914, and the second for his wife as her residence. The design of Schwerinburg incorporates an original stone structure built by Curt von François and used as a lookout post in the early days of the Schutztruppe's presence in Windhoek. Sander designed the third castle for himself in 1917.

Heinitzburg Castle on Heinitz Strasse is open to the public as a luxury hotel; however anyone can go and have coffee on the terrace which offers one of the best views of central Windhoek and the mountains of the Khomas Hochland to the W. The terrace coffee shop is open from 0700-2000 and it is well worth the effort of walking up from the city centre to enjoy the views. Sanderburg Castle is privately owned but Schwerinburg Castle, until recently home of the Italian Embassy and Ambassador's Residence is now up for sale for a reputed cool N\$5,000,000 if you fancy it.

The **Hofmeyer Walk** takes about an hour, and if you're feeling moderately energetic is worth the effort for the views it offers of the Klein Windhoek valley. The best time for the walk is Mar/Apr when a variety of aloes are in bloom. You can start the walk either in Sinclair St or at the upper end of Uhland St.

Avis Dam, on the eastern outskirts of the city on the way to the international airport, is a popular spot for birdwatchers particularly just before the first summer rains fall, when more than a hundred different species have been reported in a day.

City drive If you have a car you might be interested in taking a drive around

Aloë candelabrum

the city to get a feel for the residential areas. The Shell map of Namibia has a good map of Windhoek which also covers Katutura and Khomasdal. With this you can plan a route to take you round the city, or you can follow the signs from the city centre towards **Daan Viljoen Game Reserve** until you reach the **Western Bypass**. Take this road N and on your right between Pioneer's Park and Hochland Park you will see the site of the **Old Location**, lying cleared of its former buildings but never subsequently developed. Continue on towards **Khomasdal** which will be on your left hand side, and before you reach **Katutura** you should join **Independence Avenue**; depending on how you feel about being a wealthy foreigner and voyeur in the township, you could choose to drive into Katutura down Independence Ave and take a walk around the covered market. Alternatively, you might choose to follow the signs back towards the city centre. If on the other hand you should find someone to act as your guide, a walk through Katutura is interesting and worthwhile, not least as first-hand experience of the difference between the different parts of the city.

Back in town, drive down **Nelson Mandela Avenue** past the Indian High

Commission on your right hand side, and before reaching the **Quba Mosque** turn left and drive up any one of a series of extremely steep hills and you will find yourself in **Ludwigsdorf**, probably the most exclusive part of the city. Mansions here come fully equipped with swimming pools, gyms and even squash courts in some cases. Rejoin Mandela and turn right onto **Sam Nujoma Drive** which will take you back into the centre of town. Alternatively you can miander up the streets to the S of Nujoma to take a closer look at the three castles already mentioned, and from there make your way back into town.

MUSEUMS AND GALLERIES

The Alte Feste Display and Education Centre, Robert Mugabe Ave. Open Mon-Fri 0900-1800, Sat 1000-1245 and 1500-1800, Sun 1100-1230 and 1500-1800. Houses the historical section of the **State Museum** and is an interesting place to go to get a feel for both Namibia's colonial heritage and her fight for independence.

The **Owela Museum**, Robert Mugabe Ave next to State House. Open Mon-Fri 0900-1700, Sat and Sun 1000-1230 and 1500-1700, closed public holidays. Natural history museum with dioramas of traditional village life. Also has a permanent cheetah exhibition which seeks to educate people about Africa's most endangered cat, the largest population of which is found in Namibia.

The **National Gallery**, corner of John Meinert St and Robert Mugabe Ave. Open Mon-Fri 0900-1700, Sat 0900-1100, closed Sun. Houses a permanent display reflecting a spectrum of both historical and contemporary Namibian art, including the work of well-known artist John Mufangeyo. There are also a series of smaller galleries around the city centre displaying local art for sale. The following are a selection of these: **Spot On Gallery** on Independence Ave opposite Zoo Park, the **Kleine Gallery** is on

Bahnhof St end of Stübel St, and the **Loft Gallery** is found on Bahnhof St.

Transnamib Transport Museum, Bahnhoff St. Open weekdays 1000-1200 and 1400-1530, closed public holidays. Admission N$2 adults, N$0.50 children. Housed upstairs in the **Old Railway Station Building** has well laid out and extensive collection depicting the history of rail and other transport in Namibia over the past 100 years.

TOURS AND EXCURSIONS

As long as you are up to walking around the city there isn't really any need to sign up for an organized tour of Windhoek. Most of the tour companies (see **Information for travellers**) offer 1-day game-viewing and sundowner tours to guestfarms around Windhoek and if you're really pressed for time you might well want to consider opting for one of these. If you're in the country on business for a few days, then a day in the bush with a knowledgeable guide followed by a Sundowner and optional braai makes for a good break and is well worth it.

● **Tour companies & travel agents**
Namibian Tourist Friend, T 061-249048, F 061-233485, offers tours of the city with an optional 30 mins fly over afterwards!; *Namibia Breweries*, T 061-262915, have tours and beer tasting at their factory in the northern industrial area.

DAAN VILJOEN GAME PARK

Approach 24 km E of Windhoek on the C28. Simply find Sam Nujoma Drive and follow the signposts which take you all the way to the park's entrance. If you continue along the road it will take you further into the Khomas Hochland and eventually down into the Namib desert via the Spreethoogte Pass, just about the steepest in Namibia. Follow signs from the centre of town.

Background The park is situated at an altitude of about 1,700m in the Khomas Hochland, a landscape of rolling hills scarred by river valleys and ancient erosion. This 3,953 ha park was proclaimed in 1962 and is a very pleasant introduction to the bush experience for first time visitors. Formerly a reserve, and home to a group of Damara people, the park is named after Daan Viljoen, the former South African administrator to South West Africa.

Vegetation The vegetation in the park is typical of that of the central highlands area, with an abundance of thorn trees such as blue, mountain and red umbrella, and thorn bushes such as trumpet and honey thorn. After the summer rains the hills are covered with grass, but as the months pass they turn from green to yellow and then become barren just before the next rains. However, the views over the highlands and Windhoek itself are spectacular whatever time of year it is. There is a small dam by the picnic areas and campsite.

Game The park is well stocked with various species of antelope and other medium-sized game, and chances of seeing mountain zebra, blue wildebeest, springbok, gemsbock, kudu, red hartebeest and impala are good. Smaller mammals such as baboons and rock dassies can also be seen.

Birdlife There is an abundance of birdlife in the park including the colourful rollers and bee-eaters, hornbills and weaver birds, and by the small dam an assortment of ducks, geese and even the odd heron.

Circular drive A 6.4 km circular gravel road offers a tour of the park designed to take the visitor to where the animals are, but the real beauty of Daan Viljoen is that there is no big game, so the area can be safely explored on foot. This potentially allows you to see more game and certainly gives you more of a feeling of being in the bush.

Hiking There are three hiking trails that can be taken, the 3 km **Wag-'n-bietjie** (wait a while) trail is undemanding

Dassie
Source: Steele, David (1972) *Game sanctuaries of Southern Africa* Howard Timmins: Cape Town. Illustrated by John Perry

provided you don't set off at midday, and is suitable for anyone, whatever their level of fitness. The 9 km **Rooibos** (Red bush) trail is more demanding, but for anyone who is in reasonable shape it's a very enjoyable experience. The first part of the trail takes the hiker steadily uphill to a triangulation point at 1,763m, before descending into a river bed which meanders back to the dam area by way of a final, particularly vicious hill.

A 32 km 2-day unaccompanied trail for groups from 3-12 persons leaves from the main office every morning at 0900. Hikers must take their own food and water for the overnight stop which is spent at a shelter on the trail. Both of the last two trails are good introductions to walking in the bush for those who intend to take on the more strenuous walks such as the Ugab River, Fish River Canyon or Naukluft Park Trails. It's important to have decent walking shoes, at least two litres of water per person, and adequate sun protection for all walks. Maps for all the trails are available from the park office at the entrance.

Resort information The Park is open all year round and is very popular with both Windhoek residents and travellers passing through the area who don't wish to stop in Windhoek. It's a relaxing place to come and swim, braai and enjoy a few cold beers, so that at weekends and on public holidays the camping sites and braai facilities get full. Bookings through Central Reservations Windhoek, see page 125.

● **Accommodation D** *1 & 2 bed bunga-lows*, including breakfast, fridge, hot plate, wash basin, communal toilets, showers, field kitchens, situated by dam; **F** *caravan & camp-site*, max 8 people, 2 vehicles, 1 caravan/tent per site, communal ablution blocks, field kitchens; **F** *picnic sites*, entrance fee per day N$10 adults, N$1 children under 16, N$10 caravans and minibuses, N$8 cars. Although Nature Conservation requires that all day visitors book in advance, in practice when the park is quiet it is not necessary to do so.

● **Places to eat** A small restaurant serves meals 0730-0830, 1200-1330, 1900-2030. A small kiosk sells soft drinks and snacks.

LOCAL FESTIVALS

Apr/May: Windhoek Carnival, a 2-week traditional German festival culminates with a parade down Independence Ave. During the festival there are various cabaret evenings and an all night masked ball. Check press for details.

26 Aug: Herero Day in Okahandja commemorates fallen war heroes and involves a parade through town to the graves of former leaders.

Oct: Festival is held at the end of the month with beer and 'oompah' bands. Organized by Sportklub Windhoek, T 235521.

1-8 Oct: Windhoek Industrial and Agricultural Show.

Nov: Enjando Street Festival takes place towards the end of the month in Independence Ave with traditional music and dance. Information from Windhoek Information and Publicity, T 2902050.

LOCAL INFORMATION

Windhoek offers a good range of hotel and guesthouse accommodation, from the 4-star luxury of the *Kalahari Sands Hotel* to dormitories for backpackers at the *Cardboard Box*. As a general rule two people sharing a double room get a much better rate than one person on their own as most places don't actually have single rooms. Unless you need to be near either of the airports there is no need to look for accommodation outside the city centre whilst you are in Windhoek. The larger hotels, apart from the *Safari Hotel* by Eros Airport, are all either on or close to Independence Ave, whilst most guesthouses are found in suburbs close to the city centre.

Making a choice between staying in a hotel or a guesthouse is less about price than about atmosphere. Broadly speaking the guesthouses, many of which are run by German-speaking Namibians, tend to be smaller and more personal than the hotels, but offer similar facilities, with en suite bathrooms and televisions available in most. One major difference is that although all guesthouses listed here offer breakfast, they generally do not have restaurants or bars, so meals need to be eaten out. Room service also tends not to be on offer in the guesthouse, so if you prefer to remain relatively anonymous but still enjoy being waited on, then a hotel will be a better choice.

Price guide

AL	over N$500	**A**	N$400-499
B	N$300-399	**C**	N$200-299
D	N$100-199	**E**	N$50-99
F	under N$50		

● **Accommodation**

AL *Kalahari Sands Hotel*, Independence Ave, T 222300, F 222260, a/c, TV, restaurants, pool, gym, casino and roof-top bar, a Windhoek landmark right in the centre of the city, all you'd expect of a 4-star hotel, very popular with both local and overseas business people, good views over Windhoek; **AL** *Windhoek Country Club Resort* on the western bypass overlooking the golf course, T 2055911, F 252797, luxury rooms, casino, restaurant, nightclub, completed 1995 in time for the Miss Universe pageant hosted in the conference centre.

A *Hotel Heinitzburg*, Heinitzburg Strasse, T 249597, F 249598, stylish old world style rooms with all mod cons in this turn of the century castle, with magnificent views over the city, swimming pool, rec.

B-C *Safari Court & Hotel Safari*, Rehoboth Weg (B1 S), well placed for Eros Airport, T 240240, F 235652/223017, recently refurbished to offer two hotels in one with a/c, TV, restaurants, pool and free transport 0700-1900 into city centre; **B-D** *Continental Hotel*,

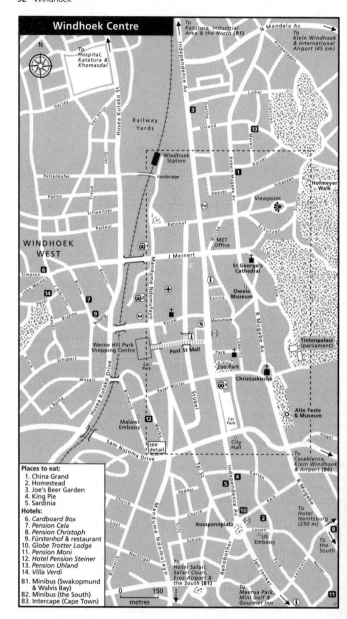

Windhoek Centre

Places to eat:
1. China Grand
2. Homestead
3. Joe's Beer Garden
4. King Pie
5. Sardinia

Hotels:
6. Cardboard Box
7. Pension Cela
8. Pension Christoph
9. Fürstenhof & restaurant
10. Globe Trotter Lodge
11. Pension Moni
12. Hotel Pension Steiner
13. Pension Uhland
14. Villa Verdi

B1. Minibus (Swakopmund & Walvis Bay)
B2. Minibus (the South)
B3. Intercape (Cape Town)

0   150
metres

Independence Ave, T 237293, F 231539, right in the middle of town has a variety of rooms from standard to luxury which includes en suite bathroom, a/c, TV, minibar, room service, the hotel also has a sauna, 2 bars, disco and restaurant.

C *Hotel Fürstenhof*, T 237380, F 228751, Bülow St, well known for the quality of its continental style restaurant, comfortable rooms, a/c, TV, bar, secure parking, within easy walking distance of the city centre; **C** *Thüringer Hof Hotel*, Independence Ave, T 226031, F 232981, known for its beer garden is a comfortable old-style hotel close to the city centre, the staff are friendly and the recently refurbished rooms have en suite bathroom, a/c, TV, rec.

Guesthouses (price generally including cooked breakfast): **C** *Villa Verdi*, Verdi St, T 221994, F 222574, within easy walking distance of the city centre, offers tasteful African theme rooms with TV, phone, pool, comfortable lounge and secure parking, rec; **C** *Kleines Heim*, Volans St, T 248200, F 248203, acquired its name from its function as a maternity home during the days of the 'Old Location', smart English cottage style rooms with showers, TV, phone, bar, conference facilities built around small pool, rec; **D** *Pension Cela*, Bülow St, T 226294/5, F 226246, centrally located, has rooms wth en suite showers, phone, mini bar, TV, laundry service and secure parking, rec; **D** *Pension Moni*, Nesser St, T 228350, F 227124, makes a pitch for the 'budget-conscious traveller' with good cooked breakfasts; **D** *Pension Uhland*, Uhland St, T 229859, F 220688, opp Ministry of Education within easy walking distance of the city centre, clean rooms with showers, TV, phone, pool and secure parking, rec; **D** *Pension Christoph*, corner of Henitzburg St and Robert Mugabe Ave, T 240777, F 248560, close to the city centre, has double rooms with showers, fans, TV, phone and swimming pool; **D** *Hotel Pension Steiner*, 11 Weckerstrasse, T 222898, F 224234, clean en suite rooms, swimming pool, braai area, lounge, rec; **E** *Hotel-Pension Alexander*, 10 Beethoven St, T 240775, behind the Werne Hill Park shopping centre close to the city centre, has en suite rooms, some with baths, TV, parking and TV lounge.

Bed and breakfast: **E** *Littlest Angel Guesthouse*, 106 Jan Jonker Weg, T 231639, 5-min drive from town has rooms in the family house with basic cooking facilities, telephone and en suite bathrooms; **E/F** *June's Place*, 91 Nelson Mandela, T 226054, F 229066, a short drive from the city centre, has en suite rooms, lounge with TV; **E/F** *Marie's Accommodation*, 156 Diaz St, Suiderhof, T 251787/251766, F 252128, 10-min drive from the city centre, variety of rooms and self-catering flats, guests can use the pool and braai area.

Backpackers: **D-F** *Globe Trotter Backpacker's Lodge*, Independence Ave, Ausspannplatz, T 223249, F 227698, is centrally located and offers secure parking, 10 en suite twin rooms and 3 rooms with 6 beds, popular with overlanders, bookings advisable especially for groups, can be noisy at night; **E-F** *Traveller's Lodge*, Andes St, T 249099, a newer option is about 15 mins walk from town, it has double rooms and dorms, free tea and coffee, a common room with TV and braai area outside, several recent poor reports: "he doesn't believe in doors even the WC/bathroom" and "this is and inadequate open plan converted garage, cold and sunless in winter"; **E-F** *Cardboard Box*, 15 Johan Albrecht St, T 228994, F 245587, long-time first choice with backpackers, is close to town and has double rooms and dorms, weekly rates also available, you might also be able to negotiate camping in the garden, there's a common room with TV, bar, cooking facilities, car hire is one of the cheapest around, notice board with travellers' information, over-subscribed by the younger set, getting grubby and run down, but still very popular; **E-F** *Chameleon Backpackers*, 22 Wagner St, T/F 247668, lies at the top of a steepish climb past the polytechnic, 10-15 mins from city centre, rooms and 4 6-bed dorms with communal kitchen and common room with TV, phone/fax, pool, secure parking and car hire also available, popular with mature travellers.

Self-catering: **C** *Jan Jonker Holiday Apartments*, 183 Jan Jonker Weg, T 225565, F 238794, fully equipped modern flats, cooking facilities, phone, TV, video, secure parking, close to city centre; **D** *Riverview Apartments*, corner of Bach St and Mercury St, T 252222, 2 and 3 bedroomed apartments, kitchen, fridge, cooker etc, within 15-min walking distance of town, secure parking, clean, no phones, new, dodgy decor, available for short or longer term bookings, 24-hr radio page booking service, business hours; **E** *The Bamboo Inn*, 5 Auob St, Eros, T 26956, separate access self-catering units with kitchenettes, pleasant decor, comfortable and clean, good value, rec.

Camping: C-F *Arebbusch Travel Lodge*, Rehoboth Weg (B1 S), on the outskirts of town, 2 and 5 bed bungalows, en suite double rooms, and camping/caravan sites, bar, shop, laundrette and pool, closest camping to centre of town; **F** *Daan Viljoen Game Park*, caravan and campsite, max 8 people, 2 vehicles, 1 caravan/tent per site, communal ablution blocks, field kitchens.

Guestfarms: C *Auas Game Lodge*, T 240042, F 248633, 16 large double rooms, swimming pool, tennis court, golf, hiking, stocked farm with giraffe, wildebeest, eland, blesbok, dam for bird watching, including breakfast. **Approach**: follow B1 23 km S of Windhoek, turn onto D1463 for 22 km to farm. **C** *Düsternbrook*, T 232572, F 234758, 4 doubles, 2 singles in old Geman colonial farmhouse, restaurant, swimming pool, stocked game farm with giraffe, eland, wildebeest, leopard for game viewing, bird-watching, hiking trails, all inclusive. **Approach**: follow B1 towards Okahandja, after 30 km take D1499, follow for 10 km and then follow sign for farm. **C** *Eagle Rock Leisure Lodge*, T/F 234542, 4 double bungalows, 1 family unit, restaurant, swimming pool, TV, video, hiking trails, horse riding, game drives in Khomas Hochland close to Daan Viljoen, all inclusive. **Approach**: follow C28 towards Swakopmund for 38 km, take D1958 for Wilhelmstal, turn off at sign for Eagle's Rock. **C** *Midgard Guestfarm*, T 0621 503888, F 0621 503818, en suite double bungalows, organic dining under poolside lapa, tennis, volleyball, badminton, hiking, horse riding, game drives in Otjihavera Mountains, rather large and impersonal though. **Approach**: follow B6 towards Gobabis for 20 km, turn onto D2102 for 60 km. **C** *Weissenfels*, T 0628 (Friedental) 1213, F 061 226999, 5 en suite rooms, pool, hiking, horse riding, game viewing, bird watching in Gamsberg Mnts. **Approach**: follow C26 towards Gamsberg Pass for 114 km, follow signs to farm.

Other guestfarms in the area: *Corona* T 0628 (Friedental) 1330, F 061 251084; *Elisenheim*, T/F 264429; *Finkenstein*, T 234751, F 238890; *Hochland*, T 232628, F 238890; *Hope*, T 0628 (Nina) 3202, F 061 223899, *Kamab*, T/F 0621 503708; *Karivo*, T 560028, F 238486; *Kuzikus Game Ranch*, T 0628 (Nina) 3102, F 061 225000; *Mountain View Game Lodge*, T 560008,, F 560009; *Niedersachsen*, T 0628 (Hochland) 1102, F 061 225820; *Okapuka Ranch*, T 234607, F 234690; *Okatore Lodge*, T/F 232840; *Ondekaremba*, T 0626

40424, F 0626 40133; *Rooisand Desert Ranch*, T 0628 (Friedental) 1302; *Silversand*, T 06202 1102, F 061 235501; *Sundown Lodge*, T 232566, F 232541; *Swarfontein*, T 0628 (Namibgrens) 1112, F 061 226999.

● **Places to eat**

There are plenty of places to eat out in Windhoek, however many restaurants offer the same meaty fare of steak, ribs, schnitzel and hamburgers. There are a small number of restaurants offering a more varied menu, but vegetarians are unlikely to find anything to write home about, as the vast majority of Namibians are serious carnivores. If you do like your meat there are some interesting game dishes on offer, gemsbok steak, kudu kebabs and crocodile tail being a few of the delicacies you can try. Prices are reasonable by European/North American standards, from around N$50 for two for a light meal with drinks up to N$150 for a serious meal and wine in one of the better establishments. **NB** Most restaurants close by 2300, after which sausage and chips from the nearest garage takeaway will be your only option.

Continental: *Homestead Restaurant*, 53 Feld St by Ausspannplatz, T 221958/221990, interesting and varied menu with pleasant seating outside on terrace or inside, friendly though rather slow service amply compensated by the quality of the food, worth making a reservation on weekends and at the end of the month, rec; *Fürstenhof Hotel*, Bülow St, T 237380, renowned for its high quality food and good service, worth making a reservation and dressing semi-smart for, rec; *Gourmet Inn*, 195 Jan Jonker Weg and corner of Centaurus St, T 232360/232882, excellent and very popular restaurant with a varied menu including fresh sea food and a range of vegetarian dishes, good service, relaxed atmosphere, bookings essential, rec; *Gathemann's Restaurant*, Gathemann Bldg, 139 Independence Ave, T 223853, upstairs dining with terrace overlooking the street, busy, smartish German restaurant specializing in hearty meat dishes and expensive wines, bookings rec for the evening; *Marco Polo*, Kaiserkrone Bldg, Post St Mall, T 230141, good quality Italian food as well as occasional Namibian specialities such as crocodile, kudu and gemsbock, pleasant outdoor courtyard seating in an historic building plus comfortable relaxed indoor section, separate 'fast' lunchtime menu to cater for central Windhoek business crowd;

Mykonos Greek Restaurant, good mézze dishes, rather ordinary main courses, inside and outside dining at trendy but overrated Windhoek nightspot, reservations recommended; *Sam's Restaurant*, 90 Sam Nujoma Drive, Klein Windhoek, T 228820, relaxed atmosphere, reasonable food, specializes in 'theme' evenings, check local press; *Sardinia*, 39 Independence Ave by Ausspannplatz, T 225600, good value Italian family run café/restaurant specializing in great pizzas, pasta and a small number of traditional Italian dishes, excellent espresso, cappuccino and ice creams in the café at the front, dining in the popular restaurant at the back, closed Mon, rec; *La Cave Restaurant*, Carl List Haus, Peter Müller St, T 224173.

Chinese: *Yangste Restaurant*, Ai Gams Shopping Mall, Sam Nujoma Drive, Klein Windhoek, T 234779, closed Sun and Mon lunchtime, popular spot, westernized meat-oriented Chinese cuisine; *China Grand Restaurant*, Kenya House, Robert Mugabe Ave, T 225751, authentic mainland Chinese cooking and decor, large portions, friendly service, rec.

Steakhouse restaurants: these are generally the most popular eating places in Windhoek and many are chain restaurants. They all serve more or less the same type of food for similar prices with the odd speciality here and there. The portions tend to be generous, the meat good quality, the service American style and the atmosphere relaxed and informal. Some are also popular drinking holes with young (white) Namibians and get pretty crowded and loud later in the evenings. Overall if meat's your thing then the following offer good value.

Grand Canyon Spur, 251 Independence Ave, T 231003, good value steaks and hamburgers as well as a variety of spicy Mexican dishes; *Saddles*, Maerua Park, Centaurus Rd, next door to the cinema with seating both inside and out; *O'Hagan's Irish Pub and Grill*, corner of Robert Mugabe and Jan Jonker sts, access via Centaurus St, T 234677, pub lunches, evening grills, popular evening drinking hole; *El Toro Steakhouse*, Snyman Circle, 4 Rehobother Weg, T 222797, Spanish style steakhouse, huge portions, good service, rec; *Mike's Kitchen*, Werne Hill Park Shopping Centre/end of Post St Mall, T 226596, ever popular restaurant with a bit more on the menu than just steak; *Wurlizer Bar & Grill*, *Thuringer Hof Hotel*, Independence Ave, popular spot with yuppie black business crowd, steaks, ribs and good beer; *Buffalo Inn*, 205 Stübel St, T 234028, busy lunchtime spot with White business crowd, good food, friendly service; *Restaurant zum Wirt*, 101 Independence Ave, T 234503, aryan in food and atmosphere.

Cafés: *Le Bistro*, corner of Post St Mall and Independence Ave, popular spot in the heart of town with seating inside and out under umbrellas, offering good cooked breakfasts, pizzas, pasta, gyros for lunch and supper, after work drinking spot for young Windhoekers; *City Treff*, Post St Mall, popular with young crowd especially Fri and weekends; *Central Cafe*, Levinson Arcade, Independence Ave, busy breakfast and lunchtime spot, schnitzels, bratwurst, plus takeaway rolls and coffee; *Cafe Schneider*, Levinson Arcade, Independence Ave, T 226304, German style restaurant popular at lunchtimes, look out for daily specials; *Gert's Klause Restaurant*, Sanlam Bldg, popular lunchtimes for snacks and light meals; *Milky Way*, Post St Mall, greasy spoon café, seating under umbrellas; *San Francisco Café*, Maerua Park Mall, Centaurus St, has an excellent variety of salad lunches, as good as anywhere in Windhoek, as well as a wide range of fresh coffees.

Fastfood: there are numerous fast food outlets all over central Windhoek, including *Kentucky Fried Chicken*, *Wimpy Bar*, *King Pie* and *Nando's Chicken*. In addition most Portuguese corner shops and many garages also have fried chicken, sausages and chips to takeaway.

● **Bars**

During the day most of the cafés mentioned also serve as bars. In the evening there is not a massive choice of drinking places, and many double as nightclubs/disco bars (listed under nightlife) charging between N$5-10 admittance. Since in Namibia a liquor license is required before a gambling permit is issued, small bars often have slot machines lining the walls. Opening hours are variable, but all are open until late. *Bulldog Pub*, Hidas Centre, Nelson Mandela Ave; *Joe's Beer House*, 440 Independence Ave, is a popular spot complete with mock olde worlde interior with barbecue and bar area round the back; *The Factory*, Tal St, popular with the Afrikaner crowd; *The Plaza Café Bistro Bar*, Maerua Park Mall, Centaurus St, is popular as an after cinema drinking spot with trendy young Windhoekers; *The Royal Hotel*, Independence Ave, Ausspanplatz, erstwhile Irish pub, now converted into a sports bar with cable TV, pool tables on one side, and all-white country music bar on the other, entrance via the car park at the back.

● **Airline offices**

For Eros Airport enquiries T 238220, International Airport T 0626 40229.

Aeroflot, Ground Floor, Sanlam Centre, Independence Ave, T 229266/229120, F 220007; **Air Namibia**, Gustav Voigts Centre, Independence Ave, T 299630, F 228763, central reservations, T 2982552, F 221382, Fares dept T 2982340; **Comair**, T 248528, F 248529; **LTU**, 141 Stübel St, T 237480; **Lufthansa**, Sanlam Centre, Independence Ave, T 226662, F 227923; **South African Airways**, Carl Lis Bldg, Independence Ave, T 231118; **TAAG** (Angolan Airline) Sanlam Bldg, Independence Ave, T 226625, F 227798.

● **Banks & money changers**

There are four main banks in Namibia, **Standard Bank**, **Bank Windhoek**, **Commercial Bank** and **First National Bank**, all of which have a number of branches in central Windhoek which change money.

● **Cultural centres**

Franco-Namibian Cultural Centre, 1 Mahler St, T 225672, exhibitions and film shows, check press for details.

● **Embassies & consulates**

Angola, 3 Ausspan St, T 227535; **Botswana**, 101 Nelson Mandela, T 221941; **Brazil**, 52 Bismarck St, T 237368; **P R China**, 13 Wecke St, T 222089; **Finland**, 5th Flr, Sanlam Bldg, Independence Ave, T 221355; **France**, 1 Goethe St, T 229021; **Germany**, 6th Flr, Sanlam Bldg, Independence Ave, T 229217; **Ghana**, 5 Nelson Mandela, T 221341; **India**, 97 Nelson Mandela, T 225936; **Italy**, Anna/Gevers St, T 228602; **Kenya**, 5th Flr, Kenya House, 134 Robert Mugabe Ave, T 226836; **Malawi**, 56 Bismarck St, T 221391; **Netherlands**, 2 Crohn St, T 223733; **Nigeria**, 4 Omuramba Rd, Eros, T 232103; **Norway**, 5th Flr, Sanlam Bldg, Independence Ave, T 227812; **Portugal**, 28 Garten St, T 228736; **Russia**, 4 Christian St, T 228671; **South Africa**, Nelson Mandela/Jan Jonker St, T 229765; **Spain**, 53 Bismarck St, T 223066; **Sweden**, 9th Flr, Sanlam Bldg, Independence Ave, T 222905; **British High Commission**, 116 Robert Mugabe Ave, T 223022; **USA**, 14 Lossen St, T 221601; **Zambia**, 22 Curt von Francois, T 237610; **Zimbabwe**, Independence Ave/Grimm St, T 228134.

● **Entertainment**

Art Galleries: The National Art Gallery, Robert Mugabe Ave and John Meinnert St, exhibitions and permanent display of Namibian and other African art.

Cinema: Sterkinekor, Maerua Park Mall, Centaurus St, T 248980, 3-screen cinema with showings from midday until 2200.

Gambling: there are numerous bars with slot machines as well as book makers covering horse racing from South Africa. In 1995 casinos were legalized and there are currrently 3 in operation in Windhoek with a further one planned for 1997. These are found at the *Windhoek Country Club Resort*, Western Bypass, T 205911; *Kalahari Sands Hotel*, Gustav Voigts Centre, Independence Ave, T 222300 and the *Hotel Safari*, on the B1 heading S towards Rehoboth.

Health clubs: *The Health and Racquet Club*, Maerua Park, Centaurus Rd, T 234399, is the largest and best equipped gym in Windhoek with indoor swimming pool, squash courts, a full range of weights machines, aerobics classes and saunas, there is a admission fee of N$50 for non-members for the day. *Nucleus Health and Fitness Centre*, 40 Tal St, T 225493, is smaller but has a good range of weight machines and also has aerobic classes.

Nightlife: *The National Theatre of Namibia*, Robert Mugabe Ave, T/F 237966 stages plays, opera, dance, mime; *The College of Arts*, Peter Müller St, T 225841, F 229007, has classical music concerts, ballet and modern dance; *The Warehouse Theatre*, 42 Tal St, is the most popular live music venue in Windhoek featuring rock, jazz and African bands from Africa and Europe, excellent atmosphere, late bar, rec, check local press for details; *Casablanca*, 90 Sam Nujoma Drive, Klein Windhoek, is a popular late night drinking and dance spot, with a disco on Wed, Fri, Sat nights and musicians night on Sun. *The Woofer*, Kelvin St, in the Southern Industrial Area is popular with the 'in' young white crowd and has a disco and late night drinking; *Snap*, Bahnhof St, mixed, young crowd, rave, rap, African music, Wed, Fri, Sat all night; *Club Thriller*, Katutura, plays a mixture of the latest club sounds and African dance music, with the occasional band outside in the courtyard, open until very late, a taxi is the best way to get there or a local guide rec; *Club Pamodze*, Antiochie St, Wanaheda, Katutura, plays up-to-date dance music until late, again you'll need to take a taxi or a local guide to find it.

● **Hospitals & medical services**

Medicity Windhoek, Private Hospital, Heliodoor St, Eros, T 222687, is the best and most expensive hospital in Windhoek; *Central State Hospital*, Florence Nightingale St, T 2039111; *Roman Catholic Hospital*, 92 Stübel St, T 237237; *Rhino Park Clinic*, Rhino Park, Hosea Kutako Drive, T 225423; *Medrescue Namibia*, 24-hr evacuation service, T 230505.

Emergencies: T 211111.

● **Libraries**
Public Library, 18 Lüderitz St, T 224163; *Estorff Reference Library/National Library of Namibia*: 11 Peter Müller St, T 2934203.

● **Places of worship**
Catholic Cathedral, Stübel St; *Anglican*, Love St; *Mosque*, Nelson Mandela Ave, Klein Windhoek.

● **Post & telecommunications**
Windhoek Post Office, Independence Ave, T 2019311, open 0800-1600 for parcel service round the side on Munamava St as are phones. Phone cards can be bought in the main hall of the post office. **Grab A Phone**, Independence Ave and Peter Müller St, T 220708, F 220820 has facilities for International calls and faxes.

● **Shopping**
Arts and crafts: *African Curiotique*, Gustav Voigts Centre, Independence Ave; *Bushman Art*, Independence Ave; *Crafts Centre*, Tal St, next to the Warehouse Theatre; *Craft Shop*, corner of Independence and Garten St, no name on front of shop!; *Master Weaver*, Werne Hill Shopping Centre, stocks wide range of southern African carpets, wall hangings and other crafts; *Namos & Tameka Crafts Shop*, Gustav Voigts Centre, Independence Ave; *Oshiwa Workshop*, 8 Sinclair St, mornings only; *Post St Mall outdoor market*; *Rogl Souvenirs*, Southern Life Bldg, Post St Mall.

Books, Magazines, Newspapers: books are unfortunately expensive in Namibia, subject as they are to 8% government sales tax (GST). Whilst there is a plethora of novels and other books available on the history and politics of South Africa, there are relatively few available on Namibia. There are however a number of excellent booklets put out by DIS-COURSE/MSORP publications, each one focusing on a different aspect of Namibia and Namibian history. These are relatively inexpensive and well worth reading and are available in most bookshops. *Bücher Keller*, Peter Müller St; *CNA*, Gustav Voigts Centre, Independence Ave and Werne Hill Shopping Cen-

tre; *New Namibia Books*, Post St Mall, especially good for books on Namibia and Southern Africa; *The Book Den*, Frans Indongo Gardens, Bülow St.

Camera equipment: *Nitzsche-Reiter*, corner of Peter Müller and Independence; *Photo World*, Independence Ave opp Bülow St.

Camping: *Cymot*, 60 Mandume Ndemufayo Ave; *Ernst Holz Safari Land*, Gustav Voigts Centre, Independence Ave, wide range of hiking and safari clothes; *Trappers Trading Co*, Post St Mall, wide range of outdoor clothes and camping equipment; *Safari Den*, 20 Bessemer St.

Clothes: *Edgars*, Post St Mall; *Foschini*, corner of Independence and Peter Müller; *Markhams*, corner of Independence and Peter Müller; *Model*, Werne Hill Shopping Centre, end Post St Mall; *Otto Mühr Mens' Outfitters*, Independence Ave; *Truworths*, Levinson Arcade.

Furs and leather: *Hamm Pelze Furs*, Gustav Voigts Centre, Independence Ave; *Nakara*, Kronprinz Bldg, Independence Ave, high quality karakul leather clothes; *Pelz Haus*, corner of Daniel Munamava and Independence Ave, karakul leather and furs.

Gems and jewellery: *G Leiten*, Gustav Voigts Centre, Independence Ave; *Namib Jewellers*, Kronprinz Bldg, Independence Ave; *Rocks and Gems*, corner of Post St and Independence, semi-precious stones and jewellery.

Maps: detailed maps are available from the Surveyor General's office in the Ministry of Justice building on Independence Av. The building is to the right of the Post Office overlooking Zoo Park. Go to the second floor, take a right and follow the corridor to the very end. The office is on the right.

Supermarkets: *Model*, Werne Hill Shopping Centre, end Post St Mall; *Okay Bazaars*, Gustav Voigts Centre, Independence Ave; *Shoprite*, Independence Ave.

● **Sports**
Spectator: football and rugby are played at their respective Independence Stadia just off the B1 heading S. Check local press for match details.

Swimming: the municipal pool is located at Maerua Park, Centaurus St.

● **Tour companies & travel agents**
There is a bewildering array of tour companies offering safaris in Namibia and southern Af-

rica, by plane, by 4WD, and on foot. If you plan to book an organized tour from your own country, the best bet is to locate a travel agent with a link to a tour company in Namibia, as they will probably be able to get you the best deals. Below is listed the main tour companies and the specialities they offer.

There are a multitude of tour operators in the country offering everything from fly-in safaris to the Skeleton Coast and Okavango Delta, hiking tours of Damaraland and canoe safaris down the Kunene River. Many companies offer guided trips to the remoter parts of the country for small groups; with some you have to come as a ready made group, with others you can join up with an existing group. As most have offices in the city centre they're easy to get to, and it's worth visiting a few in person to discuss the various options and to compare prices.

Adozu Tours, 6 Erikson St, T 236634, F 235453, will arrange off-road safaris and camping trips; *Baobab Tours*, 7 Willan St, Cultural and Environmental Tours, T 224017, F 232314; *Chameleon Safaris*, T/F 234345, offer camping safaris; *Charly's Desert Tours* in Swakopmund, T 064 404341, F 404821, specialize in 1 or ½-day guided tours of the Namib around Swakopmund; *Eden Travel Consultancy*, 6 Andraditstrasse, Eros Park, T/F 234342, arranges fly-ins to neighbouring countries; *Footprints*, 19 Johan Albrecht St, T/F 249190, specializes in eco-tourism activities, rec; *Gondwana Tours* in Keetmanshoop, T 0631 23892, will organize trips to the Fish River Canyon and Namaqualand; *Karibu Safaris*, 53 Krupp St, Suiderhof, T 251661, offer guided off-road driving and hiking trips in the bush; *Makalani Safaris*, T/F 233101, can arrange personalized off-road safaris; *Mola Mola Safaris* in Walvis Bay, T 064 205511, F 064 207593, offer ski boat fishing and dolphin viewing trips off the Namibian coast; *Namib Pappot Safaris* in Maltahöhe, T 0663 3042, F 0663 3180, arrange tours of the Namib Desert, Damaraland and Kaokoland; *Namib Sky Safari Adventures* in Maltahöhe, T 0663 25703, specialize in balloon trips above the dunes of Sossusvlei; *Namibian Tourist Friend*, T 249408, F 233485, arrange fly-drive safaris over Windhoek, the Namib and as far as Lüderitz in the S; *Olympia Reisen*, Jan Marais St, Northern Industrial Area, T 262395, F 217026, hold the concession for fly-in safaris to the Skeleton Coast; *Ondese Travel & Safaris*, Kunene Court, Heliodore St, T 220876, F 239700; *Oryx Tours*, 11 Van der Bijil St,

Northern Industrial Area, T 217454, F 263417, are of the larger tour companies offering coach tours around Namibia; *Pasjona Safaris*, T/F 223421, give guided tours; *Ritz Reise Travel Agency*, 250 Independence Ave, T 236670, F 227575; *Southern Cross Safaris*, 10 TV More St, T 221193; *SWA Safaris*, 43 Independence Ave, T 221193, F 225387, another large coach tour company; *Trip Travel Agency Independence Ave*, T 236880, F 225430, offer some of the best deals around; *Trans Namibia Tours*, 414 Independence Ave, T 221549, F 230960, also specialize in eco-tourism; *Welwitschia Travel*, Post St Mall, T 225710, are a reliable company; *WTS Travel Service*, 6 Peter Müller St, T 237946, F 225932.

● **Tourist offices**

7 Post St Mall, T 220640; Continental Bldg, Independence Ave, T 284 2111, F 221930,Internet: www.iwwn.com.na/namtour. **Tourist Info**: 138 Jan Jonker St, T 226119, F 220275, is a privately run tourist office open every day of the year offering a hotel reservations service, tours and car hire. **Wildlife Tours**, Sanlam Bldg. WTS Travel Service, Peter Müller St. **Trans-Namibia Travel Agency**, Welwitschia Travel.

● **Useful addresses**

Immigration: Department of Civic Affairs, Cohen Bldg, Kasino St, T 2929111.

Police: Main station, Bahnhoff St. Emergencies: T 211111.

● **Transport**

Windhoek is in the centre of the country, all the surfaced highways and railways radiate out from here. The pattern of the road network makes it difficult to do a circuit of the country without having to return to Windhoek at some point – unless you want to spend a lot of time driving on gravel roads of variable condition.

1,218 km to Katima Mulilo, 482 km to Keetmanshoop, 850 km to Lüderitz, 533 km to Namutoni (Etosha NP), 786 km to Noordoewer (South Africa border), 435 km to Okakuejo (Etosha NP), 350 km to Swakopmund, 1435 km to Victoria Falls (via the Caprivi Strip).

Local Car rental: Asco Car Hire, 10 Diehl St, Southern Industrial Estate, T/F 232245; **Avis**, Safari Hotel, Aviation Rd, T 233166, F 233072; **Bonanza Car and 4WD Hire**, 60 Sam Nujmaa Drive, Klein Windhoek, T 240317, F 240318; **Budget**, 72 Mandume Ndemufayo Ave, T 228720, F 227665; **Camping Car Hire**, corner of Mandume Ndemufayo Ave and Edison St, Southern Industrial Area, T 237756,

F 237757; **Champion 4WD Hire**, 165 Diaz St, Suiderhof, T 251306, F 251620; **East End Land Rover Hire**, 335 Sam Nujoma Drive, T 240390, F 228855; **Imperial**, 43 Stübel St, T 227103, F 222721; **Kessler 4WD**, 72 Mandume Ndemufayo Ave, T 233451; **Odyssey**, 36 Joule St, Southern Industrial Area, T 223269, F 228911; **Pegasus Car and Camper Hire**, 53 Bülo St, T/F 223423.

Air There are two airports serving Windhoek, which can confuse first time visitors, all the International flights arrive at a larger airport out of town, but internal flights and some regional flights use a smaller airport in the southern suburbs, the second airport is known as *Eros*. There is no regular transfer service between the two airports.

Windhoek International Airport: the airport is 45 km E of the town centre, it is used essentially for flights to/from Europe and South Africa. The Air Namibia flight to **Victoria Falls** departs from here. There is a single modern terminal building; the left end is for departures, and the right is a café and arrivals hall. The airport only comes to life for a few hours when flights to Europe are departing. There is also a bank, post office, car hire offices and a telephone bureau which is ideal for international calls. In the departure lounge there is a small duty free shop and a bar which also serves snacks. Change any remaining Namibian dollars at the bank by the arrival point, you cannot exchange the currency anywhere else.

Transport to/from airport: Intercape, the long distance coach company, run a bus between the airport and the Grab-a-Phone terminal taxi stand opposite the *Kalahari Sands Hotel*; the service connects with all major international flights. As with all airports the taxi fare is comparatively high, expect to pay in the region of N$100 to go to hotels in the centre of town.

Flights: Lufthansa are the only major European airline to provide direct flights into Windhoek. While it will add time to your journey a practical alternative route is to fly into Johannesburg or Cape Town (there are plenty of flights every day from Europe) and then transfer to a South African Airways or an Air Namibia flight to Windhoek.

Air Namibia, T 299630, fly to **Frankfurt** (9 hrs) and on to **London-Heathrow**: Wed, Fri, 2105, Sun, 2035. Their internal flight to Katima Mulilo departs from here because the plane continues to Victoria Falls in Zimbabwe

and Livingstone in Zambia. Enquiries: T (0626) 40315. **Cape Town**, daily except Sat; **Harare**, Tues only; **Johannesburg**, daily except Thur, there are 3 flights on a Fri and 2 on Tues and Sun; **Livingstone**, Fri only; **Luanda**, Sat only; **Lusaka**, Tues only; **Victoria Falls** (4 hrs, includes couple of stops): Mon, Wed, Sun, 0940 – a special 'classic' flight operates every Tues, 1115. **Internal destinations**: **Katima Mulilo/Mpacha** (2 hrs): Mon, Wed, Fri, Sun, 0940; **Walvis Bay** (45 mins): Mon, 1115, Wed, 1030, Fri, 1015, Sun, 1045.

Comair, T 248528, F 248529 **Johannesburg** (2½ hrs): Wed, 1025, Thur, 1740.

LTU, T 237480, flights to **Munich** and **Düsseldorf** on Tues, this is a day flight; LTU also fly once a week from **Cape Town** to Munich and Düsseldorf. Their flight from Germany leaves Mon eve and arrives in Windhoek early Tues morning.

Lufthansa, T 226662, flights to **Frankfurt** via Johannesburg dept Tues and Thur, late afternoon.

South African Airways, T 231118, operate direct flights to Cape Town and Johannesburg, from these two towns there are onward connections to all major towns in South Africa as well as Zimbabwe, Botswana, Malawi and Moçambique. **Cape Town** (2 hrs): Wed, 1340; Fri, 1415; Sun, 1355; **Johannesburg** (1¾ hrs): Mon, Fri, 1340; Tues, Wed, 1155, 1525; Thur, 1125, 1650; Sun, 1640.

Windhoek – Eros: this is the smaller airport which is used by **Air Namibia** for domestic flights, by tour operators, charter companies and private flights. The airport is next to the *Safari Court Hotel*, 3 km S of the town centre. There is no public transport at the airport, and you have to telephone for a taxi to come and collect you, or arrange in advance and hope the taxi company remembers. If you are travelling with very little luggage you could walk the 400m to the *Safari Court Hotel* complex, and then either ask the hotel reception to call for a taxi, or use their complimentary town centre transfer service, a mini bus which runs every 10-15 mins to the Grab-a-Phone office on Independence Ave. Here you will always find waiting taxis.

Flights: a variety of private and charter companies fly from here, if you have booked on a safari which starts with a flight out of Windhoek make sure you check which airport they are using. **Air Namibia** have at least 1 local flight a day from here, they also operate their flight to **Maun** and **Kasane** in Botswana from here as well as their stopping flight to **Cape Town**. The Air Namibia non-stop flight to Cape Town leaves from the International Airport. Details of the routes are provided below, but check with Air Namibia to confirm the exact timing of each flight. T (061) 238220, F (061) 236460.

Keetmanshoop (95 mins): Sat, 0800; **Lüderitz** (2½ hrs) via Swakopmund: Tues, Thur, Sat, 1000, Sun, 1100; **Mokuti**: Wed, Fri, 1130; Thur, 0800; Sun, 1040; **Ondangwa** (2½ hrs): Thur, 0800; Fri, 1530; Sun, 1040; **Ongava** (2 hrs): Wed, Fri, 1130; **Rundu** (2½ hrs): Mon, 0800; **Swakopmund** (45 mins): Tues, Thur, Sat, 1000; Wed, Fri, 1130; Sun, 1100; **Tsumeb** (1 hr): Mon, Thur, 0800. Flights to **Walvis Bay** and **Katima Mulilo** (Mpacha airport), fly from the International airport.

Train Gobabis (7¾ hrs), Tues, Thur, Sun, 2200; **Keetmanshoop** (11 hrs), via Rehoboth and Mariental, daily except Sat, 1900; **Swakopmund** and **Walvis Bay** (9 hrs), daily except Sat, 2000; **Tsumeb** (16 hrs), via Omaruru and Otjiwarongo, Tues, Thur, Sun, 1800.

Road Bus: Intercape, T (061) 227847, the coaches from South Africa and Swakopmund direction all terminate by the taxi rank and information booth on the corner of Independence and Müller Sts, close to the *Kalahari Sands Hotel*. Reservations must be made 72 hrs before departure. The service no longer runs to Tsumeb.

Cape Town (16 hrs), via Rehoboth, Mariental and Noordoewer (border post), Mon, Wed, Fri, Sun, 1900; **Keetmanshoop** (5 hrs), Mon, Wed, Fri, Sun, 1900; **Swakopmund** (3½ hrs), Mon, Wed, Fri, Sat, 0700; **Upington** (10 hrs), Mon, Wed, Fri, Sun, 1900; **Walvis Bay** (4 hrs), Mon, Wed, Fri, Sat, 0700.

Windhoek-Livingstone (20 hrs): **Zambezi Express**: this bus service has replaced the Victoria Falls bus, T (061) 223478. This is an 11-seater minibus which departs on Tues & Fri. The return journey departs from Livingstone in Zambia on Thur and Sun. Check noticeboards in any of the backpacker hostels for latest details of the service. It could well have closed down by the end of 1997. Cost in May 1997 (one way) N$150.

Swakopmund: a cheap (N$45) minibus service departs from the Caltex Garage by Rhino Park Hospital. You may have to wait 2-3 hrs for the bus to fill up. Take note these services may be fun and cheap, but they are dangerous. We do not advise using the service.

ROUTES The **B1** N out of Windhoek leads first to Okahandja (68 km) where it branches into the **B2** for Swakopmund (350 km) and continues N towards the Waterberg Plateau, Otjiwarongo and the 'triangle' towns of Otavi, Tsumeb and Grootfontein.

For the first 15 km the road is an impressive 4-lane highway but then, just before the turn-offs for Döbra and Brakwater, it slims down to a more modest two lanes. As well as being the main route to Swakopmund and the N, this road is a commuter route between Windhoek and Okahandja. It therefore gets very busy during 'rush' hours and on Fri and Sun afternoons with traffic leaving and returning to Windhoek. Care should be exercised driving this stretch as there are plenty of speeding, impatient drivers around who can spoil your day!

The light industry surrounding Windhoek is soon left behind and the road then snakes its way through the attractive mountainous Khomas Hochland with cattle ranches and guestfarms situated on either side of the road. About 10 km before Okahandja the road passes the Osona Military Base and soon after on the right is the turn-off for **Von Bach Dam**. Just before the turn-off for Okahandja itself the road passes over the Okahandja River, a dry, wide sandy river-bed with some market gardening practised along its banks.

OKAHANDJA

(*STD code* 0627) The small town of Okahandja is one of the oldest established settlements in Namibia and is the administrative centre of the Herero-speaking people, with a number of its former leaders buried here. A yearly procession through the town to the Herero graves commemorates Herero dead during various wars against the Nama and the Germans. As a crossroads between the routes

W to the coast and N to Etosha, Okahandja is a busy, bustling place with a railway station, a number of service stations and two large outdoor crafts markets.

The last couple of years have seen a growth in light industry in the town and the relocation of the research arm of the Ministry of Education as part of the decentralization process in the country. A new diamond cutting factory is scheduled to open here in 1998 and together with the increasing number of people choosing to live in Okahandja and work in Windhoek, the town is set to grow as a district centre.

History

Okahandja was known to the Nama as *Gei-keis* meaning 'big sandy plain', a term which aptly describes the wide sandy river bed by the town. The missionary Heinrich Schmelen visited the area briefly in 1827 and for a number of years during the first half of the 19th century the settlement was known as Schmelen's Hope by Europeans, however this name never stuck. Oral tradition suggests that Herero-speaking peoples have been living in the vicinity of Okahandja since the end of the 18th century, coinciding with their migration S from the Kaokoland from c 1750 onwards. They gave the place the name Okahandja, meaning 'little and wide' after the short, wide river here.

During the 1840s the Herero chiefs Tjamuaha and Katjihene both established themselves at Okahandja, having moved away from Oorlam leader Jonker Afrikaner's base in Windhoek, and in 1850 missionary Kolbe established a mission station here. The establishment of this mission ran contrary to the wishes of Jonker Afrikaner, at the time the most powerful leader in central Namibia, as he felt that European influence over the Herero would interfere with his self-declared rights over Herero cattle. In Aug 1850 he raided the settlement, destroying the mission and killing men, women and children indiscriminately. The site where most of the atrocities took place was named **Moordkoppie** or **Blood Hill**, in memory of those who fell there. Jonker Afrikaner himself settled at Okahandja in 1854, using the settlement as a base from which to launch his cattle raids in Hereroland, and lived here until his death in 1861.

During the turbulent 1860s Herero chief Maherero moved his base away from Okahandja to the more secure location of Otjimbingwe, but in 1868 he moved back again – ostensibly to be near the grave of his father, Tjamuaha. In 1870 the missionary Reverend Diehl built another mission station and house for himself, the latter surviving until 1990 when it was demolished. Maherero's sons, Willem and Samuel, both built themselves houses in Okahandja

Gei-keis, the big sandy plain, Okahandja shortly after its official founding in 1894.

and Samuel Maherero, who succeeded his father as the senior Herero leader in 1890, remained at Okahandja until the Herero uprising of 1904.

The official founding of Okahandja is deemed to be 1894, despite the fact that the Herero had already been living here for about 100 years, but this relates to the increasing power and influence of the German colonial presence in Namibia. Gradually, the rich grazing land around Okahandja was appropriated by white settlers, and today only a fraction of the land around the town is for communal grazing. The period of German rule saw the construction of a number of fine buildings still standing today, these include the present day library, the railway station and the riding club. Nevertheless, Okahandja still remains an important centre to the Herero-speaking peoples and the graves of many of their former leaders lie here.

Places of interest

There are a number of attractive turn-of-the-century buildings scattered around the town, unfortunately none of them have yet been turned into a museum, and apart from a casual glance, there is not much to see. The **Old Fort**, situated just along from the post office on Main St was started in 1894, the year Okahandja was officially founded, and served for many years as the police station. It now lies empty and rather forlorn and the various schemes to turn it into a museum or a rehabilitation centre have so far come to nothing.

At the northern end of Kerk St just after Voigts St by the tennis courts, is the turn-off for the **Herero Graves**. It is not possible to go into the graveyard, but this is where on 26 Aug the annual march to commemorate Herero war heroes ends up. Located here is the communal grave of the 19th century leader Maherero and his son Samuel Maherero, who lead the Herero into exile in Botswana in 1904 after a final pitched battle against the

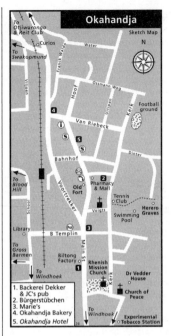

Germans at the Waterberg Plateau (see History section, page 42).

There is a cluster of buildings at the southern end of Kerk St, including the **Rhenish Mission Church** containing the grave of Willem Maherero, the eldest son of the late 19th century Herero leader Maherero. Opposite is the **Church of Peace**, consecrated in 1952, which contains the graves of three influential Namibian leaders. The 19th century Oorlam leader **Jonker Afrikaner**, who died in 1861, lies here, as does Herero leader **Chief Hosea Kutako**, widely credited as the leader of post WW2 resistance to South African rule in Namibia, and Chief Clemens Kapuuo, Kutako's successor and former Democratic Turnhalle Alliance (DTA) President, who was assassinated in 1978.

Behind the Church of Peace is the former house of **Dr H Vedder**, a pioneer in linguistic studies and oral history in Namibia during the first half of this century, viewed by some as an important Namibian historian and by others as an apologist of white, colonial rule in the country. Just round the corner from here is the old **Experimental Tobacco Station** where in 1906 the planting of tobacco and making of cigars was started. Although quite an attractive building it is now surrounded by overgrown vegetation and stands quite empty.

Across the railway line at the end of Bahnhof St is the **Library**, another attractive early 20th century building, constructed for the first district official Fromm. On the same side of the railway line on the corner of Duikerweg is **Mordkoppie/Blutkuppe** or **Blood Hill**, where in 1850, the Oorlam leader Jonker Afrikaner led a punitive raid on Chief Kahitjene's tribe of Herero speakers, killing women and children and virtually wiping out the entire tribe.

Leaving town on the main road to the N next to the National Institute for Educational Development stands the **Reit Club** with its old-fashioned green corrugated iron roof. Originally the 1909 home to Dr Fock, the first Mayor of Okahandja, today the house and grounds serve as a stables and restaurant, which can be used by anyone, despite the sign to the contrary. The building is large and impressive, and the spacious courtyard is a pleasant place to sit and have lunch before heading N.

Okahandja is a town of great significance to the Herero-speaking peoples as it contains the graves of a number of their former traditional leaders, amongst them, Maherero, Samuel Maherero and Hosea Kutako. It also contains the grave of Jonker Afrikaner, the Oorlam leader who throughout the 1840s and 1850s waged an on and off guerrilla war against the Herero. Every year on 26 Aug the Herero gather to honour their forefathers and those fallen in battle in various wars. The procession begins on the outskirts of town, and women in traditional Herero dresses and men in military uniforms march from the outskirts of town to the graves of their former leaders to pay their respects.

Local information
● Accommodation
There is a simple hotel in town, but for visitors wishing to stay in the area the accommodation at Gros Barmen hot springs and nature reserve is of more interest.

D *Okahandja Hotel*, Main St, T 503024, the only hotel in town, modest rooms, bar, only rec if you are stuck in town.

● Places to eat
Backerei Dekker & JC's Pub, Main St, pleasant bakery serving fresh rolls, pies, cakes and coffee, with bar and disco upstairs, bar has unusually shaped pool table; *Bürgerstübchen*, Posweg, T 501830, closed Sun eve, small restaurant with outdoor terrace offering steaks, game, schnitzel, reasonably priced, friendly service, rec; *Okahandja Bakery*, Voortrekker St, shady terrace and a/c dining room, serving variety of pies and hamburgers with chips, licensed.

Takeaways: there are a number of snack bars at the various service stations as well as *Marie's*, Main St and B Templin.

● Banks & money changers
Standard Bank, Main St, has a cash dispenser; Bank Windhoek, corner of Main St and Voortrekker St. Both have money changing facilities.

● Hospitals & medical services
State Hospital, Hospitalweg, T 503039.

● Post & telecommunications
Post Office: Main St, Mon-Sat 0800-1600, Sat 0800-1100.

● Shopping
Biltong: Namibia Biltong Factory, Main St, sells range of biltong ideal for car journeys if to your taste at all.

Souvenirs: there are two outdoor crafts markets in town. The one on the corner of B1 and Main St represents the **Namibian Carvers Association**, and specializes in carvings of animals, masks, drums. On Voortrekker St by railway crossing, the market has a large selection of crafts from Namibia and surrounding countries. Beware crafts from Zimbabwe being sold at vastly inflated prices.

● **Tourist offices**
Information Centre in the Municipality Bldg, Main St, little information aside from Okahandja on foot map.

● **Useful addresses**
Police Station: B Templin St.

● **Transport**
68 km to Windhoek; 278 km to Swakopmund.

Train Swakopmund and **Walvis Bay** (7 hrs): daily except Sat, 2205; **Tsumeb** (13 hrs), via Omaruru and Otjiwarongo: Tues, Thur, Sun, 1955; **Windhoek** (2 hrs): Mon, Wed, Fri, 0330.

Road Bus: Intercape, T (061) 227847, coach picks up and drops off at *Okahandja Hotel*: **Swakopmund** and **Walvis Bay** (3 hrs): Mon, Wed, Fri, Sat, 0745; **Windhoek** (1 hr): Mon, Wed, Fri, Sun, 1615.

VON BACH RESORT RECREATION AREA

Approach On the B1 about 5 km S of town, turn right onto gravel road which leads up to entrance gate.

Background The dam is the main water supply for Windhoek. For residents it is a reasonably popular place for fishing, water sports and picnics, but apart from bird watching, the dam offers little for the overseas visitor.

Resort information Reservations for both day and overnight visitors need to be made by calling T 0621 501475. **Accommodation F** *Camping*, ablution block, no power points, *Two bed hut*, no amenities, no pets, open all year round. Entrance fee per day N$10 adults, N$1 children under 16, N$10 cars.

GROS BARMEN HOT SPRINGS RESORT

Approach Turn off the B2 by the southern entrance to Okahandja onto the C87. Follow the road for 25 km to resort entrance.

Background Gros Barmen was known by the Herero as *Otjikango*, meaning 'a weak spring running over rocky ground', an apt description for the hot spring which bubbles up here. In 1844

Hugo Hahn and Heinrich Kleinschmidt established a mission station here, the first amongst the Herero-speaking people, and named the station *Neu Barmen* after Barmen, the headquarters of the Rhenish Missionary Society in Germany. Kleinschmidt and his wife left soon after to establish the mission station amongst the Swartbooi Namas at Rehoboth.

The first church was completed in Dec 1847 and consecrated early the following year. Following the building of the church growing numbers of impoverished Herero came to settle at Gros Barmen and the mission station also became a trading post. In 1849 Hahn wrote: "Who would have thought that at the very beginning – yes, even 2 years ago – that this station would become such a market place! Sometimes, the Herero come here from places several days' journey distant to trade."

During the turbulent 1860s the station was abandoned and resettled a number of times following attacks by the Afrikaner Oorlams under Jan Jonker Afrikaner. At the beginning of the 1870s, the 'decade of peace', a new, larger church was consecrated, and the mission station flourished first under missionary Brinker and then missionary Meyer.

Following the German occupation of Namibia in the 1880s, a military garrison was established at Okahandja in 1894 and a substation established at Gros Barmen. This consisted of a double-storey fort with watchtower, which allowed the soldiers to control the area within a 600m radius. In 1902 the fort was enlarged but the mission station itself was dying. Reverend Hammann commented, "As regards Gros Barmen, it is interesting to note that almost all the Herero have moved away from there. Only 4-6 families remain ...".

Following the 1904-1907 Herero-Nama uprising against the German occupation of Namibia, the colonial government approved the sale of land to white settlers, and in 1907 Gros Barmen was sold off. The Hot Springs Resort was opened in 1966 and is extremely popular with local residents as a weekend getaway. Gros Barmen is a good place to relax at for a couple of days en route for the coast or after a dusty trip in the N. It is advisable to make reservations in advance as the resort can get booked up.

Hot springs The main reasons for visiting the resort are the hot spring baths and the outdoor swimming pool, both supplied by the thermal spring. The indoor thermal hall consists of sunken baths and an artificial fountain, and with a water temperature of 65°C is an ideal place for a relaxing soak during the cooler winter months (Jun-Aug). The outdoor swimming pool and children's pool are extremely popular in summer when visitors come to braai and relax on weekends.

Hiking Although no trails have been laid out, there are some enjoyable walks around the dam and into the surrounding hills, where it is possible to see kudu, warthogs and baboons.

Bird watching The dam and surrounding reed beds attract large numbers of birds, in particular water birds such as moorhens, teals and coots. There are also large numbers of Monteiro's hornbill, lilac-breasted rollers and crimson-breasted shrikes with their distinct black and crimson markings. A path has been cut through the reedbeds, which provide an excellent habitat for a number of different species of warbler, and benches on the edge of the dam are excellent places from which to twitch.

Resort information The resort is open all year, and reservations for both day and overnight visitors need to be made by calling T 0621 501091. Picnic sites can be hired by day visitors for up to a maximum of 8 people. The resort has a shop, kiosk, restaurant and filling station.

• **Accommodation D** *5 & 2 bed bungalows*, fully equipped, fridge, cooker, utensils;

bedding; **E** *2 bed rooms*, fully equipped; **F** *Caravan & campsites*, maximum 2 vehicles, 1 caravan/tent per site, ablution blocks, field kitchens. Entrance fee N$10 adults, N$1 children under 16, N$10 cars.

Guestfarms: B *Otjisazu Guestfarm*, T 0621-501259/69, F 0621 501323, 12 en suite double rooms, 2 family units, swimming pool and thatched poolside lapa, horseriding, mountain bike trails, game drives, hiking trails in former mission station, all inclusive. **Approach**: follow D2102 out of Okahandja for 27 km. **C** *Okomi-tundu Guestfarm*, T 0621-503901, F 0621-241196, landing strip, 5 en suite rooms, swimming pool, game drives, horseriding, hiking and birdwatching, awarded 2nd prize 1995/96 in Air Namibia Guestfarm Hospitality Awards. **Approach**: follow B2 from Okahandja to Wilhelmstal, turn left onto D1967 and follow signs to farm, all inclusive. **C** *Oropoko Lodge*, T 0621-303871, F 0621-217026, smart but rather sterile guestfarm, better suited to conferences that holidays, 30 en suite double rooms, 3 suites, a/c, minibar, conference centre, swimming pool, game drives with the chance of seeing rhino and many species of antelope, aircraft charter available for flights to Etosha, Soussusvlei, Skeleton Coast, B&B. **Approach**: follow B2 from Okahandja towards Wilhelmstal, turn right onto D2156 for 18 km. **C** *Ozombanda Guestfarm*, T 0621-503870, F 503996, 3 thatched en suite double bungalows, swimming pool, game drives, hiking trails and game viewing from blinds, all inclusive. **Approach**: follow B2 30 km from Okahandja towards Swakopmund.

Other guestfarms in the area: *Khan Rivier Guestfarm*, T 0621-503883, F 0621-503884; *Matedor Gästefarm*, T 06228 4312; *Moringa*, T/F 0621-503872; *Okatjuru*, T 0621-502297, F 0621-503236; *Otjiruze Guestfarm*, T/F 0621-503719; **B** *Ovita Game Lodge*, T 0621-503882, F 061-226999, 5 en-suite double rooms, swimming pool, excellent food and hospitality, wide range of game including 17 species of antelope, giraffe, elephant and predators such as leopard and cheetah. Game drive and overnight hiking trail staying in bushcamp, guided by knowledgeable and friendly owner. All inclusive, very recommended. **Approach**: follow B1 N from Okahandja for 1 km. Turn left onto D2210 for approx 60 km and follow signs to lodge; *Wihelmstal-Nord Hase*, T/F 0621-503977.

The main road E out of Windhoek passes through the suburb of Klein Windhoek before it starts to weave its way through the Eros mountains. After passing under the railway there are a couple of curio shops and guestfarms before the airport. **Eharui**, 20 km from Windhoek, T 232236, open Mon-Fri, 0700-1900, for those who have left their curio shopping until the last minute, good selection of carvings and hunting souvenirs. **Accommodation** **C** *Airport Lodge*, T (061) 236709, 6 thatched self-catering chalets with TV and mini-bar, conference facilities, swimming pool, with such a wide range of accommodation available in Windhoek it is difficult to imagine who would stay here. Traffic is only heavy on this road, the **B6**, when there is an international flight arriving or departing from the airport, 45 km out of town. Drive carefully along here, especially at dusk, there are often loaded taxis who will overtake on blind stretches in a mad rush to the airport. The airport was built here because of the need for level land and a clear approach for larger aircraft such as the Boeing 747, closer to Windhoek there are too many mountains.

After passing the airport the road is a dull straight drive to Gobabis. The terrain is relatively flat and there are few trees. Most of the country is owned by cattle and sheep farmers. After good rains the countryside looks beautifully green, but for most of the year it is a dull burnt brown covered with a scrub vegetation. There are small hotels at **Omitara** and **Witvlei**, each can be recommended for a cool drink but little else. **Gobabis**, the regional centre, is the last settlement of any note before you reach the Botswana border. There are a couple of comfortable hotels, banks and a good range of shops. If you are planning on exploring the Kalahari in Botswana this is the best place to stock up with supplies.

DORDABIS

Before you reach the international airport, 24 km from Windhoek, is a right turning for the C23 to Dordabis and Leonardville. 66 km of gravel road brings you to Dordabis, an important regional centre for the **karakul carpet** industry. The majority of visitors head for the farm at **Ibenstein** just outside the village. Tours of the farm and weavery are possible, Mon-Fri, 0800-1200, 1430-1800. **Dorka Teppiche**, E of Dordabis towards Nina is also open for tours to see karakul carpet weaving, here you can appreciate the full range of designs on offer. A *Star Line* bus runs via Dordabis every Tues and Thur, 0700, the journey takes about 1½ hrs. If you take the Tues bus you can return to Windhoek on the same service in the afternoon at 1630.

● **Accommodation** **B** *Scheidthof*, PO Box 6292, T (0628) 1422, 5 bedrooms with full board, a perfect spot for anyone wishing to sample the peace of rural life, walking trails and 4WD on offer; **B** *Eningu Guest Lodge*, PO Box 9531, T (0628) 1402, F (061) 229189, Stefanie and Volker have built a superb guest lodge which blends into the dry landscape, 5 double rooms with en suite bathrooms, made from adobe sun-dried bricks, the patterns and artwork throughout the complex all enhance this peaceful location, central dining and lounge area, solar-heated swimming pool, outdoor whirlpool, ideal for hiking and birding plus limited game viewing opportunities, rec.

ARNHEM CAVE

If you have plenty of time or are particularly interested in caves and bats then a detour to Arnhem Cave can be recommended. The cave is situated on a private farm in the Arnhem hills S of the B6. Contact Mr Bekker, T (0628) ask for 1430 in Dordabis in advance. The easiest route to the farm is to follow the D1458 towards Nina. Entrance to the cave is N$25 per person, there are also helmets and torches available for hire.

The cave system is 2,800m long, making it the longest in Namibia. It is a dry cave and thus there are few of the typical cave formations such as stalagmites. After it was first discovered in 1930 it was exploited as a source of bat guano, today the cave remains a home to five different species of bat: the Egyptian slit-faced bat, giant leaf-nosed bat, horseshoe bat, leaf-nosed bat and the long-fingered bat.

● **Accommodation** A variety of accommodation has been developed on the farm close to the cave. **D/C** *Arnhem Cave & Restcamp*, PO Box 11354 Windhoek, consists of 4 chalets each of which can sleep 2 or 4 people and are fully equipped for self-catering, a campsite, and a swimming pool, excellent meals are available on request.

GOBABIS

(*Pop* 11,000; *Alt* 1,442m; *STD Code* 0681) Gobabis is a typical Namibian town surrounded by important cattle country. The region has some good grazing although drought in recent years has caused the numbers of cattle to decline. The name is derived from a Nama word meaning "the place where people had quarrelled". For visitors driving across the Kalahari from Maun in Botswana this is likely to be the first Namibian town they encounter. This is a very conservative place and even in the hotel bars and restaurants we found the occasional racist remark most unpleasant.

The first Europeans to settle in the district were Rhenish missionaries, in Aug 1856 Amraal Lambert decided to move to Gobabis and build a church and small school. For many years the settlement was a popular stop-over point for hunters and traders travelling between Walvis Bay, Omaruru, Rietfontein, Ghanzi and Lake Ngami. Some of the great adventurers of the period were attracted to the region: Baines, Green, Chapman, Hahn and McKiernan. But once all the profitable wild animals had been killed the trade and interest moved elsewhere.

In 1895 the town received a boost when the Germans built a military post to patrol the eastern borders of their colony, unfortunately this fort was demolished after it ceased to be used. But it was still difficult to persuade people to come and settle in this dusty region on the edge of the Kalahari. The rinderpest outbreak in 1897 killed more than 50% of the cattle in the area making the region even less attractive to potential settlers. In an effort to stimulate development the first four farms were sold to former members of the Schutztruppe in 1898, the first civilian to buy a farm was Carl Ohlsen in 1899. The post office opened in Aug 1898, but by 1913 there was still only a full mail service twice a month. The future of the town was only secured when the railway service was opened in Nov 1930, this greatly facilitated the export of cattle from the district to Windhoek and South Africa.

Although modern Gobabis is still regarded as a cattle centre the industry is always on alert for prolonged periods of drought. The 1945 drought resulted in the loss of 70% of sheep in the district; a meat processing plant built in 1983 has never been used, it is known locally as the 'Blue Elephant'. The prosperity of the town and region will be assured once the Trans-Kalahari Highway is complete. When this road is finished it will reduce the distance between Johannesburg and Walvis Bay by 400 km. This will mean that freight landed at Walvis Bay will take 6 days less to reach Johannesburg than goods offloaded at the port of Durban. Whether heavy freight traffic across the Kalahari desert is a good thing or not is another matter, and one not up for debate at present.

Local information
● **Accommodation**
The two hotels in town are the focus of most activity for the local white community, they are also the best place to eat at. Neither can be recommended for more than an overnight stop.

C *Central*, Heroes Lane, Box 233, T 2094, F 2092, 15 rooms with TV restaurant, popular bar, rooms not quite so comfortable as the

Gobabis, but little to choose between the two, the atmosphere is likely to dictate which hotel you choose to stay in; **C** *Gobabis*, Mark St, Box 942, T 2568, F 2703, 17 double rooms with TV (M-Net), small shower, clean and airy, a/c or fan, peaceful shady courtyard, restaurant, bar, swimming pool, off road parking, a single storey whitewashed building just off the main street.

E *Welcome Rest Camp*, PO Box 450, T (0681) 3762, F 3584, camp to the left as you leave town for the border, there are 5 fully equipped bungalows, camping, swimming pool.

Guestfarms: there are a variety of farms in the district which welcome visitors, in addition to providing a peaceful overnight stop these farms are an interesting insight into life on the fringes of the Kalahari desert where nothing can be taken for granted. The rates include an evening meal and breakfast, usually eaten with your host. Note trophy hunting is a popular and lucrative pastime in this region, if you don't wish to share the dinner table with a group of bloodthirsty hunters call in advance to find out how busy the farm is and what activities they have planned.

B *Harnass Lion, Leopard and Cheetah Farm*, PO Box 548, Gobabis, T (0688) 17240, 5 chalets, camping, restaurant and swimming pool, day visitors most welcome, call for directions; **B** *Ohlsenhagen*, PO Box 434, Gobabis, T (0681) 11003, 5 double rooms, small conference room, swimming pool, hunting is practised on the farm as well as game viewing; **B** *Owingi*, T (0681) 17330, hunting tours and photographic safaris to Bushmanland and Botswana.

● **Banks & money changers**
Standard Bank, Heroes Lane, opp the *Central Hotel*.

● **Shopping**
If you are travelling towards Botswana this is a good place to stock up with fresh produce and Namibian beers. On the Botswana side of the border you will only come across village stores until you reach Ghanzi. There are the usual range of chemists, supermarkets and petrol stations.

● **Tourist offices**
Kalahari-i, Eastern Tourism Forum, PO Box 33, T 2551, F 3012. A relatively new office which is responsible for promoting tourism and trophy hunting in the Eastern Region.

● **Useful addresses**
Police: T 10111.

● **Transport**
Windhoek, 330 km, Botswana border, 122 km.

If you are trying to hitch into Botswana you would be best advised to wait for a through lift as far as Ghanzi if not Maun.

Road Bus: Star Line buses run several services to outlying villages, Epukiro and Leonardville, as well as a weekly bus into Botswana. Reservations, 0800-1600, T (0681) 2416 or Windhoek (061) 2982032. **Buitepos** (3 hrs), Thur, 1000, this bus continues as far as **Ghanzi**, arriving at 1700. The return service leaves Ghanzi every Fri at 0800. **Aranos** (6 hrs), Wed, 0530.

Train Windhoek (8 hrs), Mon, Wed, Fri, 1900. This is a very slow service which more or less follows the main road all the way into Windhoek.

ROUTES The road to the Botswana border is gradually being surfaced, there is less than 50 km of gravel remaining. Visitors arriving from Botswana will find it a welcome relief to be driving on a surfaced road again, from Maun to the border is all gravel and sand, at times the going can be slow and it is tiring for the driver. Watch your speed when you first start driving on the surfaced road again, there is a great temptation to go too fast.

BUITEPOS-MAMUNO BORDER

Although this is the closest border to Windhoek there is relatively little traffic, you are more likely to be delayed by officialdom than other vehicles. Just before you arrive at the border there is a garage to the right, **D-E** *East Gate Service Station*, you can camp or stay in 3-bed bungalows, this is a welcome spot and a surprise in such a desolate region. If you wish to drive through to Maun in one stretch then it is advisable to spend the night here and cross the frontier as soon as it opens.

● **Formalities** Open 0730-1700. The Namibian office closes for an hour at lunchtime. A clearance certificate is required to take **locally registered** vehicles out of Namibia. This can be obtained from the car hire company or a police station. Documents needed for the certificate are proof of ownership and driver's passport/ID number. Sometimes you may be asked to open the bonnet so the police can check the engine and chassis number. All foreign vehicles entering Botswana are charged a road tax. Vehicles registered outside the Southern African Common Customs Area (SACCA) are required to obtain third party insurance, this can be purchased at the border post.

By starting your journey so early you will be able to make good progress before the heat becomes a factor. The first comfortable accommodation is the **B-D** *Kalahari Arms Hotel* in **Ghanzi** which has chalets and space for camping, there is also a swimming pool which is the perfect tonic after a hot day on the dusty roads. You will be able to eat plenty of meat here.

Between **Mamuno** and **Kalkfontein** the road is calcrete with corrugations and pot-holes, before you reach Ghanzi there are several sandy stretches. This journey can be done in a saloon car, but a small car with a heavy load may encounter problems, particularly if the driver has no experience of driving in these conditions.

The North

NORTH TO OTJIWARONGO

ROUTES The road N from Okahandja passes over the Khomas Hochland and heads N through an endless bushveld of cattle ranches which stretch as far N as the Etosha Pan. Two conical shaped hills on the left as you drive N of Okahandja were named *Omatako* or 'buttocks' by the Herero due to their suggested shapes. Otjiwarongo itself lies at a crossroads where the road branches NW for Etosha, Damaraland and the Kaokoland, and NE for the triangle towns. As there is no fuel on the 174 km drive to Otjiwarongo it's worth remembering to fill up before leaving Okahandja.

OTJIWARONGO

(*STD code* 0651) The town of Otjiwarongo is a small, commercial centre in the centre – N of Namibia, serving the farming communities in the surrounding area. It is also a convenient stopping-off place for people travelling to Etosha and the Waterberg Plateau. The name of the town originates from the Herero which is translated both as 'place of the fat cattle' and 'beautiful place'. Given the central role that cattle play in Herero culture, both meanings are appropriate.

The town is officially deemed to have been founded in 1906 upon the arrival of the narrow gauge railway linking the important mining centre of Tsumeb with the coast. However, as with elsewhere in many parts of Namibia, there is evidence that Bushmen were living in the area thousands of years ago. It is believed that groups of Damara settled

in the area in the late 14th century where they lived as hunter gatherers until the arrival of the Herero in the early part of the 19th century. The land was ideal for cattle grazing and the Herero gradually forced the Damaras off the land and into the surrounding mountainous areas.

In 1891 the Rhenish Mission Society secured the agreement of Herero Chief Kambazembi, and a mission was established, opening the way for adventurers and traders to move further N. The Herero 'revolt' of 1904 and the eventual retreat of the Herero nation into the Omaheke sandveld, where thousands were to die of thirst and hunger, provided the colonial authorities with the opportunity to take control of the land in the area. Following the defeat of the Herero, German and later Afrikaner farmers settled into the area as cattle ranchers.

Cheetah
Source: Steele, David (1972) *Game sanctuaries of Southern Africa* Howard Timmins: Cape Town. Illustrated by John Perry

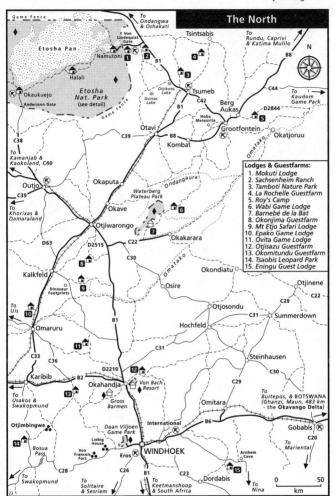

The North

Game Fence

To Ondangwa & Oshakati

Etosha Pan

Tsintsabis

To Rundu, Caprivi & Katima Mulilo

Von Lindequist Gate

Namutoni ❶ ❷

B1

❹

N

B8

Etosha Nat. Park (see detail)

Halali

Okaukuejo

Andersson Gate

❸

Tsumeb

C42

Berg Aukas

C44

To Kaudom Game Park

Otjikoto Lake

Guinas Lake

Hoba Meteorite

Grootfontein

D2844 ❺

Okatjoruu

C38

Otavi

B8

Kombat

Omatako

To Kamanjab & Kaokoland, C40

Okaputa

Ondangaura

Outjo

To Khorixas & Damaraland

C39

Okave

Waterberg Plateau Park

❻

Otjiwarongo

Lodges & Guestfarms:
1. *Mokuti Lodge*
2. *Sachsenheim Ranch*
3. *Tamboti Nature Park*
4. *La Rochelle Guestfarm*
5. *Roy's Camp*
6. *Wabi Game Lodge*
7. *Barnebé de la Bat*
8. *Okonjima Guestfarm*
9. *Mt Etjo Safari Lodge*
10. *Epako Game Lodge*
11. *Ovita Game Lodge*
12. *Otjisazu Guestfarm*
13. *Okomitundu Guestfarm*
14. *Tsaobis Leopard Park*
15. *Eningu Guest Lodge*

D63

D2515

❼

Okakarara

C22

C30

Omatako

Okondiatu

Otjinene

C29

C22

Kalkfeld

Dinosaur Footprints

❽

❾

Osire

Otjosondu

C31

Summerdown

To Uis

❿

Omaruru

B1

Hochfeld

C29

Steinhausen

C31

⓫

C33

C36

C30

Karibib

B2

D2210

⓬

C29

Okahandja

Von Bach Resort

To Buitepos, & BOTSWANA (Ghanzi, Maun, 483 km – the Okavango Delta)

To Usakos & Swakopmund

⓭

Gross Barmen

Omitara

B6

Gobabis

International

Otjimbingwe

Daan Viljoen Game Park

Liebig House

⓮

Bosua Pass

Von Francois Fort

Eros

WINDHOEK

Arnhem Cave

⓯

To Mariental

C20

To Swakopmund

C28

C26

B1

C23

Dordabis

0   50

To Solitaire & Sesriem

To Keetmanshoop & South Africa

To Nina

km

Places of interest

Although the town has a number of old buildings dating back to the early years of the century, there is nothing to match the buildings of Lüderitz or Swakopmund.

Narrow Gauge Locomotive Located in front of the station, the impressive old steam train is one of three manufactured by Hensel & Son in Germany in 1912 for Namibia's original narrow gauge railway. The locomotive remained in commission until 1960 when the track was widened from 600mm to 1,067m.

The Crocodile Ranch, T 303121, open Mon-Fri 0900-1600, Sat and Sun 1100-

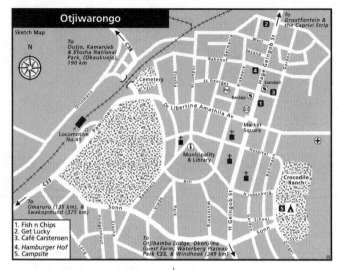

Otjiwarongo

Sketch Map

N

To
Outjo, Kamanjab
& Etosha National
Park, (Okaukuejo),
190 km

To
Grootfontein &
the Caprivi Strip

Cemetery

Locomotive
No.41

To
Omaruru (135 km), &
Swakopmund (375 km)

Dr Libertina Amathila Av

Municipality
& Library

Market
Square

Hospital

Crocodile
Ranch

School

To
Otjibamba Lodge, Okonjima
Guest Farm, Waterberg Plateau
Park C22, & Windhoek (249 km)

1. Fish n Chips
2. Get Lucky
3. Café Carstensen
4. Hamburger Hof
5. Campsite

1400, entrance fee N\$9 adults, N\$7 children. The first and only one of its kind in Namibia, the ranch is a family business started in 1985 primarily breeding crocodiles for their skins. These are then exported mainly to Europe and North America to be used to make a variety of leather goods such as shoes, wallets and briefcases. A tour takes about 30 mins and the farm is located on the corner of Zingel St and Hospital St next to the municipal campsite.

Africat Foundation The guestfarm at **Okonjima** is home to the **Africat Foundation**, a non-profit making organization dedicated to the conservation and protection of Namibia's wild cats. Visitors (overnight only) to the Lodge have the opportunity to watch wildlife, especially leopard and cheetah, from hides located on the ranch as well as get closer to the tame cheetahs rescued by the foundation. Namibia has the largest population of wild cheetahs in the world, 90% of which live outside established game reserves on livestock ranches. The foundation works in partnership with farmers, who traditionally

have regarded the cats as pests, to find ways in which to preserve the wild cheetah population, rec. **Approach**: turn off B1 48 km S of Otjiwarongo. Follow signs on D2515 to Okonjima. **Accommodation A** *Okonjima*, T 0651-304563, F 0651-304565, 10 en suite luxury rooms, restaurant, swimming pool, game drives, bird watching, hiking trails, all inclusive.

Local information
● Accommodation

C *Hamburgerhof Hotel*, Bahnhof St, T 302520, F 303607, is the only hotel actually in the town, part of the Namib Sun group, this is a medium size hotel in the town centre set in small gardens, offering reasonable value, clean, spacious en suite rooms with a/c, and TV, the hotel has a restaurant, bar with draught beers, coffee shop, curio shop with limited tourist information, off-street parking but not secure, popular with local business folk; **D** *Otjibamba Lodge*, T 303133, F 303206, 5 km S of town on the main Windhoek road is a pleasant stop-off point to or from Etosha, chalets with en suite rooms and veranda by swimming pool, the main building houses a lounge, restaurant and bar.

E *Rent-a-room*, T 302517, opp the *Hambur-*

gerhof Hotel, offers basic rooms with shared facilities.

Camping: F *Municipal Campsite*, T 302231, F 302098, adjacent to the Crocodile Farm on the corner of Zingel and Hindenburg sts. 6 sites with ablution facilities.

Guestfarms: **A** *Okonjima* (see above); **A** *Wabi Game Lodge*, T/F 0658 15313; **B** *Okaputa*, T/F 0651 302229; **C** *Oase*, T 0658 14222; **C** *M'Butu Lodge*, T 0658 (Prosit) 16322, T/F 0658 15313; **D** *Mon Desir*, T 0658 (Prosit) 14630, F 0626 40133.

● **Places to eat**
Hamburgerhof Hotel has reasonably priced meals; *Café Carstensen*, St George's St, good place to stop for coffee, cakes and light snacks; *Get Lucky*, popular lunch venue on the outskirts of town.

Takeaways: most of the garages in town sell burgers, hot dogs, chips and sandwiches.

● **Banks & money changers**
First National, St George's St; **Bank Windhoek**, Hage Geingob St; **Standard Bank**, Hage Geingob St. All offer money changing facilities.

● **Hospitals & medical services**
The State Hospital, T 302491, Hospitalweg on the eastern outskirts of the town. *Medicity Otjiwarongo Private Hospital*, T 303734/5, Son St, is a costlier option.

● **Post & telecommunications**
Post Office: Van Reebeck St, Mon-Fri 0800-1630, Sat 0800-1130.

● **Shopping**
There is a small shopping centre with most chain stores represented situated at the end of St George's St.

● **Useful addresses**
Police: St George's St, T 10111.

● **Transport**
249 km to Windhoek; 190 km Okakuejo (Etosha); 375 km to Swakopmund.

Train Windhoek (11½ hrs), Mon, Wed, Fri, 1755; Tsumeb (4 hrs), Tues, Thur, Sun, 0515; Swakopmund and Walvis Bay (7 hrs), Mon, Wed, Fri, 1655.

Road Bus: Star Line: Khorixas (5 hrs), via Outjo, Mon, 0700; Opuwo (9½ hrs), Mon, Thur, 0700; Walvis Bay (11 hrs), via Khorixas and Henties Bay, Thur, 0700.

WATERBERG PLATEAU PARK

Approach
Turn off B1 22 km S of Otjiwarongo onto C22. Follow this road for 41 km before turning left onto the D2512. Follow signs for a further 27 km to Bernabé de la Bat rest camp at Waterberg Plateau. There is no public transport to the park and once off the main road, hitchhiking may involve a long wait.

Background
Known to the Herero-speaking people as *Oueverumue* or 'narrow gate' between the Kleine and Große Waterberg, the Waterberg Plateau is Namibia's only mountain game park and is a striking sandstone mountain rising 200m above the surrounding plain, about 50 km long and 16 km wide. It can easily be seen from as far away as 50 km and the contrast between the looming mountain and the bushveld plain is one of the most spectacular sights in Namibia.

Originally part of a much larger plateau which extended as far southwards as Mount Etjo, the sediments which make up the Waterberg were originally laid down in Karoo times (290-120 million years ago). The break-up of the super-continent Gondwanaland, made up of Africa, India, Australia, Antarctica and South America, 150 million years ago caused an upswelling of lava which compacted underlying sediments into rocks. At the same time, the huge pressure caused by the break-up of the continent caused uplifting of Africa's edges.

This uplifting started an erosion cycle visible today at Waterberg, Mount Etjo and Omatako, which are remnants of the old land surface, and which are slowly being eroded down to the level of the surrounding plain. Finally, in late Karoo times, a thrust fault on the NW side of Waterberg covered part of the plateau with debris, thereby protecting it from further erosion. This part, the Okarakuvisa Mountains, is the highest

An oxwagon train slowly climbs the trail to the Waterberg Plateau.

part of the plateau today.

The mixture of very sandy soils and the Etjo sandstone cause the plateau to act like a sponge, absorbing any water that falls. The water is sucked into the soil until it reaches a layer of impermeable stone, from where it runs off underground to emerge on the SE side of the plateau as springs. It is from the springs that the plateau gets its name.

History

In 1873, two missionaries from the Rhenish Mission Society, G Beiderbecke and H Brincker, established a mission station at the largest fountain at the Waterberg, although they had been instructed only to assess the situation. Their congregation consisted of Herero, Damara and Bushmen, described by the missionaries as living in mutual distrust. In 1880 during a dispute between Damara and Herero groups, the mission station was looted and burned to the ground, and lay deserted until 1890, when Missionary Eich was sent to resurrect it. Over the next 10 years a school, church, trading post and post office were established.

However, events elsewhere in Here-roland were leading to a major confrontation between the Germans and the Herero. Unscrupulous traders encouraged and forced Herero-speaking people to buy goods against credit, and when the latter couldn't pay, the traders took land to cover these debts. Certain Herero chiefs, such as Samuel Maherero of Okahandja and Zacharias of Otjimbingwe sold off large tracts of tribal land to meet their growing desires for European manufactured goods and alcohol. Both promised their people that the land would be recovered at a later date.

In Jan 1904, facing increasing pressure to take action over the lost lands, or to stand down as Paramount Herero Chief, Samuel Maherero gave the order to drive the Germans from Herero land. Initial Herero attacks were successful, but following the appointment of General von Trotha as German commander in the middle of the year, the tide started to turn against the Herero. As a growing number of Herero men, women and children retreated to the Waterberg with their cattle, the scene was set for the crucial battle of the war.

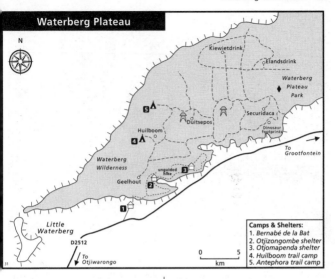

Throughout 11 Aug, skirmishes took place between the German and Herero forces. The Germans had a total of about 1,500 men, as well as 30 cannons and a dozen machine guns. Estimates of the strength of the Herero forces range from 35,000-80,000 with between 5,000 and 6,000 guns at their disposal. As the day progressed, the battle moved deeper into the bush, stretching over a 40 km front, with neither side able to establish a telling advantage. However, on the morning of 12 Aug a German signal unit on the plateau noticed a huge cloud of dust heading SE. The Herero were retreating into the Omaheke sandveld rather than surrendering to the enemy.

Over the next months thousands of Herero men, women and children, with their cattle, died of hunger and thirst on the trek into exile in Botswana. In the years immediately following the battle and the exodus of the Herero, the land around the Waterberg was sold off to European settlers. The small graveyard near the rest camp is testimony to some of those who fell during the battle.

Game

The park itself, 40,549 ha in size, was originally created as a sanctuary for rare and endangered species from around Namibia. The aim was to breed these animals and then restock the areas from where they originated. So roan and sable antelopes were relocated from the Kavango and Caprivi, eland and giraffe from Mangetti, and blue wildebeest from Daan Viljoen Park just outside Windhoek. White rhino were obtained from the Natal Parks Board, South Africa. Black rhino were reintroduced to the area from Damaraland in 1989. Today it is possible to see any one of 25 species of game including, leopard, gemsbok, kudu, jackal, hyena and baboon, as well as those animals mentioned above.

In addition to the game, the park has an estimated 200 species of birds, and in particular is home to the only breeding Cape vultures in Namibia. Other common species are birds of prey such as the black eagle, the booted eagle and the pale chanting goshawk, as well as smaller birds such as the

White Rhinocerous
Source: Steele, David (1972) *Game sanctuaries of Southern Africa* Howard Timmins: Cape Town.
Illustrated by John Perry

red-billed francolin, whose distinctive call can be heard at sunrise, five different hornbills, and the attractive rosy-faced lovebird.

The vegetation of the plateau varies from acacia savannah at the bottom of the plateau to sub-tropical woodland with tall trees and grassy plains on top, which are ideal feeding and breeding grounds for the animals.

Bird watching

More than 200 species of birds have been recorded in the park, and of particular interest are the black eagles, booted eagles, peregrine falcons and rosyfaced lovebirds. However the park is also at the centre of efforts to ensure the survival of the Cape Vulture in Namibia. This species declined from an estimated 500 birds in the late 1950s to an all-time low of 15 birds in 1987, when an intensive awareness campaign was launched by Namibian conservation officials. This aims both to educate farmers to limit the use of poisons, and seeks to reverse bush encroachment on the plateau to increase grazing land for species such as kudu and gemsbok, upon which the vultures feed. The strategies have ensured that numbers have started to climb again, and the Waterberg Plateau is the only breeding site in Namibia of the Cape Vulture.

Guided tours

Open-top game viewing vehicles set off early morning and late afternoon from the rest camp, and provide the opportunity for those unable or unwilling to hike on the plateau with the chance to see game. The tours stop at game-viewing hides which can provide good opportunities for animal watching. Bookings should be made at the camp office. Cost: N$40 adults, N$20 children.

Hiking

There are a number of different walking options on and around the plateau, designed to cater for a variety of needs. The gentle 2 and 3-hr walks around the base of the plateau are an excellent way of seeing the ruins of the Old Mission, as well as enjoying the flora and fauna without undertaking a major expedition.

Waterberg Wilderness Trail A 4-day guided wilderness trail in the Okarakuvisa Mountains, starting on every 2nd, 3rd and 4th Thur of the month (Apr to Nov) from the Onjoka Gate. Only one group (6-8 people) is permitted per week and reservations should be made well in advance at the Windhoek Reservations Office. Cost: N$150 per person, hikers must bring their own food and sleeping bag.

Waterberg Unguided Hiking Trail
This unaccompanied trail, which starts at the Bernabé de la Bat rest camp office before taking hikers up onto the plateau for 4 days, is aimed at reasonably fit, self-sufficient hikers and nature lovers who want to enjoy both the scenery and wildlife and have an adventure.

Once up on the plateau itself, the trail winds around the sandstone kopjies on the southeastern edge of the plateau, through glades of weeping wattle, silver bushwillow and laurel fig trees. Everywhere there are signs of the close presence of game, the dung piles of the white and black rhino, and the spoor of kudu, giraffe, gemsbok and baboon. It is important to take care to walk relatively slowly so as not to surprise any rhino or buffalo which might charge if frightened. If this happens the only recourse is to run and climb the nearest tree or kopjie.

The trail is divided into four stages of 13, 7, 8, and 14 km respectively, all of which can be completed in a morning's walk. The first day's walk takes you along the edge of the plateau. There are several good view points, notably Omatoko view close to Commiphora Kopje. Your first night is spent in Otjozongombe shelter. For the second day the path skirts along the rim of Ongorowe Gorge. There is no need to push yourself along this stretch, the overnight shelter – Otjomapenda – is only 7 km away. The third day can also be taken gently. The path follows an 8 km loop bringing you back to the same shelter. The final day's walking follows a different path all the way back to Bernabé de la Bat restcamp. The trail is generally well marked, but in the odd place it is necessary to look for the footprints of previous trailists, and this adds to the adventure of the walk. Although the distances are not great, and the walk is not nearly as demanding as the Naukluft and Fish River Canyon Trails, it can get very warm during the daytime, especially carrying a pack with provisions, sleeping bag, water and camping stove. Nights can be

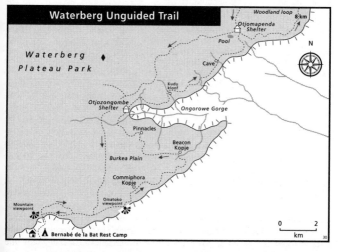

Waterberg Unguided Trail

Waterberg Plateau Park

Woodland loop — 8 km
Otjomapenda Shelter
Pool
N
Cave
Kudu kloof
Otjozongombe Shelter
Ongorowe Gorge
Pinnacles
Beacon Kopje
Burkea Plain
Commiphora Kopje
Mountain viewpoint
Omatoko viewpoint
Bernabé de la Bat Rest Camp

0   2
km

cold with sub-zero temperatures not uncommon, so it is advisable to take some warm clothes along. Accommodation is in stone shelters with pit latrines and water is also provided, otherwise hikers must take everything themselves.

As the early morning and early evening are the best times to see game, a good plan is to walk early in the day, rest up at camp during the heat of the day, and then go for another short walk just before dark. After 4 days of the solitude and silence of the plateau it can be strange going back down the mountain into civilization again.

The hikes start every Wed (April-Nov). Only one group (3-10) people is permitted each week and reservations should be made well in advance at the Windhoek Reservations Office. Cost: N$60 per person, hikers must provide their own food and equipment and the trail is undertaken at the hiker's risk.

Resort information

The park is open all year round and reservations for all accommodation should be made at the Central Reservations Office in Windhoek. The resort has a shop, restaurant, bar, filling station (no diesel) and swimming pool.

● **Accommodation D** *4 bed bungalows, 3 bed bungalows, 2 bed de luxe room*, clean, modern rooms with hot showers, all fully equipped asides from crockery and cutlery; **F** *Caravan and campsites*, maximum of 8 persons and 2 vehicles per site, ablution blocks, field kitchens. Entrance fee: N$10 adults, N$1 children under 16, N$10 cars.

OUTJO

(*Pop* 7,500; *Alt* 1,300m; *STD code* 06542) Outjo is a typical quiet, small farming centre which serves the large white owned farms of the region and more recently has developed as an important staging post for tourists on their way to the famous **Etosha National Park**. If you have been travelling in the S of the country, or have come up from the coast, you will notice a far greater number and variety of trees in the landscape. This is an area of woodland savanna which is not only good cattle country but this is also the start of plentiful game country. As you continue N towards Etosha National Park – Anderson Gate, keep an eye out for antelope sheltering in the shade of the trees.

The name comes from a Herero word, *oHutjo*, meaning 'little hills', a reference to the many small hills which surround the town. The first Europeans to settle here were big game hunters and traders; Tom Lambert is often cited as the founder of the settlement, in 1880 he arrived with his family and built a small garden on the river close to where the old **Water Tower** now stands. Before he could start cultivating the land he had to get permission from the Herero chief Manassa to build a home close to the water supply.

In 1895 part of the German army was stationed here, during their period of residence they built several solid buildings, some of which still stand today. These included the **Water Tower** (see below), the **Franke House** and a large fortress on the W bank of the river, the later no longer survives. One of the more important roles for the army when they were not at war, was to help to try and prevent the spread of Rinderpest from the Kaokoland and Angola. They also acted as early anti poaching units.

Places of interest

If you spend the night here you will not be delayed the following day by sight seeing. However for anyone with an interest in local history it is worth paying a visit to the museum as well as admiring the old **Water Tower**. The **town museum** contains an account of the local history and a collection of gemstones, many of which can be picked off the ground if you know where to look. The museum is open Mon-Fri, 1000-1230, 1430-1630, admission is free. If you particularly want to look around at other times, especially over the weekend there is a key you can

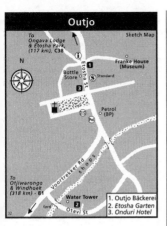

Outjo Sketch Map

To Ongava Lodge & Etosha Park, (117 km), C38

N

Bottle Store

Franke House (Museum)

Standard

Petrol (BP)

To Otjiwarongo & Windhoek (318 km) - B1

Water Tower

ford

Otavi St

1. Outjo Bäckerei
2. Etosha Garten
3. Onduri Hotel

collect from the tourist office. The **museum** building is also known as the **Franke House**. This was one of the first homes to be built in Outjo, and dates from around 1899, its first occupant was the commander of the German garrison, Major von Estorff. Major Victor Franke was one of the last local commanders who made a name for himself in leading a punitive raid against the Portuguese in Angola in 1914 (see below).

In 1900 the settlement ran into its first problems of water supply, the natural fountain could no longer provide for all the extra people and livestock. At the end of the year the German troops started to dig a well in the dry river bed and at the same time work started on the **Water Tower**. The role of the tower was to house a wooden pump which would be powered by wind sails. The 9.4m high tower is made from local stone and clay, but the sail mechanism has not survived. In Mar 1902 the first water started to flow, it was lifted into a concrete dam and then carried over 600m by pipes to the army barracks, a hospital and the stables. Today the tower stands on a stone platform between the *Etosha Garten Hotel* and the dry river bed, it is protected as a national monument and is an important local landmark, rather

like the Franke Tower in Omaruru.

A less well known monument from the past is the **Naulila memorial** standing in the old German cemetery. In Oct 1914 a group of German officials and accompanying soldiers were massacred by the Portuguese near a Fort Naulila which was on the Angolan side of the Kunene River. More troops were killed a couple of months later, on 18 December 1914, when a force under the command of Major Victor Franke was sent to avenge the earlier loss of life! In 1933 the Naulila memorial was built in memory of both expeditions.

Local information
● **Accommodation**

B *Onduri*, PO Box 1046, Windhoek, Main St, T (0654) 313405, F 313408, 45 plain a/c rooms with telephone, restaurant, peaceful palm shaded central courtyard, off-street parking, a large characterless town centre hotel; **B-C** *Etosha Garten*, PO Box 31, Outjo, Otavi St, T (0654) 313130, F 313419, 11 spacious but dull rooms, en suite bathroom, restaurant, average meals, stick to the simple dishes, bar, TV lounge, snooker table, the swimming pool is more of a plunge pool but still very welcome during the hot season, all set in a shady garden with some magnificent large Jacaranda trees, ideal for sitting in peace except for the caged birds.

F *Outjo Rest Camp*, PO Box 51, T (06542) 13, just before you arrive in town on the Otjiwarongo road, well shaded with Jacaranda trees, for a little bit more you can sleep in a self-catering bungalow, 2 or 4 bed, at busy times of the year call in advance as many local people are looking for cheaper accommodation on their way to Etosha with the family.

Guestfarms and Game Lodges: AL *Bambatsi Holiday Ranch*, PO Box 120, T (06548) 1104, F (0654) 313331, 8 double rooms, swimming pool, tennis court, game drives, excellent quality of service, a superb location with magnificent views across hills and tree tops, well run example of the guestfarm, perfect location for day trips to some special local tourist sites. **Approach**: take the C39 for Khorixas, take a right turn, 70 km from Outjo, just after the turning for the Vingerklip; **AL** *Huab Lodge*, PO Box 180, Outjo, T (061) 226979, F (061) 226999 or the local number,

T (06549) 4931, 8 thatch bungalows tasteful decor and plenty of room, private verandah, showers to remember all with a view across the Huab River, delicious meals with plenty of farm cooking and wine, swimming pool plus a hot spring to enjoy in the cool evenings, game drives, bush hikes, horse riding, not only does the countryside have plenty of wildlife to enjoy but with the help of guides there are a fascinating series of rock paintings to view, this is a perfectly luxurious lodge which will greatly enhance your stay in the bush, it is set in a private nature reserve, in 1995 it won a 'Best Lodge' award. **Approach**: take the C39 from Outjo for Khorixas, just before you reach Khorixas turn N (right) onto the C35 for Fransfontein and Kamanjab, after 46 km look out for a left turning (D2670), the Monte Carlo turnoff, lodge is signposted, it's another 35 km from the turning.

A *Namatubis*, PO Box 467, T (0654) 313061, 17 chalets, swimming pool, explore the countryside in a 4WD or on horseback, a very smart and comfortable guestfarm. **Approach**: 15 km N of Outjo on the C38 for Okaukuejo; **A Ombinda Country Lodge**, PO Box 326, Outjo, T (06548) 313181, F 313478, 15 thatch roof chalets with reed walls, en suite showers which have the exciting thrill of being open to the sky, electric lighting, colourful fabrics, plus camping facilities, meals served in a large thatched *lapa* overlooking the swimming pool which is surrounded by a lush green lawn, neat little thatched bar next to the pool, tennis courts, 9-hole golf course, the lodge also has conference facilities. **Approach**: signposted 1 km before Outjo, on the right if approaching from Windhoek; **A Otjitambi Guestfarm**, PO Box 2607, Outjo, T (06548) 4602, 7 rooms, T (061) 254322, 3 with en suite bathroom, swimming pool, game viewing, keen birder's will not be disappointed, artificial waterholes are a focal point for wild animals and bird life, hunting also possible, one of the unique attractions here is a natural hot spring to relax in, the water is a constant 40°C, if you have a head for heights the owners will take you up in their light aircraft. **Approach**: follow the C38 out of Outjo N towards Etosha, after 9 km turn left onto the C40, the turning for the farm, D3246, is almost exactly 100 km along the C40 on the left, it is another 7 km off the main road.

● **Places to eat**
Both the hotels have a restaurant and bars, but during the daytime the *Outjo Bäckerei*,

Etosha St, is to be rec, open throughout the day for breakfasts and light lunches, good cake and coffee. The *Onduri* also serves takeaways.

● **Shopping**
As a small regional centre you will find all the cool drinks and snacks you tend to buy when spending a lot of time driving in the heat on empty roads. A break in this sort of town is advisable in order to give the driver a rest and everyone a chance to stretch their legs and have some fresh air.

Ondu Radio Hardware Shop, Voortrekker Rd, camping equipment and fishing tackle for hire, most importantly for the holidaymaker is their camera repair service, something which could save someone a trip to Windhoek.

● **Tourist offices**
The Tourist Shop, Etosha St, doubles up as a shop selling postcards, and curios, they have a reasonable collection of slides depicting the Namibian landscape; very helpful on local information, also have a few maps for sale, all the information on Etosha is available in the park for the same price.

● **Transport**
318 km from Windhoek; 114 km to Okaukuejo (Etosha NP); 145 km to Kamanjab; 133 km to Khorixas; 73 km to Otjiwarongo; 688 km to Ruacana.

Road Bus: **Star Line**, Central reservations, T (061) 2982032, open 0800-1600, operate several services each week, for Windhoek it is best to change services in Otjiwarongo, from here there is a choice of bus or train. **Kamanjab** (3 hrs): Thur, 0330, Mon, 1200; **Khorixas** (3 hrs): Mon, Thur, 1100; **Otjiwarongo** (1 hr): Mon, Thur, 0600, Mon, 0730, Wed, 1300; **Opuwo** (8-10 hrs): Thur, 0330, Mon, 1200.

Train Outjo is at the end of a disused branch line, the Windhoek-Tsumeb train stops at Otjiwarongo, from here passengers for Outjo have to transfer to a bus service.

ROUTES There are several very different routes one can follow from Outjo, whichever you choose make sure you have refuelled and have plenty of water, all of the routes lead into remote regions, where there is minimal traffic and supplies in small village centres cannot be relied upon. Take the **C40** for **Kamanjab**, the **C35** then continues N into the **Kaokoland**, **Opuwo** and **Ruacana**. To complete a circuit follow the **C46** from Ruacana to

Ondangwa where you rejoin the **B1** which leads back to Tsumeb and **Otavi**. Due E from Outjo the **C39** takes you to **Khorixas** and the tourist sights around the **Brandberg**, this is the heart of **Damaraland**. Follow the **C38** N for **Etosha National Park**, this is the main route into the park, after 96 km the road reaches Andersson Gate, from here it is a further 18 km to **Okaukuejo** the main rest camp.

Springbok

ETOSHA NATIONAL PARK

Etosha is one of the great national parks in Africa, the game viewing here is on a par with Kruger, Hwange, the Masai Mara and Serengeti. The park is home to 114 mammal species, 110 reptile species and more than 340 different bird species have been identified. A large proportion of the park is either closed to the public or inaccessible, this has enabled conservationists to carry out some very important studies of wildlife. The central feature to the park is the Etosha Pan, a huge depression which in years of exceptional rainfall becomes a lake again, although in parts it is only a few centimetres deep. There are no roads into the pan, but along the southern fringe is a network of trails which offer some exceptional views of this natural feature which can be clearly seen from space. A visit to Etosha is rightly one of the highlights for any visit to Namibia.

Approach

There are two entrances to the park open to the public, **Andersson Gate** to the N of Outjo and **Von Lindequist Gate** at the eastern end of the park. There is a gate on the western side of the park, but this part of Etosha is **closed** to the public. The shortest route from Windhoek, 447 km, is to follow the **B1** N as far as Otjiwarongo, from here take the **C38** for Outjo and continue N to Andersson Gate, Okaukuejo camp is 18 km into the park from the gate. For visitors approaching from the Kavango and Caprivi regions, follow the **B8** S as far as Grootfontein, from here take the **C42** to Tsumeb where

the road joins the **B1**, follow the signs for Etosha, Ondangwa and Oshakati. The turn-off for the Von Lindequist Gate and *Mokuti Lodge* is clearly signposted 74 km from Tsumeb. Namutoni camp is just inside the park.

Each of the three camps within the park have their own airstrips which are used by tour operators and private flights. There are also scheduled Air Namibia flights to *Mokuti Lodge*, seven times a week, from here it is a couple of kilometres to Namutoni camp (see below).

Background

The central feature of Etosha is the large pan which covers 23% of the park. The first Europeans to see the pan and write about it were Charles Andersson of Sweden and Francis Galton from Britain, who came here in 1851 en route to Owamboland. They were very disappointed to find it to be bone dry having been told it was a large lake. Galton estimated the pan to be 9 miles (14 km) in breadth and at least 15 miles (24 km) wide, but as anyone standing on the southern fringe will appreciate the mirage effect had disguised its true size. Etosha Pan is 130 km long and 72 km wide, a fantastic and most unusual natural feature.

There are a couple of interpretations as to the origins of the name: the Great White Place is regarded as the most accurate, or Place of Emptiness. There

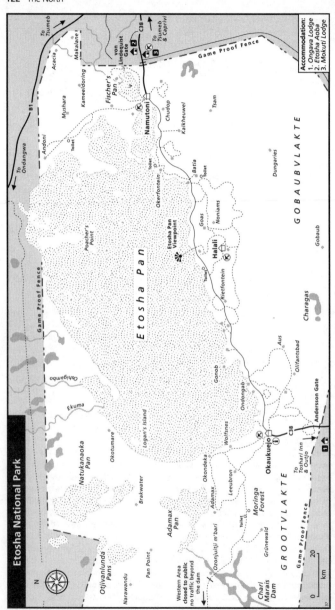

Etosha National Park

Accommodation:
1. Ongava Lodge
2. Etosha Aoba
3. Mokuti Lodge

is an old San tale which refers to a group of people who strayed into Heiqum lands only to be surrounded by some hunters who killed all the men and children. One of the young women rested under a tree with her dead child in her arms, she wept so much that her tears formed a giant lake. After the sun had dried her tears the ground was left covered in salt – and so the Etosha Pan was formed. The pan is very alkaline, sediment samples have a pH higher than 10, with a 3.25% sodium content (le Roux 1980), this high salt content is very important to the local wildlife which require salt in their diet.

The Heiqum have lived around the pan for generations, surviving as hunter-gatherers. Today many are employed as assistants in the park to watch over the animals and carry out repairs to pumps and fences. They are a group of people related to the Bushmen who live around Outjo, Tsumeb and Grootfontein, their language is a Nama dialect.

The first European interference in the region came in the 1890s when the German administration was faced with the rinderpest outbreak. To try and control the spread a livestock free buffer zone was established along the southern margins of the pan. In order to enforce the restrictions on the movement of cattle two small military units were posted in tiny forts at Namutoni and Okaukuejo. The park was created in 1907 by Governor Friedrich von Lindequist along with two other reserves. Since its inception the boundaries have been significantly changed on a number of occasions. In 1907 the new reserve incorporated an area of 93,240 sq km, this included all of the present day Kaokoland from the coast to Ruacana. In 1947 the Kaokoland was allocated to the Herero-speaking people. Less than 10 years later the Elephant Commission recommended the park also include land between the Ugab and Hoanib rivers, the new park was larger than ever at 99,526 sq km. The current size came about after the Odendaal Commission recommended the creation of a Damaraland homeland in 1970 – the new park only covered an area of 21,365 sq km.

After they had been built the German forts at Okaukuejo and Namutoni were converted into police posts to help establish control over the Owambo kingdoms to the N. The fort at Namutoni was made famous after it was attacked by several hundred Ndonga warriors serving King Nehale. On 28 January 1904 four German soldiers and three ex-servicemen managed to resist the attack during daylight hours. During the night they managed to escape from the fort before it was overwhelmed the next day and burnt to the ground. The present building at Namutoni dates from 1906 when a new and larger fort was completed. Once the new reserve had been created the military significance of the post declined, the last troops stationed here surrendered to the South African forces under the command of General Coen Britz on 6 July 1915. In 1957 the fort was restored as a tourist camp.

Best time to visit

The park is open all year but there are three distinct seasons which mean that the game viewing experience for visitors will vary throughout the year. It is widely recognized that the best time to visit the park is just before the first rains arrive, **August** and **September** are regarded as the best months. The reason for this is as for any other game park in Africa, this is when the animals congregate around the many natural and artificial waterpoints, many of which can be reached by car. The other popular time of the year for visitors is during Dec and Jan, but this is more to do with local school holidays than any particular condition within the park. It may be difficult to book park's accommodation during the most popular periods, especially at weekends, if visiting from overseas consider booking your accom-

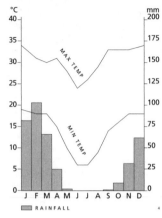

Climate: Okaukuejo Camp

modation prior to your arrival within Namibia. For the bird enthusiast the best time to visit the park is during and after the rains, Nov to Apr.

Wildlife

There are countless drives and waterholes that you can visit for game viewing purposes, they all have their different merits, but it is impossible to recommend any one point ahead of another. The wardens are the best source of advice as to where the game is congregating and where the cats and large mammals have been spotted each day. It always pays to be patient, once you have found a waterhole that appeals to you just turn the engine off, keep quiet and wait.

The most commonly occurring species are the animals which prefer open savanna country. You can expect to see large herds of blue wildebeest, gemsbok, Burchell's zebra, springbok and elephant. After the rains many of these animals migrate to pastures which are in areas closed to the public. A good reason for visiting Etosha is to see the endangered Black Rhinoceros, the resident population is reckoned to be one of the largest in Africa. While it is difficult to spot these animals in thick bushland

they frequently visit the floodlit waterhole at Okaukuejo. During the heat of the day they tend to lie up and you are very unlikely to spot them on a drive.

The park is home to three uncommon antelope species; the Black-faced impala, Damara dik-dik and Roan. The Roan were originally introduced to the park in 1970. In one of the earliest cases of moving animals by aircraft a small herd was transported by Hercules aircraft from Kaudom Game Reserve. These are shy animals and tend to be only seen in western areas. The Black-faced impala are easily recognized as an Impala but with a distinctive black facial band. They were originally located in Kaokoland before a large herd was released within the park boundary. The largest groups used to occur in the vicinity of Namutoni, but like all wild animals they will move to the water and pasture. The Damara dik-dik is the smallest antelope in Namibia, the adult only weighs 5 kg. They are shy animals which favour wooded areas, you may catch a glimpse of family groups, but such a small animal can quickly disappear.

Park information

There are three camps in the park managed by the Ministry of Environment & Tourism (MET), bookings for all accommodation are handled by the head office

Dikdik
Source: Steele, David (1972) *Game sanctuaries of Southern Africa* Howard Timmins: Cape Town. Illustrated by John Perry

in Windhoek (see page 91). The park headquarters are at **Okaukuejo**, the other two camps are **Halali** and **Namutoni**. The facilities at each camp are very similar, there is a parks office which you will have to visit first to find which accommodation unit you have been allocated, a shop which sells both curio items and food and drink for campers, a restaurant which serves three meals per day, a bar, a filling station (you can cover a surprising distance while game viewing), a swimming pool for residents, plus a post office. The speed limit throughout the park is 60 km/hr.

Entrance fees (payable at Namutoni or Okaukuejo before you enter the park): Adults: N$20 per day; Children: N$2 per day; plus N$10 per car. The *office is open*: sunrise to 1300, 1400 to sunset, all visitors staying overnight must be in the camps by sunset when the camp gate will be locked. **Do not stay out in the park after sunset**, you may find yourself in serious trouble if you fail to time your return to the camp by sunset. In the event of a breakdown or a puncture **do not leave your car**, you could easily be attacked by lion, stay in the vehicle until help arrives, for this reason make sure you always have some drinking water and light refreshments when out game viewing. The *shops are open*: Mon-Sat, 0730-0900, 1100-1400 and 1730-1930; Sun, 0800-0900, 1200-1400 and 1800-1900. Restaurant *meal times*: breakfast, 0700-0830; lunch, 1200-1330; dinner, 1800-2030. During busy periods the restaurants can get very crowded in the evening and you may have to wait for the initial rush to eat their meal before you can get a table. *Post office hours*: Mon-Fri, 0830-1300, 1400-1630.

● **Accommodation**
Although you are continually encouraged to book accommodation in advance it is possible to obtain a bungalow or campsite on the day if there is space. Check at the office at Namutoni or Okaukuejo for availability, either of these offices can advise you of the situation in all three camps.

All accommodation must be vacated by 1000, rooms can be occupied from 1200. During local school holidays visits to Etosha are limited to a maximum of three nights per camp. All the bungalows have en suite wash facilities plus towels and bedding, some have hotplates but visitors must provide their own crockery and cutlery. The central booking office for park accommodation is in Windhoek at the Kaiserliche Landesvermessung building, corner, J Meinert and Molte streets, close to the Kudu statue. T (061) 236975-8, 221132, F (061) 224900. Open: information, Mon-Fri: 0800-1700; reservations, Mon-Fri: 0800-1500. All accommodation must be paid for in advance, major credit cards are accepted. Bookings by telephone will be accepted 11 months in advance; written bookings can be made up to 18 months in advance. Written reservations should be addressed to: Director of Tourism, Reservations, Pvt Bag 13267, Windhoek. All applications should include details of accommodation required (see below for details), date of arrival and departure (give alternative dates for popular periods, see above), number of adults and children, your passport number and full home address with contact telephone numbers. While the process is clearly designed for local residents there is no reason why one should not apply from abroad several months prior to your arrival in Namibia.

Okaukuejo: 18 km from Andersson Gate, 70 km to Halali, 140 km to Namutoni. This is the largest of the three camps, the central feature of the camp is a circular limestone water tower close to the administration block, worth climbing for the superb views of the plains and Etosha Pan. In addition to luxury bungalows and simple rooms there is a camping and caravan site with communal facilities. There are three circular pools next to the restaurant which suffer from a lack of shade in the middle of the day. The restaurant is sensibly priced with a choice of dishes for each meal. Away from the offices and shops is a floodlit waterhole which is always rewarding for game viewing. Bench seats are arranged by the protective wall plus there is a covered miniature grandstand. Please refrain from talking loudly when in the vicinity of the waterhole, it is very easy to startle a shy animal, especially at night, and you will not make yourself popular with other guests. There is a good chance of seeing black rhino with young at this water hole, the three

Black Rhinocerous
Source: Steele, David (1972) *Game sanctuaries of Southern Africa* Howard Timmins: Cape Town.
Illustrated by John Perry

big cats also often drink here. **C** *Luxury Bungalow*, 2 rooms, 4 beds, en suite shower, bedding and towels provided, fridge, kettle and hotplate; **C** *Bungalow*, 2 rooms, 4 beds, similar to the luxury version but less space; **D** *Bungalow*, a single room with 3 beds, bedding and towels provided, en suite shower, fridge, hotplate, kettle; **D** *Bungalow*, single room with 2 beds, the cheapest option for bungalows, with the same facilities and equipment as the other bungalows; **D** *De Luxe Room*, 2 beds, en suite bath, fridge and kettle but no hotplate; **E** *Campsite*, dusty but well shaded with clean communal facilities with plenty of hot water; **day visitors** can hire out **picnic sites** for N\$30, plus N\$5 per adult, N\$2.50 per child over and above the first 2 occupants, visitors have use of the communal kitchens and ablution blocks.

Private lodges & camps: just before you enter Etosha National Park via Andersson Gate there are two excellent private lodges which cater for visitors looking for more comfort and attention than you will find within the park. **AL** *Ongava Lodge*, PO Box 186, Outjo, T (061) 248526, F 248529, 10 double chalets which have been furnished to an exceptional standard, the views across the mopane woodland from the swimming pool will be hard to tear yourself away from, excellent food, since the lodge was opened in 1993 it has won several awards for comfort and its wine list, excursions into Etosha are on offer every day; the lodge is set in a private game reserve which is large enough, 30,000 ha, to offer guests a genuine bush experience without having to

visit a national park, in addition to the chalets there is a tented camp where you have the opportunity to have a 'luxury bush experience!'; **A-B** *Toshari Inn*, T (06548), ask for 3702, large rooms for 4 people, en suite bathroom, restaurant, swimming pool, good alternative if Etosha National Park is fully booked; **Approach**: 26 km S of Andersson Gate, signposted off the C38.

Halali: located more or less midway, 70 km, between the two other camps. This was the third camp to be opened in the park. While it is less developed than the other two sites the camp has an excellent restaurant and a large swimming pool. The floodlit water hole is in a beautiful location at the base of a kopje, there is a short walk to the viewpoint, make sure you are quiet as you approach. Several years ago the game viewing at this hole was disappointing, but the animals have since found it, and have now become used to the lights at night. One of the advantages of staying at this camp is that you are in the centre of the park, thus there are more water holes within a short driving distance. If you are planning a visit to Etosha a recommended itinerary would be to spend your first night at either Okaukuejo or Namutoni, and then 2 nights at Halali, and exit the park at the opposite end to which you first entered. This way you will not only see all the camps, but you will see most of the park without having to double back on your route too much. **C** *Bungalow*, 2 rooms, 4 beds, en suite shower, bedding and towels provided, fridge, kettle and hotplate; **D** *Bungalow*, 2 rooms, 4 beds, en suite shower, bedding and towels provided, fridge, kettle and hotplate; **D** *De Luxe Room*, 2 beds, en suite bathroom, no hotplate; **E** *Campsite*, dusty but well shaded with clean communal facilities with plenty of hot water; **day visitors** can hire out **picnic sites** for N$30, plus N$5 per adult, N$2.50 per child over and above the first 2 occupants, visitors have use of the communal kitchens and ablution blocks. Some of the accommodation blocks are a bit close, when the camp is full you have limited privacy, the camp has plenty of trees but little grass, at the back of each bungalow is a sheltered area for brais, firewood and lighters can be bought from the shop.

Namutoni: 140 km from Okaukuejo, allow at least 3 hrs to drive between the two camps, you are always likely to stop for something, even if it is to allow some elephant to cross the road. For many visitors this is their favourite camp, however it has a busy feel to it, and you do not feel you are right in the bush with wild animals all around. While the old German fort is an interesting centrepiece the camp lacks large trees. The swimming pool is in a pleasant garden close to the restaurant. The menu here is the same as at the other two camps. There is a floodlit water hole which is surrounded by tall grasses and reeds. In 1995 most of the camp was refurbished and new accommodation blocks were built to host part of the Miss Universe contest. **C** *Bungalow*, 2 rooms, 4 beds, en suite shower, bedding and towels provided, fridge, kettle and hotplate; **D** *De Luxe Room*, 2 beds, en suite bathroom, fridge but no hotplate, all linen provided; **D** *Flat*, 2 rooms, 4 beds, en suite bathroom, fridge, hotplate and kettle; **E** *Room*, a simple room with 2 beds, en suite bathroom, no fridge or hotplate; **E** *Campsite*, a greener site than at the other 2 camps but less shade, communal kitchen and excellent ablution blocks, can get crowded; the accommodation within the restored fort has a pleasant character, but the rooms are very small and have limited light.

Many of the visitors to Etosha who enter via Andersson Gate tend to leave via the Von Lindequist Gate in the E of the park. From here it is 35 km to the main Tsumeb-Ondangwa road, B1. Just outside of the park there are a couple of luxury game lodges as well as an airfield served by Air Namibia on its domestic routes.

● **Accommodation AL** *Mokuti Lodge*, T/F (0671) 29084, F 29091 or T (061) 33145, F 34512, 216 beds in a/c thatched huts, set in a small woodland area with neat gardens, restaurant has a very high reputation, pool bar, swimming pool, childrens playground, one of the most comfortable lodges in the Namibian bush which has won awards on three occasions, it looses out to other establishments because of its size, it lacks the atmosphere of small bush camps which charge similar rates, excellent service, horse riding and bush walks, and an ideal base for spending several days exploring Etosha, popular with tour groups. **Update**: in April 1997 there was a serious fire at the lodge which destroyed the central administration and restaurant complex, none of the accommodation was damaged, the lodge has remained open but furture/potential visitors would b advised to check on conditions with their travel agent. **Approach**: as for *Etosha Aoba*, but on the left side of the main road, the turning is 500m from Von Lindequist gate. **A** *Etosha Aoba Lodge*, PO Box 469, Tsumeb, T (0671) 13503, 10 thatched bungalows, a friendly small lodge on the border of Etosha, ideal if you want something a little less crowded than Mokuti, and more upmarket than the park camps. **Approach**: drive out of Etosha from the E and the lodge is a couple of km outside the boundaries. If you are already in the N take the B1 from Tsumeb towards Oshakati, take a left onto the C38 after 73 km, the lodge is on the right just before you enter the park.

● **Transport** You can fly to the lodge with **Air Namibia** on Mon, Wed, Fri, 0940 a direct flight from Windhoek-International; there are flights from Windhoek-Eros on Wed, Thur, Fri and Sun, only the Sun flight is direct; to **Windhoek-International** (1 hr), Mon, Wed, Fri, 1805, Sun, 1700; **Windhoek-Eros**, Wed, Fri, 1500, Thur, 1715, Sun, 1215.

After a couple of days driving at slow speeds on the gravel in Etosha it feels quite strange as you drive along the C38 towards the main highway, what is most noticeable is the quiet. When you reach the **B1** there is a choice of heading NW to **Ondangwa** and **Oshakati**, or turning SE towards Tsumeb. If you choose to travel to the far N you will experience a Namibia that is totally different from the rest of the country, the most noticeable fact is the people, between 50-60% of the country's population live in the N. This region used to be known as **Owamboland**, but it has now been divided up into four new regions (see page 164 for details of the Far North).

As the road approaches Tsumeb much of the land is given over to agriculture, a whole variety of products are grown to feed the mine labour force and other local residents. Though this part of the country receives a reasonable amount of rainfall it is still necessary to irrigate crops. Since the mines came into production water has been drawn from two unusual lakes which are found in the bush close to the main road. The two lakes are known as **Lake Otjikoto** and **Lake Guinas**.

ROUTES Once in Tsumeb you are faced with another choice; if you are heading for the Caprivi region follow the **C42** to **Grootfontein** and then the **B8** to **Rundu**; or follow the B1 S towards Otavi and the middle of the country. In Otjiwarongo the road divides yet again, the **C33** will take you to the **coast**, stay on the B1 to return to Windhoek.

LAKE OTJIKOTO AND LAKE GUINAS

Approach Lake Otjikoto is 24 km N of Tsumeb on the B1. Just before you reach the lake there is another turning on the right, the D3043, if you follow this for 19 km and then take a turn onto the D3031 you will find yourself beside Lake Guinas.

Background Each of the lakes was formed by the collapse of a ceiling in a huge dolomite underground cavern. They are technically known as *'sink holes'*. The cavern had been formed after water had leaked into the dolomite rocks, following a minor earthquake which would have fractured the rocks. Once in contact with the limestone the water slowly starts to dissolve the rock. The shape of the lake can be described as an upside-down mushroom. A popu-

lar myth is that Lake Otjikoto is bottomless, this is not so, but the flooded cave system extends for much further than was originally believed. Lake Guinas is considerably deeper, it has been measured to over 200m. The levels in both lakes fluctuate as water is pumped for irrigation purposes.

Lake Otjikoto is home to an interesting range of fish, most of these fish are alien species and have been introduced by unknown people. A sub-species of the common Tilapia was introduced to the lake in the 1930s; secondly the lake is home to a very unusual type of bream. The bream has a protective habit of carrying the eggs and when they are first born, the young fish, in its mouth. The dwarf bream live in the dark depths of the lake, their Latin name is *Pseudocrenoolabrus philander dispersus*, some scientists have postulated that these fish moved to the depths because of a population explosion in shallow waters due to an absence of any natural pedators.

History The name *'Otjikoto'* is said to come from the Herero and can be loosely translated as "the place which is too deep for cattle to drink water". The first Europeans to come across these lakes were Francis Galton and Charles Anderson; they camped beside Otjikoto in May 1851. In 1915 the German army in Namibia was retreating from the South African army when the bizarre decision was taken to dump their weapons in Lake Otjikoto so the South Africans could not make use of them. There are mixed accounts about what actually was thrown in, but there is no doubt about the pieces which are on show in Tsumeb museum. A large ammunition wagon is also on display in the Alte Feste museum in Windhoek. In 1916 a team of divers under Sergeant G Crofton and J de Villiers of the Special Intelligence Unit of the Union forces was sent to try and recover some of the armaments, they managed to find a mix of small arms, and ammunition, five cannons, ten cannon chassis and three machine guns. In 1970 the ammunition wagon was found at a depth of 41m, it was in surprisingly good condition. In the early 1980s divers discovered and recovered some more pieces, including a Sandfontein cannon. All of the most recently discovered items have been carefully restored and are now on show in the Khorab room in Tsumeb museum.

Setting Lake Otjikoto is set back from the main road (B1), amongst the trees, but the position is given away by the presence of other vehicles, the collection of curio stalls, toilets and the chain fence around the lake. A small admission fee is charged, for this you can get close to the lip of the lake and take some good pictures with a wide angle lens. When the sun shines the waters of the lake look very blue and clear. It is possible to climb down to the lake shore via a rock stairway, this is not encouraged and swimming is forbidden.

Lake Guinas lies further from the road along the D3031. It is clearly signposted, but the site has not been developed. The lake was formed in the same manner, but there is no easy access to the lake shore, the sides are precipitous. If you are able to visit this lake in May you will see it at its best – surrounded by flowering aloes on the rock faces. The rusty remains of a large steam pump lie close by, in the 1920s efforts were made to irrigate some citrus orchards nearby. Both of the lakes lie on private farms and as you can imagine they are very popular with scuba divers. This is a very complex form of diving and should **not** be attempted by inexperienced divers. Prior permission is always required from the farmers.

THE TRIANGLE

When you look at a map of northern Namibia, the roads which link the towns of Otavi, Tsumeb and Grootfontein quite clearly form a triangle. They are part of a prosperous region which produces a lot of the annual maize crop and is also an important mining centre. Because of their proximity to Etosha National Park and the Waterberg Plateau, most visitors tend to pass through the towns en route to one of the national parks or one of the many luxury guestfarms in the area. The museum in Tsumeb is worth a visit and there are a couple of old buildings to look at. Grootfontein is the last town in Namibia before you leave behind the German colonial influence, N from here the countryside and the atmosphere is totally different to life in the centre and the S of the country. All three towns are suitable for stocking up with supplies and perhaps a visit to the bank, but they are not places to spend any time in.

OTAVI

(*Pop* 4,500; *STD Code* 06742) Otavi is the first of the three 'triangle' towns you reach when driving N from Windhoek on the B1. It is the smallest of the towns and easily overlooked, the history is far more interesting that the town today. In the past it was an important mining centre and the scene of many feuds between the Ovambos, Hereros and Bushmen.

It was the **copper** that brought the boom period to the town. Work on a narrow gauge railway began in November 1903 and was completed in August 1906, after being interrupted by the Herero-German war. The railway was built to carry the copper ore to Swakopmund on the Atlantic coast. The German colonial company which ran the mine and built the railway was the **Otavi Minen-und Eisenbahn-Gesellschaft (OMEG)**, there are some excellent photographs of the railway on show in the OMEG museum house in Swakopmund (see page 189 for further details). Major mining operations still continue today, but they are based in and around Tsumeb leaving Otavi with a slightly run down feel. Other minerals found in the Otavi mountains are lead, vanadium, cadmium and zinc. Just outside of the town is an Amethyst mine, this is well worth visiting to try and see some of the samples in their natural state.

The only local site is the **Khorib Memorial**, 2 km N of the town. Unlike some memorials in Namibia this one is particularly plain. There is a small stone plaque close to the railway. It was unveiled 1920 to mark the end of German rule in South West Africa in Jul 1915, when local officials surrender to the Commander of the Union Forces, General Louis Botha. The German officials were the Commander of the German forces in South West Africa, Colonel Victor Franke and the Governor of South West Africa, Dr Seitz.

Few visitors are likely to spend any time here, there is a **Spar** store in the centre of town, J Buchholz St; **Tourist information** is in the municipal building next to the *Caravan site*. All the buses and minibuses heading N have to pass through here. Although it is not as large and developed as the other two 'triangle' towns, Otavi does have a couple of processing factories which are related to the large white owned farms which dominate the district; Agra Mill processes locally grown maize meal, and the Meatco Plant prepares cattle products for export to the EEC.

● **Accommodation C** *Otavi*, Unie St, T (06742) 229, 11 simple rooms, restaurant has good selection of tasty dishes, bar, don't be put off by the outside, this is the only place to get a meal in the evenings apart from the Takeaway at the Total petrol station; **E** *Lions Caravan Park*, PO Box 59, Unie St, holiday resort and camping; **F** *Municipal Campsite*, chalets and camping, a poorly looked after venture, if you are looking for somewhere

cheap to stay then push on to *Hiker's Haven* in Tsumeb. **Guestfarms: B** *Khorab Safari Lodge*, PO Box 186, Otavi, T/F (06742) 352, 10 rooms, swimming pool; **B** *Kupferberg*, PO Box 255, Otavi, T (06742) 2211, F 2611, 5 rooms, swimming pool, game drives, with the limited number of rooms you always feel relaxed. **Approach**: follow the B8 out of Otavi towards Grootfontein, the lodge is on the left after about 32 km.

ROUTES   If you are heading for **Etosha National Park** or **Oshakati**, follow the **B1** to **Tsumeb** (63 km), where the B1 turns NW; this road takes you past **Otjikoto** and **Guinas Lakes**, after 73 km there is a left turning, **C38**, to Etosha National Park (**Von Lindequist Gate**). Follow the **B8** out of town for **Grootfontein** (92 km), Rundu and the **Caprivi Strip**. Before you reach Grootfontein there is a sign to the left for the **Hoba Meteorite** (see page 136). Visitors travelling from the N have another 353 km to **Windhoek** on the **B1** via Otjiwarongo and Okahandja.

TSUMEB

(*STD code* 067) Tsumeb is the largest of the three triangle towns in northern Namibia and is a major mining centre. The name Tsumeb derives from the Hain/Ohmbushman word *Tsomsoub* meaning 'to dig a hole in loose ground', and the Herero word *Otjitsume* meaning 'place of frogs'. The reference to frogs derives from the green, red-brown and grey streaks of copper and lead ores found in the ground in the area. These are supposed to resemble frog spawn scooped out of a water hole and sprinkled around on the surrounding rocks! The town's coat of arms acknowledges both Tsumeb's mining and frog connections by depicting a pair of frogs squatting alongside mining tools.

Thanks to the wealth generated by the mines, Tsumeb is an attractive town boasting some fine old colonial buildings and a palm tree-lined central park with wide lawns. It is also the last stop before passing N of the so-called 'red line', separating the enclosed commercial cattle farms to the S from the

One of the new mine shafts sunk by OMEG around 1905.

communally-owned lands to the N. Travelling N across the red line one moves away from European Namibia and into the heart of Owamboland, where almost half of all Namibians live.

History

There is evidence of the smelting and mining of copper in the Tsumeb area as long ago as the Stone Age, and certainly both Damara and Owambo communities were known to be skilled smelters and workers of the metal. As the different Namibian tribes came into increased contact with each other during the second half of the 19th century, so disputes arose over the ownership of the land around Tsumeb. White traders, active in Namibia by this time, were also interested in the minerals in the area and a number succeeded in gaining land concessions around Tsumeb.

Serious European interest in the area was signalled in 1892 when the London-based South West Africa Company obtained a mining concession, and early the following year the geologist Matthew Rogers visited Tsumeb to carry out further investigations. In 1900, a new company, the Otavi Minen – und Eisenbahn – Gesellschaft (OMEG), was formed in order to raise more money to develop mines in the area.

Following the construction of a road between the settlement and the mines and the sinking of two new shafts, the first 9 tonnes of copper left Tsumeb for Swakopmund at the very end of 1900. Although this first copper was carried by ox-wagon, by Aug 1906 the narrow gauge railway to Swakopmund had been constructed. This quickly proved itself to be a faster and more efficient means of exporting minerals extracted from the mine, and by 1908 the company was already generating significant profits.

This was to signal the start of almost a century of mining at Tsumeb, interrupted only by the two World Wars and the more recent miners' strike. Ownership of the mines passed into the hands of the Tsumeb Corporation (TCL) following Germany's defeat in WW2, and they continued to develop mining capacity. Tsumeb mines are today a major producer of copper, lead, zinc and precious minerals – silver and gold. The corporate tax paid by the mines contribute significantly to Namibia's overall tax revenue, and so place mining at the heart of the Namibian economy (see

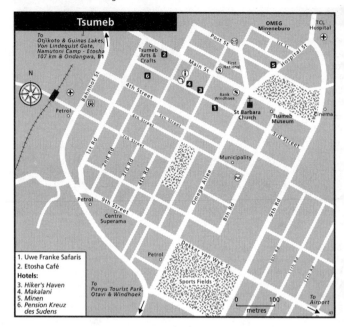

Tsumeb

To
Otjikoto & Guinas Lakes,
Von Lindequist Gate,
Namutoni Camp - Etosha
107 km & Ondangwa, B1

Tsumeb
Arts &
Crafts

Main St

Post St

OMEG
Mineneburo

TCL
Hospital

1st St

Hospital St

First
National

4th Street

Bank
Windhoek

St Barbara
Church

Tsumeb
Museum

Cinema

5th Street

5th Street

5th Street

3rd Street

Municipality

Omega Allee

Pol

Bahnhof St

1st Rd

2nd Rd

3rd Rd

4th Rd

8th Rd

9th Rd

Petrol

9th Street

Centra
Superama

Petrol

Dekker van Wyk St

Sports Fields

Petrol

To
Punyu Tourist Park,
Otavi & Windhoek

0   100
metres

11th Rd

11th Rd

To
Airport

1. Uwe Franke Safaris
2. Etosha Café
Hotels:
3. *Hiker's Haven*
4. *Makalani*
5. *Minen*
6. *Pension Kreuz des Sudens*

Horizons, page 70, for further details).

Places of interest
Tsumeb Museum, T 220447. Open
Mon-Fri 0900-1200 and 1500-1800, Sat
1500-1800, entry N$3 adults, N$2 students, N$1 children. Located in the old
German Private School building dating
back to 1915, the museum has a fine
display of the town's mining history including a display of minerals. There are
also exhibits of traditional costumes, ar-
tifacts and photographs, and a fascinating collection of German WW1 weapons
retrieved from Lake Otjikoto, where they
were dumped prior to the German surrender to South Africa in 1915.

St Barbara Catholic Church, corner
of Main and 3rd sts, consecrated in 1914
was dedicated to the patron saint of mine
workers, and for 13 years served as the
town's only church. The church dominates the centre of the town, and the

unusual tower above the entrance is particularly eye-catching.

OMEG Mineneburo, 1st St, looks
remarkably like a church, however it was
designed in 1907, by Joseph Olbrich, to
symbolize the wealth and power of the
MEG company at the time.

Local information
● **Accommodation**
D *Makalani Hotel*, 4th Rd, T 221051,
F 21575, is one of two hotels in town, 18 clean
en suite rooms, TV, phone, a/c, secure parking,
the hotel has a restaurant and pub/bar offering
lunches; **D** *Minen Hotel*, Hospital St,
T 221071, F 221750, German-owned hotel
with pleasant 'tortoise' garden at the back, 40
en suite rooms, a/c, telephone, TV, pub lunches
served in the garden, restaurant with extensive
menu, and attached bar; **D** *Hotel Pension
Kreuz des Sudens*, 3rd St, T 221005, small
friendly German-run guesthouse with 3 en
suite double rooms, fans, swimming pool,
restaurant, breakfast N$18.

F *Hiker's Haven*, 5th Rd, T 221051, clean

Trouble at TCL

On 22 August 1996 miners working at three TCL owned mines downed tools, starting Namibia's largest ever industrial dispute. The strike, which was to last for 45 days, started because of a wage dispute, however over the course of the 7 week stoppage, it became clear that the miners were fighting for much more than this. "In view of the magnitude of the dire exploitation at TCL, I do not know what the outcome of this strike will be", said Peter Nholo, Mineworkers Union Of Namibia (MUN) Secretary-General, one day before the start of the strike. "But I can assure you that when the strike ends, TCL will never be the same again," he concluded.

In effect the miners were claiming gross discrimination between white and black employees at the mines, and the payment of near slave wages to black miners. Some were taking home N$541 (£75) a month after 30 years' service at the mine. In reply TCL claimed that with a 30-35% drop in world copper prices in Jun 1996, the company could not afford to pay its miners the 13.5% increase demanded by the MUN.

The dispute was eventually settled with the help of government mediation and a wage increase of 10.5% was agreed upon, however the MUN did have to agree to the retrenchment of some workers. On the other side, a Commission of Inquiry was appointed to investigate labour practices at the mines. "There are no two ways about it ... Apartheid and Broederbond TCL must be destroyed and buried 20 million km down the earth so that it never rises again," vowed Labour Minister Moses Garoeb.

Overall the strike cost TCL over N$100 million and some observers reckon that the company will not be in a position to pay corporate tax for over a year. The effects of the strike on the Namibian economy will only start to be felt in 1997.

orms, shared facilities, central location; *Punyu Tourist Park*, B1 southern edge of own, T 220604, F 2216223, 21 caravan and ampsites, ablution block, braai sites, maxinum 6 people, 2 vehicles per site, green and pacious site, but a problem with theft, so ever leave valuables unattended.

Guestfarms: **B-F** *Tamboti Nature Park*, 220140, F 221718, one en suite luxury bungalow, TV, a/c, main accommodation in converted railway carriages, shared facilities, price inclusive of breakfast, dinner, game drives, king trail, offers the chance to see lion, cheetah and leopard feeds, 10 campsites, abution block. **Approach**: follow B1 10 km N in Etosha Rd, then follow signs for Tamboti.

Other Guestfarms in the area: **AL** *La Rochelle Hunting & Guestfarm*, T 067 221326, 220760, thatched bungalows, all facilities, photographic and hunting safaris; **D-** *Sachsenheim Game Ranch*, T 0678 (farmline) 13521, F 067 230011, simple, clean en uite and shared accommodation (7 rooms), ame drives, hunting May-Oct, campsite, resaurant, bar, curio shop.

● **Places to eat**
Makalani Hotel and *Minen Hotel* both have restaurants serving lunch and dinner; *Etosha Café*, Main St, ultra-German atmosphere created by oompapa music and pinafored waitresses, excellent cakes and coffee, light meals plus tourist shop; *Tsumeb Bakery & Toni's Café*, Main St, light meals, coffee etc.

Takeaways: most of the garages in town sell burgers, hot dogs, chips and sandwiches.

● **Banks & money changers**
Bank Windhoek, **First National Bank** and **Standard Bank** are all found on Main St. All have auto tellers and money changing facilities.

● **Hospitals & medical services**
The State Hospital, 7th St, T 221082. *Medirescue*, T 221911 for emergency airlifts.

● **Post & telecommunications**
Post Office: Post St, Mon-Fri 0800-1630, Sat 0800-1130.

Teleshop: 3rd St, for phone cards.

● **Shopping**

For those interested in buying unusual rocks and semi-precious stones, Tsumeb is the place to do your shopping. The Tourist Information Centre can give you advice on where to go.

● **Tourist offices**

Etosha-i, 24 4th Rd, PO Box 779, T 220720, F 220916. **Tourist Office**, Main St, T 220728 or T 220157 after hours, offers nationwide tourist information and bookings, as well as having a small shop selling a range of traditional local handicrafts; **Uwe Franke Safaris**, 3rd St, T 220687.

● **Useful addresses**

Police: 8th Rd, T 10111.

● **Transport**

427 km to Windhoek; 107 km to Namutoni; 247 km to Ondangwa.

Local Car hire: Avis, Jordan St, T 220520; **Imperial**, T 220728.

Air Air Namibia, T (067) 220520, F 220821. Rundu (1 hr): Mon, 0935; **Windhoek-Eros** (1 hr): Mon, 1745, Thur, 1800.

Train Windhoek (18½ hrs), via Otjiwarongo and Okahandja: Mon, Wed, Fri, 1100; **Walvis Bay** (17¾ hrs), via Otjiwarongo and Swakopmund: Mon, Wed, Fri, 1100.

Road Bus: Star Line, T (0671) 20358: Oshakati (4 hrs): Mon, Thur, Fri, Sat, 1115.

GROOTFONTEIN

(*STD code* 067) The northern market town of Grootfontein is one of the trio of towns, the others being Otavi and Tsumeb, located in the so-called maize triangle. Blessed in Namibian terms by high annual rainfall of 450-650 mm, the Grootfontein area supports a wide range of agriculture on its predominantly white-owned farms. Apart from the usual livestock farming of cattle, sheep and goats, the farms here produce most of Namibia's commercially grown maize, sorghum, cotton, peanuts and sunflower.

The town itself is a pleasant enough place with its limestone buildings and tree-lined streets, and is particularly attractive in Sep and Oct when the purple jacaranda blossom and red flamboyants appear. With two small hotels, a good

municipal campsite, and the nearby Hoba Meteorite, Grootfontein is a good place to stop between Windhoek and the Kavango-Caprivi regions.

History

With an abundant supply of water and good grazing, the area has been home to both game and humans for many thousand years. In pre-colonial times the town was known to the Herero as *Otji-wandatjongue*, meaning 'hill of the leopard'. The earlier Nama and Berg Damara inhabitants called the area *Gei-ous* meaning 'big fountain', from which the Afrikaans name Grootfontein is derived. The fountain and the Tree Park, planted by the South West African Company, can both be seen today on the northern edge of town close to the municipal swimming pool and adjacent campsite.

In the 1860s two elephant hunters, Green and Eriksson, used the fountain as a base from which to launch their hunting expeditions. However the first Europeans to settle in the area arrived around 1880, followed soon after by the so-called 'Dorsland Trekkers' who in the mid-1880s established their own Republic on land purchased from Owambo chief, Kambone. The Republic of Upingtonia, as it was called, only survived for a mere 2 years before collapsing.

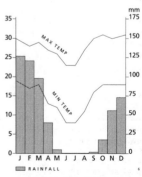

Climate: Grootfontein

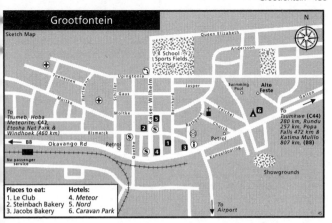

Places to eat:	Hotels:
1. Le Club	4. Meteor
2. Steinbach Bakery	5. Nord
3. Jacobs Bakery	6. Caravan Park

In 1893 the South West Africa Company established its headquarters at Grootfontein and in 1896 the settlement was enlarged by a group of settlers from the Transvaal. In the same year the *Schutztruppe* constructed a fort and administrative centre, and in 1904 a tower was constructed, providing the garrison with an excellent vantage point from which to survey the surrounding area. In 1922 the limestone extension was added.

Between 1923 and 1958 the fort served as a school hostel, after which it was abandoned. A public appeal in 1974 saved the building from demolition, and in 1975 it was used as an assembly point for Angolan refugees, before being renovated in 1977. In 1983 the **Alte Feste**, 'Old Fort' museum was opened, and today it houses a local history exhibition. Grootfontein itself officially became a town in 1907, and the following year the narrow gauge railway linked the town with Otavi and Tsumeb. The town has subsequently grown to become the centre of Namibia's cattle ranching industry.

Places of interest

The **Alte Feste Museum**, just around the corner from the municipal campsite is worth visiting for its history of the town and the local area. Exhibits include local minerals, restored carpenter's and blacksmith's shops with working machinery, and traditional crafts. Open Tues and Fri, 1600-1800, Wed 0900-1100, for access at other times call 2457, admission free.

Local information
● Accommodation

C *Le Club*, Bernhard St, T 242414, is a small, friendly guesthouse with 4 en suite rooms, a/c, phone, the restaurant specializes in steaks and fish from the nearby lakes and there's a small bar and beer garden; **C-F** *Olea Municipal Caravan Park*, corner of Okavango St, T 243101, has a 4 bed fully equipped 'luxury' bungalow, three 4 bed bungalows, bedding N$15 extra per person, and 9 shady camp/caravan sites with shared ablution block, care should be taken with valuables as the campsite is close to town and not secure, follow the main road towards Rundu, campsite on left.

D *Meteor Hotel*, Okavango Rd, T 242078/9, F 243072, is the better of the two hotels in town, and although breakfast is included, is still rather overpriced for what it offers, there are 17 en suite double rooms with telephone and a/c, and 7 rooms with shared bathrooms, bar and restaurant are both popular with locals and on Sat nights fresh pizza is served in the pleasant courtyard, the hotel has off-street parking and the local **Imperial Car Hire** office is also here.

E *Nord Hotel*, T 242049, corner of Kaiser Wilhelm and Bismarck sts, has more basic rooms, 4 en suite and 6 with shared facilities, breakfast is N\$14 extra.

Guestfarms: **C** *Dornhügel*, T (06738) 81611, F (06731) 3503, see page 141.

● **Places to eat**
Le Club Restaurant, Bernhard St, specializes in steak and fresh fish, rec; *Meteor Hotel*, restaurant also offers fish as a speciality as well as steaks, ribs and game dishes; *Backerei & Café Jakob*, Okavango St, on the way out of town, has excellent coffee and pastries, as well as a rather gruesome collection of antlers on the walls; *Backerei Steinbach & Café*, Kaiser Wilhelm St, also serves light meals, coffee and pastries throughout the day.

Takeaways: most of the garages in town sell burgers, hot dogs, chips and sandwiches.

● **Banks & money changers**
Bank Windhoek, Goethe St, **First National Bank**, Kaiser St and **Standard Bank**, Bismarck St, all change money.

● **Hospitals & medical services**
The State Hospital, Toenessen St, T 2422141.

● **Post & telecommunications**
Post Office: end Bismarck St, Mon-Fri 0800-1630, Sat 0800-1130.

● **Useful addresses**
Police: Upingtonia Rd, T 10111.

● **Transport**
460 km to Windhoek; 257 km Rundu; 280 km to Tsumkwe; 807 km to Katima Mulilo.

Road Bus: **Star Line**, T (06731) 2628: **Rundu** (3 hrs), Tues, Wed, 1300; **Tsumeb** (45 mins), Wed, Thur, 1015, Mon, Fri, 1400.

HOBA METEORITE

Approach Follow C42 towards Tsumeb for 3 km, then take D2859 for about 15 km following sign to Meteorite.

Information The Hoba Meteorite is the largest known single meteorite in the world, weighing in at around 60 tonnes and measuring 2.95m by 2.84m. It was discovered by Johannes Brits in 1920 whilst he was hunting in the area. After various people tried to get a souvenir piece of it, the meteorite was declared a national monument in 1955.

The meteorite is believed to be between 190 and 410 million years old, but fell to earth around 80,000 years ago. Made up of 82% iron, the meteorite also contains 16% nickel which South West Africa Company manager, T Tonnessen proposed mining in 1922 – fortunately he never got round to it. There are suggestions that the Hoba Meteorite is merely the largest fragment of an even larger meteorite which broke up during entry to the earth's atmosphere, in which case there may be other fragments lying around in the area waiting to be discovered.

In 1987 a small information and education centre was established, a nature trail laid out, and braai facilities provided for tourists visiting the site. There's also a small shop selling information leaflets, souvenirs and drinks. It is well worth taking the short detour to see this mysterious object from space.

DRAGON'S BREATH CAVE

In the hills around Grootfontein there are reputed to be a number of underground caves on private farms. One such cave is known as Dragon's Breath Cave, located on Haraseb farm, 41 km from Grootfontein, 61 km from Tsumeb. Unfortunately the cave is currently closed to the general public. Nevertheless we decided to include this short piece in case access is improved in the future and it once again becomes an attraction. The significance of the lake is that it is reckoned to be the largest underground lake currently known to man.

The entrance to the underground system is via a narrow crevice in some dolomite rocks. The first obstacle to negotiate is a 4m drop, this is managed with the use of a cable ladder. At the bottom you find yourself in a sloping cavern, you exit this cave onto a narrow ledge, from this ledge it is a further 18m down to the point where you can first see the lake. This viewpoint is an opening in the cavern roof directly above the lake.

waters. A rope is used for the final 25m to the water.

The surface area of the lake is almost 2 ha – that is the equivalent of 4 rugby pitches. The water in the lake is crystal clear and very deep. A small raft is required to cross the lake to a small stone beach. If any visitor using this handbook finds out any more about the possibility of visiting the lake please let us know what is on offer.

BUSHMANLAND

When you look at a road map of Namibia there is a large blank area in the NE where there are very few roads or settlements, this is the region commonly known as Bushmanland. Like the Kaokoland to the NW, this is tough country to travel in, you should not even consider exploring here unless you are familiar with 4WD driving in soft sands and off the road. There are no facilities for the tourist, visitors must be completely self-sufficient; food, water, petrol, tents and so on, must all be brought with you. If you are planning on visiting Kaudom then there must be at least two vehicles travelling together. Elsewhere in the region it would always make sense to travel with another vehicle. This is a very remote area, even by Namibian standards. In a wilderness of over 7,000 sq miles there is only one settlement of any note – **Tsumkwe**, 275 km from Grootfontein, via the **C44**.

The countryside is flat and dry, the few roads that you can see are no more than tracks in places and there are few signposts. To the S of the C44 there are a couple of pans, Kbebi Pan and Nyaenyae Pan which tend to flood after the rains and then attract wildlife from all over the Kalahari region. It is very difficult to travel in these areas after the rains, known as the Panveld, since the soils become very muddy. Dotted about this level landscape are the occasional baobab tree, patches of savanna forest and San communities.

The majority of visitors to the region are heading for **Kaudom Game Reserve**, Namibia's most remote game reserve situated along the border with Botswana. There are two roads into the reserve, if you arrive in the S it is possible to exit in the N and make your way into the Caprivi strip.

TSUMKWE

Do not be deceived by the local maps, Tsumkwe is the regional administrative centre, and the largest settlement in the region. But the town itself is no more than a ramshackle collection of shops, trading stores, bottle shops and petrol station. There is a police station and Nature Conservation have an office here. This is useful for anyone visiting Kaudom, the office will be able to advise on the condition of the roads and where the wildlife might be. Look out for a large baobab tree, Nature Conservation are close by.

● **Accommodation** Until recently there was nowhere for tourists to stay except for the Game Reserve. *Namibia Adventure Safaris & Tours* have now opened **B** *Tsumkwe Lodge*, PO Box 1899, Tsumeb, F (67) 220060,

5 thatch bungalows with en suite bathrooms, restaurant, bar, you can hire a Land Rover from here on a daily basis, with a driver and guide. It is 50 km from Tsumkwe to the southern entrance to Kaudom National Park.

KAUDOM GAME PARK

A remote park with a wide variety of animals and bird life. There are no facilities in the park, visitors have to be totally self sufficient, many of the roads are very sandy and it is easy to get stuck, for this reason the rules of admission state that you **must be travelling in a group of at least two 4WD vehicles**, more would be even better.

Approach Driving from Grootfontein on the gravel **C44** take a left just before entering Tsumkwe, follow the road behind the village school and look out for the signs to the park and Klein Döbe, before you reach the park entrance you will pass a Nature Conservation field station.

If you are to the N on the **B8** in Caprivi there is a road to the park at a village called Katere. 120 km E of Rundu. This is very easy to miss, the turning is about 75 km after the Total petrol station in Mukwe, if you are driving from Katima Mulilo. Once you are on the road driving S check with people at regular intervals that you are on the right road, there are plenty of tracks and no signposts. This is a very sandy route in parts.

Background Kaudom was proclaimed in 1989, it covers an area of 384,000 hectares along the Botswana border on the edge of the kalahari.

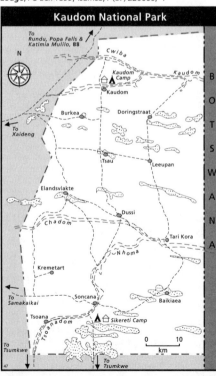

Kaudom National Park

To Rundu, Popa Falls & Katimia Mulilo, BB

N

Cwiba

Kaudom Camp

Kaudom

Kaudom

B

To Xaideng

Burkea

Doringstraat

O

T

Tsau

Leeupan

S

Elandsvlakte

W

Chadom

Dussi

A

Tari Kora

N

Kremetart

Nhoma

A

To Samakaikai

Soncana

Baikiaea

Tsoana

Tsoanadom

Sikereti Camp

To Tsumkwe

0   10
km

To Tsumkwe

47

The climate of the area has two distinct seasons; the rainy season extends from late Nov until Mar, this is also the hottest time of the year – the rest of the year is a long dry season, Apr to Nov. *Best time to visit*: after the summer rains the vegetation is very dense and the roads can become impassable. It is during the winter months, Jun-Oct, that the animal numbers seem to increase in the park, and game will be found close to the artificial waterholes along the *omiramba*. Bird life is prolific between Nov and Mar.

Vegetation and wildlife The park was established to conserve one of the few true wilderness areas in Namibia. The vegetation is dense mix of short and tall dry woodlands, in the winter most of the trees shed their leaves and game viewing is much easier. The dominant tall trees are wild teak, wild seringa and copalwood. The shorter trees, those less than 5m in height, are the Kalahari apple-leaf, silver cluster leaf and the shepherd's tree. All of these trees are able to grow on the thin sandy soils of the kalahari. Running through the park are several fossil rivers, these are known as *Omiramba*. In the N of the park, close to the campsite are the Kaudom and Cwiba omiramba, the soils which occur along the margins have a high clay content and therefore support a different climax of trees; here you will find a mix of thorn trees – camel, umbrella and candle as well as leadwood. After the first summer rains the flowering knob thorn are a special sight.

The Omiramba no longer flow as rivers, but they collect water during the rains and gradually release water as the dry season continues. They are made up of peat beds and are usually full of reed beds. The lush vegetation withi them and along their marins make them the perfect natural migration route running E-W.

Wildlife If you want your animals to be around the first corner when you drive out of the camp then this is not the game park for you. Here game viewing is a real skill, you have to be patient and know something about the animals – what do they eat, when do they eat, where do they prefer to be at different times of the day, and so on. Since very few people visit the park the animals are not used to the sound of engines and they are more likely to bolt than ignore you. There are no fences around the park so all the animals are free to move along traditional migration routes during the year, this means that a certain times of the year there are far fewer animals in the park.

The park is an excellent place to see Roan antelope and wild dogs have been seen frequently in the past. Other animals you can expect to see on a good day are kudu, eland, steenbok, gemsbok, blue wildebeest, giraffe, elephant,

Tourism and the San

The San once roamed an area several times the extent of the current 'Bushmanland' living as hunter-gatherers. Sadly this is no longer the case, more than any other ethnic group in the region they have suffered from coming into contact with the modern world. There is high unemployment and a serious problem of alcoholism in most communities. If you come into contact with the San communities be courteous at all times and respect their traditions. In most areas it is possible to pitch your camp anywhere, however if you are near a village make sure you seek their permission. Tourism has only just started to find its way into this region, the first people who pass through first must be careful to leave the right impressions.

hartebeest, reedbuck, tsessebe, jackal, spotted hyaena, lion, leopard and occasionally cheetah. The mix of vegetation habitats provides a wide variety of birds, over 300 species have been recorded. After good rains the pans and the omiramba become flooded and more than 70 migrant species have been recorded.

● **Accommodation** There are two camps in the park, Kaudom in the N and Sikereti in the S, both are run by the Ministry of Envronment and Tourism, these are very simple camps and everything needs to be brought with you, including lamps for the evenings. **E** *Kaudom*, 3 four-bed huts and campsites, you must provide your own bedding and all kitchen utensils, the wash block has showers which are heated by wood stoves; the camp is in a beautiful location beside the Kaudom *Omuramba*, overlooking the flood plain. **E** *Sikereti*, 3 four-bed huts, communal open-air kitchen, campsite, set in a pleasant woodland environment.

Wild (or hunting) dog

Bookings for the camps are made through the MET office in Windhoek as for any other Game Park in Namibia. This is probably the least visited of the parks because of the logistics of getting here, but once here the true wilderness experience is highly rewarding. **Reservations**: Pvt Bag 13267, Windhoek, T (061) 221132, F 224900; office hours: Mon-Fri, 0800-1500; the office is in the Kaiserliche Landesvermessung building, corner of J Meinert and Molte sts, opp the Kudu statue.

The North East

KAVANGO & CAPRIVI

If it were not for the Kavango and Caprivi regions you would see nothing but a dry landscape as a visitor to Namibia. But in the NE of the country you will find a landscape that is dominated by rivers and is green for the majority of the year. Here the local farmers can hoe their fields, wait for the rain with certainty and harvest a staple crop of grain each year. This is not to say that the people who live here are wealthy, but few will have suffered the hardships that Namibians in the S of the country experience. For the visitor from overseas the region presents an opportunity to view wildlife in a beautiful and unspoilt environment. It is undoubtedly a long drive from Windhoek, but for many people this is where they are likely to experience the Africa they were expecting to see.

KAVANGO

Between Grootfontein and Rundu there is nothing to detain the visitor aside from the beauty of the countryside, the most interesting aspect of this stretch is that you finally feel that the arid lands have been left behind as you approach the Angola border and Rundu. This is the wettest region of Namibia and the green vegetation and trees are a pleasing sight if you have already spent several weeks touring in the centre and S of the country. The average annual rainfall in the Kavango region is 580 mm, compared to 380 mm at Okaukuejo only 250 km to the

S, most of the rain falls between Nov and Mar. **Malaria is a risk** and you should take prophylactic drugs, especially during the wet season. Many of the tourist lodges and camps have been built along the banks of rivers.

If you prefer staying in the country rather than in town hotels there is a comfortable Guestfarm 42 km NE of Grootfontein, if you are heading for Bushmanland then this is on your route, but if you are heading for Rundu it will involve a 48 km detour; take the D2844 turning, signposted Berg Aukas.

Local information
● **Accommodation**
C *Dornhügel Guestfarm*, PO Box 173, Grootfontein, T (06738) ask exchange for 81611, F (06731) 3503, 3 double rooms, 2 single rooms, en suite shower, swimming pool, tennis, enjoy hearty farm cooking with a third generation German-speaking family, as with many guestfarms the setting is both stunning and peaceful, Gerhard and Irmgard are happy to discuss the complex problems facing the newly independent Namibia, although visitors whose first language is English may not feel so comfortable.

At 57 km there is a turning to the E (C44) for **Tsumkwe** (222 km) and **Kaudom Game Park**. This is a tough region to travel in and should not be explored if you have had no previous experience of off road driving, even if you are driving a 4WD vehicle (see page 137, the Bushmanland section for details). **Accommodation** About 1 km off the **B8** is a new bushcamp run by Marietkie and Otto Wimpie, early reports comment on a well thought out camp in a beautiful setting. Once again this represents a pleasant alternative to staying in Grootfontein. The accommodation is known as **C** *Roy's Camp*, it consists of 5 thatched stone huts made with indigenous materials, en suite bathroom, slightly unusual are the double storey huts with the bathroom downstairs, each hut has been tastefully decorated with mobiles and hessian curtains, swimming pool, there are also excellent camping facilities, rec. After the Tsumkwe turning there are no other junctions of note before the B8 reaches **Rundu**.

RUNDU

After the long straight drive N from Grootfontein the small settlement of Rundu is a welcome sight. The town is spread out along the banks of the Kavango River, the opposite bank is Angola. Since 1993 it has been the regional capital of the Okavango region and consequently is home to the usual selection of local government offices, banks, supermarkets, pharmacy, petrol stations and a hospital.

Rundu was once a thriving border town but the independence struggle brought most commercial activities to a halt. Recently several new lodges have opened along the river and by virtue of its geographic position between Katima Mulilo and the rest of Namibia quite a few organized tours overnight here. The character of the town is quite different from other Namibian towns, the Portuguese influence from across the border is very strong, and there is no legacy of the German past; gradually the town is coming back to life as stability is restored to the region on both sides of the border.

Depending upon your schedule there are several options available for continuing your journey. It is possible to drive straight through to Katima Mulilo (518 km), but you should ensure there is sufficient time to arrive in daylight. Remember to refuel before continuing, since supplies and other traffic in the Caprivi are limited. A popular option is to drive as far as Popa Falls and spend the night at the MET camp or one of the private lodges situated along the banks of the Kavango River. The next day you have the option of exploring the Mahango Game Park (see below), entering into Botswana, or continuing E through Caprivi towards Katima Mulilo. A third option is to stop-over in Rundu, there are several excellent lodges and the sunset over the Kavango is a beautiful sight.

Local information
● **Accommodation**
Look out for sign boards at junctions and petrol stations for directions to the lodges. There is a surprisingly good choice for this isolated town, not all the options have been listed below, some of the lodges are out of town. Many of the lodges advertise for boat trips on the Kavango River, these may well not be possible between May and November when water levels are too low. However for the energetic it should still be possible to paddle about in a canoe.

A *Kwasi Lodge*, PO Box 245, Grootfontein, T (06731) 2056, F 2058, Windhoek reservations, T (061) 221225, F (061) 250851. 22 km E of Rundu on the banks of the Kavango River, a luxurious lodge which is popular with tour

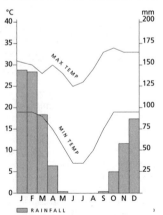

°C / mm

40 — 200
35 — 175
30 — 150
25 — 125
20 — 100
15 — 75
10 — 50
5 — 25
0 —

MAX TEMP

MIN TEMP

J F M A M J J A S O N D

▨ RAINFALL

Climate: Rundu

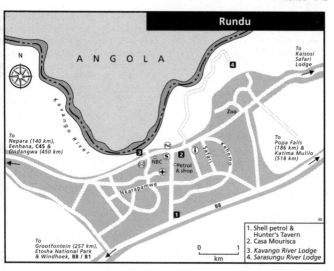

Rundu

To Kaisosi Safari Lodge

ANGOLA

N

Kavango River

To Nepara (140 km), Eenhana, C45 & Ondangwa (450 km)

Zoo

To Popa Falls (186 km) & Katima Mulilo (518 km)

Nkarapamwe

B8

48

1. Shell petrol & Hunter's Tavern
2. Casa Mourisca
3. *Kavango River Lodge*
4. *Sarasungu River Lodge*

To Grootfontein (257 km), Etosha National Park & Windhoek, B8 / B1

0   1
km

groups en route to the Victoria Falls, rooms are spacious wooden chalets, thatch roof, en suite bathroom, with patterned wood walls, there is also a neat campsite which is well shaded and has good grass cover, cosy central dining area, bar alongside the swimming pool, horse riding, canoe trips, special game viewing tours can be organized to Kaudom Game Park, this represents an excellent opportunity to visit one of the more inaccessible parks in Namibia, the whole camp is set in neat well kept grounds with plenty of shade and lawns, this is a popular spot for bird enthusiasts.

B-C *Kaisosi Safari Lodge*, PO Box 599, Rundu, T/F (067) 255265, situated 7 km E of Rundu in the riverine forest, 12 thatched chalets, some with 2 bedrooms, en suite bathroom, superb views from the first floor balcony, camping also permitted, restaurant, bar, swimming pool, the standard range of activities are on offer, boat trips and bird walks along the river banks, if you call in advance the lodge will arrange transfers to/from Rundu and the airport for US\$20 per journey; **B-C** *Omashare River Lodge*, Usivi Rd, PO Box 294, Rundu, T (067) 256101, F 256111, 20 spacious rooms with en suite bathroom, à la carte restaurant, long wooden bar, TV lounge, curio shop, conference facilities, swimming pool set in exposed grounds, the gardens have yet to take shape, relaxing views of the Kavango River

from the shady veranda, canoe trips on the river, a smart new modern hotel, more suited to the business traveller and government officials than the tourist; **B-E** *Sarasungu River Lodge*, PO Box 414, Rundu, T (067) 255161, F 256238, Windhoek bookings, T (061) 220694, simple thatched reed cottages with en suite showers, there is a more luxurious 'Honeymoon' bungalow set on stilts, for the budget traveller there is a grass camping area with braai sites and hot water, meals are served in a cosy timber dining area with a bar, pizza is their speciality, small swimming pool, informal, relaxed atmosphere, run by friendly Portuguese/German couple, Eduardo and Ines, who took over the camp in 1992 when life along the Angola border was not so safe and few visitors were travelling through Caprivi; they have now completed the rehabilitation and transformation of the camp and are well established as one of the best lodges in the N, many of the leading travel agencies use the lodge, the birding along the river is excellent, mountain bikes for hire (the tracks are very sandy in places), it is possible to arrange a canoe ride on the river, remember the far side is Angola, avoid the temptation of a short exploratory stroll; overall the perfect set up for the setting, the smaller cottages are slightly overpriced, rec and worth the stop rather than pushing on to Popa Falls or Grootfontein.

C *Kavango River Lodge*, PO Box 634, Rundu, T (067) 255244, F 255013, 10 clean a/c bungalows, en suite bathroom, TV, the best ones have private verandas, each bungalow has a fridge stocked with breakfast provisions (the room rates incl all the contents of the fridge), each bungalow has a superb sunset view of the Kavango River, no restaurant, guests can buy cool drinks, beers and braai packs from a kiosk, the braai sites are set amongst the trees with a well kept lawn overlooking the river, a relaxing feature are some hammocks slung amongst the trees, tennis courts, a variety of trips can be organized on the river – canoes, fishing trips, sunset and photographic cruises.

● **Places to eat**

There are some supermarkets in the centre of town which stock everything you need if camping. Eating out is very limited, only the lodges cater regularly to tourists. *Casa Mourisca* in the centre nr the police station, closed Tues, if you are self-catering and don't wish to cook a good range of Portuguese dishes are served; *Hunter's Tavern*, at the Shell petrol station, snack meals available all day.

● **Banks & money changers**

Open, Mon-Fri, 0900-1530, Sat 0830-1100. There is one ATM, but do not rely upon this for cash. The banks in Grootfontein are more reliable.

● **Shopping**

Local crafts: the Kavango region is known for some fine wood carvings. The **Mbangura Woodcarvers' Cooperative** run by the government is worth checking out for some items, though many pieces may be too large to carry back home. Look out for roadside stalls selling handicrafts as well as fresh fruit at certain times of the year. Household objects from the San can also be bought from roadside stalls.

● **Tourist information**

Tourism Centre, PO Box 519, Rundu, T (0671) 55909, F (0671) 55910, a mix of local information and services including a curio shop.

● **Transport**

257 km to Grootfontein, 518 km to Katima Mulilo, 438 km to Mudumu NP (Lianshulu Lodge), 186 km to Popa Falls.

Across the Kavango River is the Angolan town of Calai, you may be able to enter for the day without a visa, but check carefully with the police on both sides of the border or else you could find yourself facing a large US$ 'fine'.

Rundu-Calais border open daily: 0700-1700.

Air Local Air Namibia office, T 255854. **Windhoek-Eros** (2½ hrs), via Tsumeb, Mon, 1630. The weekly flight from Windhoek arrives at 1030 every Mon.

Road Bus: the Windhoek-Livingstone bus service stops in Rundu, T (61) 223478. This is an 11-seater minibus which departs from Windhoek on Tues and Fri. The return journey departs from Livingstone in Zambia on Thur and Sun. This is a popular service and advance reservations are recommended.

If you have driven up to Rundu from the S the chances are that you will be continuing on to **Katima Mulilo** at the eastern end of the Caprivi Strip, however there are two possible alternative routes. 120 km E of Rundu on the B8 is a small village of **Katere**, this is very easy to miss, so it is worth making a note of your milo reading as you leave Rundu. At Katere there is a turning to the S which is for **Kaudom Game Park**, the sign is not clear, and nor is the road as you travel further S into Bushmanland. You can exit the game park in the S and complete a circuit back to the main road just N of Grootfontein. The other option is to turn off the **B8** at **Bagani** and **Popa Falls** and drive S into Botswana via the Mohembo border post. If you don't turn off at Bagani for Botswana the road crosses the Kavango River and you enter the Caprivi region of Namibia.

CAPRIVI

Compared with the rest of Namibia the contrast in scenery could not be more marked. The Caprivi region is a land of fertile floodplains surrounded by perennial rivers, a far cry from the arid lands of the Kalahari or the Namib-Naukluft. An unusual feature of the area is that wherever you are no piece of land is more than 47m higher than the rest. The regional centre is Katima Mulilo, normally referred to as just 'Katima'. This is a busy commercial centre on the banks of the Zambezi. There is nothing to detain the visitor here, the attractions of the region are the game parks and the beautiful scenery. At the eastern end of Caprivi are two undeveloped game parks, Mudumu and Mamili. In the western sector you can visit Mahango Game Reserve and the Popa Falls. The narrowest part of the Caprivi strip is also a game reserve – Caprivi Game Reserve – but there are no facilities here and permits or entry fees are not required. The main road runs through the middle of this reserve. If you have driven to this part of the country from Windhoek we would advise you also allow yourself enough time to travel a little further into Botswana and Zimbabwe to experience the magnificent Chobe Game Park and the famous Victoria Falls. It is only a 4-hr drive from Katima Mulilo to the Victoria Falls.

Local history

The Caprivi Strip is a classic example of how the former colonial powers shaped the boundaries of modern Africa. The strip is 500 km long, with the Caprivi Game Reserve only 32 km wide, at the eastern end it opens up to almost 100 km wide before narrowing to a point on the Zambezi River where the boundaries of Zimbabwe, Namibia, Zambia and Botswana meet.

During the struggle for independence the Caprivi region was home to the South African Army and police, and as a consequence none really knows what went on up here. There were secret army camps, the airfield at Mpacha was used for air strikes into Angola and Zambia, and the region was closed to anyone who didn't live here or have a reason for visiting. From the early 1960s until 1990

Berlin Conference – carving up the strip

The Caprivi Strip owes its origins to the Berlin conference when the European colonial powers decided how to carve up Africa between themselves. On 1 July 1890, Britain traded Heliogoland and the Caprivi region for Zanzibar and parts of Bechuanaland, present day Botswana. Germany planned to use the strip as a trade route into central Africa, but even before the outbreak of WW1 this plan was thwarted by the activities of Cecil Rhodes in modern day Zimbabwe. The strip was named after the German Chancellor, General Count Georg Leo von Caprivi di Caprara di Montecuccoli. Unlike the rest of Namibia the region has little to show from the German period of rule. The strip returned to British control at the outbreak of WW1, less than 25 years after the Germans had assumed control of the region. The return to British control came about in a most unusual fashion. The story goes that the German governor was having afternoon tea with a senior British official from Rhodesia, when a message arrived saying that war had just been declared between the two countries. The German governor was placed under arrest and the territory under his control annexed.

In 1918 the land was incorporated into Bechuanaland and thus ruled by the British. In 1929 it was handed over to the South African ruled South West Africa, at independence it remained part of Namibia.

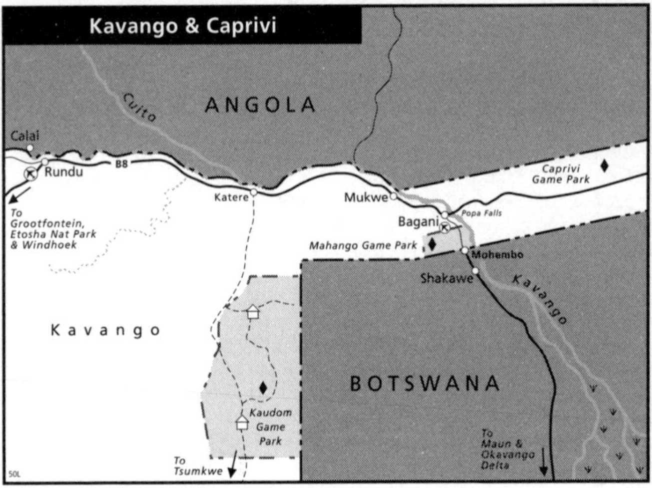

Kavango & Caprivi

the region was in a constant state of war. Today this is all the past, as far as the tourist is concerned you can safely travel through the region, when the local communities fully recover is another matter.

As you drive along the B8 towards Katima Mulilo it is hard not to think of where the international boundaries lie. The Caprivi Strip is for many travellers a special attraction, you have to travel through it because it is there. But on the other hand it is just another corner of Africa. It is a region blessed with some magnificent forests and rivers as well as a wide variety of wildlife. Visits to Mudumu and Mamili will always be remembered, but not necessarily for the wildlife. At the end of Caprivi is the isolated town of Katima Mulilo, remember where you are on the map when you pass through here. Make sure you have a cool beer by the Zambezi before pushing on, at times this could be the heart of Africa.

SOUTH TO BOTSWANA

Just before the 'Golden Highway' crosses the Kavango River into the Caprivi Strip there is a right turning by the 24-hr petrol station. The junction is marked as Divundu on most maps, although there is only the petrol station and the police checkpoint on the far side of the bridge. This gravel road follows the river S to **Mahango Game Reserve** and the border with **Botswana**. It is a relatively busy road since it is the shortest route from northern Namibia to **Maun** and the **Okavango Delta**. (A number of organized tours combine visits to Etosha National Park with trips into the Okavango Delta, Chobe National Park and the Victoria Falls.) The camp at **Popa Falls** has long been a popular overnight destination, particularly in the days when the road between Rundu and Katima Mulilo was all gravel.

BAGANI

Bagani is no more than a general store and a few buildings beside the road, from here it is a further 35 km to the border. Along this road there is a variety of accommodation reflecting the continued popularity of this route. Since the road passes through the Mahango Game Reserve you may have difficulty getting into

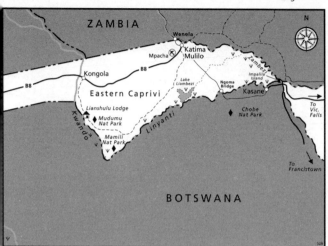

Botswana if you are on a motorbike. In fact the only legitimate way into Botswana is a roundabout route via Zambia, see box below. Popa Falls and Mahango are both run by the Ministry of Environment and Tourism, there is no accommodation in the park, MET permits are issued at the northern entrance to the park or at the Popa Falls office.

● **Accommodation** The following three options are all past the turning for Popa Falls and before the N gate to Mahango Game Reserve, each one has a pleasant riverside location. **A-B** *Ndhovu Lodge*, PO Box 894, Rundu, T (061) 220876, F (061) 239700, this lodge is wonderfully luxurious and in a beautiful spot on the banks of the Kavango River, run by Lynne and Roy Vincent; guests sleep in permanent structured tents for 2/4 people, or in a wooden chalet on stilts for 2, all with reed and thatch en suite bathrooms, price includes dinner and breakfast, packed lunches available on request, all the food is excellent, activities can be offered on a limited scale – game drives to Mahango, river trips and bush walks, the lodge has a small curio shop, guests can arrange to arrive and leave by light aircraft from Bagani airport through tour operators in Windhoek, rec; **A-E** *Suclabo Lodge*, PO Box 894, Rundu, T 6222 (number about to change), situated

between *Ndhovu Lodge* and Popa Falls, this lodge aims towards the German clientele, it is a similar price to *Ndhovu* but without the warm welcome (unless you are German), accommodation is in wooden chalets on some raised ground, camping also permitted, mixed reports, service can be erratic, the lodge is named after Suzzie, Clara and Boris; **F** *Ngepi Campsite*, take a left turning just after the airstrip, the camp is a further 4 km down a sandy track, the green location on the river bank makes up for other deficiencies, a very basic campsite which is short on ablution facilities, the bar can get quite lively, canoes for hire, don't leave yourself with a long strenuous trip back to the camp against the current.

The turning for *Ndhovu Lodge* is just before the N gate to Mahango Game Park, if you plan on driving straight through the park to the border you do not need a permit or need to pay any park fees. This system does to a certain extent rely upon honesty, please don't abuse the trust, without the income it would be even more difficult than it already is for the parks to be managed and preserved. The **Mohembo border post** with Botswana is **open** between 0600-1900. The quality of the road on the Botswana side used to have a bad

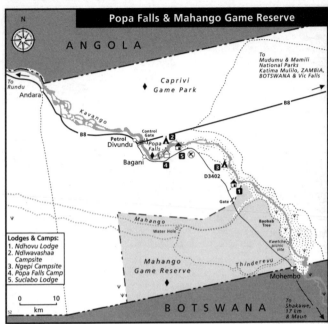

Popa Falls & Mahango Game Reserve

ANGOLA

To
Mudumu & Mamili
National Parks
Katima Mulilo, ZAMBIA,
BOTSWANA & Vic Falls

To
Rundu

Andara

*Caprivi
Game Park*

Kavango

B8

B8

Control
Gate

Petrol
Divundu

Popa
Falls

Bagani

D3402

Gate

Baobab
Tree

Kwetcher
picnic
site

Mahango

Water Hole

Mahango
Game Reserve

Thinderevu

Mohembo

Lodges & Camps:
1. Ndhovu Lodge
2. Ndiwavashaa
   Campsite
3. Ngepi Campsite
4. Popa Falls Camp
5. Suclabo Lodge

0   10
km

BOTSWANA

To
Shakawe,
17 km
& Maun

reputation, it is now surfaced. The first settlement on the Botswana side is Shakawe, 17 km from the border, this road continues S with the 'panhandle' of the Okavango delta to the E. The first accommodation you reach is *Shakawe Fishing Camp*, 15 km further S. Welcome to Botswana, Namibia never seemed so cheap!

POPA FALLS

Many visitors speak of their disappointment when they discover that the Popa Falls are **not falls** at all, rather a series of rapids, waterways and islands on the Kavango River. When the river is very low the highest visible drop is about 3m. There is a walkway into the middle of the river, after this you are free to scramble over the rocks in the middle of the river. At this point the channel is about 1 km wide with the river split into a series of channels making their way through the rocks. The area is a popular camping spot for travellers on the way to Botswana, or a convenient stopping place when travelling between Kavango and E Caprivi. The area is protected as a National Park, but apart from birdlife, a few hippo and some crocodile there is little wildlife to be seen at the site. **Warning** do not swim in the river, in addition to the presence of crocodile there is bilharzia in the water.

● **Accommodation** **D-E** *Wooden chalet* for 4, with bedding, communal washing facilities, no restaurant but communal cooking facilities and a small kiosk which only stock basic tinned supplies and cool drinks; camping also permitted but you might be better off at Ngepi a little further downstream if Popa Fall is busy, the office will issue fishing permits on the way, this camp always has mixed report but it will remain popular as long as it is kept clean and the alternatives in the area remain expensive.

Motorbikes & animals do not go together

Both Namibia and Botswana have a policy which does not permit motorbikes in National Parks and Game Reserves. This is understandable when one considers the potential dangers posed by a herd of elephant or buffalo. The down side of this policy is that it makes it quite difficult for anyone on a motorbike to exit from the Caprivi Strip region of Namibia into Botswana. It is not possible to cross the border between Namibia and Botswana at Mohembo since the road passes through Mahango Game Reserve.

At the eastern end of Caprivi it is not possible to enter Botswana via Ngoma Bridge because the road runs through Chobe National Park until you reach Kasane. Mark Easterbrook writes that you have to drive to Katima Mulilo and then go via Zambia (Wenela border) – the road on the Zambia side is as bad as all reports, in fact you will be lucky to drive at much more than 10 mph. Unless you really wish to see the Caprivi region it would probably be easier to exit Namibia via the B6 from Windhoek to Gobabis and Buitepos. You are then faced with a long dusty road via Ghanzi to Maun.

MAHANGO GAME PARK

This is a pleasant small reserve which borders the perennial Kavango River, a 4WD vehicle is required to explore the side roads. If you are travelling through the Caprivi region it is worth allowing sufficient time to enjoy a day by the river, even if you do not see the large herds of elephant, the mixed forest and bush country is very beautiful and full of life. The main road to Botswana passes through the park so there is always a chance of seeing game even if you are just passing through.

Approach It is quite conceivable that this park would be the first park you visit in Namibia if approaching from Botswana through the Mohembo border post. The northern gate is 232 km from Rundu or 310 km from Katima Mulilo. The signpost for Popa Falls on the B8 is very clear, it is only a further 12 km from the falls to the park.

Background Mahango has a lot in common with Kaudom Game Park, both are in a remote region with a common boundary with Botswana, neither have been developed beyond the cutting of a few tracks which are only suitable for 4WD vehicles and both were created in 1989 just before Namibian independence.

It is worth noting that some people believe the parks were created for the wrong reasons, but like Mudumu and Mamili National Parks to the E, if these areas had not been declared as parks they would have quickly fallen prey to woodcutters, hunters and poaching and Namibia would have lost a unique and valuable tourist resource. All of these game parks are set in beautiful countryside that is threatened from all sides. You only have to compare the appearance of the land on either side of the boundary lines to appreciate the importance and value of the parks.

Mahango is a relatively small park, being only 28,000 ha in area, the southern boundary is the border with Botswana, and its eastern boundary is the Kavango River. The year-round supply of water in the river helps ensure that the game remains in the vicinity of the park. Although there are no fences the presence of man outside of the park helps to act as a barrier to movement, although the animals which traditionally migrate between Angola to the N and the Okavango delta to the S still pass freely through the region, although not without causing damage to crops and other problems with the local communities.

There are two distinct climate seasons for the area; the rains fall between Dec and the end of Mar, between 500 and 600 mm is expected, this is also the warmest time of year, the average daily maximum temperature is over 30°C. The dry season extends from Apr to Nov, no rain is expected in the middle of winter when in the evening temperatures can fall to around 7°C. *Best time to visit*: during the winter months, Jun-Oct, the game will be found close to the river and waterholes. Bird life is prolific between Nov and Mar, after the rains many of the trees flower and carry fruit all of which are an attraction for the birds.

Vegetation One of the attractions of Mahango is the variety of vegetation in such a small area, there are three distinct habitats, and with each comes different bird life and conditions for the wild animals. The river provides a mix of trees, reeds and grasses along its banks and on the floodplains. The dominant tree species are Kalahari apple-leaf, water pear and jackal-berry, along the floodplain margins you will see the wild date palm. If you visit one of the private camps or Popa Falls restcamp you will find many of the riverine trees have been labelled to help with identification as visitors start to take an interest in the whole environment rather than just the wild animals. A tree which every visitor quickly learns to recognize is the large baobab. There are several groups within the park, including a distinctive clump just before the Kwetche picnic site, this is one spot where the track runs close to the main river channel.

Away from the river the vegetation is predominantly open dry woodland, aside from a couple of *omiramba*, fossil rivers (see Kaudom Game Park, page 138) which run W-E towards the Kavango River. The omiramba are covered with open grasslands with tall acacia and bushwillows along their margins. For a few months after the rains pools of water collect along the omiramba, these are always good locations for viewing game. Between Mahango omiramba in the N and Thinderevu omiramba to the S the vegetation is dry woodland with some dense patches of Zambezi teak, wild seringa and wild teak. This is beautiful country to walk in, but it is also very easy for animals to blend in at a surprisingly short distance. Although walking is permitted in the park you should exercise great caution, we would advise against it if you have no previous experience of hiking in the bush, zebra and kudu may well run before you are close to them, buffalo and elephant do not.

Wildlife If you are fortunate you will encounter a wide variety of animals in this small park. It is home to the following less common antelope species for Namibia; sable, roan, reedbuck, tsessebe and sitatunga. The sitatunga is very difficult to spot since it lives in thick swamp areas, if you manage to see one consider yourself very lucky. They are only found in large numbers in the Okavango Delta. Reedbuck are also quite difficult to spot, they tend to inhabit the floodplains where you also have a good chance of spotting the red lechwe. One other antelope to look out for along the river front is the Chobe bushbuck. Away from the river in the thick woodlands you have a chance of seeing roan and sable, two very fine antelope species, but both are quite shy and difficult to spot deep in the woods. Their magnificent curved horns will help distinguish them from any other type of antelope, kudu are the most common antelope in the woodlands of the park.

In addition to a variety of antelope you can expect to see elephant, warthog, duiker, steenbok, hippo, crocodile and the occasional lion or leopard. Local residents often talk of large herds of elephant, but these are not resident animals, they merely pass through this re-

Tsessebe
Source: Steele, David (1972) *Game sanctuaries of Southern Africa* Howard Timmins: Cape Town.
Illustrated by John Perry

gion on their annual migrations during the dry season.

Compared to most game parks there are few roads for game viewing purposes. In addition to the main road running through the park there are two side tracks, each of which is only suitable for 4WD vehicles. The track to the E follows the margins of the flood plain, when the river is full flood this drive presents a very different impression of the park when compared to the dry season. This track is about 12 km long, there is a popular picnic spot overlooking the river, Kwetche, but be on the look-out for game all along this drive. The second trail in the park follows the course of the two *omiramba* in the park, see above.

These roads are very sandy in the dry season, and after the rains there are plenty of spots where you can get stuck. Nevertheless this is a special drive through unspoilt bush country and it makes one appreciate what national parks are trying to preserve.

Finally it is important not to forget the bird life in the park, over 300 species have been recorded throughout the year, you can quite easily identify over 50 different birds in a few hours walking in the bush without really trying. The different habitats in the park help attract such a variety of species; it is interesting to compare the birds you will see along the river banks with those that you come across in the woodlands –

even an amateur can quickly start to recognize how the species vary between different areas of the park.

Park information Entry permits are issued at the northern park gate, they are also available in advance from the MET offices in Windhoek or Rundu. If you are just passing through en route to/from the Botswana border a permit is not required. Fishing permits can be issued with the permit. If you are planning on using the 4WD trails to the W of the main road you may be required to travel with a minimum of two vehicles in convoy. This is a sensible practice, which is enforced in many of the more remote regions of Namibia. If you have limited 4WD driving experience it is best to stay on the busier roads. There is **no accommodation** in the park, there is a Ministry of the Environment and Tourism (MET) restcamp at **Popa Falls**, plus several private lodges off the road leading into Botswana.

CAPRIVI GAME PARK

Although officially a game park, this 204 km stretch has no stopping places, side roads for viewing or facilities. A couple of community based projects are starting to emerge (see below). Game can sometimes be seen, especially elephant herds which cross the strip to get to water in the drier season. Driving can be hazardous in the wet season as most of the strip is slippery sand and gravel. The strip is slowly being tarred, so far 70 km at the Bagani end is finished and completion of the entire strip is aimed at Oct 1998. There is no fuel available on the strip and sometimes the fuel station at Bagani runs out of petrol, although diesel is usually available. If this is the case and you need to fill up before reaching the Engen station at Kongola (the Caprivi-end of the strip) there is a BP fuel station on the road opposite the Popa Falls turn-off signposted for Divundu. Alternatively, turn off the tar road when approaching

from Rundu about 30 km before Bagani, signposted Shamangorwa, for a quicker route to the BP station.

A short distance after the police checkpoint at Bagani Bridge is a turn off to the right to a new community based project – **Ndlwavashaa Community Campsite**, this is clearly signposted and the track to the campsite can be used by a saloon car. This is an initiative started by the local Barakwena community living near the Popa Falls. The project is in line with the Ministry of Environment and Tourism's (MET) new policy to involve communities in conservation and ensure that the people who live in areas with wildlife derive direct benefits from this valuable resource rather than continually suffering from the negative impact of wild animals, destroyed crops and the loss of livestock to predators. This scheme has received assistance from IRDNC, a Namibian non-governmental organization, any profits will be used to repay the loan and contribute towards future community self-help projects.

● **Services F** *Campsite* offers basic, but exclusive sites in a prime position overlooking the Popa Falls on the eastern bank of the Kavango River. At the time of writing there were four sites with reed chalets for changing and ablutions, braai places and a bush style toilet, the 'long drop'. None of the sites impose on the privacy of the other sites. Only firewood is available. Visitors must be fully self sufficient including drinking water. The nearest shops are at Divundu and Mukwe, 15 km towards Andara. Instead of rushing off the next morning try a guided walk with the local people, for a small fee you will be introduced to the incredible traditional knowledge of plants and how they have been used in the day-to-day life of local people. Another local attraction are the Mushangara Rock Pools. If you are not keen on walking try some fishing or bird watching.

During the independence struggle this area was the South African Army Buffalo Base, the training grounds for the infamous 32nd battalion and Third Force. Sadly the army was responsible for the hunting out of much of the game in this region. It is said that the Western Caprivi was kept as the private hunting ground for John Vorster who used to come up here and go hunting from helicopters. With a bit of care the animals will return, but their hunters are long gone.

In addition to the campsite the local community have two other tourism projects in the district. Continuing along the B8 towards Katima Mulilo, 10 km from the Bagani police checkpoint there is a sign for the **Xhacho** picnic site, there is a community museum here to browse around while you eat lunch, the whole site overlooks the Kavango River. The third part of the Ndlwavashaa Community project is a craft shop – Mashi Crafts, located at the eastern end of the Caprivi strip by the Kongola T-junction. The shop is open Mon-Fri, and sells a mixture of traditional handicrafts from the E and W Caprivi. These items can be less expensive than those that are for sale in Katima, but check the finish closely. For these projects to really succeed there is no point in allowing the people who are making the crafts to think they can get away with selling substandard items at inflated prices.

EAST CAPRIVI

One of the most important issues facing the inhabitants of the E Caprivi region is how to establish a balance between the needs of the local people and develop the tremendous tourist potential of the region. In Sep 1989 the Caprivi Wildlife and Tourism Association and the Mafwe Tribal Authority came into being to investigate the means by which they could, "conserve the environment and preserve current ecological processes and survival systems". There were plans to develop a series of tourist sights along the Kwando and Zambezi rivers, including the protection of Nambweza Forest Reserve, the only remaining indigenous riverine forest along the Zambezi in Namibia.

Shortly after independence the association published a follow-up report in May 1990 which emphasized the region's position in relation to the tourist centres of Victoria Falls, Chobe National Park and the Western Caprivi. To date nothing further has come about from the association's ideas.

But in April 1992 a workshop was held at Lianshulu Lodge to discuss ways in which the local communities might benefit from environmental conservation with special emphasis on the region's wildlife. This marked the start of a vibrant and at times controversial programme that to a large part has depended upon the energies of Grant Burton and Marie Holstenson, the managers of Lianshulu Lodge. The ideas and projects make a lot of sense, but nothing is ever that simple in Africa, especially when it involves land, money and success.

It was quickly recognized that if the local community were to respect the newly formed Mudumu National Park they would have to be shown that the park and tourism could directly benefit them. A proportion of local opposition was the result of damage caused by elephant and hippo to farm crops, plus the occasional loss of livestock to lion and crocodile. In this scenario there are two options, kill the problem animals, or make them worth more than the damage they cause. Aside from a few local conservation jobs the local community usually gains no direct benefits from wildlife.

Lianshulu along with an NGO and the department of Integrated Rural Development and Nature Conservation established a fund which could be used to pay people involved in various conservation efforts and compensate people for the loss of livestock and crops. Monies for this fund come from a tourist bed levy, every visitor to Lianshulu pays an additional N$20 per night. The fund is jointly administered by local leaders and those involved in community-based conservation programmes. The Lizauli community has developed a traditional village which is open for visitors (see below), within a few years this project has rightly gained a lot of recognition and is one that might serve as an example for other rural areas in Namibia.

Kongola

The police checkpoint at the eastern end of the Caprivi strip is at Kongola, like many villages in the area this is no more than a petrol station, a few buildings and a series of signposts advertising camps and lodges along the road to **Mudumu National Park** and **Mamili National Park**, to the S of the main road.

Between the eastern end of Caprivi Game Park and the police checkpoint at Kongola, the road crosses the Kwando River which rises in Angola and forms the border between Namibia and Botswana to the S of here. The small area of land between the river and the game park is known as the **Susuwe or West Caprivi Triangle**. This land does not fall within the Caprivi Game Park, however it is rich in wildlife and is open to travellers. Before you explore the area you must report at the Susuwe Ranger station, 3 km N of the main road. The turning is just before the road crosses the Kwando River flood plain. To the S of the road there is a track which follows the W bank of the river. You will need a 4WD vehicle for this drive. About 5 km along this road you reach Sikwekwe Pool, a right turn here will take you back to the main road. If you continue to follow the river S for another 5 km you will reach the very basic campsite at **Nambwa**. Camping here you have a great sense of peace and isolation, but you need to be completely self sufficient and constantly on the look out for wild animals – elephants could quite easily pass through your camp at night.

A short distance beyond the police checkpoint is the Kongola junction for

two of Namibia's least developed National Parks, Mudumu and Mamili. Both of these parks are set in beautiful countryside, and both are just starting to see the return of wildlife which had been displaced and killed during the independence war and South African occupation.

MUDUMU NATIONAL PARK

Mudumu National Park is one of Namibia's least developed parks, but if conservation programmes succeed and the wildlife returns in its former numbers then this area has the potential to become one of the most enjoyable wildlife experiences in the region. If you plan on visiting the park then your whole experience will be enhanced by staying at *Lianshulu Lodge*. This is a very special place, it may not have the variety of game that Etosha or Chobe have, but here you will truly experience and enjoy the bush, with all the necessary comfort which enables one to continue on your tour/holiday in good health and relaxed mind.

Approach Turn off the main road by the Engen petrol station at Kongola, about 110 km from Katima Mulilo before you cross the Kwando River and enter the Caprivi strip. This is a good gravel road with a couple of sandy hills. The entrance to the national park is marked only by the cutline and a sign, however the density of trees and lack of land cleared for millet fields also indicates you are in the park. It is 40 km from the main road to the turning for *Lianshulu Lodge*, the only accommodation within the park. A couple of other lodges and camps are passed before the park boundary.

Background Mudumu National Park was proclaimed in 1990 just before independence. The South African administration was worried that the area was about to be allocated to a private hunting concession and that after independence nothing would be done to protect the region. In the early 1960s the Eastern

Mudumu & Mamili

ANGOLA

Susuwe
Triangle

To
Popa Falls
& Rundu

B8

Caprivi
Game Park

check point
Kongola
(petrol)

To
Katima Mulilo
& Victoria Falls

B8

N

Nandavu
Pan

Sachona

Lizauli
village

Mudumu

National Park

To
Linyanti
& Lake
Liambezi

BOTSWANA

Mudumu
Mulapo

Sangwali

D3511

Mashi

Mamili
Nat Park   Lupala

Linyanti

Nkasa

0   10
km

Lodges & Campsites:
1. Nambwa campsite
2. Namushasha Lodge
3. Lianshulu Lodge
4. Nakatwa campsite
5. Shibumu campsite
6. Lyadura campsite
7. Nzalu campsite

Caprivi had the greatest concentration of wildlife in Namibia. Between 1974 and the early 1980s the Mudumu region was managed as a private hunting concession during which most of the game was shot out. Part of the independence process agreed that no pre-independence proclamations would be changed. While this might appear to be good news for the protection of wildlife in Mudumu and Mamili it is worth noting that the creation of these two parks was against the will of the local people, there was no proper consultation with the villagers. Since independence there has been a conscious effort to establish community-based conservation projects in the region which are paving the way for tourism to directly generate revenue for the local communities. (see above). At present the park remains a backwater

as far as the MET is concerned, there are no gates at the entrance to the park, and you are unlikely to meet anyone from the wildlife department as you drive along the few tracks which follow the river bank.

Before the park had been proclaimed a concession was granted to the management team of *Lianshulu Lodge* along the banks of the Kwando River. After independence and the creation of the national park it was a coincidence in part that this lodge should fall within the boundaries of the park. Today the lodge is very much associated with the park, although on one level they have nothing to do with the day-to-day management of the park. But as noted above Lianshulu has played an active role in trying to get local communities involved in the parks and tourism process. At present the lodge is helping provide a limited income for local villages, in the future anything could happen, but the effort and the projects in place are undoubtedly one way forward in the future.

Vegetation A large part of Mudumu is dominated by mopane woodland. This is some of the most beautiful woodland that you can find in southern Africa. Within the woods are depressions which become flooded after the rains. The western boundary of the park is marked by the Kwando River, there are remnants of riverine forest along the banks as well as well grassed flood plains which are home to reedbuck, hippo and lechwe. The soils within the park are primarily kalahari sandveld with belts of clay and alluvium where the forest occurs. Apart from the mopane tree you will come across camel thorn, Natal mahogany and mangosteen. An early morning walk in the park will quickly make one aware of the innate beauty of this bush, enjoy it and at the same time remember where you come from – this type of country is continually under threat, the wildlife may return, but once the vegetation has been cleared this beauty is lost.

Wildlife A recent survey of larger mammals in Mudumu recorded 45 species. This figure includes nocturnal animals and creatures which are very rarely seen, or perhaps the only evidence of their presence has been their spoor or droppings. The best time for game viewing is the winter season, Apr-Oct, before the rains come. As in all game parks the game quickly disperses once seasonal ponds of water start to form in the bush away from the perennial rivers such as the Kwando. The animals you are most likely to see are hippo (a family lives in the river more or less opposite *Lianshulu Lodge*), elephant, buffalo, kudu, impala, steenbok, warthog, Burchell's zebra, southern reedbuck, red lechwe, oribi (a family lives by the airstrip) and baboon.

Lechwe
Source: Steele, David (1972) *Game sanctuaries of Southern Africa* Howard Timmins: Cape Town. Illustrated by John Perry

If you are lucky you may catch a glimpse of tsessebe, roan, sable, sitatunga, duiker, spotted hyena and lion. Leopard and cheetah are known to be in the area, but they are extremely rare. Unfortunately the casualties of hunting are giraffe, eland, wildebeast and waterbuck. None of the animals occur in the park and their return is inhibited by the Kwando River which they will not normally cross. Poaching is still a problem, but only for food, but nevertheless the amount of game in the park is improving each year.

Park information Mudumu has a MET office at Nakatwa camp, but there is no reason for going here if you are staying at *Lianshulu Lodge*. At present the park is really only MET in name, there are few visitors here and there are no government managed facilities.

● **Accommodation** There is a **F** *Campsite* just S of Nakatwa but this is no more than a clear bit of land overlooking the river with a long drop on the other side of the track. Anyone staying here would have to be totally self sufficient. There are no signs for the campsite, if you wish to stay here we would recommend you call in at Lianshulu and ask for directions. It is not far but there are plenty of unmarked tracks in the area. The jewel in the crown is the privately run lodge, **AL** *Lianshulu*

Lodge, PO Box 142, Katima Mulilo, F (064) 207497, attention 1277, which is located within a private concession on the banks of the Kwando River. Pick up any tourist guide book to Namibia and you will read about how good this lodge is and how welcoming Grant and Marie are – it's all true, this is a very special place, but the guests as well as your hosts make it so, there are 8 A-frame en suite chalets all hidden in the forest along the river banks, number 6 has the best views, at the far end of the camp are two superior chalets, none will forget their stay in these, especially the shower in number 9, all of the accommodation is set in a pleasant garden with plenty of green lawns, nevertheless you still need to be wary of wild animals as you walk back to bed in the evening, the food here is excellent it is worth stopping off for lunch, the lounge area has a small reference library and a bar, but all of this is being redeveloped in 1997, when finished you will be able to enjoy meals from a platform overlooking the river as well as cool off in the pool at the end of the day, the lodge is well equipped to offer game drives twice a day plus boat trips on the river, for the energetic a walk in the bush at dawn is strongly rec, fishing is not possible nor are trips to Mamili National Park, despite what other publications might say, finally, like everyone who has been here before us, one can only speak in glowing terms of this lodge, but it is also worth remembering that it is down to the people who run the lodge, Grant and Marie, and not the invisible players behind the scenes who often have a different agenda, enjoy your stay, these are the places you hope to discover when on holiday.

There are two other places to stay within the vicinity of the park, both are off the road leading to Mudumu and Mamili parks, **A Na-mushasha Lodge** is a former police recreation camp run by Manfred, it is situated on the Kwando River, 10 decent reed and thatch chalets, camping is not allowed, the food is reasonable, activities include game drives into Golden Triangle, boat trips and fishing, the location of this lodge will always satisfy the visitor, but the welcome from the managers, if you meet them, cannot be guaranteed, during the research for this guide there were too many negative stories about this lodge, but one can never be sure, if you enjoy your brandy and coke then this is the place for you, if not then you may not be what they are looking for, when guests from overseas are told there are no afternoon activities because they arrived too late you start to wonder who the lodge is being run for; **F Open Skies**, a simple campsite on the river, this camp suffers from being surrounded by local villages, run by African Safaris, if you wish to camp then go to the national park site just S of Nakatwa; finally avoid *Aloe Hunting*.

Lizauli traditional village

A short distance from Lianshulu Lodge is Lizauli village, part of the success story in getting the local communities involved in tourism projects which will directly benefit themselves. As you drive back towards Kongola from Mudumu National Park the turning for the village is on the left just outside the park boundary.

This is a traditional village in appearance and layout, but one that has been constructed for the benefit of tourists. During the day a group of local people pass their time here waiting to show visitors around and explain a variety of rural activities. One of the most comforting aspects of a visit here is that you do not feel like an intruder walking around private homes, and yet what you see does not have that theme park feel.

The complete tour lasts at least an hour, after which you have ample opportunity to ask questions about all aspects of rural life. On a typical visit you will be shown a collection of household objects and how they are used, including a crude but effective mouse trap, the girls will perform a couple of dances and the village blacksmith will demonstrate how the farm implements are forged. The tour finishes with the whole group acting out a village dispute with the elders being called upon to resolve the matter. This is an enjoyable introduction to a way of life far removed from that of the tourist from overseas. There is a collection of curio items for sale, but some of these are overpriced and the quality needs to improve before they could be considered a good buy, nevertheless you know your money is going to a good cause.

MAMILI NATIONAL PARK

A seldom visited park tucked in the corner of Eastern Caprivi with a common boundary with Botswana. There are no facilities here and visitors must travel in a group of at least two 4WD vehicles. This is the only protected swampland in Namibia, for several months each year, after the rains, this region resembles the Okavango delta in Botswana, but with none of the development. Whenever you visit you are likely to be the only people in the park. This is a difficult area to visit, but if you have the right vehicles and experience it can be most rewarding.

Approach As for Mudumu, but continue to follow the road through Mudumu until you see the signposts for Mamili. Like Mudumu the Ministry of the Environment and Tourism has a very limited presence here. The road to Linyandi, the D3511, is not maintained, you could easily get lost along here. There are sporadic supplies of petrol in Linyandi, 80 km from Katima Mulilo.

Background Mamili was created at the same time as Mudumu, these are the only two protected areas in Eastern Caprivi, an area which 35 years ago had the richest concentration of wildlife in Namibia. The park is considerably smaller than Mudumu, 32,000 ha, but it encompasses a unique environment which has tremendous tourist potential. After good rains most of the park is turned into a swampland similar in make up to the Okavango delta in Botswana. There are no reliable maps and it is possible to get lost between the main road and the informal campsites. The park is usually flooded between May and Aug, but this depends in part on how much rain has fallen elsewhere and what the level of water is in the local rivers (see below), in years of good rains the two large islands, **Nkasa** and **Lupala**, are cut off from the main road for a few months. During the dry season these islands disappear into the undulating landscape.

Best time to visit This to a large extent depends upon how much rain there has been and whether the park is completely inundated or not. Most of the rain falls between Dec and Mar, this is a good time for viewing birds, but it can be very difficult to get about the park. After the rains there tends to be more wildlife in the park, but then as already noted, this is when most of the tracks are likely to be impassable.

Wildlife The variety of animals you can expect to see is more or less the same as for Mudumu. The large area of swampland means that you are more likely to see the antelope which favour this environment – red lechwe, sitatunga and waterbuck are fairly common. If you are lucky you may also see puku, another swamp antelope which is only found along the Chobe River, and is quite rare. Unlike Mudumu you may also come across giraffe in the woodlands. Overall the game viewing in this park is unpredictable, a large proportion of the animals still migrate between Angola and Botswana. Poaching and hunting have also left their mark. During the dry season the park has a reputation for large herds of buffalo, but as with all game there are no guarantees you will see them. Lion and leopard also live in the park, but you are only likely to see their spoor.

Park information Although the park remains undeveloped visitors must still report at the Ranger station at the entrance to the park, this is 8 km from Sangwali on the Kongola-Mudumu road. Entry and camping permits should be obtained in advance from Windhoek or Katima Mulilo. As noted above the park is only accessible to 4WD vehicles, whether dry or wet you will require prior experience to driving in such conditions. **Do not take risks**, if you get stuck it might be a long wait before help arrives. Rangers do patrol the park on the look-out for poachers and squatters, but if you have failed to report to the station it could be several days before you are found.

● **Accommodation** There are three campsites, both as basic as they come, one at **F** *Lyadura* on the Linyanti River and the other at **F** *Shibumu* which is on a river channel. As with the campsite in Mudumu you will have to be completely self sufficient, this includes water unless you are equipped with an efficient purifying kit; **F** *Nzalu*, in the NE corner of the park.

The rivers of Eastern Caprivi

A closer look at a map of Eastern Caprivi reveals the unusual feature that, except for a 90 km strip of land between the Kwando River and the Zambezi River, the region is completely surrounded by rivers. The Kwando-Linyanti-Chobe forms the border to the W, S and E, while the Zambezi marks the border with Zambia in the NE. Enclosed by these rivers is a landscape which is relatively flat with numerous floodplains, ox-bow lakes, swamps and seasonal channels.

The hydrography of the area is particularly interesting because in years of high floods and good rains the flow of water in stretches of the rivers can be reversed and water actually spill over into the Okavango delta system, a completely different watershed. At present most of the river system is drying up, the Kwando, Zambezi and Okavango are at their lowest recorded levels. **Lake Liambezi** does not currently exist, since May 1985 it has been dry, when full it covered an area of 100 sq km and was an important source of food and water for the surrounding villages.

The complexities of the river system start in Angola where the river **Cuando** rises in the Luchazes mountains. As this river flows SE it forms the border between Angola and Zambia before it cuts across the eastern end of the narrowest part of the Caprivi Strip. Where the river cuts though Namibia by Kongola it is known as the **Kwando**. Having cut

across Caprivi the river once again becomes an international boundary, this time between Botswana and Namibia. The western bank which forms the border with Botswana is known as the **Mashi** until the river reaches Nkasa island, this is in the SW corner of Caprivi in Mamili National Park. At this point the main river channel turns sharply to the NE and becomes known as the **Linyanti** river until it reaches the dry **Lake Liambezi**; from the lake until the point where it flows into the Zambezi it assumes yet another name, the **Chobe**.

When the Zambezi is exceptionally high the flow of water in the Chobe and Linyanti can be reversed. Water flows back up the Chobe and then spills into the depression which is Lake Liambezi, in exceptional seasons water from the Zambezi has been known to flood across the plains between Katima and Ngoma bridge and drain into the northern shores of Lake Liambezi via a depression known as the **Bukalo Channel**.

Occasionally water from the Kwando River can enter the Okavango system via a channel known as the **Selinda Spillway** or **Magwegqana Channel**. Because of the difference in elevation the waters usually only flow a few kilometres to the W, however this channel drains into the **Mababe depression** via the **Savuti Channel** and in very wet years water from the Kwando has been known to drain into the Savuti Marsh in Botswana.

Between Kongola and Katima Mulilo the main road, **B8**, passes through mopane woodland which has been cleared close to the road to make way for millet fields, a trend which is understandable, but which needs to be halted before the local environment is completely destroyed. Most of the signs along the roadside are for village schools and churches, evidence of extensive missionary influence. About 20 km short of Katima is a sign for Mpacha Army Base on the left, this is also Mpacha airport served by Air Namibia flights. The road ends at a T-junction with the Zambezi River straight ahead; a left turn takes you towards Zambia, a right into the town. At the other side of town the road continues to the border with Botswana at Ngoma Bridge.

KATIMA MULILO

(*STD Code* 0677) Katima is the regional capital of Caprivi, a fairly large and picturesque town with good facilities. These include a post office, pharmacy, Bank Windhoek, Air Namibia office, shops and supermarkets, all are situated around a tree-lined central square which is the centre of all activity. Most businesses are open between 0900-1700 with a lunch break from 1300-1400. Watch out however for different times (for example 0800-1600) in the winter when the clocks change and shops side by side can be operating on different times; Namibia or South Africa time. The hospital is seen from the square a little way up the main road and there is a private clinic near the Air Namibia office, if you don't mind paying more and don't want to wait a long time before being seen. Fuel is available

at several stations including 24-hr Engen, and Shell both on the way into town.

Local information
● **Accommodation**

There are several comfortable lodges on the banks of the Zambezi, if you are looking for a cheap option the campsites attached to the lodges are good value, you benefit from the location and is just a short walk to the bar or restaurant. If you wish to take a boat trip on the river we would recommend you wait until you are in Kasane or Victoria Falls, assuming you are travelling in this direction. Trips are offered by the lodges in Katima but most visitors are just passing through, there are good game parks to the E and to the W.

C-F *Kalizo Lodge*, reservations, PO Box 70378, Bryanston 2021, South Africa; T/F (11) 7067207, primarily for fishing which is excellent, situated off the Ngoma Bridge road, turn left just before you come onto the gravel from the tar road, from the turn off it is approx 22 km of gravel and sandy roads, in the wet season 4WD is necessary, the lodge is set on a wide, sweeping curve of the river and while wildlife is limited, there are many species of bird to be seen and the occasional crocodile, accommodation is in A-frame wood, reed and thatch chalets overlooking the river, good beds, but rooms are a bit tatty for what they charge, the food is excellent, camping facilities are also available but you need to be fully equipped; **C-F** *Zambezi Lodge*, PO Box 98, Katima Mulilo, T (067) 352203; set amongst the trees high on the river bank over-looking the Zambezi, 32 a/c rooms, most are spacious and spotless, restaurant, lunch time terrace snack bar, indoor bar with pool table, swimming pool, a famous floating bar which is really no more than a few oil drums strapped together and covered by planks but this is still a very relaxing location for your sun downer, but for residents only, overall the lodge has a perfect location but occasionally one feels the management are resting on their laurels and the service can be a little too sleepy and indifferent, but that is also a reflection of life in Katima, enjoy your stay here but don't be surprised if you are treated as just another traveller passing through, camping also permitted upstream from the main complex, good shady location with plenty of grass.

D *Guinea Fowl Inn*, this is the cheapest lodge

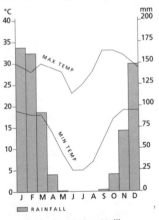

Climate: Katima Mulilo

n the area, it can be found by following the bird signs behind the back of the police station, although set in a beautiful position on lawns which slope down to the Zambezi the hotel itself is a little run down, all the rooms are set off a single corridor and separated by thin walls, restaurant has been fairly good in the past but now meals can take several hours to appear, camping on the lawns is sometimes permitted, no activities on offer, the lodge has recently been taken over so conditions may well have improved under the new management; **D Hippo Lodge**, T 3685; situated 6 km out of town on the Ngoma/Botswana road, his lodge has a relaxed atmosphere set on the river surrounded by banana trees, palms, grassy lawns. Unlike *Zambezi Lodge* it is made from local products – wood, reeds and thatching, it is also quite a lot cheaper, guests can camp or stay in little chalets, there is a bar and platform overlooking the river which is a good spot for watching bird and hippo, restaurant s a little haphazard in terms of quality, meals seems to depend on the staff working there at the time, activities from the lodge include boat trips and fishing trips with the occasional braai thrown in, this lodge has a wonderful potential that has not yet been achieved, the campsite is part of an old army camp but all the facilities are now run down.

E Caprivi Guesthouse, situated on the town square this is newly opened, very cheap, meals available, a little dubious and rumour says it may double as a brothel, but it might be the adventure you are looking for.

● **Places to eat**

Apart from the hotels, there are several bars which also serve food. These are the *SOS Club* formerly serving the South African Defence Force) and the *Golf Club*. The former is situated opposite the 'Boma' on the turn-off signposted for the government garage and the latter just past *Zambezi Lodge* on the road to Botswana. Both serve good food although the golf club is only open at the weekend.

Takeaways: are available at the *Coimbra* supermarket in the main square; *Zambezi Take-away* at the Shell station and the Engen station.

● **Banks & money changers**

Bank Windhoek, open Mon-Fri, 0900-1245, 1400-1530, the **only** bank in town, a new building on the corner of the market square close to the post office. Transactions can take some time here (at the end of the week and each month), as it is the only bank in the region, fortunately it has an efficient a/c system. There are two sets of ATMs close by, but these are likely to be as busy as inside. If you are planning on obtaining Namibian dollars using your credit card there is a limit of N\$200 after which they will have to call Pretoria (South Africa) for clearance, it might be easier using the ATMs assuming you have a PIN for the card, there are currently two machines.

If you are heading for Botswana then it is a good idea to buy some Pula here since the officials at the Ngoma Bridge border often find something to charge you for, the nearest bank in Botswana is 54 km away in Kasane. If you have just entered Namibia the next banking facilities are in Rundu and then Grootfontein.

● **Shopping**

As you enter from Caprivi there is a large warehouse structure on the left before you reach the river, this is the only source for groceries in Katima. Most of the shops around the market square consist of furniture stores, clothes shops and bottle stores.

There is a well stocked craft market next to the hospital with locally made products and those from bordering countries. Nearby is a food market selling some fruit, vegetables, and fish along with a clothes market selling the locally-worn '*shitenges*', women's wrap around skirts.

● **Useful addresses**

The **Police station** is found at the *boma*, an area of government offices on the road to Ngoma Bridge and Botswana. This is where clearance certificates need to be obtained to take **locally registered** vehicles out of Namibia. It is best to go to the police station for these a day in advance in case the office is closed. Documents needed for the certificate are proof of ownership and driver's passport/ID number. Sometimes you may be asked to open the bonnet so the police can check the engine and chassis number.

● **Transport**

1,361 km from Windhoek, 660 km to Rundu, 1,485 km to Swakopmund, 3,340 km to Johannesburg.

Katima Mulilo is an ideal stopping place on the way to or from Zambia, Botswana and the rest of Namibia with good accommodation and places to eat. Lifts for hitch hikers can be arranged nr the Shell fuel station. There is no public transport as such, although buses running between Victoria Falls (Zimbabwe) and Windhoek can be sometimes caught by the Engen station (see below).

Air Air Namibia, T/F (0677) 3191, office located on the main square in Katima. Mpacha airport is 20 km SW of town off the road to Rundu, look out for the signs for the army base, the airport is not signposted. This was an important military base during the occupation by the South African army (it is now used by the Namibian army), you can still see the remains of the mortar proof parking shelters for the South African airforce beside the runway. If you are arriving by air make sure you have arranged in advance to be collected by your hotel, there are no taxis or buses. There is a card telephone outside the terminal building and a kiosk selling cool drinks.

Victoria Falls (30 mins), Sun, 1225; Mon and Wed, 1330; **Windhoek International** (3 hrs), via Mokuti Lodge (Etosha NP), Sun, 1455, Mon, Wed, Fri, 1600. Passengers travelling from Victoria Falls have to disembark and clear customs formalities, consequently the plane is usually on the ground for about 1¼ hrs. There is nothing to see or do at the airport except to sit on incredibly uncomfortable wood and brick seats.

Road Bus: the Windhoek-Livingstone bus service stops in Katima, T (61) 223478. This is an 11-seater minibus which departs from Windhoek on Tues and Fri. The return journey departs from Livingstone in Zambia on Thur and Sun. This is a popular service and advance reservations are recommended. From Katima the bus stops in Kasane (Botswana) and Victoria Falls (Zimbabwe) before entering into Zambia. It is the passengers responsibility to have all the necessary visas.

IMPALILA ISLAND

At the eastern tip of Caprivi, by the confluence of the Chobe and Zambezi rivers is the last piece of Namibia – **Impalila Island**. The island is formed by the Kasai Channel which flows between the Zambezi and Chobe. At the eastern end of the island is another small island, Kakumba, which lies opposite the Botswana town of Kazangula. This is the point where the borders of Zimbabwe, Zambia, Botswana and Namibia all meet in the middle of the great Zambezi.

During the last couple of years two new tourist camps have been developed on Impalila island. Although they lie within Namibia they are usually accessed by boat from Kasane in Botswana. There is a surfaced airfield on the island which is suitable for small aircraft. There are customs and immigration facilities on the island. Visitors to the island can enjoy some superb fishing on the Zambezi and Chobe, just upstream there are two sets of **rapids** to explore – **Mombova** and **Chobe**. At the western end of the island you can take a boat up the Indibi River and look for game amongst the papyrus fringed flood plain. There are several trails on the island which will take you past the local villages. The only drawback to a stay on the island is that it is heavily populated, there are a lot of cattle and rubbish. Since the camps were established a clean up programme has been put into place, reports of how successful this has been would be most welcome.

● **Accommodation AL** *Impalila Island Lodge*, PO Box 70378, Bryanston 2021, South Africa, T/F (011) 7067207, T (00267) 650763, 6 chalets with en suite bathrooms overlooking the Mombova rapids, the centrepiece of the dining area is a large baobab tree, from the elevated platforms by the bar you can enjoy your sundowner watching the birds and bats with the continual roar of the rapids in the background, the lodge also has a swimming pool, an excellent camp in a most exclusive location; **A** *Ichingo River Camp*, PO Box 206, Kasane, Botswana, T (267) 650143, F (267) 650223 or a South African contact, T/F (011) 7082020, 7 luxury tents with open air bathrooms, each tent has been decorated with care and is a comfortable place to return to at the end of a day on the river, hidden in the riverine forest each tent has its own viewing platform overlooking the Chobe, there is a central restaurant, lounge and bar which has also been designed to blend in with the surroundings, this camp has a good ambience and the food is excellent, while many of the visitors come here for the fishing, the camp also caters for the visitor who wishes to just cruise along the

Zambezi or just drift along in a *mokoro* on the Caprivi flood plain, this is a superior camp run by Andre and Karin which every visitor will leave feeling most privileged, this is truly the beauty of Africa.

NGOMA BORDER POST (BOTSWANA)

This border separates Namibia from Botswana and is 60 km from Katima on a gravel road which can be quite hazardous in the wet season and very dusty in the dry months. A clearance certificate, available from the police station in Katima, is required to take your vehicle out of Namibia. It is wise to have some pula ready to buy an insurance paper needed to drive through Botswana. It is very cheap and is valid for a year, but a trip to the bank in Kasane and then back to the border post is an irritating 100 km plus round trip. **Border open**: 0800-1800, but beware of time changes. All foreign vehicles entering Botswana are charged a road tax. Vehicles registered outside the Southern African Common Customs Area (SACCA) are required to obtain third party insurance, this can be purchased at the border post.

The Botswana post is at the far end of the bridge, you will have to drive through a disinfectant dip as well as walk through it, all immigration formalities are completed here, there is no need to report to the police at a later stage.

WENELA BORDER POST (ZAMBIA)

This post separates Namibia from Zambia. It is situated 6 km up a gravel road (Wenela road) at the end of the Rundu-Katima road. A clearance certificate, available from the police station in Katima, is required to take Namibian registered vehicles out of Namibia. The route can either take you up along the Zambezi River, or you can take the car ferry across the Zambezi to Sesheke. **Border open**: 0800-1800. **NB** The road on the Zambian side is notoriously bad, only take this route if you have to.

The Far North

THE FAR NORTH has little to offer the international, hotel acclimatized holidaymaker. Although the region is developing rapidly, tourism is low on the agenda in this former war zone. For the more discerning visitor there is plenty of intrigue; the nightlife, the Portuguese/Angolan influence, the rich businessmen, the range of NGOs all superimposed on the Ovambo traditions and the beauty of the *oshanas* after heavy rains – when they come.

Formerly known as Owamboland the far N of Namibia – now divided into four political regions (Oshikoto, Ohangwena, Omusati and Oshana) – is home to 50-60% of the country's population. Between Tsumeb and Ondangwa, at Oshivelo, the B1 crosses the 'Red Line', the veterinary fence which separates the commercial farms from the communal land. The movement of livestock across this line is forbidden. Farmers are still concerned about possible outbreaks of foot and mouth or rinderpest. Animals to the N, bred on the communal lines are not sold to the overseas markets.

From this point onwards there is increasing evidence of a different relationship between people and the land – herds of small livestock and cattle cris cross the main road and wooden, fenced homesteads are visible. After the vast, uninhabited expanses of fenced farmland, it is a refreshing reminder of humanity – strings of children along the roadside at the end of the school day, travellers on bicycles, donkey carts or on foot and the tireless collectors of water.

CLIMATE

Although they seem to be increasingly unreliable, the rains which lead to the extensive flooding, known as the *Efundja*, and the resultant filling of the *oshana*, should arrive at the beginning of the year, making Mar-May the best months to visit. The average annual rainfall ranges from less than 300 mm in the W to more than 500 mm in the E. When the rain falls it is usually as a heavy thunderstorm causing severe damage to crops. By Jun/Jul most of the *oshanas* have already dried up, the evenings feel cool and the sun will have set by six.

Before the rains it can be unbearably hot and dusty. As the temperatures soar expectations of rain increase, but the hot winds just blow the clouds away and dust storms fill the skies instead of rain

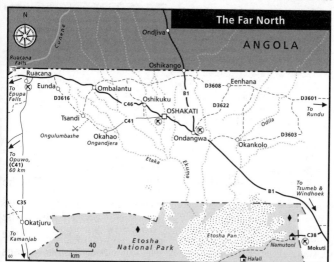

The Far North

ANGOLA

Some days the dust is like a mist, headlights are needed for driving and the landscape becomes surreal and moon-like. For your comfort this period is best avoided. The highest temperatures are recorded in Dec and Jan, 26°C, during Jul the mean daytime temperature is only 17°C.

The Oshana environment

More than 620,000 people live in the northern area of Namibia that borders Angola, this is approximately a third of the total population. Few overseas visitors get to see this region for a variety of reasons, but those who do venture here will be rewarded with an insight into a unique natural environment and ecosystem which is wholly responsible for enabling so many Namibians to live off the land in such concentrated numbers. The features are known as the 'Oshana' environment.

The *oshanas* are a system of shallow water courses and *vleis* which first appear in south-central Angola and reach all the way into Namibia as far as the Etosha Pan. Most of these 'rivers' are several hundred kilometres long, but they only flow for a few months each year after the rains. In years of exceptionally heavy rainfall there can be widespread flooding, these floods are known as the *Efundja*. The last major *efundja* was recorded in 1954. If there were to be a similar size flood today many farms which have been built close to the oshanas would be washed away.

Overhead satellite imagery or simple aerial photography immediately reveals the pattern of watercourses which if they were flowing into an ocean would be instantly recognized as a delta. Today they no longer flow but the pan is evidence of a period when water did flow so far, depositing alluvium and leaving behind a high concentration of salts once the water had evaporated.

Given the large numbers of people living in the region off the land, the *oshanas* are a vital natural system that the government must protect and manage sensibly whatever the cost. In recent years a growing population and an erratic rainfall pattern has placed a severe strain upon the system. Without good rains the land is never able to fully re-cover and the basic farm crops such as *omahangu* (millet) marula nuts cannot mature. The *oshanas* perform several roles to the average family; they carry water across large areas replenishing the groundwater in areas where there may have been no rainfall above, the pastures quickly recover providing vital food for the livestock, the standing water is a drinking supply for the people and live-stock, and for a few months before they start to dry up there is the added bonus of freshwater fish.

The whole economic basis of the area is dependent upon two factors, money brought in from migrant labour and pensions and agriculture. The agricul-tural season, and in turn the lives of the people, is dominated by the rains and the availability of water in the *oshanas*. The rains usually start in Nov and Dec, there is water in the *oshanas* from about Jan until Jun – this will depend upon their size, depth and how much rain as fallen across the region. With the first rains the farmers start to prepare their fields and cattle are brought back from distant pastures to benefit from the new pastures. The presence of livestock close to the home helps to enrich people's diet with milk products.

Since independence the develop-ment of the region has been vital, but there are signs of population pressure getting the better of the environment – over grazing, soil erosion, deminishing wood fuel supplies, lack of water and problems of soil salinity. Taken as a whole these symptoms are a serious threat to the natural ecosystem of the oshanas. For the government the sensi-ble management of the oshana environ-ment in the future is one of it's greatest challenges, they cannot afford to get it wrong since there is virtually nowhere else in Namibia that such a concentra-tion of people can go and live. But with-out good rainfall there is nothing that can be done.

OVAMBO

ONDANGWA

(*STD code* 06756) As you approach On-dangwa, the number of small commer-cial centres increases – wooden sheltered market stalls and shacks as well as depots of the larger regional traders line the roads. This is the second largest town in this populous region but like all of the settlements in the area the commercial centre is very limited, everything runs alongside the main roads. For much of the year the earth is desolate and sandy but in spite of overgrazing it does sustain some plant life, but for how much longer. The **makalani palm** trees are the most attractive plants, gracing the harsh land-scape with their delicate silhouettes at sunset. A few weeks after the heavy rains, the *oshana* fill with water and pale pink and white lilies miraculously appear. De-pending on the time of year, you will see cone shaped fishing baskets in use. As the connecting channels dry up, the fish grow to an impressive size in their shrink-ing *oshanas* – often little more than big puddles.

Coming through Ondangwa there is a sense of having arrived somewhere. The traffic flow increases and develop-ments extend further away from the road. In the last couple of years the banks and insurance companies have built impressive shopping centres – mostly housing furniture stores where 'lay-byes' and monthly payments can secure you formica room dividers and velour sofa sets. Of more interest are the innumerable '*cuca*' shops. Cuca, the im-ported Angolan beer has long since gone, but bars remain 'cuca shops'. Play spot the most unusual name on the way in to Oshakati and you'll notice little else – 'No Money No Life', 'Corner Life', 'Tenacity Centre' and 'Friendship Only' are but a few signs to look out for.

Local information

● Accommodation

During the week most of the hotels and guesthouses are fully booked with business people, government officials and NGO staff. Standards and the quality of service will vary considerably.

D *Punyu International*, approaching from Windhoek take a right turn on the tar road to Onandjokwe and Eenhana, the hotel is on the right, Oniipa St, PO Box 247, T 40556, 30 a/c rooms with en suite bathroom, TV, breakfast incl, restaurant with pleasant outdoor seating during summer months, car hire including 4WD vehicles, inconvenient location and neither the rooms or the restaurant are particularly special, check out the alternatives in town before choosing to stay here.

F *Ondangwa Rest Camp*, T 40310, approaching from Windhoek turn right on to the gravel road by the pink First National Bank Centre, the camp is on the right, and clearly visible from the tar road, always has a good range of tasty snacks to eat, particularly their chips, a restaurant with a varied menu should be in place soon.

● Shopping

Crafts: approaching Ondangwa from the S there are roadside stalls selling traditional baskets, bowls and calabashes. They may look unattended but stop your car, and someone will be there in a flash. The markets in Ondangwa and Oshakati are also worth browsing about for carved cups, bowls, snuff containers and knives. None of these are produced for the tourist, they are the preferred implements and containers at the homesteads.

● Transport

686 km from Windhoek; 256 km from Tsumeb; 35 km from Oshakati.

Air Air Namibia, T 40655, F 40656, flies 3 times a week to **Windhoek** – Eros airport, Tues, 1620, via Mokuti Lodge and Tsumeb, Fri 1710, Sun, 1310.

Road Bus: check the **SWAPO** buses which transport people back to rural areas from Windhoek.

ONDANGWA TO ANGOLA

The situation in Angola is changing rapidly and links with the N of Namibia are getting stronger. The commercial impact of Angola has always been felt in Oshakati and Ondangwa, with Angolan businesses taking an ever higher profile. The presence of Angolans and the use of Portuguese is increasing – more Angolans are venturing S to take advantage of their recent US$ payouts and the availability of goods S of the border. In recent years Namibians have ventured in the other direction, but only for cheap petrol, cattle and goats. For the visitor, however, in search of a different flavour, an afternoon in the Angolan village of **Santa Clara** (**Oshikango**) is worth the experience.

The road from Ondangwa to the border is busy with Angolan trucks and for the last kilometre the road is lined with traders. The customs and immigration offices on the Namibian side are a brick and mortar statement of national pride. Angola can hardly compete on 'peace and stability' – in fact the buildings on their side of the border show no sign of repair and all the evidence of war damage. It is possible, with a minimum of red tape, to go over to **Santa Clara** for a few hours. It is advisable to walk the short distance, you may invite unnecessary problems by trying to take a car over. There do not appear to be formal immigration checkpoints so respond helpfully to officials who may approach you – they are most likely to be Angolan police dressed in Namibian uniforms with the insignia removed. The border is open between 0600-1900.

In the centre of **Santa Clara**, about 400m from the border there are several bars on the right which are worth a try, Namibian dollars can be used. **NB** For 6 months of the year there is a time difference between Namibia and Angola, and although there are no signs to warn you, vehicles drive on the right.

● Accommodation

D *Namib Contract Haulage Investment Centre Motel*, T (061) 234164/65, 5 km from the border on the road to Engela and Okalongo, a new development which in time must become known by some shorter name, at the time of writing there are only 4 rm, more are being built, all have en suite bathrooms, a/c and TV; **D** *Peter's*, T (06751) 61545, on the right 500m before the border, you can't miss the large signs, 12 rm with fans.

WEST TO RUACANA

At **Ongwediva**, 10 km before Oshakati, there is a small **craft shop** at the Oshiko centre run by the **Council of Churches** which caters for tourists. A short distance further on, opposite the *Pelican Café* is a signpost for the **Traditional Shop**, set back from the road the shop has a good selection of Owambo and Himba jewellery, traditional dresses and skins. The ENGEN Service Station has a spacious takeaway, but your choice is limited to fish and chips or chicken and chips.

OSHAKATI

(*STD code* 06751) The commercial centre of Oshakati and the N happens where the high street banks and the open market, *Omatala*, face each other across the dusty main road. Oshakati has many faces; there is the 'town', the former South African military base, where government employees, expatriates and the successful live in detached houses set in leafy gardens close to the video shops, private schools and public library. Then there are the various 'locations' where shanty type dwellings of corrugated iron and scrap metal are dotted with NGO and municipality built public lavatories and stand pipes. In between these extremes are those who have housing and services of a basic standard. The lasting impression, however, is that life in Oshakati is hard.

Local information
● **Accommodation**

B-C *Santorini Inn*, T 20457, Greek only in name, recently extended the accommodation with a second storey, a rarity in Oshakati, mix of small and large a/c rooms, plus chalets, all have en suite bathroom, TV and phone, and are of a good standard, room rate incl breakfast, restaurant, bar and gardens are well kept and service is efficient, but this is not the place for those who may want to question recent history and the behaviour of the South African occupying forces, the most expensive option in the area.

C *International Guesthouse*, PO Box 542, T 20175, F 21189, all rooms a/c with en suite bathroom, TV and phone, comfortable accommodation that has been upgraded since the

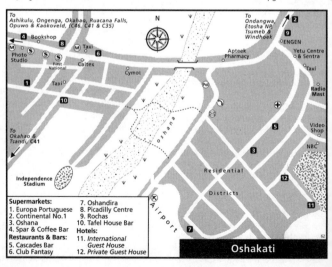

To Ashikulu, Ongenga, Okahao, Ruacana Falls, Opuwo & Kaokoveld, (C46, C41 & C35)

To Ondangwa, Etosha NP, Tsumeb & Windhoek

Apteek Pharmacy

Yetu Centre & Sentra

Radio Mast

Video Shop

NBC

Residential

Districts

To Okahao & Tsandi, C41

Independence Stadium

Oshana

Airport

Supermarkets:
1. Europa Portuguese
2. Continental No.1
3. Oshana
4. Spar & Coffee Bar
Restaurants & Bars:
5. Cascades Bar
6. Club Fantasy
7. Oshandira
8. Picadilly Centre
9. Rochas
10. Tafel House Bar
Hotels:
11. *International Guest House*
12. *Private Guest House*

Oshakati

UNTAG personnel left, restaurant is similar to the *Oshandira Lodge* but lacks the atmosphere; **C** *Okave Club*, T 20892, coming from Windhoek, turn left by the new shopping centre (the radio mast is a useful landmark here), 500m before the shopping centre is a sign for the club – turn left by the mast on to a gravel road, after a further 500m take a right and the club is visible straight ahead, a limited number of rooms, singles available, all rooms a/c with en suite bathroom, breakfast incl; **C** *Oshandira Lodge*, T 20443, next to the air strip, a/c rooms with TV and phone, set in well watered green gardens with a few caged parrots, restaurant can get very busy, you can either sit indoors or around the swimming pool, as one of the best local options it can get very busy; *AMCOM*, a former South African social club which now offers reasonable B&B, once again after a few drinks don't bother trying to question the past, the conversation will be an unwelcome eye opener to those unfamiliar with recent local events.

D *Continental*, T 20257, between Ongwediva and Oshakati on the left of the main road, next to the Caltex service station, all rooms have en suite bathroom, some a/c, breakfast extra.

● **Places to eat**
In addition to the places listed below there are a number of locally owned, well equipped takeaway snack bars where you can enjoy fresh and tasty food in relative comfort.

In the centre of town the Caltex service station has a reasonable takeaway counter; the best place to eat is probably the *Picadilly Centre* opp the banks, here you will not only have a good choice of dishes but you can enjoy your meal in comfort.

Club Fantasy, on weekday evenings the bar is frequented by businessmen, visitors and anyone else who is passing through, the bar is arranged around a collection of armchairs and low tables which successfully encourages the mixing between groups, come here to find out what is new and going on in town, open Wed, Fri and Sat, expect to hear and dance to South African disco hits, along with a good dose of *soukous* – the infectious Zairean dance plus the Angolan *kazomba*; *Yetu* shopping centre, the same finger lickin' pieces you find worldwide; *Rochas*, a new restaurant opened late 1996, serving simple, well prepared Portuguese cuisine – Portuguese chicken, steak and cod are the specialities, a friendly atmosphere, the table settings and decor are pleasant but not fussy, as the evening progresses it is easy to forget you are sitting beside the roadside in Oshakati, there is a bar next door with a couple of pool tables; *Tafel House*, Okahao Rd, beer garden has picnic benches under thatched roof, good for a draught beer, meals are simple but well prepared, nicely served and a reasonable price, at weekends there is a disco which is cheaper and more intimate than *Club Fantasy*.

● **Shopping**
Continental Supermarket: is something of an Oshakati institution, it sells everything you need for basic survival in a rural setting – cast iron cooking pots, car stereo systems, saddles, water drums, nylon leopard skin underwear, curtain hooks and plenty more. It also has an amazingly well-stocked and reasonably priced bottle store. The range of spirits and special liqueurs is final evidence, if necessary, of Namibian's love of drinking. There cannot be many places in Africa which offer five different brands of Tequila! The store is part of Frans (Oupa) Indongo's empire – the wealthiest Owambo businessman, and a very powerful Namibian figure. Continental No 2 is in Ongwediva and No 3 is now the new **Spar Supermarket** in the centre of Oshakati, which has a coffee bar inside. The **Europa Portuguese Supermarket** is another good store for camping supplies.

● **Transport**
721 km from Windhoek; 35 km to Ondangwa; 152 km to Ruacana.

Continuing through and beyond **Oshakati**, the sense of 'somewhere' becomes elusive as the ribbon development peters out. Only the scattered homesteads and schools are a reminder that this is still one of the most densely populated parts of Namibia. The direct route from **Oshakati** to **Ruacana** follows 160 km of good tar road, **C46**, alongside the **Ogongo canal**. This route will take you through **Oshikuku**, 28 km, and Uutapi (**Ombalantu**), 100 km. Depending upon the time of year you will either pass through flood plains (Mar-May), or dry sandy pans, dotted with clusters of **Makalani palms**, homesteads and *mahangu* fields. The most striking feature of the landscape is its flatness. Instead of passing straight through the region for Kaokoland, consider making a short detour to explore some of the villages of the Oshana and Omusati regions. This will take you through country which for the majority of Namibians is what they consider to be home.

ROUTES   The road to **Okahao** is 60 km of good tar, it is clearly signposted from the centre of **Oshakati**, **C41**. **President Sam Nujoma** was born in a village close to Okahao. After Okahao it turns into a good gravel road heading due W to **Tsandi**, a further 30 km. From Tsandi there is another 30 km of good gravel before you rejoin the main Oshakati – Ruacana tar road at **Ombalantu**. Alternatively you can stick to back roads and follow the **D3616** to **Eunda** and **Ruacana**.

While these gravel roads are of good quality you may not wish to inflict the damage to your saloon car. As with all such roads in Namibia do not let the needle go above 80 km per hour, there are many fatal accidents involving visitors each year on such roads.

OKAHAO AND ONGANDJERA

Ongandjera is the birthplace of **President Sam Nujoma**; while **Okahao** is the largest village in the region, just a kilometre away from the president's traditional homestead. This is where his elderly mother still lives and to where he still makes frequent visits. As the road turns into the village the homestead can clearly be seen. Separated from the road by mahangu fields, the homestead looks just like any other – a huddle of traditional huts with one zinc roofed brick building. In this case the building is painted pink and there is usually a SWAPO flag in the tree.

The road to **Tsandi** in Uukwaludhi takes you deeper into the Oshana region where *mopane* trees dominate with the occasional *baobab* along with the usual *makalani palms*. Just before the road turns into Tsandi there is a signpost for

Ongulumbashe (see below), scene of an important event in the struggle for independence.

Tsandi is a more attractive village than Okahao, and if time permits it is worth stopping here for a while to savour a different pace of life and take in a little refreshment. There are several well-stocked, up-market bars which are very popular and full of drunken characters.

As you turn N to **Ombalantu** there is a huge baobab tree, but this is not as well known as the **baobab at Outapi** which has served as a prison and now a church. **Outapi** is the main town of Ombalantu and is developing rapidly. As you approach from the S you will notice the large number of newly constructed government buildings and shops. To visit the baobab, check first at the police station – at present it is necessary to obtain permission to go in as it is something of a national monument. If you are planning on driving on to **Ruacana** and the **Kunene** make sure you stop here for fuel since supplies in Ruacana and **Opuwo** are unreliable. The *Super Foods* restaurant opposite the hospital and the *Onawa Supermarket* at the junction with the main road are the best options to stock up on food and drink.

ONGULUMBASHE

Soon to be declared a national monument, this is the historic site where the first shots of the liberation struggle were fired in 1966. Deep in the bush, SW of the current president's birth place, a group of PLAN (Peoples Liberation Army Namibia) combatants were ambushed by South African soldiers having been betrayed by a high ranking soldier who, it later emerged, had been trained in espionage by the South Africans in the 1950s. When visiting the site it is hard to believe that the PLAN combatants were not totally taken aback by the South African's precise knowledge of their whereabouts. It really is the middle of nowhere;

Heroes Day

On Heroes Day (26 Aug) the site becomes the focus of national interest. Given Namibia's tiny population, national events are normally characterized by empty stadiums and skilful camera work making small huddles of people look like throngs. At Ongulumbashe on Heroes Day, Namibia can honestly boast a crowd of several thousand. Over the past few years this annual event has developed into a symbol of both national pride and reconciliation. Lasting one full day, with visitors camping out before and after the event, the events of 1966 are commemorated and those who fought during the struggle are honoured. Performance and cultural presentations are made by representatives of the 13 regions – traditional praise songs and colourful dances in traditional costumes. The most popular of these is a dramatic re-enactment of the battle of Ongulumbashe complete with carved wooden AK 47s. The victorious combatants end by raising the Namibian flag as did the real fighters after each victory in the bush. The flag was flown then lowered and carried with the unit wherever they went. As far as is known, at no point during the bush war did the SAD succeed in capturing the Namibian flag.

Along with the performances speeches are made and prayers said before the people – civilians, heroes, heroines and politicians alike sit down and eat together. Away from the pompousness of Windhoek, the bush is a great leveller and you are likely to find yourself filling your plate shoulder to shoulder with some of the most powerful men in the country.

Namibia's recent history is still painfully fresh and the culture of commemoration is only just developing. If Ongulumbashe is anything to go by then there is a good chance that in spite of the past Namibia may yet develop a national, historic identity which is both meaningful and dignified.

far from any main routes or settlements and not a hint of landscape – the countryside is just flat, scrubby mopane woodland. Before setting their ambush the South Africans apparently harassed the civilian population in their search for the 'terrorists'. It is hard to imagine who they found to harass. In spite of their opponents' distinct advantage the PLAN fighters won the battle of Ongulumbashe and the struggle for Namibian independence was born.

Today the site is marked with a monument to the heroes and heroines of the liberation struggle and there is talk of setting up a permanent exhibition. Otherwise there is little to see or do here, although the original bunkers dug by the combatants in 1966 are still in tact somewhere in the vicinity. Interestingly the replica bunkers constructed in 1990 as a commemoration have long since caved in.

RUACANA AND RUACANA FALLS

Ruacana is the last centre for supplies in the N for those people who plan on exploring the **Kaokoland**. The town only came into being as a camp for all the workers involved with the construction of the underground Ruacana Hydroelectric Project. This is now an important source of power for Namibia. Some of the river is also diverted for irrigation purposes in Owamboland, the water is carried by the **Ogongo canal** alongside the C46 to lands beyond Oshakati. The palm fringed river is a refreshing site but the Ruacana Falls have lost some of their appeal since the Angolans built a dam upstream.

Ruacana Town is 3 km off the main

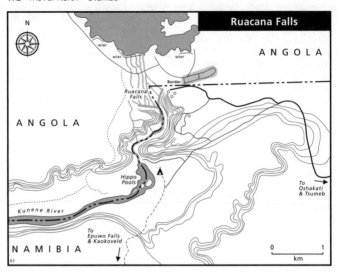

Ruacana Falls

ANGOLA

ANGOLA

NAMIBIA

Ruacana Falls

Border

Hippo Pools

Kunene River

To Oshakati & Tsumeb

To Epuwo Falls & Kaokoveld

0   1
km

road, take a left just after the airfield. One of the many legacies of the armed conflict in the area is that there is only one entrance into the settlement. This was an important South African military base – barbed wire, bomb shelters and other buildings from the military occupation can still be seen. Look out for the signs, do not go wandering too far in the bush because of **mines**. There is a **BP Petrol Station** – closed at night, this is the only source of fuel in the area. The small market serves as a vivid reminder as to how far you have now travelled from the capital, Windhoek.

● **Accommodation D** *Kunene River Lodge*, PO Box 643, Ondangwa, T (06756) 40310, F 40820, follow the main tar road straight ahead past the Ruacana Falls and the Angolan border post. At Hippo Pools where a campsite is currently being developed the road becomes gravel; the lodge is a further 49 km. **NB** After rain a good 4WD vehicle is necessary, the road is very rough, it could easily take 2 hrs to cover the gravel section. Limited fuel is available at the lodge. There are currently four bungalows with en suite bathrooms, more are planned, camping is also permitted, a superb location, Giel Grobler is your host); **D-E** *NAM-*

POWER Guesthouse, T (06758) 51, from the main tar road turn left following the sign for Ruacana, the road curves over a long distance before entering the town through the old security checkpoint, the guesthouse is just beyond the service station on the left, it is set behind high fences in a well-watered garden, all rooms have en suite bathroom, fans and a fridge, TV lounge, bar, price includes breakfast.

● **Transport** 162 km to Epupa Falls (the D3700 follows the Kunene River); 150 km to Opuwo; 272 km to Kamanjab; 243 km to Hobatere Lodge; 302 km to Sesfontein.

ROUTES All of the country around Ruacana is tough going, **you must travel in a minimum of two vehicles per group**. If you have approached through Oshakati you can avoid back-tracking by leaving the region via the **C35** towards the western end of Etosha National Park, **Kamanjab** and **Khorixas**. All of the roads in the **Kaokoland** are for **4WD vehicles only**. If you follow the **D3700** along the banks of the Kunene in a westerly direction you will eventually reach the **Epupa Falls**, 162 km, one of the most isolated tourist sites in Namibia. Few overseas visitors visit these areas under their own steam – most will join organized tours (see page 179).

Ruacana Falls

Ruacana Falls are 15 km from Ruacana, follow the signs marked 'valle'. The falls are divided by the border, one of the view points is close to the run down border hut. Since the flow of the river was checked the views are disappointing for most of the year. The overall flow of the river is now controlled by the Calueque Dam, built 50 km upstream in Angola, this has had the effect of checking any floods and ensuring a steady flow throughout the year. Much closer to the falls are a system of intake weirs designed to collect water for the hydroelectric plant. The combination of these two artificial barriers means that the falls are rarely flooding in their full splendour. If all the conditions are right, Apr is the best month to appreciate the falls. Below the falls is a 2 km long gorge which ends at **Hippo Pools** where there are a couple of small islands in the middle of the channel. It used to possible to climb down to the bottom of the gorge, check in Ruacana at the police station, the frontier runs down the middle of the river below the main falls. **NB** There are nearly 500 steps to the bottom of the gorge. Overlooking the Hippo pools is a **F** *Campsite*, this was very run down but has recently been renovated, hopefully all the work is now complete. We would welcome any information.

From the Ruacana Falls to the Atlantic Ocean the **Kunene river** makes up the border between Namibia and Angola. It is a pleasant and welcome sight as it weaves its way through the Ehomba Mountains, and then the Zebra Mountains, before plunging over the much smaller **Epupa Falls** (32m high), 175 km W of Ruacana. There are also two sets of rapids at **Enyandi** and **Ondorusu**. The river enters the Atlantic Ocean along the northern extremity of the Skeleton Coast National Park, this also marks the northern limits of the giant sand dunes which first appeared 1,700 km S, along the banks of the Orange River. The name Kunene was given to the river by the Hereros. In their language it means, 'right-hand side'; the name refers to the land N of the river. The lands to the S are known as the **Kaokoland**, 'land on the left-hand side'. In Angola the local name for the river is *Omulongo*, 'the stream'. Most visitors to Kaokoland approach it from the S via Kamanjab and Sesfontein, or they fly in on excellent, but expensive organized safaris. (see Windhoek – Tour companies & travel agents).

The North West

One of the last true wilderness areas in southern Africa, Kaokoland lies in the extreme NW of Namibia. Bounded by the Kunene River and Angola to the N, the Skeleton Coast Park and Atlantic Ocean to the W, Owamboland and Etosha to the W and Damaraland to the S, the area is a rugged, mountainous wilderness. Geographically, Kaokoland is part of the larger Kaokoveld encompassing Damaraland to the S, the two areas together making up the Kunene political region. Kaokoland is a world unto itself offering a glimpse into the past, whilst at the same time being on the verge massive and fundamental change.

KAOKOLAND

Topographically the region can be divided into the interior highlands and the pro-Namib plains to the W. These two sub-regions are divided by a rugged escarpment crossed by numerous E-W running river courses which only flow in the summer rainy season. The Kunene River, which marks the border with Angola, is the only perennial river in the area and runs W from near Ruacana through the Zebra Mountains before reaching the **Epupa Falls**. From here it continues its journey towards the Atlantic via the remote Baynes and Otjihipa Mountains on through the Hartmann Mountains before arriving at the bleak Skeleton Coast.

Despite the concerted efforts of hunters and poachers to decimate the game population in Kaokoland, the region is still home to a wide range of animals. The legendary **desert elephant** survives here, specially adapted to life in the dry Kaokoland and the sand dunes of the Skeleton Coast. With their extra long legs these creatures often walk up to 70 km in a day in search of food and water and can survive 4 or 5 days without drinking. The black rhino also survives here, the last place in the world where it can roam free.

The region also supports populations of gemsbok, zebra, giraffe and springbok, as well as smaller numbers of predators such as lions, leopard and cheetah. Despite the harsh, inhospitable conditions the game survives, although as with elsewhere pressure from humans threatens the habitats of these animals. Plans have been afoot for a number of years to declare the western part of

Kaokoland a conservation area, and although the last proposal was turned down by the government, a new scheme will be put forward in 1997. If this is successful then at least this part of this great wilderness area will be preserved for the future.

Kaokoland is sparsely populated with just under 30,000 inhabitants, mainly Herero and Himba. The much filmed, photographed and talked about Himba people are the descendants of the earliest Hereros, who migrated into this area early in the 16th century. Around the middle of the 18th century the pressure of too many people and cattle in this dry, fragile environment led to the migration of the mainly body of the Herero

to the rich pasturelands further S leaving behind the Himba.

The Himba are a semi-nomadic pastoral people who follow their cattle and goats in search of good grazing. Until relatively recently they lived almost untouched by the 20th century and this has made them an attraction both to anthropologists wishing to study their customs and culture and tourists wanting a glimpse into a 'romantic' notion of Africa and her peoples. However today the Himba and their old way of life are threatened by the intrusion of traders, tourists and in particular by the proposed **Epupa Dam Scheme** (see box). More Himba are starting to live in permanent settlements, such as the regional 'capital' **Opuwo**, and many are adapting their customs and lifestyles as they come into contact with the rest of the world and attempt to meet the demands of living in the late 20th century.

Just as the Nama and Herero peoples were exploited by European traders who introduced strong, mass produced alcohol during the 19th century, much the same is happening today to many Himba communities. Traders from Angola and Namibia have penetrated the most isolated areas, bringing with them liquor which is sold to the Himba in exchange for goats or cattle. The drunker and more dependent on alcohol the Himba become the easier it is for unscrupulous traders to take advantage of them.

Tourists too pose a threat as they come into contact with a culture they know little or nothing about; by encouraging the Himba to sell their images for the tourist camera in exchange for cigarettes, sweets and tobacco a proud and highly successful people are turned into a cliché of the 'noble savage'. Whilst there is undoubtedly a place for tourism in the Kaokoland and for contact with the Himba, caution and sensitivity should be exercised at all times. If possible a local guide should liaise between tourists and the Himba to ensure that local customs and people are respected. A number of community projects (see Purros Conservation Project page 181) have developed in response to this need for controlled and non-exploitative form of tourism. Visitors to Kaokoland may well want to support these local initiatives.

Travelling in Kaokoland Maps of the area may give the misleading impression that there is a well established system of roads allowing free access to many parts of Kaokoland. However nothing could be further from the truth. So-called roads are often little more than dirt tracks which become unpassable bogs during the rainy season and the rocky, mountainous terrain of much of the region makes all travel extremely slow and hazardous **Note: do not** drive up Van Zyl's Pass; only travel from east to west betwen Okongwati, Otjitanda

---

Do and don'ts of travelling in Kaokoland

● Do not travel on E-W running water courses as these are migration routes for animals. Approaching vehicles will frighten animals and may cause stress or even injury to game which cannot escape up steep slopes out of the river course.

● Do not camp in river courses, both to avoid night time encounters with large game and the risk of flash floods in summer during the rainy season.

● Ensure that all rubbish is taken out of the area. Do not bury or leave anything for scavengers to get at.

● Do not camp at water holes or springs. Animals have to travel long distances to reach water and if you are camped there game will be too scared too drink. Likewise never wash anything in the springs or water holes as they provide local inhabitants, both people and animals, with drinking water.

● Respect the customs of the Himba and never enter seemingly deserted settlements. As a semi-nomadic people, the Himba move around with their animals to return later to villages which may appear abandoned but in reality are not.

● Do not enter a kraal uninvited and when inside never walk between the sacred fire and the main hut. Never take photographs without first having obtained permission and negotiate payment beforehand if you must take photos.

The Dorsland Trekkers of Kaokoland

In the remote northwestern corner of Namibia there are several monuments to one of the most unusual and hardy group of trekkers to leave South Africa during the 19th century. The origins of this trek date back to 1872 when the Rev Thomas Burgers was elected president of the Transvaal. On hearing of the election results a highly religious group known as the '*doppers*' decided to leave the Transvaal because they opposed the teachings of their new president.

The term *doppers*, meaning dampers, was used because the group had a reputation for opposing all forms of social-progress. One of their arguments that is frequently quoted was their claim that the construction of railway lines was the work of Satan. So in 1874 a group suddenly abandoned their homes, packed the wagons and set off into the Kalahari desert with absolutely no idea of the climatic and physical perils that lay ahead. They were driven by the belief that the trek was necessary to bring them to the land of *Beulah* (after the biblical land of rest). As they journeyed further into the Kalahari many of the women, children and livestock died from fever, heat exhaustion and dysentery. They came to be known as the 'Dorsland Trekkers' – or the thirstland trekkers. By 1876 part of the group had reached the grasslands that are now part of Etosha National Park. Close to the perennial spring, which they renamed *Rietfontein* (reed fountain), is a lone mopane tree providing the shade for the grave of a trekker woman, Johanna Alberts (1841-1876).

Eventually a group of trekkers reached Humpata in Angola, having passed through Kaokoland. Within Kaokoland there are a couple of monuments to the trek, one at Otjitunduwa, 90 km north of Hobatere Lodge; and a second at Swartbooisdrift where they crossed the Kunene into Angola. In between the two monuments are the ruins of a small church at Kaoko Otavi in the Joubert mountains. Within a couple of years the trekkers were quarrelling amongst themselves and the group started to fragment. Some of the party decided to return to the Transvaal, others returned as far as Grootfontein where they set up the capital of the Republic of Upingtonia, after buying some land from a local Owambo chief. The republic was abandoned in 1893 when the South West Africa Company started to prospect for minerals in the area. The Dorsland Trekkers never fulfilled their dreams of *Beulah* but they are a tremendous example of the toughness and the will power required of people if they wished to travel in Namibia before the arrival of the Germans at the end of the 19th century.

and Marienfluß valley. Furthermore, outside of Opuwo the region is devoid of facilities for tourists – no hotels, no garages, no shops, no telephones, just the vast wilderness and small isolated communities living a subsistence existence off the land. Fuel is only available at Opuwo or Ruacana.

It is therefore absolutely essential to travel in a 4WD off-road vehicle, preferably two in convey, in case one runs into trouble. Vehicles should carry two spare tires and puncture repair kits, basic spares such as oil and fuel filters, all the fuel, water and food needed and a decent medical kit. Drivers must stick to existing tracks so as not to damage this fragile environment and leave scars on the landscape that may last for the next 50-100 years. There are a few campsites in the area (see below) and although camping is permitted in the veld the following guidelines should always be observed.

If after all this you are still determined to undertake an unaccompanied trip in Kaokoland, allow plenty of time for travelling and read up beforehand on the flora and fauna of the area in order to fully appreciate you environment. The best map currently available is the Shell Kaokoland Kunene Region Tourist Map.

● **Tour companies & travel agents**

If you are unable or unwilling to make an independent trip to Kaokoland there is always the option of an organized tour. Whilst these are not cheap they offer specialist trips lead by guides familiar with the terrain and the people and usually employ local guides too. It may be worth balancing the cost of hiring two 4WD vehicles plus the risks and pitfalls involved with independent travel with the cost of one of these guided tours. *Desert Safari Adventures*, T/F 064 404072, runs *Serra Cafema Private Camp* in Hartmann's Valley on the banks of the Kunene River, Organizes fly-in tours with 4WD trips to Epupa Falls and other parts of the region; *Ermo Safaris*, T 061 257123, run *Omarunga Camp* at Epupa Falls and also offer safaris in the region; *Kaokohimba Safaris*, T/F 061 222378, run *Camp Syncro* in the Marienfluß by the Kunene River, the camp is not open to casual visitors but arrangements can be made in advance, the company organizes fly-in hiking and 4WD cultural tours using local guides; *Ohakene Guesthouse* in Opuwo also offers tours and day trips in the region as well as accommodation in Opuwo itself.

OPUWO

(*STD code* 06562) Surrounded by low-lying hills, Opuwo, which means 'the end' in Oshiherero, is a small and uninspiring town in the middle of the bush. The town grew into a permanent settlement and administrative centre for the region during the bush war prior to Independence, when the South Africa Defense Force used it as a base from which to launch expeditions into the surrounding area.

Opuwo's name is indeed appropriate as it both the first and last place offering supplies, accommodation and telecommunications in the region, although there are at present no bank facilities. The town consists of a main street with a garage, a few shops and bars and two distinct residential areas. A few streets of bungalows, built during the bush war for army and government personnel, house government officials and the few business people in the area. Not far away are the Himba and Herero settlements consisting of huts and shacks.

Places of Interest

If you fancy a walk around the 'township' where the Himba live ask at the garage for a guide. These will usually be unemployed school leavers who will speak English and therefore be able to translate for you. It is also a way of putting a little money into the local economy as crafts and other souvenirs can be bought directly from the people themselves. Do not take photos without negotiating first.

Local information
● **Accommodation**

Options are unsurpisingly limited as few tourists actually spend any time in Opuwo, most using it merely as a brief stop-over en-route in or out of the region. The Catholic Guesthouse which used to offer accommodation to travellers is now reported to be no longer willing to do so. It may though still be worth checking out this option. **C** *Ohakene Guesthouse*, T 31, F 25, located behind the petrol station offers en-suite double rooms includes full board with bar and swimming pool, it is also possible to arrange trips to Epupa Falls from here; **E** *Guesthouse*, ask for directions at Opuwo Wholesale Supermarket, has recently renovated rooms and bungalows, some en-suite, it may be possible to camp in the grounds here.

● **Places to eat**

Ohakene Guesthouse generally only provides food to guests but it is always worth asking. The best bet is the *Bakery* which offers takeaway hamburgers as a speciality. There are also a couple of takeaways specialising in goat meat and chips located along the main drag.

● **Bars**

Don't be put off by the rather seedy-looking bars. People in town are generally friendly and interested in visitors and chatting over a beer or two is a natural way of getting to meet people. *Verona Bar* and *Cuvelai No 1* both have pool tables where strangers are welcome to take on the locals, a mixed bunch some in traditional dress others in jeans and t-shirts; *Pedro's Disco* is also a popular spot for a late night drink and a bop. Ask anyone where it is.

● **Shopping**

The local crafts shop, set up by missionaries, is located on the one main street and sells locally made and used baskets, jewellery and ornaments. If you intend buying these kinds of souvenirs this is the place to do so, as the money goes directly to the makers of these items, which furthermore are a fraction of the price in Windhoek.

● **Transport**

235 km Khorixas; 290 km Oshakati.

Local Bus: Starline: Otjiwarongo (7 hrs 30), via Outjo Tues 1000, Fri 0700; **Opuwo Line**: private service **Windhoek** departs Fri returns Sun destination Katutura Singles Quarters.

EPUPA FALLS

Approach 177 km NW of Opuwo on the D3700. This dirt road passes through the Otjiveze Mountains then past the Traditional **Himba Demonstration Kraal** at Omuhunga, where tourists can view a traditional Himba homestead and take photographs if so inclined, before heading due N to the falls. It is essential to take spare fuel as there is none at Epupa.

Background The falls are a series of cascades where the Kunene River drops a total of 60m over a distance of about 1.5m. As the river drops it divides into a multitude of channels and forms rock pools where it is possible to bathe – beware of crocodiles though. Over the past few years Epupa has become a focus of tourist activity in Kaokoland with the numbers of tourists steadily increasing as both tour companies and independent travellers alike have flocked to the site.

It is possible to go for walks along the river past the falls although it may be a good idea to take a local guide with you if you intend to walk far. Be careful of crocodiles and snakes.

The Community campsite evolved gradually from just a place where people camped into an organized campsite in response to the growing number of tourists in the area. The camp is maintained by local people, paid by **Kaokohimba Safaris** who contribute 20% of the income into a fund administered by the Namibia Nature Foundation. This money is available to the local community for development purposes.

The **Epupa Camp**, somewhat more upmarket than the community campsite, was originally built for the various consultants and other experts involved in the feasibility study (see box) for the Epupa Dam project. However it has also gradually evolved into a site for the general tourist. There have been some accusations that the money to build the campsite, which is privately owned and managed, came from feasibility study funds – however these remain mere muttered rumours.

● **Accommodation F** *Community Campsite*, campsites with fire places for cooing, running water for showers and toilets; **D** *Epupa Camp* situated under makalani palm trees, has permanent tents, running water for showers and toilets, a lapa with eating area and bar, price is inclusive of breakfast and dinner. **Private camp: A** *Omarunga Camp* owned by Ermo Safaris (see Tour companies and travel agents) is a well equipped private lodge for fly-in safari clients, it may be possible to stay here without joining a tour if you book in advance, the price is all inclusive.

MARIENFLUß & HARTMANN'S VALLEYS – THE KUNENE RIVER

Approach The extreme NW of Kaokoland can be reached by taking the D3703 from Opuwo for about 140 km before it joins another branch of the same road at Otjitanda. From here the road heads W over Van Zyl's Pass before entering the spectacular Marienfluß valley and heading due N to the Kunene. Hartmann's Valley is reached by turning S at the entrance to Marienfluß valley, heading W past the Red Drum – and then N up Hartmann's Valley to the Kunene. **Note**: do not attempt to cross Van Zyl's Pass from west to east.

● **Accommodtion Camping**: **Marienfluß Valley**: F *Public Campsite* by the Kunene River, shaded campsites, long drop latrines but no water, so you will have to be totally self-sufficient; *Camp Syncro* run by Kaokohimba Safaris is not open to the public, but arrangements may be made in advance by contacting the company in Windhoek. **Hartmann's Valley**: *Serra Cafema* run by DAS in

Swakopmund is also a private campsite only for clients of fly-in safaris.

SOUTH TO DAMARALAND

Approach   Either SW on the D3707 towards the Etendeka Mountains and Purros Village or S on the D3704 towards Sesfontein. The fastest route out of Kaokoland S is via the D3709 onto the main C35 gravel road running parallel to Etosha and onto Kamanjab.

Epupa Dam Project

The proposed Epupa Dam & hydroelectric power plant is one of the most controversial projects in Namibia at the moment and has ranged politicians, civil servants, anthropologists, civil engineers, community leaders and conservationists up against one another.

The Epupa scheme is intended to meet Namibia's energy needs for the future, thereby reducing her dependency on importing energy from South Africa. In addition power generated here will also be used to pump water through the proposed Okavango pipeline bringing water from the Okavango River to Windhoek, which cannot grow unless it solves its water problems.

Those in favour of the project argue that the dam will offer the country a renewable source of energy and will also bring much needed development to Kaokoland, bringing schools, clinics and businesses to a remote and underdeveloped area. Those against the scheme argue that the dam will adversely affect the Himba communities living in the area. Ancestral land will be swallowed up by the lake forcing the Himba off the land where they can support themselves and in so doing destroy their traditional way of life and culture.

The Himba themselves are divided on the issue although it appears as if they have little power to influence the decision anyway. Senior government officials have come out firmly in favour of the dam and Prime Minister Hage Geingob recently hit out at what he sees as negative foreign interference in the project. It appears as if the Namibian government has decided that the dam must go ahead in order to bring development to the Kaokoland area.

However it is by no means certain that the project will go ahead, if for no other reason than financial. At present, sources of loans for the project are thin on the ground and it is doubtful that Namibia can finance such a huge project herself. There is also a possible alternative source of energy which may prove both more financially viable and less controversial than the Epupa Scheme.

The Kudu gas field – a vast reserve of natural gas situated under the seabed off the SW coast of Namibia – is also the subject of a feasibility study. In this case the question is to establish whether the expense of running a gas pipeline 1,000 km to the Cape Province is worth it. If this plan were to go ahead it would no longer be necessary to develop Epupa.

Whatever the case, the debate over the Epupa Dam project highlights the conflict between those who wish to preserve the last remnants of the old Africa and those who see the need to adapt in a rapidly changing world in order to survive.

PURROS CONSERVATION AND ECO-TOURISM PROJECT

Background This is a joint project between the local community at Purros Village and Integrated Rural Development and Nature Conservation (IRDNC) based in Swakopmund. The idea behind the project is to develop sustainable tourism in the area which benefits both tourists and the local community and helps to preserve the environment and the wildlife. Community game guards, funded by the World Wide Fund for Nature (WWF) through IRDNC, help to protect the game from poachers so that the community can benefit from this natural resource.

Game drives and hikes This area supports populations of desert elephants, black rhinos, giraffe, gemsbok, ostrich and small numbers of predators such as leopard, cheetah and lion. Local guides offer game drives or hikes into the surrounding area as well as a plant trail intended to educate visitors about plants used in traditional medicines.

Cultural visits Guided visits to local Himba or Herero families where the emphasis is on tourists behaving as guests, spending some time talking with local people, rather than treating them as if they were attractions in a zoo.

● **Accommodation Camping**: F *Ngatu-tunge Pamwe Campsite*, 5 shady sites each with flush toilet, shower and braai facilities, visitors must bring all food and equipment with them, a percentage of the fee goes to Purros Development Committee Fund to be used for small scale development projects in the area.

DAMARALAND

Damaraland covers the southern half of the Kaokoland, the vast wilderness area of NW Namibia, and together with Kaokoland forms the Kunene political region. A huge area stretching almost 600 km N to S and 200 km E to W, Damaraland is bordered by the Hoanib River to the N, the tar road to Swakopmund to the S, the Skeleton Coast to the W and an invisible line running just W of Omaruru and Outjo.

This sparsely populated region is a highland desert wilderness, home to uniquely-adapted animal species such as the desert elephant, as well being a refuge for the last free roaming black rhinos in the world. The region also encompasses some of Namibia's most dramatic natural features such as the **Spitzkoppe** and **Brandberg** mountain ranges, the **Petrified Forest** close to Khorixas and **Verbrandeberge** or 'burned mountain' and the **Organ Pipes** near **Twyfelfontein**, site of Namibia's largest collection of Bushman rock art. Other less accessible places of interest are the **Numas Ravine**, another site of Bushman paintings and the **Messum Crater**, a huge ancient volcanic crater W of Brandberg.

Inhabited for centuries by the Damara people, the area around Okombahe (between Omaruru and Uis) was first proclaimed as a 'reserve' for the Damara by the German colonial administration in 1906. Following the Odendaal Commission report in 1964 which led to the creation of Bantustans in Namibia, a separate Damara tribal homeland was proclaimed in this region. Further acts in 1968 and 1969 cemented this arrangement and in 1971 a Damara Advisory Council was formed. This was part of an overall strategy on the part of the South African government to incorporate Namibia as the country's fifth Province and mirrored similar policies in South Africa itself. Following Independence Damaraland was incorporated into the newly proclaimed Kunene Region.

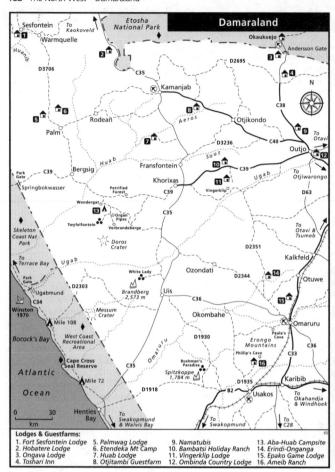

Damaraland

Lodges & Guestfarms:
1. Fort Sesfontein Lodge
2. Hobatere Lodge
3. Ongava Lodge
4. Toshari Inn
5. Palmwag Lodge
6. Etendeka Mt Camp
7. Huab Lodge
8. Otjitambi Guestfarm
9. Namatubis
10. Bambatsi Holiday Ranch
11. Vingerklip Lodge
12. Ombinda Country Lodge
13. Aba-Huab Campsite
14. Erindi-Onganga
15. Epako Game Lodge
16. Ameib Ranch

Damaraland is sparsely inhabited with the majority of the population engaged in subsistence livestock farming. There are no sizeable towns in the region which is for the most part devoid of tourist facilities, however a network of lodges and campsites, a number of them community-run, allow visitors to explore this stunningly beautiful region. Travellers should be as self-sufficient as possible and always carry spare fuel, water and food when travelling in Damaraland. Since virtually all the roads in the region are gravel, it is advisable, although not essential, to drive with a pick-up truck (bakkie) or 4WD. There are also a number of tour companies offering specialist guided hiking and driving trips in the region.

● **Tour companies & travel agents**
Damaraland Trails and Tours, T 061 234610, F 061 239616, offer 2 and 3 week

guided tours which incl a number of days hiking, good for those who would like a 'bush experience'; **Desert Adventure Safaris**, T 064 404459, F 064 404664, fly and drive safaris, using *Palmwag Camp* as a base (see below); **Footprints**, T/F 061 249190, cultural and nature camping tours, focusing on interaction with local people; **Nawa Safaris**, T/F 061 227893, guided driving safaris with the option to design your own trip.

KHORIXAS

(*STD code* 065712) The town lies at the junctions of the C39 route from Outjo and the C35 between Kamanjab and Uis. Although Khorixas is the administrative centre of the Kunene Region, in truth it is hard to see much evidence of this. There is a pleasant rest camp located just outside town and in town itself a bank, garage and a few shops, otherwise Khorixas is devoid of interest to the tourist.

Local information
● **Accommodation**
The *Khorixas Rest Camp* is the only place to stay in town and if you are happy to pay the price of the bungalows, is a pleasant enough place. However for campers interested in Twyfelfontein, the Aba-Huab Campsite is a much better option. **A-C** *Khorixas Rest Camp*, T 196, F 388, pleasant, pricy en suite bungalows set in green gardens with swimming pool, restaurant and bar, dusty campsites, communal facilities.

● **Places to eat**
Khorixas Rest Camp just outside town has good food. The only other option is the bakery in town which serves good coffee and cakes and is an interesting place to sit and people watch.

● **Banks & money changers**
Standard Bank, may not be the best place to rely on to change money.

● **Shopping**
There is a small community crafts shop in town.

● **Transport**
441 km to Windhoek; 133 km to Outjo.

Local Bus: Star Line: Otjiwarongo (4 hrs 30 mins), via Outjo: Mon, 1200.

PETRIFIED FOREST

Approach 42 km W of Khorixas on C39.

Background Declared a national monument in 1950 the Petrified Forest lies on a sandstone rise in the Aba-Huab Valley affording a fine view of the surrounding countryside. Around 50 fossilized trees reckoned to be 260 million years old lie scattered over an area roughly 800m by 300m, some of them so perfectly preserved that it is hard to believe that they aren't still alive.

The absence of roots and branches suggests that the trees in the Petrified Forest do not originate from this area, rather it is believed that they were carried here by floodwaters resulting from retreating glaciers. After being deposited here the logs were saturated with silica-rich water which penetrated into the cells of the trees, gradually causing petrification.

The largest trees here measure more than 30m in length with a circumference of 6m and belong to a type of cone-bearing plant which flourished between 300 and 200 million years ago. Amongst the fallen trees are some fine examples of *welwitschia mirabilis* ancient-looking, desert-dwelling plants, some of which are over 1,000 years old.

Entrance There is a small entrance fee to the forest and visitors are also obliged to engage the services of a local 'guide', some better than others, to show them around and prevent any smaller specimens from the forest being stolen.

TWYFELFONTEIN, VERBRANDEBERGE, ORGAN PIPES, WONDERGAT

These sites all lie within a few kilometres of each other and can comfortably be visited in a day. Better light and cooler temperatures mean that early morning and late afternoon are probably the best times to visit.

Twyfelfontein lies at the end of the D3214 26 km off the C39 and is the site of one of the largest known collections of rock art in Africa. The rock engraving have been carved into boulders situated on a hillside overlooking a picturesque valley near the Aba-Huab River.

Early inhabitants of the area must have been attracted to the valley by the small fresh water spring on the hillside and by the game grazing in the valley below. The Damara who lived here named the valley **Uri-Ais** or 'jumping fountain' after this source of fresh water. However it was renamed **Twyfelfontein** or 'doubtful fountain' in 1947 by the first white farmer to acquire the land who considered the fountain too weak to support much life.

The site was declared a national monument in 1952, however this did not prevent many of the engravings being defaced or even stolen, and the local people who act as guides are now understandably very protective of the engravings.

A total of over 2,500 engravings cut into the rock-face of the huge boulders strewn around have been identified. These engravings have been categorized into six phases ranging in age from around 300 BC to as recent as the 19th century. The majority of the engravings depict a wide range of different species of game, including elephant, rhino, lion and various types of antelope. There are interestingly far fewer depictions of human figures.

Although experts believe that rock paintings and engravings featured in ceremonies intended to imbue the hunters with the power to catch game, the picture of a seal on one of the rocks is particularly interesting considering that this site is over 100 km from the sea. This suggests that some engravings may literally have been items in a gallery of game the Bushmen were familiar with.

There are two loop trails which visitors can follow and a guide must be engaged to ensure that no further damage is caused to the engravings. The two trails take a leisurely 2 hrs to complete it is advisable to wear a hat, stout shoes and to carry water with you. Even if you are not especially interested in rock art, Twyfelfontein is a fantastic place to come and watch the sunset, whilst imagining what life must have been like for earliest inhabitants of the area.

Entrance N$5 per person and similarly sized tip should be given to your guide.

The **Verbrandeberge** or **Burnt mountain** at the end of the D3214 is a section of a 12 km long mountain rising some 200m above the plain. During the daytime the mountain merely looks bleak and uninviting, however the distinctive colouring of the rocks appears clearly at sunrise and sunset when the mountain appears to be on fire. At the base of the mountain a curious pile of rocks, closely resembling a slag heap, sit in a desolate patch of ground.

The Organ Pipes are a series of perpendicular dolerite columns closely resembling set at the bottom of a shallow gorge 3 km after the turn-off onto the D2354. These elegant rocks, some up to 5m long, were formed 120 million years ago when the cooling dolerite split into distinct columns which form the pipes we see today.

The Wondergat, set down a short track off the D3254, 3 km before reaching Aba-Huab campsite, offers an interesting view into the bowels of the earth. The hole is believed to have been created when a subterranean river washed away a chunk of earth.

● **Accommodation** There are a number of different options for accommodation in this area, ranging from the inexpensive, basic *Aba-Huab Campsite* (see below) to the expensive tented comfort of the *Damaraland Camp*. Alternatively visitors can stay in Khorixas itself (see above) or at the *Vingerklip Lodge* (see below), both of which are convenient bases to explore the area. **AL** *Damaraland Camp*, PO Box 6850, Windhoek, this camp is a joint Wilderness Safaris and Bergsig Community project, reservations are handled by the **Namib Travel Shop**, 8 Bismarck St, Windhoek, T 225178, F 239455. This has been developed as an exclusive camp, set in an area of wilderness that is one of the great attractions of Namibia. Peter Ward of Wilderness Safaris has carefully monitored the progress of the project and the camp has quickly established itself with a high reputation. In order to retain the peace & protect the environment numbers are limited to a max of 16 at any one time; guests stay in 8 2-bed tents with en suite bathrooms, shady veranda looking over the valley, central block has a bar and dining area, in the cool evenings the fire is a welcome sight, swimming pool, curio shop. The price quoted usually includes all meals and 'activities', 4WD trips are organised to Twyfelfontein & Brandberg, but perhaps the most exciting aspect of a stay in the camp is the opportunity to go walking in the magnificent landscape with an enthusiast and expert who can and will bring to your attention many tales of desert life for plants and animals, if you are very lucky you might just see the elusive desert elephants, the area is also rich in rock engravings. **Approach**: 110 km W of Khorixas on the D2620, guests leave their own vehicles at a point 3 km from the camp, from here you are transferred by a 4WD vehicle; **F** *Aba-Huab Community Campsite*, a frame shelters with braai facilities; alternatively visitors can pitch a tent on the site, communal wash and toilet facilities with hot water in winter, small bar serving cold beers and soft drinks, visitors must bring everything else with them, located on the banks of a tributary of the Huab River this attractive and friendly campsite is run by local people. It is an ideal place for short walks around the area where there is plenty of bird life; an additional thrill is the chance to see some of the elephants living in the area and which are common night time visitors at the campsite. **Approach**: 73 km from Khorixas on D3254, 11 km before Twyfelfontein. The campsite is on the right-hand side of the gravel road.

Vingerklip

Approach 54 km W of Khorixas on C39 turn onto D2743 for about 22 km.

Background Also known as the **Kalk Kegel** or 'limestone skittle' the Vingerklip is a 35m high limestone rock sitting on a 44m circumference base. The formation of this unusual landmark was caused by erosion of the Ugab River floodplain over a period of 30 million years.

● **Accommodation C** *Vingerklip Lodge*, T (0651) 302063, comfortable en-suite double rooms, restaurant, bar, swimming pool, day trips to local places of interest; **C** *Hobatere Lodge*, T 06552 (farmline) 2022, 12 en-suite bungalows, bar, restaurant, swimming pool, water hole. Trips into the western part of Etosha can be organized from here, as well as hiking and game drives on the ranch itself. **Approach**: follow C35 N out of Kamanjab for 80 km then follow sign. **C/F** *Kaross Guestfarm & Otjombungu Camp*, T 06552 (farmline) 1430, 5 en-suite double rooms, restaurant, swimming pool, nature trail and trips into the W of Etosha, campsite also available with braai sites and shared ablution facilities rec.

Kamanjab

Heading N of Khorixas en route for Kaokoland the C35 passes through the settlement of Kamanjab which offers the last source of fuel before reaching either Sesfontein or Opuwo. Although there is no accommodation in Kamanjab itself there are three guestfarms in the area.

● **Accommodation C** *Cheetah Guestfarm*, T 06552 (farmline) 1111, F 06552 (farmline) 11, 5 en-suite rooms in thatched lodge, restaurant, swimming pool, both tame and wild cheetahs live on the ranch and organized feeding sessions allow visitors good photographic opportunities, hiking trails, game drives all inclusive. **Approach**: located on Farm Sendeling 24 km E of Kamanjab.

NORTH DAMARALAND

About 70 km W of Khorixas on the C39 the road curves to the N heading towards Sesfontein on the northern edge of Damaraland and Kaokoland beyond. There are a number of campsites and lodges in this area which can be used as bases for drives or hikes into the surrounding countryside.

● **Accommodation A/C** *Palmwag Lodge*, T 064 404459, F 064 402434, run by *Desert Adventure Safaris* in Swakopmund, the lodge has 7 en-suite bungalows set amongst makalani palm trees close to a water hole, excellent opportunities especially in winter months to see desert elephants as they come to drink, restaurant, bar and swimming pool for those staying in camp, hiking trails and game drives into the surrounding area especially around the Uniab River course; **A** *Etendeka Mountain Camp*, T 061 226979, 8 tents with beds, showers, meals included, located on the slopes of the Grootberg Mountain, *Etendeka* specializes in bush hikes aimed to give visitors a real bush tracking experience, the highlight of the hikes is the possibility of seeing the last free-roaming black rhino in the world in their natural environment. The camp collects a voluntary bed-levy from visitors which is then placed into a fund for development projects in the local communities which are actively involved with nature conservation in the area. Presenting the first amount of N\$40,000 to the fund administered by Integrated Rural Development and Nature Conservation (IRDNC) in Nov 1996, camp owner Denis Liebenberg stated "My policy is to promote non-consumptive tourism and I hope to share the concept with the community ... I believe that for any conservation policy to be successful, community involvement is essential." *Bircornis Safaris*, T 064 404459, F 064 404664, in conjunction with **Save The Rhino Trust** run specialist rhino tracking safaris using and *Etendeka Mountain Camp* as a base. Close to Sesfontein are two small community bush camps: **F** *Khowarib Camp*, 3 km E of Khowarib village on D3706, 6 traditional huts, 4 campsites with A-frame shelters, communal ablution blocks, hiking and donkey trail, visitors must bring all supplies with them; **F** *Ongongo Campsite*, 6 km from Warmquelle up a narrow track, 6 campsites, communal ablution facilities, visitors must bring all supplies with them. The main attraction of this site is the chance to bathe in the natural pool or even take a shower under the waterfall during the rainy season (Jan-March).

Sesfontein

Approach Sesfontein lies 31 km N of the Hoanib River on the D3706 and is the northernmost point in Damaraland. The place was named after six springs which surface in the area.

Background In 1896 following the devastating rinderpest epidemic which killed off huge numbers of both livestock and game, the German colonial authorities established a number of control checkpoints across the country – the so-called Red Line. Sesfontein formed the most westerly in a string of such checkpoints which still survive today and which demarcate the areas of commercial and subsistence livestock farming in the country.

Following the construction of a road between Outjo and Sesfontein in 1901, the German authorities transported materials to build a military outpost. This was designed to assist in the prevention of poaching and gun running in the are and although a fort complete with vegetable garden was built, by 1909 Sesfontein had been relegated to the status of police outpost before being finally abandoned in 1914. The fort gradually fell into disrepair but was given a reprieve in 1987 when the former Damara administration renovated it. Today the fort has found a new role as home to the Fort *Sesfontein Lodge*.

● **Accommodation C/F** *Fort Sesfontein Lodge*, T 061 228257, F 061 220103, has 13 en-suite rooms, price includes B&B and campsites with communal facilities. Tours and hikes of northern Damaraland and Kaokoland can also be arranged here.

SOUTHERN DAMARALAND

Brandberg – the White Lady

Approach From Uis follow the C35 N for 14 km then turn W onto D2359 for a further 28 km.

Background The immense Brandberg Massif lying due S of the Ugab River and about 40 km NW of Uis is the site of Namibia's highest peak, Königstein, at 2,573m. It is also the site of one of Namibia's most intriguing pieces of Bushman art – the so-called White Lady. Like the **Verbrandeberge** or 'burned mountain' further N, the Brandberg owes its name to its glowing red appearance at sunset.

Nowadays the site of the White Lady is protected by some rather unsightly iron railings, made necessary by previous visitors throwing water on the

White Lady

The White Lady is the best known of a number of bushmen paintings situated in a 1.5 km radius of each other in the Tsisab Ravine. The first paintings in the area were 'discovered' in 1909 by a German soldier, Hugo Jochmann, however the White Lady itself was only found in 1918 following a successful ascent of the Königstein peak by three friends, Reinard Mack, A Griess and George Schultz.

Initially the paintings were believed to have been influenced by early Mediterranean art, mainly due to their superficial resemblance to early Cretan art, but also as a result of contemporary European belief that nothing original could possibly have originated from southern Africa. (This same line of thinking also attributed Mediterranean origins to the Great Zimbabwe Ruins in neighbouring Zimbabwe.)

The main authority on rock art at the time, Abbé Henri Breuil, was shown a watercolour of the White Lady at a science congress in Johannesburg in 1929, and concluded that the main figure in the painting was a woman of European origin. This theory came to be widely accepted however more recently, after detailed further research, it has been concluded that the painting is indeed of local origin, most likely the work of Bushmen. The White Lady is no longer believe to be a woman at all, rather it is thought that the figure is actually a man, probably a **shaman** or medicine man daubed with white body paint.

paintings to make them stand out more clearly – at the same time slowly destroying them. The sites of the other paintings are rather difficult to find, and involve clambering over huge boulders.

Getting to the paintings involves an energetic hike up a well-marked track from the car park at the end of the D2359. Depending on your level of fitness the walk will take 30-60 mins each way, but even if you are not fascinated by bushmen paintings, the walk itself up the Tsisab Ravine is interesting enough. There is plenty of bird life and the chance of seeing klipspringer and mountain zebra as well as a range of smaller mammals.

Wear a hat and decent walking shoes and take a minimum of 2 litres of water per person with you. The relative cool of early morning and late afternoon is the best time to make this walk.

Numas Ravine

Located on the southern side of the Brandberg, Numas Ravine is the site of numerous rock paintings believed to be the work of Stone Age inhabitants.

However locating the paintings without the help of a guide is likely to be extremely difficult, furthermore the road up to the ravine is not suitable for sedan cars.

Messum and Doros Craters

Both these sites are accessible only by 4WD vehicles and are best visited with a guide. A permit is also necessary for Doros Crater and you should contact Nature Conservation in Windhoek for further details.

UIS TOWN

(*STD code* 064) Lying 102 km NE of Henties Bay on the C35 and 121 km W of Omaruru on the C36, Uis was once an important tin mining town, but today is a forlorn shadow of its former self. As a company town the lifeblood was drained from it when the mine was closed after having been deemed to be no longer profitable, and the majority of the population able to do so moved away.

Although small scale tin mining had taken place in the area in the first half of this century, it was not until 1951 that a full scale mining operation was started. In 1958 the South African mining giant ISCOR took over the mining rights and built the town, which flourished until the mine's closure shortly after Independence. Today local miners, with overseas donor assistance, are once again mining on a small scale.

● **Accommodation B/D/F** *Brandberg Rest Camp*, T/F 064 504038, offers en-suite family houses and 4 bed flats, and campsites with communal facilities, restaurant and bar, pool and tennis courts, snooker table, badminton court, plus a 9-hole golf course, a genuine oasis in this rather forlorn town, a good base from which to explore Brandberg.

● **Shopping** The *Gemstone Factory* on the main street is a two person operation polishing and selling locally found semi-precious stones and is worth a visit. The **Brandberg Community Craft Project** located in the township (follow signs) was set up by a small group of local women in 1996 with help in the form of a start-up loan from the Rossing Foundation. The women make and sell crafts and souvenirs using locally available recycled materials.

SPITZKOPPE

Approach Turn off the B2 Swakopmund-Usakos road onto D1930 23 km outside Usakos. Continue on this road for a further 29 km. Actually in the Erongo Region, Spitzkoppe is nevertheless geologically linked to the other mountains in Damaraland.

Background One of Namibia's most recognizable landmarks, the 1,784m high **Spitzkoppe** or 'pointed hill', rises some 700m above the surrounding plain. The mountain's distinctive shape has given rise to its nickname as the Matterhorn Africa. The main peak, or **Gross Spitzkoppe** is one of three mountains making in the area, the others being the **Klein Spitzkoppe** at 1,572m and the dome-shaped **Pondok Mountain**.

Geologically these three mountains are in fact are can be grouped with the **Erongo Massif** to the E and the **Brandberg** to the N – all of which are ancient volcanoes. The violent break up of Gondwanaland 750-500 million years caused vast amounts of lava to burst up through these volcanoes whose granite cores have been exposed by millions of years of erosion, creating the **inselbergs** or 'island mountains' that we see today.

The NW face of Spitzkoppe was first climbed in 1946 and the W face in 1960 and today the mountain is still popular with climbers. Alternative attractions are the sites of a number of Bushmen paintings – the best known found at the so-called **Bushman's Paradise**. The area is also a great place to camp and hike and enjoy the clear desert air and fine views.

Rock art Follow the road to the base of Pondok Mountain E of Spitzkoppe past a small dam built by the German colonial authorities in 1896 as part of a farming operation. Shortly after is the steep climb up to Bushman's Paradise – the smooth slopes made easier thanks to the help of a chain. At the top is a richly vegetated natural amphitheatre and the large overhang which hides the paintings. These have unfortunately been vandalized, nevertheless the views of the surrounding countryside make the climb worthwhile. Local guides will be able to show visitors the sites of bushmen paintings, in particular the **Golden Snake** and **Small Bushman's Paradise**.

● **Accommodation Camping:** in 1993 the community of the nearby village of Spitzkoppe, encouraged by government policy that communities should be more involved in conservation and tourism, decided to establish a small campsite here. All income derived from the campsite directly benefits the community and serves to strengthen the partnership between conservation, development and tourism. Visitors are asked to make a donation for staying at the campsite and encouraged to buy souvenirs from the small crafts shop. **F** *Spitzkoppe Community Tourist Camp*, basic campsites with braai facilities and pit latrines. Water is in short supply and should be brought along by visitors together with all other supplies.

The Coast

FOR MANY visitors to Namibia the coast could easily be passed over as they go in search of wildlife and the Africa that is portrayed in many brochures. But for Namibians the coast provides a relaxing and cool contrast to the interior. Each year thousands descend on the resorts for a few weeks of fishing, boating and a bit of swimming. The contrast between the arid desert and Atlantic ocean is one that creates many unusual scenes. Here you can experience a wild coast where many have lost their lives, but if you pay the money you can explore one of the most evocative wilderness regions in the world – the Skeleton Coast. As with so many of the great wildernesses in the world you will probably end your day with more questions than answers, enjoy, but remember this is a unique place and it needs to be protected.

SWAKOPMUND

(*STD code* 064) Seen from the air Swakopmund is surrounded on three sides by the arid Namib desert, with the cold waters of the Atlantic to the W. This is one of the most unusual and fascinating colonial towns in the whole of Africa. In a period of a little more than 25 years the German Imperial Government built a succession of extravagant buildings which today represent one of the best preserved collections of German colonial architecture still standing. This is Namibia's premier holiday resort, during Dec and Jan thousands of people descend from the hot interior to enjoy the temperate climate of the coast.

History

"The municipality since 1909 has made every effort to create an up-to-date township. The water supply is the best in the whole Protectorate and shortage is never felt in the town. There is an Electric Power Station, Ice and Mineral Waters Factories, a first class Hospital and Nursing Home, Public Library, German, Dutch and English Churches, High-class Schools and Hostels and a lot of Corporations and Clubs." *Swakopmund Publicity Association*, 1924/25.

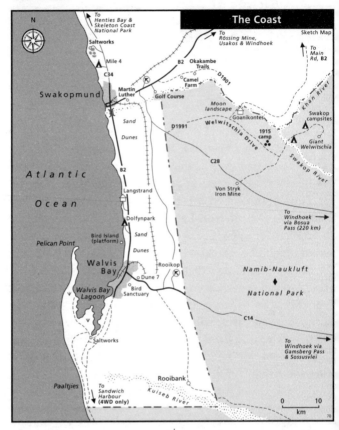

And so the town proudly promoted itself during the interwar years, and yet less than 30 years earlier no more than 30 Europeans lived in this newly established town. Many of the key events that are part of the history of Swakopmund are outlined below, but as a visitor to this modern town it is always worth pausing and questioning why and how the town came to be here. If ever there was a town in Africa that owed its origins to colonialism it was Swakopmund.

The first Europeans to encounter the barren Namibian coastline did not stop here; the Portuguese sailors left monuments to mark the points where they had ventured ashore, but there was no attempt made to settle anywhere along this section of the Atlantic coast. But when the German protectorate was proclaimed in 1884 the British had already claimed possession of Walvis Bay, forcing the Germans to look elsewhere for a suitable coastal port. The choice of Swakopmund had a lot to do with the immediate availability of fresh water. While there were other more suitable sites along the coast the

Germans selected Swakopmund as the point to develop a future harbour and settlement for two reasons; firstly the immediate hinterland was not a mass of sand dunes which inhibited the inland development of transport routes, and secondly a short distance up the Swakop River valley there was a fresh water supply.

In Aug 1892 the German gunboat, *Hyena*, landed just N of the Swakop River and two beacons were raised by the crew to mark their position. At the time this was one of many possible locations for a port along the coast that the Germans were looking for. Today history recounts that the landing in 1892 marked the origins of Swakopmund, however it was a combination of chance and a tough spirit that saw the establishment and growth of a town at this point on the coast. The first 40 settlers were landed in 1893 by four boats, but thereafter they had to fend for themselves. There was no accommodation, there was nothing; many of these early settlers ended up living in what have been described as 'caves', on the beaches. Today the town can be a grim place on a misty day, imagine how it was for the first settlers at the turn of the century. Gradually a town developed and people were able to move inland and establish trading posts and mission stations, but it was the resilience of the earliest settlers that set the pattern. After WW1 the town fell into decline as the nearby port of Walvis Bay assumed the role as the premier town on the coast. Many businesses and government offices also moved.

Until the 1970s Swakopmund may have been a forgotten town, but many of the citizens made their mark – today this is one of the most unusual and vibrant communities along the western coast of Africa; and what's more it has a special place in German history. The modern town is experiencing a building boom that is taking many people by surprise. Tourism is now an integral part of the local economy, many people in the area depend upon the thousands of visitors each year. During the month of Dec the population on the coast is said to double, hotels are full, restaurants require a booking and to the frustration of local residents there are no parking places in the town centre.

Climate

Although the town lies in a true arid desert, the cold Benguela current, which flows from S to N along the coast acts as a moderating influence. The climate on the coast is temperate, temperatures range between 15-25°C. The sea temperature ranges between 14-18°C, too cold for swimming for any period without a wet suit. Swakopmund receives less than 15 mm of rain per year, this is because the rain clouds have to travel all the way over Africa from the Indian Ocean. As you walk about the town note how most buildings have no gutters or drain pipes. The only moisture comes in the form of a sea mist that can reach up to 3 km inland. It is because of this mist that the coastal strip of the Namib desert has a unique living environment. There is sufficient moisture to support over 50 different lichen species and many other larger plants. These plants in turn provide food and water for hardy animals such as the Gemsbok and Springbok which also live in the desert.

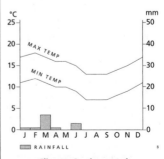

Climate: Swakopmund

Locomotive number 174 from the Tsumeb mine
being unloaded on the OMEG railway line

Roads, railways and the desert

Much of Swakopmund's early history was a battle to establish a port that could effectively supply the settlements inland. Like all colonial regimes of the period, the colonies were regarded as an important source of raw materials and new territories for trade. If they were to effectively exploit the interior the Germans had to somehow overcome the inhospitable Namib desert, which in age before railways and motorcars represented a tremendous natural barrier.

The first road to be built between the coast and the interior was known as the '**Baaiweg**'. It was built by the local leader Jan Jonker in 1844. Most of the early traffic consisted of ox wagons carrying copper from Matchless Mine to Walvis Bay, but the 350 km journey proved to be uneconomic and the route was then seldom used. All this changed when a harbour was built at Swakopmund, in 1896 records show that 880 ox wagons used this road. But this heavy traffic quickly exposed the local weaknesses; each year more than 12,000 oxen had to be fed and watered across the Namib desert, there were no waterholes and no suitable pastures, losses were very high. In 1897 the government was forced to turn to the railways to try and overcome the problems posed by the desert.

Work on the first railway started in Sep 1897, and like the mole construction project the work greatly contributed to the growth of the town as workshops, supplies and storage sheds were provided. This first railway was a narrow gauge (60 cm), considering the obstacles and the remoteness of the colony it was a great achievement for the times. The first stage went as far as Jakalsswater, 100 km inland, by Jul 1900 the railway had reached Karabib, and on 19 June 1902 the first train from Swakopmund arrived in Windhoek, a journey of 382 km. This part of the state railway remained open until Mar 1910.

In 1903 work had begun on a second narrow gauge railway, this was known as the Otavi Railway line. In 1900 the Otavi Mine and Railway Company – **OMEG** (Otavi Minen-und Eisenbahngesellschaft) had started to mine copper ore in Tsumeb, but because of the unreliable state service they opted to build their own railway line. Their chosen route into the interior proved to be a more sensible one than that followed by the state railway, and the quality of engineering was much higher. When the full line opened on 12 November 1906 it was the longest narrow gauge line in the world at 567 km. The running of the line was taken over by the government when he State railway was closed in 1910. The stretch between Tsumeb and Usakos was only widened in 1960.

Up until 1914 all the German efforts had been concentrated on connecting the port of Swakopmund with the rest of the country. But once the colony had been taken over by the British, Swakopmund quickly fell into disuse since the far more favourable site of Walvis Bay could be exploited. During WW1 the troops from the Union of South Africa built a railway line between Walvis Bay and the Swakop River in just over 2 months, but unlike the German-built railways this was a broad gauge track, measuring 106.7 cm. The problem proved to be crossing the Swakop River; the first railway bridge was washed away in 1917. As the German army retreated inland they destroyed the existing narrow gauge railway, but this merely paved the way for the South African engineers to replace the tracks with a broad gauge railway. Following the Treaty of Versailles the railway network was taken over by the South African Railways and Harbour Administration. While the network was improved and extended in the interior the problem of crossing the Swakop River remained unaddressed. A railway bridge was built between 1925-6, but in Jan 1931 the structure was washed away by the river in flood. It was not until 1935 that a secure bridge was built across the river, a short distance inland from the current road bridge. Any visitor in the 1990s to Swakopmund may well wonder what all the fuss was about, but during the early years of Swakopmund the river caused great damage as well as loss of life. The dry river bed may well look innocuous today, but with sufficient rainfall inland the flood waters have it in them to drastically alter the current landscape.

As you drive along the surfaced road between Swakopmund and Walvis Bay it is worth remembering that this stretch of road was first opened in Aug 1959, and only surfaced in 1970. The railway that ran between the two towns had to be re-routed in 1980 when the sand dunes finally reclaimed another transport route. You will feel very safe driving between the two towns today, but a hundred years ago the Namib was a real threat.

Places of interest

For Namibian residents Swakopmund is popular as a beach resort which provides a comfortable contrast to the hot interior. International visitors come here for the sea, the desert and the fine collection of German colonial buildings. Many of these old buildings are closed to the public, but much of their elegance is in their exterior. The buildings are listed in a sequence that could be followed in a walk starting from the *Strand Hotel*. If you choose to follow the route allow a couple of hours and avoid the hottest part of the day. There are plenty of cafés and bars to call in on along the route.

The *Strand Hotel* was built close to the point where **The Mole** joined the mainland. As noted in the history section Swakopmund was never the ideal place for a harbour or port, there was no natural bay or sheltered spot as at Walvis Bay and Lüderitz. In 1898 the government decided that a mole should be built in order to create an artificial harbour basin. The whole project acted as a great stimulus for the fledgling settlement, such a giant engineering project required a lot of preparation and additional facilities; these took more than 10 months to put in place and included a piped water supply for making cement, a small railway line, the opening up of a quarry and the provision of housing for the labour force. The foundation stone was laid on 2 September 1899, and the mole officially opened on 12 February 1903. It had proved to be a far greater job than imagined, the 375m construction had cost 2.5 million marks. Along the mole were three steam powered cranes which could transfer the freight from ships to barges. Unfortunately the planners were totally ignorant to the ocean currents and within 2 years of completion large amounts of silt started to build up on the S side of the mole, by Jul 1904 the tugs could only enter the artificial basin at high tide. By 1906 the whole basin had silted up and in the process created Palm Beach that is so enjoyed by the modern day tourist. After the Herero War the government looked for an alternative solution and plans were drawn up for the construction of a jetty. A wooden jetty was quickly built, which in turn was replaced by the iron jetty which can still be seen today (see below). These days the mole is used as a launch point for pleasure boats and the original harbour basin is a pleasant sheltered swimming area. If you are lucky you may see a dolphin or two swimming around in the bay as you walk out to the end of the mole.

Tucked away in the gardens behind the museum is the port **Lighthouse**. The first version, built in 1903, stood at only 11m; in 1910 a further 10m was added. The lighthouse marked the harbour as well as warning ships off the treacherous skeleton coast, the light can be seen more than 30 km out to sea. Next to the lighthouse is the **Kaiserliches Bezirksgericht** which serves as the Presidential holiday home. The presence of heavily armed soldiers will alert you to his presence, it is advisable to keep well clear during such visits. It seems there is no such thing as an 'innocent' tourist to the young soldiers. The building was originally the first magistrates court in Swakopmund.

Close to the lighthouse is the **Marine Memorial**, a monument to members of the First Marine Expedition Corps who died during the Herero War, 1904-1905. The statue was designed and cast in Berlin, it was presented to the town by the crew of the German gunboat, '*Panther*' in Jul 1908. The figure represents a marine standing by his wounded colleague, ready for action.

As you walk N along the beach look out for Ludwig Koch St just beyond the municipal swimming pool. There are a couple of contrasting colonial buildings along the seafront. At No 5 is **Vierkantvilla**, this was the last house assembled by the 'Hafenbauamt' for the construction of the harbour mole. The interesting thing about this building is that it was prefabricated by Fa. Zadek in Germany for the Kasier government. It was shipped out to Africa and erected on a stone foundation in 1899. Further along the street is a solid double storey building built in 1901 for the Eastern and South Africa Telegraph company. **Kabelmesse** was the principal office for the employees who installed the undersea cable from Europe to Cape Town. A branch from this cable surfaced a few kilometres N of Kuisebmond. When the railway was first built between Walvi Bay and Swakopmund it ran right along the beach; there was a siding at the spot where the cable ran ashore, named "Cables". This area of beach is still known as cables and appears as so on many maps. At the outbreak of WW1 the cable was severed, and then removed when the wireless telegraph was installed.

Away from the centre of the town i the **Alte Gefängnis** (Old Prison), Nor dring St. When the prison was completed in 1909 it stood right out of the town. The original tender was awarded to Heinrich Bause in Dec 1907, the prison and the living quarters for prison personnel was built for approximately 24,000 marks. The building has such a fine façade that it has frequently been mistaken as a hotel or private mansion There is a tale which recounts the firs visit of an official in the South Wes Africa administration who on seeing the solitary building for the first time ex claimed: "I wouldn't mind staying there The local dignitaries politely replied "that your honour is the prison". It is stil

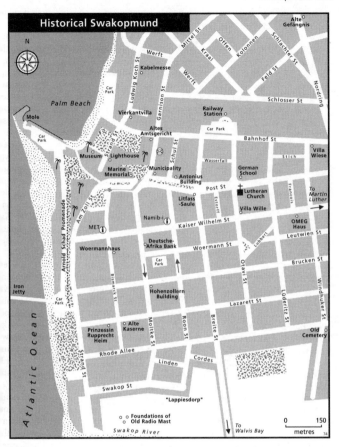

Historical Swakopmund

N

Alte Gefängnis

Mittel St

Offen

Kraal

Kolonnen

Schlachter St

Feld St

Nordring

Werft

Kabelmesse

Ludwig Koch St

Car Park

Garnison St

Werft

Schlosser St

Palm Beach

Mole

Car Park

Vierkantvilla

Railway Station

Car Park

Bahnhof St

Stich

Villa Wiese

Altes Amtsgericht

Museum

Lighthouse

Schul St

Wasserfall

German School

To Martin Luther

Marine Memorial

Municipality

Antonius Building

Post St

Lutheran Church

Francois

Litfass -Saule

Villa Wille

Arnold Schad Promenade

Am Zoll St

Namib-i

MET-i

Kaiser Wilhelm St

Lindequist

Deutsche- Afrika Bank

Woermann St

Lossen

Lüderitz

OMEG Haus

Leutwien St

Woermannhaus

Car Park

Otavi St

Brucken St

Iron Jetty

Car Park

Hohenzollern Building

Lazarett St

Lüderitz St

Windhuker St

Bismarck St

Moltke St

Prinzessin Rupprecht Heim

Alte Kaserne

Roon St

Breite St

Old Cemetery

Rhode Allee

Linden

Cordes

St Pauls

Swakop St

"Lappiesdorp"

To Walvis Bay

Foundations of Old Radio Mast

Swakop River

Atlantic Ocean

0   150
metres   74

used as a prison today so be very discreet when trying to take a photograph.

Close to the police station on the corner of Bahnhof and Garnison streets is a lemon yellow building in a well kept garden full of succulents and palm trees. This is the **Altes Amtsgericht**, built in 1906 as a school but then used as the magistrates office after the state had to finish the building when the private source of funds ran out. After falling into disrepair the building was restored in 1976. During office hours you may be

able to get a glimpse of the interior. The building was designed by Otto Ertl who was also responsible for designing the prison and the Lutheran church; notice how features such as the gables and turrets are similar between these buildings.

A short walk along Bahnhof St will bring you to *Swakopmund Hotel & Entertainment Centre*, the newest and most comfortable hotel in town. Until the early 1990s this was the **Railway Station**, and passengers from Windhoek would alight here into this fine colonial building. While all the building work has destroyed all trace of the railway line there are plenty of old photographs on show in the hotel restaurant and reception area which capture the scene perfectly. Before the conversion took place there was only one structure here, the building which is now the hotel reception and evening bar. The original platform is the terrace which overlooks the swimming pool. The building was designed by the architect C Schmidt, and built in 1901. The central tower was added at a later date by W Sander. In 1910 the main railway line was closed, but the station continued to act as a terminus for the narrow gauge railway, the Otavi Railway Company (see box below). After WW1 the broad gauge railway was once again opened and continued to terminate here until a new station was built a short distance inland on the other side of Nordring. In Oct 1972 the building was declared a national monument, so guaranteeing its future.

It may not be the most interesting sight but the **Litfass-Saule** on the corner of Post and Breite streets has an unusual background. This rather tatty looking pillar is an original advertising post dating from the days before radio and television. There were similar posts all over the town to which people used to stick their promotional posters. This is the only post still standing. Litfass was a printer in Berlin who first thought of the pillars in 1855. Post St is a pleasant wide road with some palm trees on the centre island, as you can see there are a variety of old buildings to admire all along this street.

The **Municipality** dates from 1907, it started life as a post office, telephone exchange and living quarters for the personnel. Perhaps one of the reasons this and many other buildings are still standing is due to the high standard of craftsmanship and attention to detail that was typical of the period. The architect, Redecker, included the following clause in the contract with the builders: "the building must be built as stipulated in the contract and associated plans; all wood must be seasoned and dry; qualified artisans must be engaged for each task; the roof nails must be 4 cm apart and countersunk". A short distance along Post St is the **Antonius Building**. Over the years there have been many additions to this building, but between Mar 1908 and 1987 it was Swakopmund's only hospital. In the early days it was staffed by sisters of the Franciscan order, later on it was run by the Roman Catholic church.

Across the road from the Lutheran Church is the **Old German School** building, this is still in use as a school, the new extension to the right may be more practical but it has none of the style of the original school building. This Baroque style building was opened in 1913, it was designed to fit in with the church.

The **German Evangelical Lutheran Church**, was designed in the neo-Baroque style by the government builder, Otto Ertl in 1909, it was built by FH Schmidt. On 7 January 1912 the inaugural dedication service was held in this grand building, the parsonage was completed in 1911. As with several other important buildings and homes of the wealthy the church roof was covered with copper. The congregation was led by Dr H Vedder. The total white population of Swakopmund was estimated to be 1,400 in 1912.

Villa Wille, Otavi St, is a fine example of a comfortable private residence. Hermann Wille was responsible for building some of the most elegant buildings in Swakopmund, this was his private home. He designed it as a bungalow but then decided to add a second floor. This is one of the most noteworthy buildings in Swakopmund, it has a fine balcony and a turret (a popular feature of the time) with a copper roof. Hermann Wille only enjoyed a short life in Swakopmund, he was killed in action in 1915.

If you walk along Kaiser Wilhelm St for a couple of blocks you will have reached the **OMEG Haus** and museum next to a small botanical garden. Around the corner in Windhuker St is the excellent Sam Cohen library (see below).

One of the finest colonial buildings in Swakopmund is the **Hohenzollern Building**, on the corner of Brucken and Moltke streets. The most obvious feature is the statue of Atlas on the roof above the front door, he is kneeling holding up a globe of the world. In 1988 the original cement figure had to be replaced with the present plaster-of-paris version, from street level it is impossible to tell the difference. The building dates from 1909 when it started life as a hotel built by Mr Herman Dietz. But in 1912 the building was taken over by the Municipality after the hotel licence had been revoked by the local magistrate. The hotel had become a well known gambling den. When the municipality moved out the building was converted into private flats.

The **Alte Kaserne (Old Schütznhaus)**, was built in 1906 as a fort for the Second Railway Company who were involved with the construction of a wooden jetty. The style of the fort was considerably different from other forts of the period, notably Fort Namutoni. The front of the building measured 55m with a tower in the centre facing out to sea, the other sides measured 45.5m. A turret was built at each corner, the turret loopholes were included more for decoration than practical purposes. Today the most interesting feature is to be found in the entrance hall directly below the main tower. Now used as a reception for the youth hostel the walls are covered with original paintings which represent the 26 emblems of the German Alliance States which were united in 1871 to form a unified German nation state. There is also a plaque with the names of the soldiers who died during the Herero War. Even if you are not staying here they are well worth closer examination.

On the opposite corner of Bismarck and Lazarett streets is another original colonial building that is now a pension for visitors. The **Prinzessin Rupprecht Heim** is a fine single storey building dating from 1902. It was first used as a military hospital, but in 1914 it was taken over by the Bavarian Women's Red Cross who renamed the building after their patron, Princess Rupprecht, the wife of the crown prince of Bavaria. For many years the building served as a peaceful nursing home until it was converted, and some outbuildings added, into a private guesthouse.

Heading back along Bismarck St the **Woermannhaus** is easily recognized as the building on the high ground with a decorated tower. Until recently part of the building housed the Namib-i tourist office, now it is home to the AA, but visitors can still climb the tower and visit an art gallery on the first floor and the local library (the tower key is kept in the library and the Art Gallery, 1000-1200, 1500-1700). The Woermannhaus dates from 1905, it was designed by Friedrich Höft as an office for the Damara and Namaqua Trading Company. In 1909 the building was bought by another trading company, Woermann, Brock & Co. The Damara Tower was used as a lookout position to see when ships arrived at sea, and when ox wagons arrived from the desert. Between 1924 and 1972 the building served as a school hostel. When it was closed in 1972 it was in such a poor state of repair that the municipality planned to demolish the building, fortunately a successful campaign organized by Dr A Weber and Mrs O Levinson saved the building; restoration was completed in 1975 and the public library moved into part of the building.

At the lower end of Brücken St you can view the town from a different angle by walking to the end of the jetty. In 1910 the German government decided that it was time to build a permanent **Iron**

Jetty. A contract was entered with the bridge builders, Flender, Grund and Bilfinger to complete the jetty in 3½ years for a cost of 3.5 million marks. Before work on the jetty could start workshops and storage rooms had to be built on the shore, these were only finished in Nov 1911. The original plans were to build a bridge reaching 640m out to sea, this would carry two parallel railway lines of 490m. These lines would carry a loading platform with two cranes, 3 and 5 tonnes respectively. A third crane was planned for the shipping of marble from the Karibib region. Each of the iron posts supporting the jetty were filled with cement. Progress was slower than planned, by Sep 1912 only 100m had been completed. At this stage the contractors ran into the first problems with shifting sand banks. When work stopped at the outbreak of WW1 a third of the jetty had been completed for a cost of 2.5 million marks. In 1919 one side of the jetty was covered with planks so that it could be used by visitors and fishermen. In 1931 and 1934 the Swakop River flowed for more than 4 months after exceptionally good rains in the interior. In 1934 parts of the town were destroyed by the floodwaters and silt from the Swakop River pushed the sea 3 km back from the present coastline. The jetty stood high and dry with a set of steps added at the end to help people get to the ocean. Slowly the sea washed away the silt and the present coastline was restored. In 1985 the jetty had to be closed for safety reasons. The following year an appeal raised Rand 300,000 to pay for the necessary repairs, more than 60% of the money came from public donations. Today the jetty stands safe and solid, although only half the width is covered.

If you have been following the recommended walk this marks the end of the tour, the *Tug* by the jetty is as pleasant a place as any for a sundowner and a good fish meal. Alternatively you could walk along the cool **Arnold Schad Promenade** back to the *Strand Hotel*.

At the southern end of Strand St behind the new Fisheries and Marine Centre are three small buildings which were once the anchor points for the **radio mast** used by the Germans until 1914. In Dec 1911 the Germans erected a strong transmitter which could communicate with Windhoek, ships along the coast as well as a similar transmitter in Duala, in the German Cameroons. This 85m high steel tower became of great strategic importance at the outbreak of WW1 since it enabled the German navy to operate in the South Atlantic and threaten all the allies' shipping. When the British government asked the Union of South Africa to invade German South West Africa it was to both silence this radio and gain control of it for themselves. On 14 September 1914 the British auxiliary cruiser – *Armadale Castle* – started to bombard the radio mast, but failed to score a hit. At the time they did not know that the Germans had already dismantled the equipment and moved the radio inland on 13 Aug. To try and stop the bombardment the remaining personnel cut two of the cables causing the tower to collapse, no more shots were fired at the town that day. 10 days later the British cruiser *Kinfauns Castle* bombarded the town hitting the customs shed by the lighthouse with a lucky shot. 40 years later these ruins were converted into Swakopmund Museum.

Museums and libraries

Close to the *Strand Hotel*, by the Mole, is the **Swakopmund Museum**, founded in 1951 by Dr Alfons Weber. Open Mon-Fri, 1000-1300, 1400-1700, adults N$7, children N$3. The collection is very strong on local German history and the geography of the Namib desert. A small museum shop stocks a wide selection of historical leaflets (mostly in German) plus the usual choice of postcards, slides and books on Namibia. Visitors interested in rocks and minerals will find an impressive collection to the right of the entrance. Next door to the uranium mine showcases are a series of shops and rooms recreating the days of German occupation, this is one of the most interesting displays in the museum. Overall this is a worthwhile museum which both educates and entertains, there are not that many museums worth visiting in Namibia, but an hour spent here should be of interest to most visitors.

There is a very interesting small museum in the **OMEG Haus**, Kaiser Wilhelm St, devoted to transport and photography in and around Swakopmund during the German occupation. Open 1000-1300, 1400-1700, no charge. Note the couple of diving helmets that were used during the construction of the jetty, each weighs 15 kg. Outside in the courtyard are a couple of restored items from the Otavi railway. This was the site of the first station for the railway line. At a later date the railway was moved to the state railway station, the present day *Swakopmund Hotel*. The OMEG house was the goods shed.

Anyone with a keen interest in Namibian history should visit the excellent **Sam Cohen Library**, next to the OMEG Haus, open 0900-1300, 1500-1700. Here you will find most of the material that has ever been published on Swakopmund; of particular interest is the collection of historical photographs and old newspapers. Anyone able to read German will find plenty of fascinating reading here. The town reading library is housed in the Woermannhaus, Bismarck St.

National Marine Aquarium, Strand St. Open Tues-Fri 1000-1600, Sat 1000-1600, Sun 1100-1700, adults N\$6. Fish are fed daily at 1500, on Tues, Sat and Sun the fish are hand fed by divers. The new centre has a large central tank with a walk-through tunnel, the tank contains some sharks and sting rays plus a mix of smaller fish. There are smaller tanks with lobster, crabs and prawns. A fascinating glimpse at marine life, allow about 30 mins unless you are there during feeding time.

Excursions

The **Saltworks**, 6 km to the N of town off the Henties Bay road, C34, are a must for any keen birder. Follow the dirt track around the salt lakes, on the coastal side is the Seabird Guano House, drivers in a saloon car will have to stop by the fence. The terrain is a mix of ponds and canals surrounded by a gravel plain, off the sandy beach is a guano platform. It is advisable to arrive here in the early morning before human activity at the works and on the beach disturb the birds. In addition to the resident population of waders there are many migrants to be seen between Sep and Apr each year. A comprehensive list of birds to be seen here has been put together by Dr G Friede, this small booklet can be found at the museum, any keen birder should buy this. The following list is a summary of some of the species recorded at the saltworks, resident: avocets, chestnut-banded plover, oyster catcher, cape teal, cape shoveller, grey heron, blackwinged stilts, the pelicans and cormorants breed on the guano platform. Migrants: whimbrel, turnstones, little stint, knot, ringed plover, sanderling and bartailed godwit. Salt no longer naturally occurs in the area, however water is pumped from the ocean into the shallow pans, and during the next 15 months evaporation results in the formation of salt crystals which are then collected. The whole area is a private nature reserve.

There are several other popular local sites for bird watching. The **Swakop estuary**, just beyond the *Hotel Garni Adler* can easily be visited by foot from the centre of town. Here there is a mix of reed beds and the sandy beach, find a sheltered spot and you should be rewarded with a variety of waders and land birds. The **Sewage Works** are another site for birds, visitors must obtain a permit at the Altes Amtsgericht, Garniston St, access is limited to working hours, 0800-1700. The final recommended location for birding is 10 km to the E of town. Follow the road towards the airport and Windhoek, take a right turning for the camel farm and look out for a castle-like building on a small hill. This is **Nonidas Castle**, behind the building are a couple of vleis surrounded by reed beds and shrubs. Here you can expect to see moorhen, redbilled teal, dabchick,

marsh warblers, swallows and martins. A visit here can be easily combined with a tour of the camel farm or horse riding with **Okakambe Trails** (see below).

Assuming you have your own vehicle there are several other popular day trips. For most visitors a drive up to Henties Bay and **Cape Cross Seal Reserve** will be all they see of the infamous Skeleton Coast. This is a bleak coastline and after several hours of driving most visitors will get the picture, there is little variation in the scenery all the way to An-

---

Martin Luther – the steam ox

Just out of town beside a clump of palm trees on the Windhoek road stands one of Swakopmund's most famous historical monuments, a rusty old steam engine known as "Martin Luther". In 1896 a First Lieutenant Edmund Troost of the Imperial Schutztruppe on a trip back to Germany came across a mobile steam engine at the engineering works in Halberstadt. Aware of the heavy losses suffered by the ox wagons he saw this new machine as the answer to Swakopmund's problems. He was so sure of the idea that he paid for the steam engine out of his own pocket and arranged for its transportation from Hamburg to Swakopmund. But when the ship arrived in Swakopmund the offloading equipment could not cope with the 280 cwt iron machine, so the boat proceeded to Walvis Bay where the engine was successfully landed. Troost was forced to leave the machine at the harbour for 4 months because of his military obligations elsewhere. When he finally returned to Walvis Bay he found that the engineer he had retained to drive the steam engine had left and returned home when his initial 5 month contract had expired.

The first attempt to drive the steam engine to Swakopmund was undertaken by an American who it quickly became apparent knew little about such machines. But the going was very tough, the machine continually got stuck in the sand, by the time a Boer completed the journey for Troost a further 3 months had elapsed. The whole venture was never that successful, apart from the problems of weight the machine also consumed vast amounts of water and there was no one able to carry out regular maintenance and repairs. In all about 30,000 lbs of freight were transported inland; two trips were made to Heigamchab and several journeys to Nonidas, the first source of water inland. In 1897 the engine broke down where it stands today and Troost was forced to give up his venture. Fortunately by now the government in Germany had released funds for the construction of a railway.

One of the most frequent stories you will come across in Swakopmund is how the steam engine got its name. The tale goes that shortly after it had ground to a halt a Dr Max Rhode is reputed to have said during a meeting at the Bismarck Hotel: "Did you know that the steam ox is called 'Martin Luther' now because it can also say – 'here I stand; I cannot do otherwise'?" The original statement was made by the German reformer, Martin Luther, in 1521 in front of the German parliament in Worms.

gola. See page 214 for information on the coast N of Swakopmund. Another popular excursion is to follow the **Welwitschia Plains** drive in the Namib section of the Namib-Naukluft National Park. The full route is about 135 km long and can be covered in 4-5 hrs, however if you take a picnic this can be turned into a pleasant leisurely day trip. Follow the B2 out of town for the airport and Windhoek, take a right turn on to the C28 signposted for Windhoek via the Bosua Pass. **NB** Permits for the Namib Desert and Welwitschia Plains must be purchased in advance from the Min of Environment & Tourism, Bismarck St, see below for full details.

One of the more interesting ways of enjoying the desert landscape is to ride on a camel. 12 km from the town centre, off the B2, is a **Camel Farm**, T 400363. Rides can be organized every afternoon between 1400-1700, advance notice advised. As you drive out to the farm there is a large pipeline visible to the right of the main road, this is the water supply for Swakopmund; the pipe supplies over 11.5 million cubic metres a year, most of the water comes from the Omaruru and Kuiseb rivers.

Every Fri morning (0800-1200), a tour to **Rössing Uranium Mine** leaves from by the *Schweizerhaus Hotel*. Bookings must be made in advance at the Swakopmund museum, N$10 for adults. While this is undoubtedly a fascinating glimpse into a major mining operation, like everything associated with the nuclear industry there is a sense of 'look how good and safe we are'. Even if this is the case, the giant scar on the landscape could never be passed off as environmentally sound. Recommended if you are free on a Fri.

Tours

While there are plenty of tour companies to choose from in Swakopmund and Walvis Bay there is little variation in the destinations on offer, below is a brief summary of the most popular sights, details for many of the locations are described elsewhere in the text, particularly those in Damaraland, the Namib desert and the Skeleton Coast National Park. The value of joining a tour depends upon the quality of your guide and which off-road locations you are taken to. If you have already hired a car then trips to Cape Cross, Walvis Bay and Spitzkoppe can easily be done under your own steam. The prices shown here are only intended as a guide, small groups may be asked to pay a little more. **NB** Although many companies still advertise trips to Sandwich Harbour it is unlikely they will run it. The road is very difficult and most of the birds have gone, the lagoon has been filled with sand and should no longer be considered as an attraction. A good place to see flamingos are the fresh water pools inland from Walvis Bay close to the dairy-farm and the saltworks N of Swakopmund.

Town tours of Swakopmund are only worth going on if you don't have your own vehicle or find it too hot to walk around. Many of the most interesting buildings are only a short walk from the hotels and restaurants. Many of these buildings are not open to the public (N$50). The Namib desert tour is one of the most worthwhile trips on offer, while many of the companies no longer go into the national park you will still get to see all of the desert sights. Most tours criss-cross the country to the N of the Swakop River, here you will drive through the amazing moon landscape, be introduced to many of the unusual plants which manage to survive in this arid environment and see some spectacular rock formations, some desert tours include a visit to Goanikontes spring (N$165). Tours to Cape Cross Seal Reserve involve a lot of driving and limited sight seeing, the landscape is typical of much of the skeleton coast, but after a while it becomes very repetitive. The outing should include a stop at the saltworks, a good location for birds (see above) and the fishing resort – Henties Bay. Total distance, 250 km (N$160). A variation on the full desert tour will combine a visit to Walvis Bay (there is little of interest here) with a visit to the impressive dunes which line the road between Swakopmund and Walvis Bay. (N$125). If you have no plans to travel in Damaraland then a tour to Spitzkoppe should be considered. This is a long day trip and you can expect to spend a lot of time in the vehicle, over 400 km are driven. The tour will start by driving up the coast as far as Henties Bay before turning inland towards the mountains. Around the Spitzkoppe are a number of interesting rock paintings. Some companies will include a visit to a small mineral mine where you can buy semi-precious stones. This and the desert tour are probably the two most interesting outings on offer (N$170).

Local information
● Accommodation

Swakopmund has a wide choice of rooms covering all budgets. There are several points worth bearing in mind when choosing your room; many of the establishments are run by the minority German speaking community, if you are not from Germany as well as presentable you may not feel that welcome; the smaller establishments will only serve breakfast; during the peak Christmas period everywhere is booked months in advance, during the busiest periods many places lose their friendly touch and you tend to feel like a number that is being processed as quickly as possible. You will only experience good service and facilities in the large hotels.

AL-A *Swakopmund & Entertainment Centre* (known locally as the Entertainment Centre), PO Box 616, Bahnhof St, T 400800, F 400801, 90 a/c rm, light and airy rooms with M-TV, the split level restaurant has a limited à la carte menu but the buffets are of the highest standard, heated swimming pool, shops, an excellent hotel that caters primarily for international visitors, the service here is of a higher standard than the Windhoek hotels, the only drawback is the hotel bar (a gloomy back room) which has been positioned away from

all the guest rooms, currently the management open a temporary bar in the reception area in the evenings – hopefully in the future the right sort of bar will be created as befits a hotel of this standard, the casino and amusement arcade tend to appeal more to the Swakopmund residents than any of the guests at the hotel, the front building is the original railway station built in 1901, look at the old photographs to see where the trains used to pull up, by far the best of the three principal hotels in town, rec; **A-B** *Hansa*, PO Box 44, 3 Roon St, T 400311, F 402732, until the old railway station was converted this was for many years the top hotel in town, 55 rm arranged around a garden courtyard with palm trees, restaurant has good selection, bar, spacious and comfortable guest lounge, a smoothly run hotel in the centre of town which has recently been refurbished in parts, rec; **A-B** *Strand*, PO Box 20, on the beach front close to the lighthouse, T 400315, F 404942, 45 rm, restaurant, a shady terrace bar serves light lunches, popular family holiday hotel, the only hotel right on the beach with ocean views.

B *Garni Adler*, PO Box 1497, 3 Strand St, T 405045, F 404206, 14 rm, TV, breakfast room, but no evening meals, residents bar, indoor heated swimming pool and sauna, private and sheltered sun deck on the roof, a very clean and neat hotel, secure off-street parking, the new fisheries building has partly spoilt the location but this remains a pleasant and peaceful location, popular with German tour groups, but rec outside busy periods; **B** *Schweizerhaus*, PO Box 445, 1 Bismarck St, T 400331, F 405850, 24 rm on the first floor, some with ocean views, short beds, clean and spacious rooms, bath and shower, TV, rooms on the inside overlook a courtyard which is also an aviary for parrots, unfortunately this means the balconies are not very clean, restaurant, private residents bar in the back garden, while this is a fully fledged hotel the reception area doubles up as the popular *Café Anton*, it is a bit strange checking in with all your baggage while everyone is enjoying coffee and cakes, a good value hotel still under family management, helpful and friendly young staff, rec; **B-C** *Europa Hof*, PO Box 1333, 39 Bismarck St, T 405898, F 402391, 35 rm, cool but gloomy restaurant with a menu anyone from Germany will feel at home with, secure off-street parking, popular with organized tour groups, the whole building looks totally out of place in

Swakopmund, the timber frame and flower boxes would not seem out of place in the Alps.

C *Atlanta*, PO Box 456, Roon St, T 402360, F 405649, 10 rm, en suite bathroom and TV, good restaurant, Fagin's bar is a lively local drinking haunt, secure parking; **C** *Brigadoon*, PO Box 1930, 16 Ludwig Koch St, T 406064, F 464195, 3 comfortable self contained cot-

tages with small garden overlooking Palm Beach, ideal for a family or visitors wishing to avoid hotels, secure parking, a short walk from the museum and post office, run by the friendly Bruce and Bubble from Scotland, a very pleasant change to all things German, rec; **C** *Haus Garnison*, 4 Garnison St, T 404456, F 405246, holiday apartments suitable for anyone considering a longer stay, secure parking,

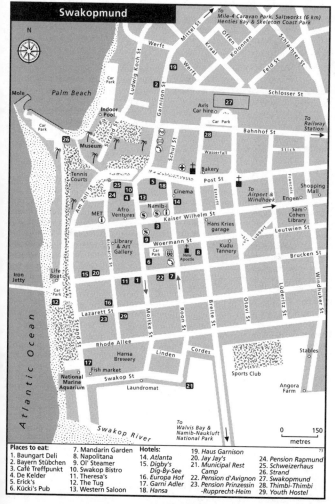

Swakopmund

To Mile-4 Caravan Park, Saltworks (6 km) Henties Bay & Skeleton Coast Park

To Railway Station

To Airport & Windhoek

To Walvis Bay & Namib-Naukluft National Park

Atlantic Ocean

Swakop River

0   150
metres

Places to eat:		Hotels:	
1. Baungart Deli	7. Mandarin Garden	14. *Atlanta*	19. *Haus Garnison*	24. *Pension Rapmund*
2. Bayern Stübchen	8. Napolitana	15. *Digby's*	20. *Jay Jay's*	25. *Schweizerhaus*
3. Café Treffpunkt	9. Ol' Steamer	*Dig-By-See*	21. *Municipal Rest*	26. *Strand*
4. De Kelder	10. Swakop Bistro	16. *Europa Hof*	*Camp*	27. *Swakopmund*
5. Erick's	11. Theresa's	17. *Garni Adler*	22. *Pension d'Avignon*	28. *Thimbi-Thimbi*
6. Kücki's Pub	12. The Tug	18. *Hansa*	23. *Pension Prinzessin*	29. *Youth Hostel*
	13. Western Saloon		*-Rupprecht-Heim*	

Lappiesdorp – Tent City on the Beach

In 1947 the municipality set aside an area, close to the present day Municipal Bungalow Park, as a temporary campsite with 10 tents to cope with the large number of holidaymakers. This proved to be a great success and the following year 50 tents were erected on the site which became known as "Lappiesdorp". In 1949 the site had swollen to 400 tents occupied by an estimated 2,000 people. Each year the council was faced with the same problem of providing enough accommodation for the Christmas influx of holidaymakers. In 1952 the council built the first small bungalows (which are still in use today); by 1972 more than 200 bungalows had been built, ranging from luxury self catering units to the basic of shelters. The camp continues to be very popular, particularly since most hotels in Swakopmund are too expensive for the average Namibian. Just below the camp is the sandy bed of the Swakop River, the original concrete pillars from the first railway bridge can still be seen leaning in all directions after being washed away by the great flood in 1932.

will be fully booked during peak periods, but competitive rates might be negotiated during the slack season; **C** *Pension Prinzessin-Rupprecht-Heim*, PO Box 124, 15 Lazarett St, T 402231, F 402019, 20 rm some with shared bathroom, a quiet and somewhat staid pension, good value for anyone on a medium budget, off-street parking and a sheltered garden at the back; **C** *Pension Rapmund*, PO Box 425, 6 Bismarck St, T 402035, F 404524, 25 rm, breakfast available but no restaurant, one of the most welcoming and friendly pensions, often full, call in advance, rec; **C** *Seagull*, PO Box 1162, 60 Strand St, T/F 405287, B&B, 3 double rm with en suite bathroom and TV, lounge, self-catering facilities also available, short walk from the shops and beach; **C-D** *Digby's Dig-By-See*, PO Box 1530, 4 Brücken St, T 404130, F 404170, 12 rm, chintzy breakfast room, across the road is a 2 bedroom, self-catering flat, lounge with TV, kitchen, ideal for anyone on a long trip looking for a change from hotels and campsites, run by Stella and Manfred.

D *Pension D'Avignon*, PO Box 1222, 25 Brücken St, T 405821, F 405542, 10 rm, clean but a little cramped, no restaurant, TV lounge, sheltered swimming pool, visitors from Germany will feel most welcome, for the rest of us look elsewhere; **D-E** *Jay Jay's*, PO Box 835, Brücken St, restaurant, bar with pool table, well established cheapo hotel, the bar can get a bit rough and rowdy, a mix of small rooms and dorm in a old rundown building, short walk from the town centre; **D-F** *Municipal Rest Camp*, Swakop St, T 402807, advance reservations through the municipality, a mix of bungalows which can sleep 2-6 people, the most basic are FISH 2 which have bunk beds, shower, small seating area with a hot plate, thin walls; at the other end of the scale are luxury bungalows with 2 bedrooms, bathroom, lounge/dining area, kitchen with crockery (no glasses or towels provided), the 4 bed bungalows and flats are clean and good value, A-frames have a lot of character; out of season the camp is frequently rec as a good value self-catering setup, the camp is to the left of the main road after crossing the bridge on the Walvis Bay road.

E-F *Youth Hostel*, Lazarett St, in the converted Alte Kaserne (old barracks), dorms, double rooms, camping, communal washing facilities, off-street parking in a sheltered courtyard with a small patch of lawn and some shade, only open for young people, 15-30 years.

F *Alternative Space*, PO Box 1388, 46 Dr Alfons Weber St, T/F 402713, small dorms, twin attic alcoves, kitchen, laundry, free pickup, quiet location on the outskirts of town beyond the palm trees leading out towards the airport, a long walk from the town centre but a good new establishment, very friendly; **F** *Thimbi-Thimbi*, 13 Bahnhof St, T 402449, converted modern bungalow, 3 rm each with 4 beds, pool room, small garden, convenient for shops and restaurants, the standard budget option, next to a lively café.

● **Places to eat**

Most of the major hotels have attached restaurants but after several meals their menus can seem a little limited, Swakopmund has the best choice of restaurants in Namibia outside of Windhoek. Check opening times, quite a few will be closed Sun or Mon evenings.

Baungart Deli, Brücken St, a welcome but an unusual sight in southern Africa, a health food shop, if you have suffered a diet of meat with meat for several weeks this shop will seem like paradise, let's hope it survives, rec for all things fresh and green; *Bayern Stübchen*, Garnison St, popular amongst those looking for the traditional German meal, excellent food, but not everyone's cup of tea; *Café Anton*, Bismarck St, a very popular bakery in the lobby of the *Schweizerhaus Hotel*, a good range of cakes and pastries to takeaway, rec; *De Kelder*, 11 Moltke St, T 402433, closed Sun, steaks, seafood with a couple of vegetarian choices, set back from the road in an arcade, uninspiring interior; *Erick's*, Post St, dull tiled interior but a vibrant seafood restaurant during the season, closed Sun; *Kücki's Pub*, Moltke St, have a drink and make up your own mind, good food but it's all down to where you want to spend the evening; *Mandarin Garden*, Roon St, T 402081, reasonable Chinese food which makes a pleasant change to the range of dishes on offer elsewhere; *Napolitana*, 32 Breite St, T 402773, good value pizza, pasta dishes and some TexMex, delivery service, popular and rec for anyone on a budget; *The Ol' Steamer*, Moltke St, T 404806, standard Namibian selection, steaks, fish dishes and German fare, OK for lunch but there are more exciting menus in town, separate bar; *Platform One*, Bahnhof St, this is the *Swakopmund Hotel* restaurant, a smart room which has been decorated with railway memorabilia, the Sun eve buffet is to be rec, plenty of fresh seafood and a wide selection of meat dishes, booking is only necessary during the busy Christmas period, good attentive service; *Putensen Café Treffpunkt*, Kaiser Wilhelm St, coffee, cakes, bit of a time warp; *Swakopmund Bistro*, Moltke St, popular young persons café with small street terrace, sports bar upstairs, *The Kalabash*; *The Tug*, Strand St, by the iron jetty, cool beers, a great sunset and ocean view, what more do you want, come here, relax and enjoy the break, good seafood, sister restaurant to *The Raft* in Walvis Bay, rec; *Theresa's*, Brücken St, cheap fast foods, chips, burgers and pies, good value; *Western Saloon*, 8 Moltke St, the name sums up the interior, the seafood is good and so are the steaks, easy-going medium priced restaurant.

● **Banks & money changers**

All the main banks have an office in the centre of town, they all have 24-hr ATMs. Avoid payday at the end of each month, it can be chaos in small branches.

Commercial Bank of Namibia, Kaiser Wilhelm St; **First National Bank**, Moltke St, **Windhoek Bank**, Kaiser Wilhelm St.

● **Post & telecommunications**

The **Main Post Office** is in Garnison St next to the police station. Open Mon-Fri, 0830-1300, 1400-1630, Sat 0900-1200. Outside the post office are some public telephones and a booth selling phone cards, this is the cheapest place to make international calls from. Faxes can be sent from 55 Kaiser Wilhelm St, but this service is only available Mon-Fri, 0830-1300.

● **Shopping**

As Namibia's principal domestic resort Swakopmund has a particularly good selection of shops selling tourist items, not all of these are as tacky as you might imagine; there are some excellent cloth shops and some interesting art studios. It may seem a strange item to buy on holiday but the locally made kudu shoes from the *Swakopmund Tannery*, 7 Leutwien St, are highly regarded and will last for many years, the factory shop also stocks handbags and smaller leather goods.

Desert Gems, Roon St, opp the *Hansa Hotel* for anyone interested in buying gem stones, polished or in their natural state; *Karakulia*, NDC Craft Centre, good selection of karakul rugs and wall hangings, some of the finest Namibian products to take back home, all of a high standard; *Peter's Antiques*, 24 Moltke St, a must for anyone interested in German colonial history, excellent collection of Africana books; *Safariland*, Kaiser Wilhelm St, large selection of smart safari clothes and T-shirts, not cheap, but the quality is excellent.

● **Sports**

Fishing: the coastline either side of Swakopmund is famous for its superb fishing. Many of the local cars seem to have a set of rods permanently attached to the roof. Check at the MET office for details of the strict regulations which control angling. Fishing trips are run by several operators, see below for details.

Golf: Rossmund golf course has 18 holes with grass greens, palm trees and shrubs add to the character. There is a restaurant in the club house, golf clubs can be hired, T 405644. Avoid trying to play a round in the heat of the day.

Horse riding: Okakambe Trails, 11 km from town centre, follow the B2 towards the airport, take a right turn, D1901, the stables are close to the camel farm, T 404747, 405258, a variety of day, half-day or longer rides are possible, if you are an experienced rider this is one of the most pleasant ways to explore the amazing desert landscape, good fun, rec, overnight rooms available.

Skydiving: the local club meet at the airport at weekends, lessons are available, ask for a contact number at the tourist office. **NB** In 1996 there were several fatal accidents in Namibia (not in Swakopmund), if you are experienced check all the equipment closely.

Swimming: there is an indoor heated pool next to the museum, Strand St, closed during the middle of the day. Within the complex is the *Swakop Hydro*, T 402866, a fully equipped health centre with a sauna, steam bath, aromatherapy and a range of beauty treatments.

● **Tourist offices**

Ministry of Environment & Tourism, Bismarck St. Open Mon-Fri, 0800-1700. A helpful office whose principal role is to issue permits for visits to the Skeleton Coast National Park (Torra and Terrace Bay), the Namib-Naukluft desert and to receive payment for MET campsites. The office can provide a little local information, but the Namib-i office is the best source for specific tourist information. When this office is closed permits can be issued from **Hans Kries** garage, Kaiser Wilhelm St or **CWV Service Station** and **Sud-West Service Station** in Walvis Bay. There is no excuse for not having a permit if stopped. The desert is well patrolled by MET staff, make sure you observe all the regulations and respect the fragility of the local environment. Do not litter, and that includes cigarettes. **Namib-i**, PO Box 1236, T 402224, F 405101, corner of Roon and Kaiser Wilhelm sts, a well run office, Elizabeth is very helpful, in addition to local tourist information covering accommodation and tour operators you will find **Air Namibia**, T 405123, have a desk here where you can confirm and purchase tickets.

● **Tour companies & travel agents**

All of the companies in Swakopmund, Walvis

Bay and Henties Bay offer a selection of similar tours. It will always pay to shop around and ask fellow guests at your hotel whether they might recommend anyone. Prices do vary, but then so to does the quality of the guide, the maximum group size, the comfort of the vehicle and the quality of any food and drink that might be included in the tour price. Prices range from N$130-250 pp for day tours.

Before you make your choice find out how many people will be in the group and what their nationalities are, a mixed language group will get far less out of their guide – it can get very hot in the middle of the day, this is not the time to find yourself squashed in the back of a Land Rover with an awkward view. If the tour you wish to go on is not being run on the day that suits your timetable don't be persuaded into joining another tour, check with another company, there is plenty of choice. Finally if you are not happy with the tour inform the local tourist office, some companies are not yet accustomed to providing the level of service and value that international visitors expect.

Afro Ventures, PO Box 1772, Hertzog Berlin Bldg, 14a Kaiser Wilhelm St, T 463812, F 400216, one of the most professional operators on the coast, friendly and helpful, rec; **Charly's Safaris**, PO Box 1400, 11 Kaiser Wilhelm St, a well established operator who we found to be off-hand and dismissive during our research, being placed on a tour with a group of Germans showed a complete lack of thought for the customer and also meant the guide had to repeat everything twice, the least impressive of the companies we visited in Swakopmund; **Desert Adventure Safaris**, PO Box 1428, Roon St, T/F 404072, slightly cheaper than other companies, longer tours for small groups can be put together to suit your needs; **Desert Explorers**, PO Box 456, Roon St, T 406096, F 405649, located in the *Atlanta Hotel* building, this is for the young, local tours with a difference, on 'Quad bikes', helmets and goggles provided, good fun, but what are 'environment friendly riding methods'; **Namibia Photo Tours**, PO Box 442, 8 Roon St, T/F 404561, fishing trips as well as sightseeing; **Namibia Safari Trails**, PO Box 1946, T 404158, F 406098, local day tours (6 hrs), longer trips to Brandberg or Kuiseb Canyon; **Pleasure Flights & Safaris**, PO Box 537, T/F 404500, strongly rec if you wish to appreciate the Namibian landscape from the air, flights as far S as Lüderitz possible; **West Coast**

Angling & Tours, Otavi St, your first port of call for keen fishermen.

● Transport

30 km to Walvis Bay; 395 km to Windhoek; 76 km Henties Bay; 120 km to Cape Cross.

Air Air Namibia, T 405123, have regular flights between Swakopmund and other regional centres in Namibia. The airport is a small room with some seats and toilets, there is a public telephone and boxes to deposit hired car keys at the end of your trip. These flights are rarely fully booked, but if the plane has a lot of baggage it will take fewer passengers to keep to a safe weight. If you have not arranged to collect a hire car on your arrival make sure you arrange with your hotel to collect you from the airport. The local taxis do not make a habit of going to the airport to meet each flight. The local Avis representatives may give you a lift into town, assuming they are meeting the flight. If it looks as if you are stranded, walk to the main road and you should not have to wait long for a welcome lift into town. The walk into town is too far in the heat, even without luggage.

Lüderitz, 75 mins: Tues, Thur, Sat, 1115; Sun, 1215 (this is the slow flight to Cape Town: Windhoek-Swakopmund-Lüderitz-Oranjemund-Cape Town; with stops the journey takes 6 hrs, compared to 2 hrs for the direct flight. Having said that this route takes you over some magnificent scenery which is crying for identification from the crew, sadly only a couple of pilots describe the prominent features). **Windhoek-Eros**, 45 mins: Wed, Fri, 1505, 1715; Mon, Sun, 1505.

Road Car hire: all the major companies have an office in Swakopmund, staff will meet flights at the airport where you will be able to pick up your car. **Avis**, Bahnhof St, T 402527, in the Entertainment Centre. **Into Namibia**, 1 Moltke St, T 464157, F 464158, 4WD and organized tours; **Kessler 4WD**, Kaiser Wilhelm St, T 404118, F 404117. **Coach**: **Intercape**, coaches drop passengers off by *The Talk*, Roon St, this is a café with an attached information service, it is also a convenient place to make telephone calls from. **Windhoek** (4 hrs), via Karibib and Okahandja: Mon, Wed, Fri, Sun, 1215. **Taxi**: there are a couple of local services, this is the safest and easiest way to get to Walvis Bay for a look around. **Raiwin Call Car**, T cell 081 1281289 (0700-2100), expect to pay N$100 for a lift to Walvis Bay.

Train The railway station is on the desert side of Nordring St; reservations, T 643538. If time is not an issue then the service between Windhoek and Swakopmund/Walvis Bay is a comfortable alternative to the long distance coach. But note, Namibian railway must rate as one of the slowest services in Africa. In Apr 1997 a new luxury service was introduced – *The Desert Express*, the train and whole service has been modelled around existing luxury services in South Africa. **Windhoek** (10 hrs): check-in 1300, Mon, Wed and Sat. The service arrives in Windhoek at 1000 the next morning. **Tsumeb** (16 hrs): Tues, Thur, Sun, 1830 (via Omaruru and Otavi); **Walvis Bay** (80 mins): daily except Sat, 0540; **Windhoek** (9½ hrs): daily except Sat, 2035.

SOUTH OF SWAKOPMUND

Cross the river by the only bridge S of town, before Walvis Bay was returned to Namibia there was a immigration control on the far side of the river, from here it is a good tar road to Walvis Bay. At certain times of day this is quite an atmospheric drive, giant sand dunes on your left, the Atlantic Ocean on the right. Midway between the towns is the **C-E** *Langstraat Resort*, Pvt Bag X5017, a popular holiday centre with plenty of facilities for children.

Just before you reach the outskirts of Walvis Bay look out for a large wooden platform in the sea. This is known as **Bird Island** and was built to provide a nesting site for seabirds from which man could collect guano. Still in use today the platform can yield close on 1,000 tonnes in a single year. There are always plenty of sea birds to watch in the vicinity.

WALVIS BAY

(*STD Code* 064) Compared with Swakopmund the port of Walvis Bay has far less to offer the overseas visitor, but for residents it is popular amongst those keen on fishing and boating. There are a couple of comfortable hotels and a limited selection of shops. Unless you have a particular reason for staying here it is more practical to visit Walvis Bay on a day trip from Swakopmund. Much of the town is a grid of characterless modern buildings. If it had not been for two colonial powers seeking to gain a foothold on this remote coastline it is likely that only one town would have flourished here.

History

The first known European to visit Walvis Bay was **Bartholomeu Dias** who entered the bay on 8 December 1487 in his flagship, the *Sao Christovao*, while searching for the tip of Africa and a possible sea route to Asia. He named the sheltered lagoon the *Golfo de Santa Maria de Conceicao*. The bay was one of the finest natural harbours along a barren coast, it

had been formed by the flood waters of the Kuiseb River, before the natural silt load blocked the delta. The modern town of Walvis Bay is located on the edge of this deep water bay and tidal lagoon. An 18 km long sandspit forms a natural breakwater against the Atlantic Ocean. The tip of the spit is marked by an automatic lighthouse and known as Pelican Point, where the spit joins the mainland to the S of Walvis Bay is a shallow lagoon famous for its superb variety of birdlife. A total of 45,000 ha are now protected as a nature reserve. Back in 1487 it was not the birdlife that was of interest to the Portuguese sailors, it was the shelter from the ocean, but when they landed and found there to be no surface fresh water Dias named the area the Sands of Hell. This was not the wealthy country they were seeking to trade with and so they pushed on further south.

The name Walvis Bay is a distortion originating from the 16th century Portuguese maps which showed the bay as **Bahia das Bahleas**, bay of whales. In 1487 Bartholomeu Dias and his crew had taken note of the abundance of fish in the coastal waters. When the first chart of the area was drawn up Bartholomeu Dias had called the area around the bay, **Praia dos Sardinha**, the coast of sardines. During the 17th century the British and American ships frequented the area in search of whale meat and seals, from time to time they used the natural harbours at Walvis Bay and Sandwich Bay but there were no attempts made to explore the interior. Eventually the Dutch in Cape Town decided to investigate the hinterland, prompted by the rumours of great cattle and copper wealth. On 26 February 1793 Captain F Duminy in the ship *Meermin* landed and annexed the 'Bahia das Bahleas', renaming it Walvis Bay. But the land remained in Dutch hands for only a few years; in 1795 the British occupied the Cape and Captain Alexander travelled up the coast to Walvis Bay, where he hoisted the British flag.

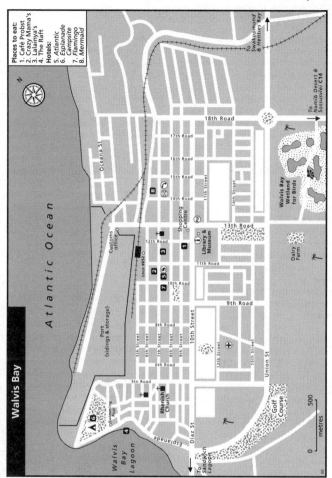

Places to eat:
1. Café Probst
2. Crazy Mama's
3. Lalainya's
4. The Raft

Hotels:
5. Atlantic
6. Esplanade Campsite
7. Flamingo
8. Mermaid

The growth of the settlement was very slow, a few traders made the epic journey from Cape Town and some missionaries passed through for the Rhenish Missionary Society. Up until the time that the Germans started to develop Swakopmund the small community at Walvis Bay prospered on the cattle trade, and copper from Matchless Mine. As noted in the Swakopmund section the coast at this time was linked with the interior by a road known as the '**Baaiweg**', built by the local leader Jan Jonker in 1844. Most of the early traffic consisted of ox wagons.

During the 1870s there was a lot of unrest in the interior and the British government in the Cape was asked to intervene; however true to their interests the British concluded that the lands were too poor to make it worth their while to add the territory to the British Empire. Instead it was decided to consolidate their position at Walvis Bay and hopefully by controlling the movement of goods and people to the interior they might be able to influence or even control the events inland. On 12 March 1878 Commander RC Dyer formally annexed the area, the boundaries were described as follows: "on the south by a line from a point on the coast 15 miles south of Pelican Point to Scheppmansdorf; on the east by a line from Scheppmansdorf to the Rooibank, including the Plateau, and thence to 10 miles inland from the mouth of the Swakop River; on the north by the last 10 miles of the course of the said Swakop River". Rooibank had been included since it was the closest place where there was fresh water and greenery, the rest of the 750 sq km enclave was desert.

For the next 50 years the fortunes of Walvis Bay were influenced by the development of the German colony of South West Africa; as Swakopmund grew and prospered so the amount of traffic using Walvis Bay declined. The outbreak of WW1 was to change everything for good. Once the South African troops had built the broad gauge railway the port was quick to develop, in 1927 a newly dredged harbour was opened by the Earl of Athlone, Governor-General of South Africa. At the same time a new source of fresh water was discovered in the bed of the Kuiseb River, which helped guarantees the future of the town.

At the end of WW1 Walvis Bay was given to South Africa as part of the mandated territory of South West Africa, to govern. This remained the case until 1977 when South Africa declared Walvis Bay to be part of the Cape province. Despite pressure from the United Nations South Africa refused to give up the small enclave, it had become an important port and economic centre for South Africa. For several years after Namibian independence the territory remained as South Africa and there were border and custom controls along the main roads to Swakopmund and the interior. In 1992 South Africa relented and agreed to a joint administration without any border controls; on 28 February 1994 South Africa gave Walvis Bay back to Namibia. The port represents a great asset for Namibia which if properly developed and well managed can challenge ports such as Durban and Maputo for trade destined for countries such as Zimbabwe, Botswana, Zambia and even Malawi. It is for this reason that Namibia is investing heavily in upgrading the road through the Caprivi Strip and the road across the Kalahari via Gobabis into Botswana.

Places of interest

Despite its long history the town has surprisingly few old buildings, for most visitors the attractions here are in the sea, not on the land. The earliest building in Walvis Bay is the **Rhenish Mission Church**, 5th Rd, a small structure surrounded by modern private homes. It was made in Hamburg as a prefabricated kit in 1879, in 1880 the wooden building was erected on the water front. As the harbour grew in importance it was decided to move the church to its present site. Once it had been reassembled the wooden walls were plastered to help prevent wood rot. The last service was held here in 1966.

On the inland side of the town is a small **Bird Sanctuary** built around several fresh water ponds. If you follow 13th Rd inland, take a left by the signpost close to the dairy farm. The track climbs over a couple of dunes before you reach a hide on stilts overlooking two pools. There are often flamingos and pelicans to be seen here. If you follow the road past another pool you will join the main surfaced road to the airport.

Other minor attractions include

The amazing Benguela Current

The Benguela Current plays a very important role in contributing to the well being of Namibia. As already noted in the piece on the economy, the fishing sector provided 22% of all exports in 1994 and remains a large source of employment in the private sector. In addition to providing the ideal conditions for fish to breed in, the cold waters of the current cool the air over the ocean, which when it comes into contact with the hot dry desert air produces a mist. As this mist drifts inland it brings moisture to a desert which otherwise would be almost completely devoid of life.

The fish equation is quite simple; the ocean current is rich in nitrogen which supports an excess of plankton, the plankton is the favourite diet of whales and pelagic fish such as pilchards and anchovies, which live in giant shoals. The abundance of fish attracts seabirds, seals and man.

Dune 7, on the outskirts of town, C14, the highest dune in the area. A small picnic site has been set up amongst some palm trees. The best time of the day to visit the dune is close to sunset, not only are the views spectacular, but the sand is not so hot for walking on.

Local information
● **Accommodation**

B-C *Atlantic*, PO Box 46, 7th Ave, T 202811, F 205063, 18 rm, restaurant has a good reputation, bar, the principal hotel in town.

C *Flamingo*, PO Box 30, corner of 7th St and 10th Ave, T 203011, F 204097, tidy but plain rooms, average setup with a rowdy bar at the weekend; **C** *Levo*, PO Box 1860, T/F 207555, guesthouse and self-catering chalets with sea views, a well run small establishment, rec for anyone interested in fishing, a full range of fishing trips and cruises can be organized from here; **C-D** *Esplanade Bungalows*, Pvt Bag 5017, T 206145, self-catering bungalows suitable for 5-7 people, simple but clean, TV, close to the sea, good value accommodation provided by the municipality.

D *The Courtyard*, PO Box 2416, 16 3rd Rd, T 206252, F 207271, 17 rm, indoor swimming pool, no restaurant; **D** *Mermaid*, PO Box 1763, T 206212, F 206211, a real downtown establishment, cheap but not that secure, popular amongst sailors looking for fun.

● **Places to eat**

Café Probst, 9th St and 12th Rd, very popular German bakery, rec for light lunches and snacks; *Crazy Mama's*, good value steaks, pizza and seafood, popular in some circles;

Hickory Creek, 140 9th St, T 6427990, part of the Spur chain, solid South African fare, always good value, filling and friendly service, children well catered for, salad bar, same menu throughout the region; *Lalainya's*, 7th St, the smart place to eat in town, rec if you are looking to eat good seafood with a choice of good wines; *The Raft*, T 204877, a newly opened restaurant which has quickly gained a good reputation, probably the best place to eat, definitely the best location, rec.

● **Tour companies & travel agents**

Inshore Safaris, PO Box 2444, 12th Rd, T 202609, F 202198, a flexible outfit happy to tailor the tour to suit your timetable and budget; *Levo*, PO Box 1860, T 207555, quality fishing tours, fish from boats or remote beach locations, deep sea trips also available; *Mola Mola Safaris*, PO Box 980, T 205511, F 207593, daily boat trips for fishing enthusiasts or birders.

● **Tourist offices**

The tourist office is located in the large Civic Centre, 12th and 10th sts, worth a visit if you are looking for holiday accommodation and to find out about the state of the road leading down to Sandwich Harbour, at the time of writing this was closed due to high tides washing away segments.

● **Transport**

30 km to Swakopmund; 389 km to Windhoek.

Local Car hire: **Budget**, T 204624, F 202931; **Imperial**, T 207391.

Air There is an airport at Rooikop, 10 km E of town off the C14. There are direct flights to Windhoek, Johannesburg and Cape Town. **SA Express** fly from South Africa.

Air Namibia, T (064) 203102, F 202928, **Cape Town**, (2 hrs): Mon, 1230; Wed, 1145; Fri, 1130; Sun, 1200. **Windhoek** (45 mins): Mon, 1745; Tues, 1615; Fri, 1850; Sun, 1815.

Train T 208504. If you are not in a hurry there is an overnight train service to Windhoek. This train is a useful way of returning to Swakopmund if you have been visiting Walvis Bay on a day trip without your own vehicle. **Tsumeb** via Usakos and Otjiwarongo (16 hrs): Tues, Thur, Sun, 1700; **Windhoek** (11 hrs): daily except Sat, 1850. The journey time to Swakopmund is just over an hour.

Road Coach: **Dolphin Express**, T 204118, a cheap daily service to Windhoek; **Intercape**, luxury service to Windhoek via Swakopmund. **Windhoek** (4 hrs): Mon, Wed, Fri, Sun, 1200.

NORTH OF SWAKOPMUND – THE SKELETON COAST

HENTIES BAY

(*STD Code* 064) The settlement is named after Major Hentie van der Merwe who started fishing here in 1929. It is the most northerly settlement of any note on the Namibian Atlantic seaboard. For much of the year it is just a quiet collection of bungalows on a windswept, bleak coast, and then during the season it is overwhelmed with 10,000 plus visitors. The majority of people come here to fish; international visitors will find little of interest here, but if you are looking for solitude then this is the place. The rock lobsters are reputed to be some of the best in the world.

● **Accommodation** Most of the accommodation consists of holiday flats and apartments which get booked months in advance over the peak Christmas period. For the remainder of the year there should be no difficulty in finding somewhere to stay unless you happen to coincide with a fishing tournament or festival. **C** *Hotel de Duine*, PO Box 1, T 500001, F 500724, 20 rm with TV and en suite bathroom, restaurant known for its good seafood, bar with slot machines, odd shape pool tables, swimming pool, squash court, recently refurbished, clear views across Atlantic from its high perch, close to the beach and golf course, the last comfortable hotel N of Swakopmund on the coast; **D** *Eagle Holiday Flats*, PO Box 20, 175 Jakkelsputz Rd, T 500032, F 500299, white washed self-catering flats, clean with tiled floors, TV, a bit stark, part of the Eagle Centre complex where there is a supermarket, restaurant, bottle store and Total petrol.

● **Shopping** As you approach from Swakopmund look out for a petrol station on the left just before a right turn to Usakos.

● **Post & telecommunications** Beyond the petrol station is the **Post Office** on the corner of Pelican St. A left here will take you to the seafront.

● **Sports Golf**: opp the *Hotel de Duine* is a dramatic golf course with grass greens set in a valley leading down to the beach. A round here will test your ability to cope with windy conditions.

● **Useful services** Just beyond the Usakos turning, on the right, is the **Namib-i** tourism office, housed in a new brick building. The police station is just behind the building. The first main road to the left after the tourist office is called Duineweg, this leads to the main hotel in the town. As you turn left look out for Benguella St on the left, this leads to all the shops in Henties Bay.

ROUTES Driving out of Henties Bay there are three different routes to explore, assuming that you have approached from Swakopmund. The easiest route to follow is the **D1918** inland, this road passes close to the **Klein Spitzkoppe** (1,572m) and **Gross Spitzkoppe** (1,784m) before joining the **B2** near **Usakos**. The other two routes will take you into some of Namibia's finest wilderness areas. Just N of the village the **C35** turns E into the heart of **Damaraland**, this is the road to **Uis** and the **Brandberg** (2,573m). Finally you can follow the **C34** along the coast, this road will take you as far as you are allowed to self drive in the **Skeleton Coast National Park** – the government run camp at **Terrace Bay**, which is 273 km from Henties Bay. En route you will pass the camps at Mile 108 and Torra Bay.

Unless you are just visiting **Cape Cross** for the day it is advisable to be self-sufficient if you continue to drive N along the coast. Make sure you fill up with petrol in Henties Bay as well as drinking water and food. As noted above it is possible to drive as far N as Terrace Bay, once you have crossed the **Ugab River** you are in the **Skeleton Coast National Park** (southern section). To travel beyond the Ugab River requires a MET permit from the office in Swakopmund or any other MET office. It is possible to stay at **Torra Bay** and **Terrace Bay**, Terrace Bay is approximately 273 km from Henties Bay, petrol is available here. There are two roads which lead inland from the coast, this is a sparsely populated region and care should be taken when

The Skeleton Coast

Note: Beyond *Seal Beach* is the **Skeleton Coast Wilderness** region. Access to this area is strictly limited. Expensive Fly-In Safaris are operated by a single official concessionaire. The granting of this concession in 1994, for a ten-year period was surrounded with a lot of ill feeling, but this is the ONLY way you can legitimately visit this part of the park. The extreme North is only open for research.

Möwe Bay
Lighthouse
Hoanib
Skeleton Coast Park
4x4 only
Hunkab
Seal Beach
dunes
Terrace Bay
Terrace Bay
D2302
Atlantic 1977
Uniab Delta
To Palm & Sesfontein
Torra Bay
Uniab
Torra Bay
Henrietta 1968
NP gate
Springbokwasser
D2620
Koichab
Montrose II 1973
C34
Salt Pans
C39
Bergsig
Luanda 1969
Toscanini diamond mine
Huab
Atlantic Pride
oil rig
sand dunes
Ambrose Bay
gravel plains
To Twyfelfontein & Khorixas
South West Sea - 1976
Ugab
Park boundary
Durissa Bay
NP gate
hike
Brandberg West
Winston 1970
Salt Pans
D2303
Mile 108
D2342
Messum
Bocock's Bay
Horing Bay
National West Coast Rec Area
Messum Crater
To Khorixas
Seal Reserve
Cape Cross
Cape Cross
Mile 72
C35
Henties Bay
Omaruru
Cape Farilhao
Jakkalspütz
D1918
To Spitzkoppe
C34
lichen fields
Rock Bay
To Windhoek
Mile 14
B2
SWAKOPMUND
Khan
Pelican Point
Rössing Mine
0   30
Walvis Bay
km

driving on these gravel and sand roads, if you have an accident or a breakdown you may have a long wait before the next vehicle comes along. Once you have driven as far as Cape Cross you should be well aware of the possible dangers.

NATIONAL WEST COAST RECREATIONAL AREA

The southern boundary for the recreational area is the northern boundary of the Namib-Naukluft National Park. This is an area of the Skeleton Coast which is protected but not subject to quite the same stringent controls which apply to areas of the Skeleton Coast National Park. The area is open all year round and there are no restrictions on when you can travel through here. For most visitors the only area of interest is the seal colony at Cape Cross; the rest of the coastline is dull and flat and only attractive to the fishermen. If you are not visiting the Skeleton Coast National Park there is no point travelling beyond Cape Cross. **Accommodation** Between Swakopmund and the National Park there are four campsites managed by the Ministry of Environment and Tourism, MET; **Mile 14**, **Jakkalspütz**, **Mile 72** and **Mile 108**. These are all very basic sites which were designed to serve the needs of the angler more than the holidaymaker. Each site has communal washing facilities, kitchens with gas stoves and sheltered eating areas. Anyone looking for more comfort should stay in Swakopmund or try the *Hotel de Duine* in Henties Bay. There are no shops at these sites.

CAPE CROSS SEAL RESERVE

Pick up any tour brochure in Swakopmund and you will see trips to Cape Cross being advertised. There are 23 breeding colonies of **Cape fur seals**, *Arctocephalus pusillus*, along the coast of South Africa and Namibia, this is reputed to be one of the largest and best known. Apart from being the location of an important seal colony the reserve has had an interesting history.

Approach The reserve is 55 km N of Henties Bay just off the C34. The entrance gate is 3 km from the junction, a short distance into the reserve is an office.

Background In 1485 the Portuguese navigator, Diego Co landed at Cape Cross. This was the furthest any European had so far reached down the coast of Africa. To mark the event Diego Co erected a stone cross on the isolated stoney headland; he inscribed the following words on the cross: 'Since the creation of the world 6,684 years have passed and since the birth of Christ, 1,484 years and so the Illustrious Don John has ordered this pillar to be erected here by Diego Co, his knight'.

Diego Co died at Cape Cross and was buried in some high ground close by, his original cross was later removed and taken to Berlin by the Oceanographical Museum. In 1974 the whole area was landscaped and a couple of replica crosses now stand amongst the rocks.

As you walk to the shoreline from the office you pass a small graveyard which dates from the turn of the century. Between 1899-1903 there was a small thriving community at Cape Cross which was involved in the collection of guano from nearby islands in a salt pan. The records show that 124 people died and were buried here. Around 1900 this was a busy little port which was even served by a railway. The guano industry was so prosperous that a 16 km railway track was laid across the salt pan to facilitate the collection of guano. In its heyday there were steam locomotives working here.

The Seals Estimates as to the number of seals here vary between 80,000 and as many as 200,000 during the breeding season (Nov/Dec). The bulls start to arrive here in Oct to claim the land for their cows. The whole scene during the birth of the young pups can be quite disturbing. Many of the newly born seals get crushed by adults, others drown and then there is always the threat posed by jackals and Hyaenas. The colony is located just beyond the crosses.

Information The seal reserve is open from 1000-1700, daily. The only facilities here are some toilets and fresh drinking water. The closest accommodation is just to the S at Mile 72.

About 33 km N of Cape Cross the salt road divides in two; the salt road, **C34**, continues to follow the coastline towards the campsite at '**Mile 108**', while the side road, **D2303**, turns inland and heads towards the Brandberg Wes Copper Mine. This road is heavily corrugated and best driven in a 4WD. As you approach the entrance gate to the Skeleton Coast National Park there is a signpost for the wreck – Winston, a fishing boat. Do not drive on the salt pans, despite their dry appearance, it is easy to get stuck here. Visitors with the correct permit can drive on into the national park.

A pleasant alternative to visiting the Skeleton Coast is to join the **Ugab River Hike**. Every month on the second and fourth Tues a guided hike starts from Ugabmund. The full hike is 50 km long and lasts for almost 3 days. This is a very interesting way of learning about the environment and life on the Skeleton Coast. The hike only runs between the months of Apr and Oct. It is limited to a maximum of 8 people and costs N\$150 per head. Hikers must bring and carry all their own food and bedding for the duration. As with the Fish River Canyon hike a medical certificate must be handed over to the trails officer. The hike follows the river inland before looping through some hills where there are some caves and natural springs. If your timing is right this is a walk worth joining.

SKELETON COAST NATIONAL PARK

The Atlantic coast between Swakopmund and the Kunene River along Namibia's border with Angola has proved to be a great hazard to shipping over the years, this is the region known as the Skeleton Coast. The term was first used in 1933 by a newspaperman, Sam Davis, who was reporting on the search for a Swiss airman, Carl Nauer, whose plane had disappeared along the coast while trying to break the Cape Town to London solo air record. No trace was ever found, but the term stuck. Today it is the elements that were responsible for so much loss of life – the desert, wide open space, isolation and solitude – that attract the majority of visitors to the coast. The Skeleton Coast is one of the finest and most unusual coastal wildernesses in the world. *Best time to visit*: the park is open all the year round, but the camp at Torra Bay is only open for Dec and Jan. During the Christmas period both Torra Bay and Terrace Bay get quickly booked up, mostly by local fishermen. As in Swakopmund it never gets too hot thanks to the cooling influence of the ocean, but during the winter months it can get cold at night.

Approach

The park can be entered in the S, from the West Coast Recreational Area, or it can be reached in the E from Damaraland. Whichever gate you enter by you must make sure there are sufficient hours of daylight to either travel through the park or reach your camp. The southern gate by the Ugab River is known as **Ugabmund**, this is approximately 207 km from Swakopmund, it is a further 162 km to the camp at Terrace Bay. The eastern gate is called **Springbokwasser**, which is 178 km from Khorixas, the quality of the road heading inland is not as good as the coast road. Torra Bay is 50 km from the gate,

Terrace Bay is 98 km from Springbok-wasser gate. Permits are required to travel in the park, and all accommodation must be booked and paid for in advance.

Background

In order to get the maximum out of the park it is worth making the arduous journey as far N as Terrace Bay, assuming there is accommodation available. Driving between Swakopmund and Henties Bay will quickly make you realize how repetitive and dull much of this coastline is, but once you start to get out of the vehicle and start to explore the dry rivers and the occasional salt pans on foot, the park can be enjoyed at a different level. The peace and solitude is amazing, the air is clean and fresh and at night the stars are like you've never seen them before. If this does sound like fun then proceed no further N than Henties Bay, where you can take the C35 and head inland for a different area of Namibia.

Shipwrecks

For many people the Skeleton Coast and shipwrecks go together, just about every photograph promoting the wild coastline will include a rusting, beached, hull. The Portuguese used to call the area the Sands of Hell. Before the days of modern communications and transport this 1,600 km long coastline represented a real threat to shipping. Sailors knew that if they did survive a wrecked ship then their problems had only just begun. The land behind them was a dry desert, and there were very few known natural sources of drinking water. The few places that did occasionally have drinking water (the river beds) were home to wild animals such as lion, leopard and elephant, which in turn represented another threat to the sailors' lives. A third factor that added to the dangers for survivors was the remoteness, before 1893, when the first people were landed at Swakopmund, there was no settlement of note along more than 1,000 km of coastline. Which way did you

head off if you had survived. Unfortunately the most spectacular wrecks are all found in the areas which are closed to the public in the far N. A little background to some of the wrecks has been included in the route description below.

Wildlife

Between Ugabmund and Terrace Bay the coastal road crosses four westward flowing rivers: the Ugab, Huab, Koichab and Uniab; under normal climatic conditions these only flow for a short period each year. For the rest of the year they represent long narrow oases which are home to migratory birds, animals and the few plants that can flourish under drought conditions.

The animals which may be seen in the park have all adapted in different ways to overcome some of the problems the desert creates. The smaller species such as genet, caracal, baboon, springbok, jackal and brown hyaena live in the desert all year round; the larger animals, such as black rhinoceros, elephant and lion tend to migrate along the channels in search of food and water. The lion may well no longer occur along the coast, but when they were roaming the beaches they were known to have fed upon Cape cormorants, seals and the occasional stranded whale. Gemsbok, kudu and zebra are occasionally seen inland in the mountainous regions, while at the coast the Uniab Delta is a good location for viewing gemsbok. During low tide

Genet
Source: Steele, David (1972) *Game sanctuaries of Southern Africa* Howard Timmins: Cape Town. Illustrated by John Perry

Twitching for a Tern

If you are not fishing on the Skeleton Coast there is a high chance you will be looking at the birds which at times seem to be everywhere. It has been estimated that over 300,000 wading birds seasonally visit the Namib coast. Some of the most popular birds are also those that are the easiest to identify: plovers, cormorants, sandpipers, flamingos and white pelicans. But this stretch of coast is also home to one of the rarest and smallest terns found in the world, the Damara tern (*Sterna balaenarum*).

It has been estimated that of the 2,000 breeding pairs left in the world, 1,800 inhabit Namibia; the rest are found close by along the coast in South Africa and Angola, where they favour the open coastline and its sandy bays. The Damara tern is only 23 cm long, with a white breast and a black head. In flight it is similar to a swallow. Such a small bird is not able to carry much food for the young so to limit the amount of flying they have to do they tend to nest close to the food supply. Their size also influences the more precise location of their nests. They are unable to defend their nests against jackals and hyenas; so to try and avoid predators they nest on the salt pans and the gravel plains up to 5 km inland. This is another reason for observing the park off-road regulations, once disturbed a breeding pair will abandon the chick.

Black-backed jackals can be seen on the beach scavenging on dead birds, fish and seals. There is stiff competition for scraps, there are the hyaena and ghost crabs along with the crows and the gulls.

While the sighting of an elephant or some kudu would be a great thrill most visitors to the coast are on the lookout for the diverse birdlife. More than 200 bird species have been recorded in the park, this figure includes vagrants which have been blown off course during the winter. Most of the birds live along the coast since there are few areas of wetlands with fresh water. At the seashore look out for sanderling, turnstone, several species of plover as well as cormorants and Arctic terns. Further inland along the river beds you will come across birds which favour gravel plains and cliff faces. Along the Ugab River hiking trail the augur buzzard, peregrine falcon, black eagle and rock kestrel have all been seen; after a little rain the reedbeds are home to a few weavers and warblers.

Vegetation

Like much of the wildlife, most of the plants growing in the park occur in the four major river beds which dissect the park. Two of the most common shrubs are the **dollar bush**, *Zygophyllum stapfii* and **brakspekbos** *Zygophyllum simplex*, both can be found in the river beds; the former is a semi-deciduous shrub with small leaves shaped like a 'dollar' coin. Brakspekbos can be recognized by looking for an off-green carpet in a shallow depression where rainwater would drain. It is eaten by the Black rhinoceros. The dollar bush will only grow where there is some groundwater, it has not adapted to make use of the sea mist.

The only other vegetation you are likely to come across are the amazing variety of lichens. The bright orange lichens which cling to rock outcrops facing the ocean add a welcome splash of colour to the grey landscape. Over a hundred different species have been recorded in the Skeleton Coast National Park, all depend upon the coastal fog for moisture, in the moist air the plants become soft and many change colour.

Park information

To travel N of the Ugab River you must

have a permit; entry permits are available from the MET office in Bismarck St, Swakopmund. No motorcycles are allowed into the park. You will not be allowed to cross the Ugab River after 1500 or to pass the gate at Springbokwasser after 1700 if heading for Terrace Bay. Each gate can issue a day permit to drive directly through the park, you must enter the park before 1500 to allow sufficient time for the journey; *entrance charge*: adults, N$10 per day, car N$10. Petrol is available at Terrace Bay all year round, and Torra Bay for the 2 months it is open for. There is also a basic groceries store at Terrace Bay. All camps have plenty of freezer space for anglers.

● **Accommodation**
All campsites and rooms have to be booked in advance through the Ministry of Environment and Tourism. There are only two sites within the National Park, **Terrace Bay** and **Torra Bay**, see below for details. Torra Bay is **only open** during Dec and Jan. Accommodation at Terrace Bay is all-inclusive; Torra Bay is a basic campsite, you have to bring everything with you, the water for the showers has to be trucked in.

DURISSA BAY TO TERRACE BAY

The boundary between the National West Coast Recreational Area and the Skeleton Coast National Park is marked by the **Ugab River** which flows into Durissa Bay. The Ugab is one of Namibia's major rivers, it rises over 500 km inland, E of Outjo, after good rains it is an important source of water in Damaraland. A giant skull and crossbones adorns the gate by the Ugabmund park office. If you are staying in the park you must produce your booking permit at the office. **NB** This gate closes at 1500 each day for traffic going as far as Terrace Bay or Springbokwasser. If you are staying at *Mile 108* you can go into the park at a later time so long as you return to Ugabmund by sunset.

As you cross the wide river notice the variety of trees and shrubs growing in the sandy bed. Some of the well established plants are stunted since they have had to survive in windswept conditions with long periods of moisture stress. Whenever you approach these river beds try to be as quiet as possible since there is always a chance of seeing a small herd of springbok resting in the shade or a shy family of kudu browsing the acacia trees.

Once across the river the salt road stays close to shore, one of the first shipwrecks you see is the *South West Sea*, wrecked in 1976. Just after you have crossed the **Huab River** there is a signpost indicating an **old oil rig**. While you will see the remains of various mining ventures along the coast, this is the only case of oil exploration. In the 1960s Ben du Preez went ahead and erected the rig despite numerous warnings that the scheme was unlikely to succeed. Today the rusty rig lies on its side providing the perfect nesting place for a breeding colony of Cape Cormorants. Between Sep and Mar visitors are asked to stay in the car park so as not to disturb the birds during the breeding season. On the beach you can visit the wreck of the fishing schooner, *Atlantic Pride*.

50 km from the park entrance you reach the point marked Toscanini on most maps. This is the site of a derelict **diamond-mine**, only a few small diamonds were ever found. Today the legacy of the operations are a few cement slabs which acted as foundations for the buildings and the ruins of the sorting plant. There are a couple more wrecks in the ocean here, but there is little to see.

Soon after crossing the Koichab River, which has more sand than vegetation, there is a junction in the road. This is the only other access road for the Skeleton Coast Park, C39, a right here leads inland to **Springbokwasser** gate 40 km. There are some fine sand dunes along this stretch of road as well as some *welwitschia* plants growing in the dry river beds.

Continuing N on the salt road you reach the seasonal fishing resort, **Torra Bay**. In the 16th century Portuguese sailors named it Dark Hill after the dark capped hills which they could see while they were looking for fresh water. These days there is a very simple, **F** *Campsite* at Torra Bay, managed by the MET. This site is only open for Dec and Jan. Anyone planning on staying here must be totally self-sufficient, during the holiday season petrol and a few basic groceries are also available. Aside from the solitude the great attraction for this site is the excellent fishing. During the few months the camp is open it is necessary to book a pitch if you plan on spending a night here. Despite restrictions on where to fish and drive there has been extensive damage caused by vehicles on the beaches.

Between the temporary camp at Torra Bay and the permanent camp at Terrace Bay is one of the most interesting attractions in the southern part of the Skeleton Coast National Park, the **Uniab River Delta**. The river has split into five main channels plus a number of reed ringed pools which are formed by seepage from the river bed. After good rains this is the perfect spot for birders. There are a number of walks in the delta, including a trail to a waterfall and a small canyon, which lie between the road and the beach. Check with the park's authorities what the situation here is from year to year since the amount of rainfall and the size of the flood can change the lay of the land between seasons. But if you hear there is water here then it is well worth the drive. Within the delta are several hides and parking spaces, each with a different view of the system. Look out for the shipwreck, *Atlantic*, at the river mouth.

Having enjoyed the delta it is a short drive to the final destination, **Terrace Bay**. The camp and all the outbuildings were once part of the mining operation owned by Ben du Preez, when the company was declared bankrupt the state inherited all the facilities at the camp. **Accommodation** here consists of **B** *Bungalows* with en suite facilities, the price includes all 3 meals. There is also a grocery shop and petrol available. The camp is built next to an old mine dump. There is an airfield to the N of the complex. Visitors to the park are allowed to drive a further 14 km along the coast to Seal Beach, this is the absolute northern limit for private visitors. At this point you are over 380 km from Swakopmund in the heart of the Skeleton Coast National Park.

SKELETON COAST WILDERNESS

A recurrent theme when reading about Namibia's desert from Oranjemund to the Angolan border, is the emphasis placed upon how fragile the desert environment is, and the need to control man's access to the most sensitive areas. When the Skeleton Coast National Park was proclaimed in 1967 the park was divided into two zones, each one about 800,000 ha in extent. The southern zone is the 210 km long coastal strip between the Ugab River in the S and the Hoanib River to the N. The boundary of the park extends no more than 40 km inland. Details of the attractions and access to this zone are related above. Access to the northern zone is tightly controlled, and for the tourist, limited to those who join the exclusive Fly-In Safaris which are organized by the sole concessionaire in Windhoek.

The northern section of the park extends from the Hoanib River (although tourists are only permitted to travel 14 km N from Terrace Bay camp, as far as Seal Beach), to the Kunene River, which forms the border with Angola – a distance of about 290 km. This section of the National Park is managed as a wilderness area and is sometimes referred to as the **Skeleton Coast Wilderness**. While the government has chosen to allow a private operator access to this wilderness there are still tight controls in place on how the operation must be run, in order to guarantee a minimum of environmental impact with each tour group. In addition to the regulations most of the area is also off limits to the concession holder. Access to the northern section is limited to the area between the Hoarusib and Nadas rivers, a strip of coastline measuring about 90 km long and 30 km wide.

Information As noted above there is only one company which holds the rights to organize Fly-In Safaris to the wilderness areas of the Skeleton Coast. This is not to say that other operators do not try to sell their own version of a Skeleton Coast safari. A typical 'alternative' safari might fly you into a private camp in the Huab Valley, visit Terrace Bay for the morning and then fly on to a camp in Kaokoland near the Kunene River before returning to Windhoek. On such a trip you will certainly get to see plenty of the Skeleton Coast as well as the remote NE, but you will have not set foot in the wilderness areas where only a thousand or so visitors go each year. The cost of such a 4-day trip would be in the region of US$1,700 pp.

Official tours *Olympia Reisen*, PO Box 5017, Windhoek, T (061) 262395, 218672. Their quoted cost for 1997, for a 3 nights/4 days tour with a minimum of 4 people is N$7,000, full board. You are flown into a camp on the Khumib River, stay in small pre-fab huts using solar heated showers. In such a small group you are able to choose which activities interest you most; there are a variety of locations along the coast where there are further seal colonies, shipwrecks as well as magnificent landscapes and the solitude. This is the Namibia which has been frequently used to promote the country as a tourist destination, ironically little more than a thousand people get to enjoy it each year.

As noted on the Skeleton Coast map all is not well with the awarding of the concession, many local tour operators refuse to deal with *Olympia Reisen*; a variety of reasons are cited, from the way in which they won the contract to the manner in which the tours are now being conducted. Perhaps the greatest crime of all is that rules designed to protect and preserve the Skeleton Coast wilderness are not doing so, and man's impact in the region is being far greater and visible than planned. Ask around before you go on one of the official tours, during our research we were frequently told bad things, but then this may all have just been professional jealousy.

THE HINTERLAND

ROUTES There are several possible routes one can take between Windhoek and Swakopmund/Walvis Bay. The most straightforward is to take the main B2 via Okahandja, Karibib and Usakos, which will take between 3 and 4 hrs. More interesting however is to take one of the three passes, the Bosua, Ushoogte or Gamsberg. Of the three the Bosua is probably the quickest and provides the opportunity to stop and see the ruins of **Liebig Haus** and **Von François Fort**, whilst the Gamsberg is certainly the most dramatic.

All three routes are gravel roads without any garages or other amenities on the way; furthermore they are all extremely steep and if there have been heavy rain may present some difficulties to low-slung saloon cars. Having said that it is definitely worth taking one of the passes either to or from the coast to enjoy the spectacular views.

The Khomas Hochland is the rugged, upland area, lying between 1,750m and 2,000m, which joins the central highland plateau with the escarpment, where the land falls dramatically away to the gravel plains of the central Namib. The surface of the Hochland was laid down in Karoo times some 180-300 million years ago and subsequent erosion has carved out the sharp ridges and rolling hills characteristic of the area.

Bosua Pass

Following the C28 out of Windhoek past Daan Viljoen Game Park, the tar road

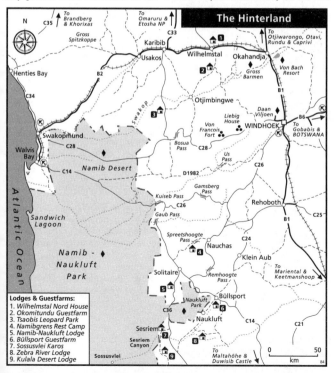

Lodges & Guestfarms:
1. *Wilhelmstal Nord House*
2. *Okomitundu Guestfarm*
3. *Tsaobis Leopard Park*
4. *Namibgrens Rest Camp*
5. *Namib-Naukluft Lodge*
6. *Büllsport Guestfarm*
7. *Sossusvlei Karos*
8. *Zebra River Lodge*
9. *Kulala Desert Lodge*

turns to gravel passing the first landmark, the **Matchless Mine**. Archaeological evidence suggests that copper mining and smelting was taking place in the Khomas Hochland area some 200-300 years ago, although commercial exploitation of the copper reserves only started in 1856.

The first manager of the mine, run by the Walvis Bay Mining Company, was Charles John Andersson (see page 226). In 1860 the mine was closed down for the first time, reopened briefly but without success in 1902 by the Deutsche Kolonialgesellschaft, and then reopened for the third time between 1970 and 1983 by the Tsumeb Corporation Limited (TCL). The collapse of world copper prices during the 1980s once more forced the closure of the mine which is now abandoned and closed to the public.

16 km further down the road is the abandoned **Liebig House**, built in 1912 for Dr R Hartig, director of the Deutsche Farmgesellschaft. This double storey house must once have been a splendid place to live, with its fountain in the main downstairs room and fine views over the surrounding rolling highlands. A little further on lie the ruins of **Von François Fort** named after the 'founder' of Windhoek (see Windhoek introduction, page 83). The fort was one of a number of military outposts built after Von François established his headquarters in Windhoek, and was designed to protect the route between Windhoek and Swakopmund. It was, however, later turned into a **Trockenposten** or 'drying-out post' for alcoholic German soldiers!

The pass itself is a 1:5 descent down to the gravel plains of the Namib and is not suitable for trailers or caravans. After this the road heads straight through the Namib on a long, straight stretch before reaching Swakopmund.

Ushoogte Pass

Take the main road towards the University of Namibia (UNAM) and ignore the turn-off S towards Rehoboth. Continue straight on past the University out of town on the C26 until the road branches right onto the D1982. This road continues down towards the 1:10 Ushoogte Pass before eventually joining the main C14 highway to Walvis Bay.

Gamsberg Pass

Probably the most popular of the three passes, the Gamsberg is sometimes called Namibia's Garden Route. The name is a mixture of the Nama word *gan* meaning 'closed' or 'shut' and the German *berg* meaning 'mountain', and refers to the flat-topped Gamsberg mountain which dominates the view. This 1,000 million year old granite mountain rises 500m above the surrounding highlands and has survived further erosion, thanks to a sandstone cap formed about 200 million years ago when most of this area was covered by an inland sea.

It is worth stopping at the top of the pass to enjoy the views of the surrounding hills and to contemplate the snaking descent the pass makes towards the desert floor.

Before reaching the Namib, however, the road must still make its way through the Kuiseb Pass (see Kuiseb Canyon Namnauk, page 232) after which it joins the C14 for the final 110 km stretch to Walvis Bay.

USAKOS

(*STD code* 064) The first town E of the Namib desert on the main B2 route from Swakopmund, Usakos lies on the southern bank of the Khan River on the edge of the Namib, overlooking a vast expanse of nothingness. The town originally developed around the railway workshops which were built to service the narrow-gauge Otavi line completed in 1906. Until 1960 the town prospered but when the old steam locomotives were replaced by diesel engines it relapsed into its present sleepy state.

Nowadays the town's main role is one

of service centre to the cars, buses and trucks plying their way to and from Swakopmund and Walvis Bay. Although there is a small hotel in town there doesn't seem any reason to stay here.

Places of interest

Locomotive no 40, which stands in front of the railway station, is one of three Henschel steam trains built in Germany for her colony's narrow gauge railway. It stands as a reminder of the town's heyday.

Local information
● **Accommodation**

D *Usakos Hotel*, T 064 530259, F 064 530267, 10 clean double en suite rooms, half with a/c, off-street parking, restaurant, the only place to stay in town.

● **Places to eat**

There is a takeaway at the Shell garage as you enter town from the Windhoek side, it also has limited tourist information. On the way out of town towards Swakopmund there are a couple of other small takeaways.

● **Bank & money changers**

The only bank in town is **First National**.

● **Hospitals & medical services**

The *State Hospital*, T 530067, is located just outside town on the Okombahe Rd.

● **Transport**

211 km to Windhoek; 147 km to Swakopmund.

Train Swakopmund (3¹⁄₄ hrs), Mon, Wed, Fri 2255, daily except Sat 0155; **Windhoek**, via Okahandja (6 hrs), daily except Sat, 0045; Tsumeb (11¹⁄₂ hrs), via Otjiwarongo, Tues, Thur, Sun, 2155.

ERONGO MOUNTAINS

The Erongo Massif, towering granite mountains, stands about 40 km N of Usakos and Karibib, and like the **Brandberg** and **Spitzkoppe** inselberg (see page 188) is the remnant of an ancient volcano. Although most of the range is only accessible with 4WD, it is possible to visit the **Ameib Ranch**, and get a first hand taste of the mountains and some rather interesting rock formations there. A further attraction is the **Phillip's Cave** National

Monument, containing a number of bushmen paintings first made famous by the prehistorian Abbé Breuil (see page 188).

● **Accommodation** Guestfarms: **C-E** *Ameib Ranch*, T 06228 (farmline) 1111, F 061 235742, 8 en suite double rooms, 2 cottages, 3 chalets, pleasant gardens, small dip pool, restaurant and bar, Rest Camp with 4 bungalows and camping facilities, communal ablution block, braai facilities, water hole close to main house, good bird-viewing, rec.

Animal Sanctuary Bears more resemblance to a small private zoo than a sanctuary and houses cheetahs, elephants, zebra, bat-eared foxes, jackals and warthogs.

Phillips Cave After a short drive from the main house a 20-30 min walk over a series of low hills takes hikers up to the cave. This is in fact an overhang on one of the highest hills in the area and offers, excellent views over surrounding countryside, making it easy to see why bushmen used this place. There are numerous paintings of the bushmen themselves, as well as buffalo and the famous white elephant.

Bull's Party and Elephant Head Both sites have interesting rock formations, in particular the 'balancing' rocks at the Bull's Head.

Approach At Usakos turn onto D1935 towards Okombahe, after 12 km turn right onto D1937 to the farmhouse.

KARIBIB

(*STD code* 064) This tiny bustling town lies almost exactly half-way between Windhoek and Swakopmund on the main B2 highway, and although most people zip through on their way to and from the coast, there is more to the town than first meets the eye. There are a number of fine old colonial buildings on the main street, the **Navachab Gold Mine** just S of town and the **Marmorwerke** or marble works lying to the N of the town.

Places of interest

In the early years of the century the train between Windhoek and Swakopmund only travelled during the daytime, and so passengers needed hotels for the overnight stop in Karibib. The present day **bakery**, on the left hand side coming from Okahandja, was one of these hotels and survived until 1950 when it was converted into a bakery.

The Rösemann Building, a little further down the road was built in 1900 and the façade has remained virtually unchanged since. Originally the headquarters of the trading firm Rösemann and Kronewitter, it was later converted into a hotel. The **granite building** further down the street, looking a bit like a church, was in fact used by a local merchant, George Woll, as both shop and living quarters. The **Christuskirche**, made partially of marble from the nearby marble works dates back to 1910.

The **Marmorwerke** close to town was started in 1904 and produces high quality marble, considered to be the hardest in the world. About 100 tonnes of marble is quarried each month and this is first cut up into smaller blocks and then processed into floor and bathroom tiles, ornaments and tombstones. It is hard to believe but marble from Karibib is exported to Italy – the words 'coals' and 'Newcastle' spring to mind.

The **Navachab Gold Mine** lying SW of town was started in 1987 2 years after gold was discovered on Navachab Farm. The gold is actually of quite low quality requiring 750,000 tonnes of rock to be processed each year.

Local information
● **Accommodation**

D *Hotel Erongoblick*, T 064 550009, 15 double rooms, 11 en suite, swimming pool, squash court, sauna, restaurant, off-street parking in this former boarding school, Sundowner drives to a private game ranch arranged, rec; **D** *Hotel Stroblhof*, T/F 064 550081, 11 double rooms, 6 en suite, swimming pool, restaurant, off-street parking.

Guestfarms: **B** *Albrechtshöhe Guestfarm*, T/F 0621 503363, 5 en suite double rooms in this turn of the century fort, restaurant, swimming pool, game drives, hiking and hunting; **C** *Etusis Lodge*, T 0628 1603, F 061 223994, en suite thatched bungalows and bush tents, restaurant, bar, swimming pool, waterhole. **Approach**: 36 km from Karibib, follow the signs from town.

● **Places to eat**
Choice is fairly limited and apart from the 2 hotels, the other options are *Springbok Steakhouse* and the *Karibib Bakery & Café*.

● **Banks & money changers**
First National Bank which has a cash dispenser and **Standard Bank** which does not, are both located on the one main street.

● **Tourist offices**
There is a small tourist office in the **Wolfgang Henckert Centre** which is the place to ask about tours to the goldmine and marble quarry.

● **Transport**
175 km to Swakopmund; 181 km to Windhoek.

Train Windhoek (4½ hrs), via Okahandja, daily except Sat; Swakopmund (7 hrs), daily except Sat.

Road **Bus**: *Intercape*, bus stops by the *Stroblhof Hotel*: **Swakopmund** and **Walvis Bay** (3 hrs), Mon, Wed, Fri, Sat, 0900; **Windhoek** (2 hrs), Mon, Wed, Fri, Sun, 1500.

OTJIMBINGWE

Once the administrative centre of German South West Africa, now a forgotten, dusty village in the bush, Otjimbingwe is situated S of Karibib at the junction of the Swakop and Omusema rivers. Opinions on the origins of the name of the town differ, however the most common meaning given is 'place of refreshment', referring to the spring in the Omusema River.

The town rose to prominence due to its position on an established ox-wagon route halfway between Windhoek and Walvis Bay. A mission station was established here in 1849 by the Rhenish Missionary Johannes Rath, although it was not until 1867 that the first church was

Deutsch-Südwestafrika. **OTJIMBINGWE.**

One of the original German administration buildings at Otjimbingwe

built. However, it was Otjimbingwe's role as a trading post that made it an important centre.

In 1854 the Walvisch Bay Mining Company had made the settlement its headquarters after the discovery of copper in the area. A trading post was set up and soon a roaring trade – typical of the time – was going on in arms, ammunition, alcohol and livestock. In 1860 the hunter, explorer and trader Charles John Andersson (see page 226) established his headquarters here, the first permanent trading post in the area. His subsequent involvement in the Herero-Nama wars to defend his trade routes was significant in drawing the small European population into Namibian tribal conflict, and further focused attention on Otjimbingwe.

However, after Curt von François moved his small garrison to Windhoek in 1890, the town started to decline, and following the construction of the narrow gauge railway between Windhoek and Swakopmund in 1902 which bypassed the town, Otjimbingwe became increasingly irrelevant. A few historical monuments do still make the town of interest to students of 19th century Namibian history.

Places of interest The **church**, completed in 1867, is the oldest to have been built to serve the Herero community and although Herero leader Zeraua was not himself a Christian he arranged for 10,000 bricks to be made for the church. As with other early mission stations, the church doubled both as place of worship and mini-fort during the on-off Herero-Nama wars of the time. The tower was only added later in 1899.

The **old powder magazine**, an 8m tower, was originally built by the *Missionhandelgesellschaft* or mission station trading company, to protect its goods during attacks by the Nama, but following the collapse of the company in 1882, the tower passed into the hands of the Hälbich trading firm.

The **wind motor** was put up in 1896 by the Hälbich family in order to generate power for their machinery in the wagon factory next door. The motor also pumped water to the settlement from a nearby fountain.

Approach 55 km S of Karibib on the D1953.

● **Accommodation Guestfarms**: **D** *Tsaobis Leopard Nature Park*, T 0662252 1304,

10 2-bed self-catering bungalows, swimming pool, hiking trails, game viewing, established as a leopard sanctuary in 1969, offers good hiking in rugged bush country with the chance of seeing the elusive leopard in its natural habitat.

OMARURU

(*STD code* 064) The C33 tar road heads due N from just outside Karibib and 48 km later arrives at the small historical town of Omaruru. Set in the heart of game farm country, the town is surrounded by an impressive array of mountains, the most prominent being the *Oruwe* or Omaruru koppie SE of town.

History

The area around the town has been home both to humans and game for thousands of years, evident from the numerous sites of bushmen art found here. Following in the footsteps of the Bushmen were the Damara and then the Herero who were probably grazing their cattle here from early in the 19th century. In fact, the name Omaruru is derived from the Herero *omaere omaruru* meaning 'bitter curd' which is apparently how the cattle's milk tasted after eating one particular local bush.

The first European to reach the area was the missionary Hugo Hahn on a visit to Omburo, E of Omaruru, in 1851. In 1867 the evangelist Daniel Cloete arrived with a group of Damara, however due to drought, they left the following year. In 1868 Herero Chief Zeraua settled down here but it was only after another missionary, Gottlieb Viehe, arrived in 1870 that the town was 'officially' founded.

In 1858 Charles Andersson, attracted by the area's plentiful game, established a hunting camp on the banks of the Omaruru River. Later, in 1870 the hunter Axel Eriksson and brewer Anders Ohissen formed a partnership to exploit the game and by 1880 they had succeeded in wiping out all the elephants, rhinos, lions and giraffes that had once lived in the area.

Throughout the 1880s Omaruru was a focal point for the continuing Herero-Nama battles, and was attacked repeatedly before peace was finally secured in 1889. As part of the consolidation of German rule in Namibia, a garrison was stationed here at the end of 1894, and following this the town took on a more permanent status and started to grow. The first postal agency was opened in 1895 and in 1896 the garrison moved into a new fort – today serving as the magistrate's court. By the end of 1896 Omaruru had the largest population of European settlers in Namibia.

However, the great rinderpest epidemic of 1897 wiped out the last remaining game in the area as well as taking a heavy toll on the settlers' cattle and many were forced to leave the area. Nevertheless, the military garrison continued to grow and a new barracks and sick bay were completed by 1901.

In 1904 the Herero rose up against the German occupiers and the town was besieged. At the time the military commander, Captain Franke was away in the S helping to put down the Bondelswart uprising. Nevertheless, he marched 900 km in 20 days and broke the siege by leading a cavalry charge, thereby defeating the Herero. In 1907, to commemorate Franke's victory, work began on the **Franke Tower**, which was officially opened the following year.

In 1909 the town received full municipal status and over the course of this century continued to steadily grow. Today, Omaruru is a sleepy little town in the heart of guestfarm country.

Places of interest

Franke Tower is on the southern bank of the Omaruru River on the corner of Monument St. The tower was declared a

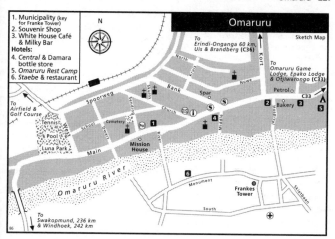

1. Municipality (key for Franke Tower)
2. Souvenir Shop
3. White House Café & Milky Bar
Hotels:
4. Central & Damara bottle store
5. Omaruru Rest Camp
6. Staebe & restaurant

Omaruru
Sketch Map

To Erindi-Onganga 60 km, Uis & Brandberg (C36)

To Omaruru Game Lodge, Epako Lodge & Otjiwarongo (C33)

To Airfield & Golf Course

To Swakopmund, 236 km & Windhoek, 242 km

Omaruru River

Mission House

Frankes Tower

national monument in 1963 and offers a good view over the town. Usually kept locked, the key is available at either the *Central Hotel* or *Hotel Staebe*. Check the staircase inside: it looks a bit fragile.

The **Old Mission House**, the oldest building in Omaruru, now serves as the town museum, focusing on the early history of the area. Made from clay bricks, the house was built by missionary Gottleib Viehe and completed in 1872, and was where he made the first translation of the gospel into Oshiherero. Later the house also served as a temporary military post and a meeting place between Herero and German leaders. Collect the key from the tourist office at the Municipality building on Main St. The **Omaruru Game Park** is only 800 ha in size, but home to a wide variety of animals and rare birds. It is a well vegetated park with plenty of old large trees and water points. You can expect to see giraffe, zebra, kudu, gemsbok, eland and klipspringer. For the keen birder there are eight species of birds to be seen which only occur in the Erongo region. Day trips to the park are organized by the Omaruru Caravan Park, minimum 4 and maximum 7 people per trip; tours

depart at 1000 and return by 1700. Bring your own packed lunch and drinks. If you have the extra day this is a most enjoyable outing, rec.

Local festivals

Every year on the last weekend before 10 Oct, the Herero hold a march to and from the cemetery where former leader Willhelm Zeraua is buried. Worth a visit if you are in the area.

Local information
● **Accommodation**

D *Central Hotel*, Main St, T 570030, F 570481, 10 double rm, 2 with en suite bathroom, a slightly run down colonial building with a classic shaded veranda, cool rooms, spacious bar decorated with animal skins and trophies, restaurant, swimming pool; **D** *Hotel Staebe*, Monument St, T 570035, F 570450, on the southern side of the river, larger of the 2 hotels with 24 double en suite rooms, nice touch to have a cold water fridge for guest use, phones, large, stark dining room which caters for tour groups, good steak and salad, small bar with draught beer, swimming pool, off-street parking, an immaculate, clean hotel run by an old German couple, 5 mins walk from the Franke Tower, rec.

Camping: **D-F** *Omaruru Caravan Park*, PO Box 400, Main St, T 570516, F 570261, choice of chalets, bungalows and campsites, all with braai facilities, simple, clean ablution block with plenty of hot water, a shady leafy site which is always very clean, new lush lawns, excellent value meals available, the camp has recently been taken over by Errol and Karin McCullogh who have already made good progress in reviving this peaceful site.

● **Places to eat**
Apart from the 2 hotel restaurants the *White House Café* serves breakfast and lunchtime snacks and takeaways, rec.

● **Banks & money changers**
First National Bank, corner of Main and Bank sts; **Standard Bank**, opp First National, corner of Bank St and Main St.

● **Hospitals & medical services**
Doctor: T 570033.

Hospital: *The State Hospital*, T 570037, on South St over the river.

● **Post & telecommunications**
Post Office: corner of Church and Main sts, Mon-Fri 0800-1630, Sat 0800-1130.

● **Shopping**
Souvenir Shop, Main St, open 0900-1700, a very good shop with items from all over Namibia, there is a wide choice of T-shirts.

● **Sports**
Golf: *Club House*, T 570516, 9-hole course with grass greens.

Swimming: the pool next to the tennis club is Olympic size.

● **Tourist offices**
Namib-i, Main St, T 570261, next to the Post Office. The best source of information about the many excellent guestfarms in the area. Here you can find out about facilities, how to get to the farms and the cost. A short visit to this office will greatly enhance your stay in the region.

● **Useful addresses**
Police: nr corner of Sending St and Main St, T 570010.

● **Transport**
242 km to Windhoek; 236 km to Swakopmund.

Train Windhoek (9 hrs) via Okahandja, Mon, Wed, Fri, 2130; Swakopmund (5½ hrs), Mon, Wed, Fri, 2035; Tsumeb (9 hrs), via Otjiwarongo, Tues, Thur, Sun, 0025.

ROCK ART
Anibib Farm is said to have one of the largest collections of rock paintings in Namibia. Covering an area of 2,000 ha are a host of rock paintings depicting both humans and animals, as well as a range of Stone Age tools and jewellery which have been left in their original spots.

There are two guided trips per day intended to give visitors a real insight into the paintings and tools and to ensure the preservation of the sites. Bookings should be made beforehand on T 0662232 (farmline) 1711.

Approach   52m W of Omaruru on D2315, follow signs.

● **Accommodation Guestfarms: A** *Epako Lodge*, T 064 570551/2, F 064 570553, luxurious, well stocked game farm, 25 en suite double rooms, a/c, telephone, mini-bar, excellent French restaurant, swimming pool, game drives, chance to see elephant, rhino, cheetah, leopard and wide range of antelope, rec. **Approach**: 22 km N of Omaruru on C33. **A** *Erongo Lodge*, T 06228 (farmline) 1631, F 064 570017, 5 en suite double rooms, bungalows, swimming pool, mainly a hunting farm, also has rock art in impressive Erongo Massif. **Approach**: 45 km SE of Omaruru – ask for specific directions. **B** *Erindi-Onganga*, T 06532 (farmline) 1202, F 061 224863, 4 en suite double rooms, home cooking, swimming pool, hiking, game drives, donkey cart rides, quiet, low-key guestfarm. **Approach**: take C36 towards Uis and after 6 km turn right onto D2344. After a further 35 km turn onto D2351 and drive for 27 km, following signs to guestfarm. **B-C** *Omaruru Game Lodge*, T 064 570044, F 064 570134, 30 en suite double bedrooms with a/c, 17 self-catering bungalows set in beautiful tree-lined gardens, restaurant, bar, swimming pool, game shelters in stocked game park, expect to see all major antelopes, elephant, zebra, giraffe and maybe leopard, rec. **Approach**: 15 km E of Omaruru on D2329. **Other Guestfarms: B** *Immenhof Hunting & Guestfarm*, T/F 0651 304431, 9 en suite double rooms, swimming pool, game drives, horse riding, hiking trails, hunting; **C** *Schönfeld Guestfarm*, T/F 0651 304571, 8 en suite double rooms, swimming pool, horse riding, game drives, cheetah feed and hunting.

DINOSAUR FOOTPRINTS – OTJIHAENAMAPERERO FARM

During the period 150-200 million years ago the 25m tracks of a 2-legged, 3-toed dinosaur were embedded in the (at the time) soft, red Etjo sandstone. The dinosaur was probably one of the forerunners of modern birds, and much like an ostrich, had powerful hind legs. Declared a National Monument in 1951, the site is well worth a visit. Stop at farmhouse and ask permission first.

Approach 29 km from Kalkveld on D2414.

● **Accommodation Guestfarms**: **A** *Mount Etjo Safari Lodge*, T 0651 4462, F 0651 4035, 13 luxurious en suite double rooms, 14 family rooms, set in gardens around a hippo pool, game drives, escorted game walk, overnight rhino camp on this superbly-stocked game farm, expect to see white and black rhino, lion, leopard, cheetah, elephants and a host of antelope, the lodge was the site for the historic Mount Etjo Declaration supervised by the UN, which effectively ended the bush war and gave birth to a new independent Namibia, all inclusive, rec.

The Namib-Naukluft

FIRST PROCLAIMED in 1907 and progressively enlarged over the years until it reached its present size in 1986, the Namib-Naukluft Park is the largest nature reserve in Africa and covers a vast area of nearly 5 million hectares. Geographically the park is divided into four distinct areas of which three are covered here, the mountainous Naukluft Park area, the gravel plains of the central Namib between the Swakop and Kuiseb rivers and the wandering sand dunes found south of the Kuiseb River incorporating the massive dunes at Sossusvlei.

THE NAMIB DESERT

The Namib desert is a narrow strip of land stretching for 2,000 km N to S and never extending more than 200 km from W to E. Bounded by the cold waters of the South Atlantic Ocean on its W and the escarpment to the E, the Namib passes through three countries, South Africa, Namibia and Angola. This section deals with the area from Walvis Bay S to the dune fields of Sossusvlei.

The Namib is generally believed to be the 'oldest' desert in the world, having enjoyed or endured arid and semi-arid conditions for around 80 million years. This does not mean that the climate has remained static during that period, nor that the dunes are that old. On the contrary the desert itself has been changing as a result of climatic shifts, one of the most significant being the development of the cold Benguela Current, about 5 million years ago, which plays an important part in maintaining the Namib's extremely arid conditions.

The great sand dune fields visible at Sossusvlei are also more 'recent' occurrences, probably having developed after the Benguela Current was formed, and are still migrating N and W in a constant cycle.

Although the common perception of a desert is a hot, dry barren wilderness, the Namib actually has distinct climate zones. Cooled at the coast by the off-shore winds and the cold Benguela current, further inland between an altitude of 300-600m the desert is watered each morning by a rolling fog caused by the cool off-shore air meeting the hot dry air from the land. This fog allows a host of life forms, such as lichens, succulents and small bushes and the insects and animals that feed off them, to exist in an otherwise inhospitable environment.

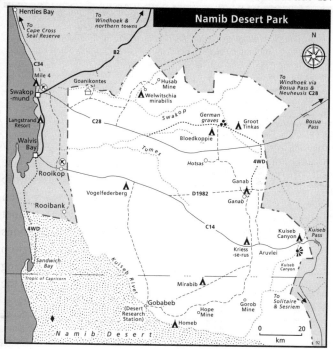

Closer to the escarpment, beyond the reach of the daily fog, the desert is hot and dry, sustaining only the hardiest forms of life. The *gemsbok* for example is specially adapted to these conditions and has an in-built cooling system to keep the blood flowing to its brain cool enough to survive in otherwise intolerable temperatures. *Ground squirrels* position themselves so that their upturned tails serve as sunshades, and a number of species of *beetle* have extra long legs which allow them to 'stilt'. Raising their bodies above the surface of the desert allows them to benefit from cooler air just above ground level. Other insects and animals have developed different strategies to allow them to survive in this environment, some simply retreat below the surface of the desert, either into the dunes themselves or by burrowing into

the desert floor.

The desert is also an archaeological storehouse, abounding in a whole range of stone tools, pieces of pottery or paintings left by the earliest inhabitants of this region. As such they play an important role in informing us how early humans made use of the natural resources of the desert in order to survive. They also beg the question as to *why* did humans spend periods of time in the desert when there was an abundance of better-watered land further inland?

The desert is a fragile environment and both plant and animal species struggle to survive here. Visitors to the desert should therefore be extra-sensitive to this environment and abide by the following rules:

● When driving, stick to existing roads and tracks, as tyre marks can scar the

Nara melons

The Nara melon is endemic to the Namib desert, in particular the Kuiseb River area. A member of the cucumber family, the nara grows in sandy places where its roots are able to burrow deep down into the earth as far as the water table. In order to reduce water loss, the stems of the plant are almost leafless thereby also preventing animals from eating it. The nara is *dioecious* meaning it has separate male and female plants, the male plant which flowers for most of the year provides a ready source of food for one particular species of dune beetle. One crop of the melons, which grow to about 15 cm in diameter, is produced each year in late summer providing food for desert dwellers such as jackals, gerbils, crickets and beetles.

Traditionally the nara has also been a source of food for the *Topnaar* Namas, who have lived around the lower reaches of the Kuiseb River for several centuries. At harvest time the fruit is collected on donkey carts and carried back to camp, where the flesh and seeds are separated from the rind and roasted over a fire. The seeds are then separated from the pulp which can be eaten as it is or dried and eaten at a later date. Archaeological sites in the Namib provide evidence in the form of seeds that the nara melon was an important source of desert food to prehistoric humans.

desert floor for decades. Similarly lichens and other fragile plants which play an important role in the ecology of the desert can be easily destroyed.

● Do not collect any samples of plant or vegetable life from the desert. Take photos or make sketches to keep as souvenirs. Any archaeological objects should also be left where they are.

● When camping in the desert take firewood with you, never collect wood. Even dead-looking trees or bushes will come alive again when it rains.

● Discoveries of fossils or archaeological sites can be sent to the Desert Ecology Research Unit, located at Goabeb at DERU PO Box 1592, Swakopmund. Unfortunately the research unit is not open to the public.

● **Accommodation**
Camping: there are 8 small campsites in the central Namib, all of which need to be booked in advance. Visitors to these campsites need to ensure that they are entirely self-sufficient, taking water and firewood with them. The only other amenities are drop toilets, fireplaces and picnic sites.

Permits
These are not necessary for visitors trav-elling on the main routes through the park. However, those people planning to travel on any of the sign-posted tourist roads, or stay at any of the campsites here, must obtain a permit beforehand. These can be obtained from Central Reservations in Windhoek, Hardap, Sesriem, Lüderitz and the tourist office in Swakopmund. On weekends these permits can be obtained from Hans Kries Service Station and the Namib I office in Swakopmund, and from CWB Service Station and Suidwes Diensstasie in Walvis Bay.

KUISEB CANYON

Background "We stared down in fascination. It was an impressive and intimidating sight, landscape inconceivable under a more temperate sky and in milder latitudes. Barren cliffs fell away steeply into deep ravines all around the main canyon like a wild and gigantic maze. They had a name, the "gramadoelas" and as someone had aptly said, they looked as though the Devil had created them in an idle hour." So wrote Henno Martin, a German geologist, who during WW2 spent 2½ years with his friend Hermann Korn living in the desert in order to avoid internment. His book *The Sheltering Desert* describes their experiences as they struggled to survive in the harsh and unforgiving Namib environment and is well worth reading for anyone interested in the Namib.

The campsite is located by the Kuiseb River bridge in the river course. The river may flood during the rainy season and visitors should check when booking the site.

Approach On the C14 at the bottom of the Kuiseb Pass.

KRIESS-SE-RUS

Named after an early European resident of Swakopmund who was interested in the game in the Namib area, this site is located in a dry water-course surrounded by camel thorn trees. Short walks around the area give visitors access to three typical central Namib habitats, the water-course, calcrete plain and the schist or crystalline rock.

Approach 107 km E of Walvis Bay on the C14.

MIRABIB

This is a granite inselberg rising above the desert floor accommodating two groups at a time. Rocky overhangs offer protection from the sun and carbon dating has revealed that early humans took advantage of this site some 8,500 years ago. There is also evidence of more recent visits by pastoralists about 1,600 years ago. A small water hole, *Zebra Pan* located 35 km SE of here is visited by mountain zebra, ostrich and gemsbok.

Approach Off the C14 in the direction of Gobabeb.

HOMEB

Located on the banks of the Kuiseb River, this campsite is capable of accommodating several parties, offers excellent views of the nearby sand dunes. Although the river only flows when good rains are received in the highland areas W of Wind-

hoek, this site demonstrates the role of the Kuiseb River in preventing the huge dune field S of here from encroaching onto the gravel plains to the N.

Seasonal water from the river and occasional rain means that there is a sufficient supply of underground water to support substantial riverine vegetation and to provide water for animals and humans. The *Topnaar* Namas, one of the groups of original Khoi living in Namibia, have their home at a village at Homeb. Sometimes called the *Naranin* or Nara people due to their close dependence on the nara melon which grows here (see box), most of the Topnaars now look for work in Walvis Bay or Swakopmund.

There is a good chance at Homeb of seeing game such as steenbok, gemsbok and baboons, as well as a fairly large number of birds. In particular look out for birds of prey such as the lappet-faced vulture, black eagle and booted eagles, as well as the noisy red-billed francolin, the well-camouflaged Namaqualand sandgrouse and the attractive swallow-tailed bee-eater.

Approach Turn off C14 towards Zebra Pan and continue on this track as far as the Kuiseb River.

GANAB

This site near a dry water-course is named after the Nama word for the camelthorn trees which are found here. Although rather a dusty site it gives the visitor a good idea of the expanse of the

Gemsbok

Namib desert, and the nearby bore-hole and windmill are an attraction for game. A host of mammals have been spotted here, including gemsbok, springbok and zebra, as well as predators such as spotted hyena, aardwolf, bat-eared fox and caracal.

Approach Turn off the C14 onto the D1982 in the direction of Windhoek.

GROOT TINKAS

Only accessible by 4WD this campsite is often deserted, which may well make it an ideal place to camp in the Namib. The surrounding area is an interesting place for hikes, although the heat means that early morning and late afternoon are the best times to do this. After good summer rains the nearby dam, an unusual site in the middle of the desert, is full of water and attracts both game and birdlife.

Approach Turn N off the C28 from Swakopmund to Windhoek, or N on the small track leading from Ganab.

BLOEDKOPPIE

Close to Groot Tinkas stands the *blood hill* granite inselberg, a popular place to camp in the Namib. The sites on the western side of the hill are very sandy, requiring 4WD to get there. It is well worth exploring the immediate area, not least for the fascinating rock formations found here. Also about 5 km E of the campsite lies the ruin of a German colonial police station and the graves of two policemen which date back to 1895.

Approach 55 km NE of the C28 from Swakopmund.

VOGELFEDEBERG

A smaller inselberg than Bloedkoppie, nevertheless an interesting place to visit, especially after summer rains. Water collects in a number of rock pools which, for a short while, become home to a host of small invertebrates, such as the crab-like *triops*. The development of all these creatures has to be rapid as the water only

African wild cat
Source: Steele, David (1972) *Game sanctuaries of Southern Africa* Howard Timmins: Cape Town. Illustrated by John Perry

remains in the pools for a few weeks. During this brief period the eggs which have been lying waiting for the rain must hatch, the creatures must mature, mate and lay eggs for the next generation to emerge when the rain returns.

South of Vogelfedeberg lie the **Hamilton Mountains**, not officially on the tourist route, but nevertheless an interesting place to go for a hike for those with the energy. This limestone range climbs between 300m and 600m above the Namib plain and benefits from enough fog-water to allow a fascinating range of plants to grow here. In particular look out for blooming succulents following summer rains as well as the occasional lily.

Approach From Walvis Bay take the C14 E for 51 km and then turn off at the sign.

THE NAUKLUFT PARK

Approach

The entrance to the park is 10 km S of Büllsport on the D854 and can be approached from a number of directions. From Windhoek take the B1 S to Rehoboth and then immediately S of the town turn W onto the gravel road C24. This passes the small settlements of Klein Aub and Rietoog (petrol during daylight hours) before gradually descending from the central highlands into the semi-desert around Büllsport. From the coast the C14 passes through the central Namib climbing steeply and tortuously winding through the Kuiseb and Gaub passes past Solitaire to Büllsport. From the S the most direct route is on the C14 out of Maltahöhe.

Background

The park was proclaimed in 1964 as a sanctuary for the Hartmann's mountain zebra before being joined with the Namib Desert Park in 1979 to form the Namib-Naukluft Park. The name Naukluft derives from the narrow *kloof* or gorge on the eastern side of the mountain range. This rugged, mountainous area hides deep ravines, plunging gorges, crystal clear rock pools and a variety of game totally at odds with the desolate surrounding desert. Accessible only on foot or on horseback the Naukluft Park is an ideal place for hiking and has a number of superb trails, ranging from the 10 km Olive Trail to the 120 km 8-day Naukluft Hiking Trail.

Geology

The geological history of the area starts

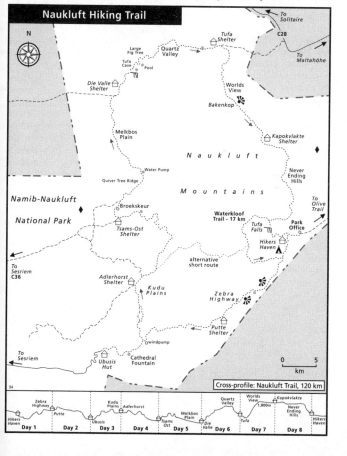

Naukluft Hiking Trail

between 1,000-2,000 million years ago when the base of the mountains was formed by volcanic rocks, granites, and gneisses. Between 750 and 650 million years ago the whole of this part of Namibia was flooded by a shallow tropical sea which formed the next layer of rock – mainly black limestone. The actual mountains themselves were formed between 550 and 500 million years ago during a period of crustal movement when large sheets of sedimentary rock formed and were set in place. These rock sheets give the tops of the Naukluft mountain

War in the Nuakluft Mountains

In 1894 the Naukluft Mountains were the setting for a series of skirmishes and battles between the Nama leader Hendrik Witbooi, and the German Imperial lead by Theodor Leutwein. The outcome of these battles played an important role in the consolidation of German control over Namibia.

In Apr 1893, the German forces, led by Captain Curt von François, had attacked Witbooi's stronghold at Hoornkrans W of Rehoboth, forcing Witbooi and his followers to flee. Signed affidavits by survivors of the attack (Hendrik Witbooi Papers Appendix 3) give a vivid picture of this bloody raid. "A little before sunrise the German soldiers opened fire on us and stormed the place. ... When we heard the firing we ran out of our houses; we had no opportunity of making resistance but fled. ... Houses were set on fire and burned over the bodies of dead women and children."

Following this attack Witbooi pursued a guerrilla war against the Germans, using his superior knowledge of the countryside to harass and outwit the German forces. Finally however, Witbooi was forced to retreat and chose the inaccessible Naukluft Mountains as the last refuge for his followers, including women, children and livestock. The decisive battles of the war took place in the Naukluft between 27 Aug and 5 Sep 1894.

An account of the fighting by German commander Major Leutwein gives an idea of how tough it must have been for both sides to have waged a war in these mountains. "The troops followed the tracks left by the Hottentots' livestock; more often than not, however, it was extremely difficult to discern these tracks on the rocky ground. For this reason, the enemy could be pursued only during the day ... the sun burned down from a cloudless sky, while the temperature dropped to several degrees below zero during the night ... no fires could be lit. ... The troops were exhausted, clothing and shoes in tatters; casualties had reduced their already thin ranks ...".

Despite superiority in arms and ammunition these deprivations prevented the German forces from defeating Witbooi, on the other hand Witbooi was not able to successfully break out of the siege. Eventually, the two sides fought each other to a standstill and on 15 Sep Witbooi signed a conditional surrender which required him and his supporters to return to Gibeon, to accept the paramountcy of the German Empire and the stationing of a German garrison at Gibeon. In return Witbooi retained jurisdiction over his land and people, and the right to keep guns and ammunition.

Concluding his account of the battle in the Naukluft, Leutwein wrote, "The enemy had suffered only minor losses. ... It proved that the Hottentot was far superior to us when it came to marching, enduring deprivation and knowledge of and ability to use the terrain ... it was only in weaponry, courage, perseverance and discipline that the troops surpassed the enemy."

Baboons

Baboons are a common sight on the trails in the park but are a real nuisance around the campsite, where they will steal anything you take your eyes off for a few seconds. Although still wary of people they will hang around a few metres away from your campsite and wait their moment. Their keen sense of smell means that should you leave anything tasty in your tent whilst you are hiking, you are likely to find your tent damaged and the edibles gone by the time you return. Although some visitors may be tempted to offer the odd morsel to vagrant baboons these animals soon become trouble makers around the campsite and consequently have to be shot.

their characteristic nappes or folds. Porous limestone deposits caused by evaporating limestone-rich water are also common all over the range and suggest a much wetter past.

Vegetation
For such a harsh environment the mountains are home to a surprisingly large number of plants and trees. These range from common gravel plain species such as corkwood trees and wild raisin bushes to mountain species such as shepherd's tree, quiver tree and mountain thorn bushes. The deep gorges with their perennial streams are home to a wide range of different species such as sweet thorn and cluster figs which attract large numbers of birds.

Game
The park is home to a host of small mammals, many of them nocturnal and therefore easily missed. These include Cape hare, ground squirrel, badger, and yellow mongoose, as well as the common and easily spotted rock dassies, which make up the bulk of the black eagle's diet. Of the larger mammals, the Naukluft Park is home to the unique Hartmann's mountain zebra which live only in Southern Angola and Namibia. A zebra sub-species, the Hartmann's differ from plains zebras by being about 14 cm taller

and also by virtue of a slightly different pattern of stripes on the lower back. Antelopes such as klipspringers are common and easily spotted as they bounce from rock to rock, as are duiker and steenbok. The mountains with their rocky overhangs, gorges and caves are an ideal home to leopards, shy animals not easily spotted, but nevertheless the most significant predators in the area. Smaller predators like black-backed jackal, bat-eared fox, African wild cats and aard-wolfs are also common in the park, although like many of the smaller animals, most of these are nocturnal and therefore difficult to spot.

Birds
Due to its position between the desert to the W and the highlands to the E, the park lies at the limits of the distribution of a large number of endemic Namibian species. Furthermore the perennial streams in the deep kloofs attracts birds that otherwise would not be found in this environment. Late summer (Feb-Mar) is an excellent time for bird-spotting in the park when species such as the Herero chat, Rüppell's korhan, Monteiro's hornbill, cinnamon-breasted warblers and African black ducks can be seen.

Hiking
Without a doubt some of the most excit-

The Dune Sea

The sand dunes of the Namibia S of the Kuiseb River are sometimes referred to as a **dune sea**. This is because the dunes are not stationary, on the contrary they are ever-moving and ever-changing as the wind blows the sand in different directions.

All the dunes in the Namib are composed of grains of quartz with a few heavy minerals, such as ilmenite, also present. The dunes rest on a base of sand where the so-called 'mega-ripples' are found; these can be as large as 50 cm high and are shaped by the wind. Above this base is the 'dune slope' and then the 'slipface', the area at the top of the dune where the sand is constantly cascading. Try walking up to the top of a dune and you will feel the effects of the slipface as you seem to endlessly climb without ever reaching the top!

Sand dunes come in many shapes and forms and of the most common types are found in the Namib. South of Walvis Bay and close to the coast are the *transverse* dunes, so-called because the axis of the dune lies perpendicular to the strong winds blowing mainly from the S. Around Sossusvlei are found *parabolic* or *multi-cycle* dunes, formed by winds of more or less equal strength blowing from every direction. The third kind, the *parallal linear* dunes are most commonly found in the Homeb area. It is believed that this series of 100m high N-S dunes, which generally lie about 1 km apart, are caused by strong S and E winds which blow at different times of the year. The most mobile dunes, the *barchans* are most visible in the Lüderitz area, especially at the deserted town of Kolmanskop, where the dunes have invaded the abandoned houses.

The distinct, different types of sand found in the Sossusvlei area, are the result of wind and water acting together. The yellow sand originates in the Namib itself, but the deep red sand usually found in the Kalahari desert has reached the Namib by being washed down into the Orange River far to the S before being blown by the wind northwards again into the Namib. Standing on top of a dune at Sossusvlei one can see the rippling dune sea extending far into the distance.

The mobility of dunes varies. The largest move perhaps no more than a metre each year. Barchans can, especially if of low altitude, travel more quickly – at up to 50m per year. Mobile dunes create a hazard for transport since roads can be covered quickly in high wind conditions. Elsewhere, cultivated lands can slowly be inundated with sand.

Stabilizing sand dunes is a difficult matter. The large dune systems are unstoppable and man's attempts to halt their advance have rarely  succeeded for long. Smaller dunes can be stabilized by planting them with a close graticule of drought resistant grass or other plants, which once established can be inter-planted with desert bushes and shrubs. This process is slow and expensive though generally very effective even in very dry conditions. More cheap and dramatic is to build sand fences to catch moving sand, tar-spraying dunes or layering dunes with a plastic net. The results are less aesthetically pleasing than using the traditional vegetation cover system and are less long-lasting unless combined with planting, though in the driest areas of the Sahara these are the only possible methods of fixing mobile dunes.

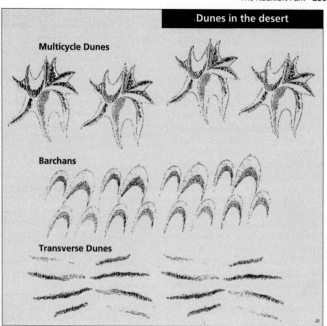

Dunes in the desert

Multicycle Dunes

Barchans

Transverse Dunes

ing hiking country in Namibia is found here in the Naukluft mountains and there are hikes to suit just about anyone. Nevertheless the conditions are hard and all hikers should make sure they come properly equipped with decent boots and a hat as well as ensuring they take enough water with them (minimum 2 litres per person per day). For those people planning longer hikes involving overnight stops in the mountains it is absolutely essential to take warm clothing as the temperature at night time, even in summer, can drop close to freezing.

Olive Trail A 10 km 4-5 hr hike, ideal as a starter for those unaccustomed to the conditions. The walk gets its name from the preponderance of wild olive trees encountered en route. The trail starts from the car park close to the campsite with a steep climb to the top of a plateau giving great views of the main Naukluft gorge. From here the path continues NW as far as a huge social weaver nest, and then turns E into a river valley. This valley gradually deepens until a narrow gorge has to be crossed with the assistance of chains anchored into the rocks. From here onwards the trail more or less follows a jeep track back to the starting point.

Waterkloof Trail A 17 km 7-hr trail, considerably more demanding than the Olive Trail, although well worth it. This hike starts from the campsite and is an anti-clockwise circular route which first leads past a weir up to a series of beautifully clear rock pools which, although cold, make for wonderful swimming pools. From here the trail climbs steadily up to a high point of 1,910m just over halfway round from where there are stunning views over the whole mountain range. As the path descends it follows part of an old German cannon road used in the campaign against Hendrik Witbooi in 1894. The last 6 km of the walk follow the Naukluft River back to the campsite.

Naukluft Hiking Trail Reputed to be one of the toughest hiking trails in southern Africa, the full distance of 120 km is normally completed in 8 days, although it is possible to shorten this to a 4 day 58 km trail. Due to extreme summer temperatures the trail is only open between 1 Mar and the third Fri in Oct to groups of between 3 and 12 people who must book in advance. Accommodation on the trail consists of a farmhouse on the first, third and last nights and simple stone shelters on the other nights. Water is provided at the overnight stops but fires are not permitted, making a lightweight camping stove essential. It goes without saying that this trail is only for the fit and experienced hiker! A good map of the trail is available from tourist information on Independence Ave in Windhoek.

Park information

Open to day visitors, campers must book well in advance. Admission N$10 adults, N$1 children, N$10 cars.

● **Accommodation**

F *Koedoesrus Campsite*, 8 campsites with braai facilities, shared ablution block with hot showers, no shop, drinking water and firewood available. A small information centre next to the office gives some interesting information on the flora and fauna in the park.

Guestfarms: **B** *Gästefarm Ababis*, T 06638 (farmline) 3340, F 061 220275, German run establishment offers 5 en suite double rooms, game drives and hiking trails in the surrounding Naukluft Mountains, all inclusive. **Approach**: at the junction of the D1261 and C14 between Solitaire and Büllsport. **C** *Büllsport Guestfarm*, T 06638 (farmline) 3302, F 061 235453, c/o Adozu Tours, well established guestfarm close to the Naukluft Mountains, 7 en suite double rooms with facilities for the disabled, swimming pool, petrol station, small store, horse riding and hiking trails on the farm and guided tours of the Naukluft and Sossusvlei, includes B&B. **Approach**: on C14 between Solitaire and Maltahöhe by the junction with the D854. **C** *Haruchas Guestfarm*, T 06638 (farmline) 4202, F 061 242 934, 4 en suite double rooms, swimming pool, hiking, 4WD trails and game drives on the farm, organized trips to the Naukluft, Sossusvlei and Duwisib Castle, dinner, B&B all inclusive. **Approach**: 255 km S of Windhoek on D855. **C** *Zebra River Lodge*, T 06638 (farmline) 4530 or c/o Namib Travel Shop: T 061 225178, F 061 239 455, in the heart of the Tsaris Mountains close to Naukluft, 5 en suite double rooms, swimming pool, 4WD, hiking to rock pools in the mountains, self-catering cottage also available close to farmhouse, rec. **Approach**: take the C14 to Büllsport, turn onto D854, after 42 km turn onto D850, farm is signposted 19 km down this road.

SESRIEM

ROUTES The C36 gravel road winds out of Solitaire and S into the Namib desert, through a 20 km section of the Namib Naukluft Park where there is a good chance of seeing wild ostriches, springbok and gemsbok. The C36 itself continues up through the pass in the **Tsaris Mountains** before eventually reaching the small town of **Maltahöhe**. The D826 is the turn-off for Sesriem approximately 80 km from Solitaire and is well indicated.

SESRIEM CANYON

Background The name Sesriem is derived from the *ses riems* or six lengths of rope that were needed to haul water out of the gorge from the top. This narrow gorge is a deep slash in the earth 1 km long and up to 30m deep running W before eventually flattening out as it approaches Sossusvlei.

Geology The Tsauchab River, which today only runs after good rains fall in the Naukluft mountains, cut the gorge some 15-18 million years ago during a significantly wetter period in the Namib's history. The canyon itself was created by continental upheaval somewhere between 2-4 million years which resulted in the creation of most of the westward flowing rivers in the Namib desert region.

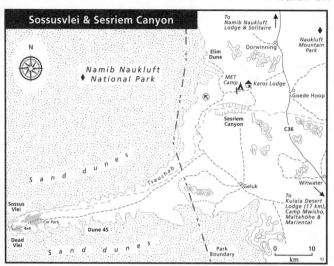

SOSSUSVLEI

Background One of most visitors' highlights of Namibia is a trip to the massive sand dunes at Sossusvlei, and well worth the effort of getting there.

Sossusvlei is actually a huge pan surrounded by towering sand dunes, reputed to be the highest in the world, surely an exaggeration, but certainly some of the highest in the Namib Desert. In years of extraordinary rains, such as early 1997, the Tsauchab River breaks through the sand and flows all the way to Sossusvlei filling the pan with water, a surreal site in the midst of the desert. The water attracts ducks and even flamingoes and gradually seeps into the ground to provide underground water for the camel thorn trees and nara plants living here.

Access to the *vlei* itself is either by 4WD or on foot after parking ordinary vehicles 4 km from the pan. Early morning and late afternoon are the best times to go into the park both for photography and to avoid the intense heat experienced for most of the year. Try climbing some of the surrounding dunes and look out over the dune sea which extends to around 100 km in all directions.

It is extremely important to respect Nature Conservation's request that whilst in the park, vehicles must remain on the road in order not to damage the fragile desert environment. Walking is permitted anywhere and good walking shoes and plenty of water are strongly recommended. Entry into the park is N$20 per person and N$20 for a car.

Approach The gravel road to **Sossusvlei** lies beyond a gate inside the rest camp where a permit must be obtained before driving into the park. It is 65 km down an often corrugated track to the pan itself, but on the way it's worth stopping at Dune 45 and (if you've got the energy) climbing to the top for the view of the surrounding dune sea.

● **Accommodation E** *Sesriem Rest Camp*, 10 camping sites, maximum 8 people per site with braai facilities, there are ablution blocks and a small shop selling wood, drinks and basic foodstuffs, bookings must be made in advance at Nature Conservation in Windhoek. The campsite is often booked out and if you arrive without a booking you'll spend the night in the desert outside the gate.

Sesriem Canyon lies 4 km down a narrow gravel road from inside the campsite and is an interesting place to walk and look at the different rock layers exposed

Balloon trips

Balloon trips over the Namib desert are organized by Namib Sky Safari Adventures and start either from Sesriem or from Camp Mishwo (see below). The trips start at sunrise when the pilot and assistants unfold the balloon with the aid of a petrol driven fan before attaching the basket in which the pilot and passengers will ride. The pilot then lights the propane gas lines and gradually inflates the balloon with blasts of hot air until it is vertical and the basket is resting on the ground below it. Take-off is barely noticeable and within a few minutes the balloon is high above the desert floor.

Depending on the direction and intensity of the wind, the balloon heads off into the desert and passengers get a spectacular bird's eye view of the dunes and the desert itself, where the innumerable tracks of ostrich, springbok, gemsbok and other desert dwellers are clearly visible in the sand. The flight itself is incredibly gentle, only punctuated by blasts of burning gas from the propane tanks, and lasts for about an hour. Landing offers the greatest sensation of the trip as the balloon steadily loses altitude before bumping along the ground and scrapping against the sand before eventually lurching to a halt.

After landing a back-up car arrives carrying everything necessary for a champagne breakfast in the desert, after which passengers are driven back to Sesriem. Trips cost N$900 per person and can be arranged by calling 06632 and asking for 5703.

there. After good rains pools of water form at the bottom of the gorge where one can take a dip.

● **Accommodation Guestfarms & lodges**: **AL** *Sossusvlei Karos Lodge*, T 0638 (farmline) 4322, 45 tent-cum-bungalow structures designed to blend into the desert, comfortable, en suite solar powered double rooms, restaurant, bar with nature videos shown in the evening, the view from the bar is very special, swimming pool, friendly service, 4WD hire, all inclusive, rec. **Approach**: entrance is immediately before the entrance gate to Sossusvlei. **B** *Kulala Desert Lodge*, T 061 221994, F 061 222574, 12 thatched 'kulalas', en suite double room, verandah, horse riding, day trips to Sossusvlei, includes dinner, B&B. **Approach**: 17 km S of Sesriem on D826. **B** *Namib-Naukluft Lodge*, T 061 263082, F 061 215356, 14 en suite double rooms, verandah, restaurant, bar, swimming pool, game drives, good service, day trips to Sossusvlei, all inclusive, rec. **Approach**: 19 km south of Solitaire on C36. **B-D** *Hammerstein Rest Camp*, T 06638 (farmline) 5111, 10 en suite double rooms, 5 bungalows and camping facilities, swimming pool, scenic drives, day trips to Sossusvlei, voted best rest camp 1994-95. **Approach**: 6 km from Sesriem on D826. **B-D** *Namib Rest Camp*, T 06638 (farmline) 3211, 5 bungalows, 4 en suite double rooms, swimming pool, excursions to Sossusvlei, all inclusive. **Approach**: 16 km S of Solitaire on C36. **C** *Camp Mishwo*, T 0663 3234, situated on the largest private game ranch in southern Africa, the camp is the base for balloon safaris (see box) over the Namib desert and guests stay in 6 double en suite tents. **Approach**: signposted off the D826 close to the junction with the D845. **D** *Namibgrens Rest Camp*, T 0628 (farmline) 1322, 7 double bed rooms, shared facilities, self-catering or B&B, situated on the Spreetshoogte Pass offering superb views of the desert floor below, has hiking trails with overnight stops in basic huts. **Approach**: take D1275 to the Spreetshoogte Pass and follow the signs.

SOLITAIRE

Recently immortalized in the Toyota Camry advertisement, Solitaire is a privately-owned farm set deep in the heart of the dunes of the southern Namib with a filling station and small shop selling soft drinks, snacks and basic supplies. For a nominal fee of N$5 the owners will allow camping under the trees by the farm buildings.

The name Solitaire is derived from the lone dead tree standing next to the service station, a motif frequently seen on publicity posters for tourism in Namibia. The mountains to the E are an extension of the Naukluft Mountains and to the E lie the massive red dunes of the heart of the Namibia.

The South

THE SOUTH of Namibia encompasses all the land from just North of Rehoboth to the South Africa border in the extreme south of the country. To the east lie the borders with Botswana and South Africa in the red-duned Kalahari desert and to the west lies the ancient Namib desert and the cold waters of the South Atlantic Ocean. The central highland plateau runs like a spine down the middle of the region and it is along this narrow strip of land that the majority of the population live.

Physically, the S is a semi-arid region of vast plains stretching as far as the eye can see. To the W lie a series of mountain ranges demarcating the edge of the plateau and the pro-Namib desert region. Just N of Keetmanshoop stands the ancient volcano Brukkaros, towering 650m above the surrounding plain, and in the moonscape of the far S lies the Fish River Canyon, an artery of the earth through which the Fish River carries water down to its confluence with the Orange River.

Politically the S is divided into the Hardap and Karas Regions, with their administrative centres at Mariental and Keetmanshoop respectively. The only other towns of significant size are Rehoboth and the old German coastal town of Lüderitz. However, all over the S there are a scattering of smaller towns and settlements, many of them dating back to the days of the first European missionaries.

The economy of the S has always been based around livestock farming. In pre-colonial times the Nama people grazed their animals on the vast plains of the S, watering them at the springs of Rehoboth, Hoachanas, Gibeon, Berseba, and Bethanie, now all small settlements. Following the arrival of European missionaries and traders, the majority of the land was turned into vast white-owned ranches, many consisting of 10,000 ha and more, and for much of this century the wealth of these farmers was built on the back of the karakul trade (see page 55). Although the Basters in Rehoboth managed to hold on to their land, following the Odendaal Commission Report in 1962, the Nama people were forced into a Namaland Bantustan located W of the main road between Mariental and Keetmanshoop.

Attractions in this region are the Oanob Lake Resort and Reho Spa Hot Springs in Rehoboth and the Hardap Dam Resort and Game Park near Mari-

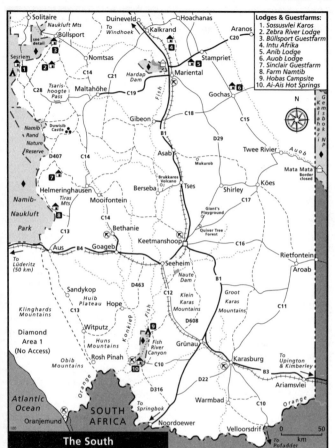

Lodges & Guestfarms:
1. Sossusvlei Karos
2. Zebra River Lodge
3. Büllsport Guestfarm
4. Intu Afrika
5. Anib Lodge
6. Auob Lodge
7. Sinclair Guestfarm
8. Farm Namtib
9. Hobas Campsite
10. Ai-Ais Hot Springs

The South

ental. On the edge of the Namib Desert is the delicate Duwisib Castle, an outpost of European elegance in the middle of the veld, and further S lies the Quiver Tree Forest, the vast Fish River Canyon and Ai-Ais Hot Springs Resort.

For hiking enthusiasts there are two tough trails – the Naukluft Trail running through the rugged, spectacular Naukluft Mountains where Nama leader Hendrik Witbooi made a stand against the German forces in 1894. The other is

the 84 km Fish River Canyon Hiking Trail, one of the toughest in southern Africa, a 4-day walk along the Fish River as it snakes its way S from the observation point at Hobas to the hot springs at Ai-Ais.

This region is the size of Germany, and with the towns and settlements spread far apart, is difficult to explore properly without a vehicle. The rail network runs through Mariental and Keetmanshoop as far as Karasburg and the border at Ariamsvlei, and there are very limited bus services to the settlements around the region. However to get to the sites of interest – in particular the Fish River Canyon – the only option to driving is hitch-hiking, which will invariably involve long waits in the hot sun, with lifts few and far between.

ROUTES The main B1 route S is a good, tarred road leading all the way to the two main southern border crossings at Noordoewer, 800 km, and Ariamsvlei 855 km from Windhoek respectively. In places the road does become quite narrow though, and great care should be exercised when overtaking the large trucks which ply their way up and down the highway between Cape Town, Johannesburg and Windhoek, particularly at night.

During the past year the B1 has acquired the unfortunate nickname of 'the road of death' due to the high number of fatal accidents that have taken place on it. **If at all possible avoid driving this road at night**. Similarly, during morning and afternoon rush hours, large numbers of Rehobothers commute in cars, pick-up trucks and mini-buses to and from their jobs in Windhoek. At such times this stretch of the road is uncharacteristically crowded by Namibian standards.

Despite its rather sinister nickname, the road between Windhoek and Rehoboth is a beautiful route, winding through the picturesque ranchland of the Auas Mountains. Approximately 30 km S of Windhoek is the *Aris Hotel*, a pleasant place to stop for coffee or a meal. On this stretch of the road troops of baboons rooting around in the bush for food are a common sight. Mongoose, ground squirrels, guinea fowl and yellow-billed hornbills are also common on this stretch of the road.

A few km S of Rehoboth the C24 branches W off the main B1 and leads to the Reemhoogte Pass, one of three spectacular routes which descend to the Namib desert floor. From here you can head W into the Naukluft Mountains or SW towards Sossusvlei.

REHOBOTH

(*STD code* 0627) Situated 87 km S of Windhoek at the foot of the Auas Mountains, Rehoboth is home to the Basters, a

The police station at Rehoboth

fiercly independent people who are the descendants of a group of farmers of mixed European and Khoisan blood. These people first migrated to the area from the Cape in 1870 and under the leadership of Hemanus van Wyk established a settlement at the site of the abandoned Rhenish mission station.

The hot springs at Rehoboth had been known for centuries by the Swartobooi Namas who called the place *Anhes*, meaning 'smoke', which referred to the steam rising from the hot water. A more permanent settlement was established in 1844 by Rhenish Missionary, Heinrich Kleinschmidt. This original mission station lasted for 20 years before being abandoned in 1864 following an attack by the Oorlam Afrikaners under Jonker Afrikaner. Kleinschmidt's congregation dispersed following their defeat and Kleinschmidt and his family walked through the bush for 4 days before reaching the safety of the mission station at Otjimbinwge, where Kleinschmidt laid down and died.

In the years following the arrival of van Wyk and his people in 1870, the mission station was rebuilt, one of the earliest buildings to be completed being the Lutheran Church in Church St. With its distinctive brickwork it is reminiscent of the Putz architechtural style of the Ombudsman's Office in Windhoek.

The Baster Community has traditionally been a farming community, living a more or less self-sufficient existence on their farms, similar to that of the white Afrikaner settlers. Fiercely independent, Christian and western-oriented in their culture, the Baster community has managed to hold on to their land despite attempts by the German and South African colonial governments to take it away from them.

From the 1920s up until Independence, the Rehoboth community was governed by a Kaptein and his *Raad* or council who had jurisdiction over all aspects of community life except for the law. A white magistrate appointed by the colonial government held these powers. Matters concerning agriculture, education, local government and health were all managed by the Raad assisted by seven *volksraad* or 'people's councils' from around the region. In effect the Rehoboth District existed as a semi-autonomous region within Namibia.

Since independence, a section of the Baster community, under the leadership of the former Kaptein (traditional leader), Hans Diergaardt, have been fighting a court battle with the central government to keep control over the traditional communal land of the town itself and the land in a radius of 10 km around it. The most recent Supreme Court ruling in 1996 handed control of the land to the government, to be administered by the town council, thus depriving the traditional leadership of the right to administer the land. However, Diergaardt and his followers have vowed to continue fighting for what they see as their 'blood land'.

Places of interest

The Rehoboth Museum is located in the former residence of the town's first postmaster. Built in 1903, it houses an interesting record of the community's history and culture, as well as details of the flora and fauna in the area. In the garden in front of the museum there is a display of traditional huts of the different ethnic groups in Namibia.

Local information
● Accommodation

The only option for accommodation in Rehoboth itself is the hot springs, whilst outside of town there are camping facilities at the *Oanob Lake Resort*. See relevant sections below.

● Places to eat

Apart from takeaways at the various garages in town, there are only two restaurants. Sigi's and *The Pin Palace*, which doubles at the town's No 1 casino.

● Post & telecommunications

The Post Office is next to the museum.

● Transport

87 km to Windhoek.

Train Windhoek (2 hrs), daily except Sat, 0332; Keetmanshoop (8½ hrs), via Mariental, daily except Sat, 2131.

Road Bus: *Intercape*, T (061) 227847, coach picks up and drops off at Echo Service Station: **Cape Town** (15 hrs), Mon, Wed, Fri, Sun, 2000; **Keetmanshoop** (4 hrs), Mon, Wed, Fri, Sun, 2000; **Upington** (9 hrs), Mon, Wed, Fri, Sun, 2000; **Windhoek** (1 hr), Mon, Wed, Fri, Sat, 0530. Local minibuses run from the main road to and from the bus station behind Wernhill Park shopping centre in Windhoek.

REHO SPA RECREATION RESORT

Approach Follow the signs off the main road onto the dirt road and turn right immediately after the Catholic Church. The road curves to the left before reaching a crossroads. Turn right here and the entrance to the resort is a further 400m on the right.

Background Known to the indigenous Nama people for centuries, the hot springs here have been developed into an attractive spa resort. This consists of a fine swimming-pool sized indoor thermal bath, an outdoor cold water swimming pool and a number of bungalows complete with braai areas.

Resort information The resort is open all year round and reservations for accommodation must be made with central reservations in Windhoek. Picnic/braai sites are available for day visitors.

● **Accommodation D-F** *6 bed 2 room bungalows, 5 and 4 bed one room bungalows*, all fully equipped except for crockery and cutlery. *Camping and caravan sites*, maximum 8 persons per site, communal ablution and cooking facilities. Admission for day visitors is N$10 for adults and N$5 for children. It costs a further N$2 for adults and N$1 for children to enter the thermal baths.

OANOB LAKE RESORT

Approach There are well signposted turn-offs to the Resort on the B1 immediately to the S and N of Rehoboth.

Background The dam was completed in 1990 and supplies Rehoboth with its water. Originally there were plans to set up some irrigated crop cultivation by the dam, but so far this has not been realized. The blue water of the lake is a welcome sight amidst the arid thorn veld of the surrounding countryside, and is a popular weekend and holiday spot with local residents. The number of tourists visiting the resort is gradually increasing, and with further development of accommodation by the dam, this is likely to become a popular stop-off place for travellers in this part of Namibia.

Bird watching There are colonies of cormorants, pelicans, darters and other water birds living on and alongside the lake.

Hiking There are a number of walks laid out around the lake, along which it is possible to spot springbok, baboons and other smaller mammals.

Watersports A speed boat ride and tour of the lake costs N$7 per person. For the adventurous there is a jet ski available for N$20; visitors can also hire pedalos or canoes for N$7.50 per person. People with their own windsurfers can also make use of the lake, however there are none at present available for hire.

Resort information The resort is open all year round and visitors can just turn up at the office. There are shaded, grassy braai sites for day visitors at N$30 per site, as well as two thatched-roofed bar/restaurants.

● **Accommodation** F *Camping & caravan sites*, with limited toilet and washing facilities, although these will be improved in the future. Entrance fee is cars N$10 plus N$2 entrance per person.

MARIENTAL

ROUTES The road S from Rehoboth passes through the ranching land of the Baster community, before reaching the village of Kalkrand with its garage, bottle store and takeaway stand. About 20 km N of Kalkrand, at the Duineveld Crossroads, there are a number of roadside stalls where springbok skin rugs are sold by locals from Duineveld. The skins themselves are bought from commercial farmers and then stitched together and lined with karakul fur before being sold. The sale of these rugs plays an important role in the economy of the village.

(*STD code* 0661, code to change to 063 late in 1997 and all numbers to add 240 prefix) Mariental is a small, quietly flourishing market town in the heart of southern Namibia and is the administrative centre of the Hardap Region. The nearby Hardap Dam – the largest reservoir in Namibia – provides water for irrigation, making it possible to cultivate animal fodder, as well as some fruit and vegetables. The recently built ostrich abattoir caters for this increasingly important industry in the S of Namibia, and what survives of the karakul trade in the S is centred around Mariental. Sitting astride the main routes into the Kalahari and Namib deserts, Mariental also services the needs of farmers in these areas.

Despite Mariental's quiet success, it is not however the most exciting or interesting place in Namibia. Wind-swept and dusty in spring and autumn, ferociously hot in summer and bitterly cold in winter, Mariental is home to a large number of Nama-speaking people, descendants of the early Khoi inhabitants of Namibia.

History
Mariental was officially founded in 1920 following the construction of Namibia's first Dutch Reform Church, however it was well known to the early Nama inhabitants who referred to the place as *Zaragaeiba* meaning 'dusty'. The present name – 'Marie's valley' – was bestowed upon the settlement by the first white settler, Herman Brandt, in honour of his wife. Following some rather turbulent early years during the anti-German war of 1904-1907 and the arrival of the railway in 1912, Mariental settled down to life as a quiet *dorp* in the middle of the veld.

Local information
● **Accommodation**
D *Mariental Hotel*, Marie Brandt St, T 2466/7/8, F 2493 is the most comfortable place to stay in town. Renovated in 1995, the hotel has 18 en suite rooms with a/c and phone, there is a tiny swimming pool in the courtyard and secure off-street parking, the restaurant is surprisingly good, although the menu is of the standard schnitzel, steak, chicken and fish variety, 2 bars to choose from; **D** *Sandberg Hotel*, Marie Brandt St, T/F 2291, is an acceptable but rather rundown

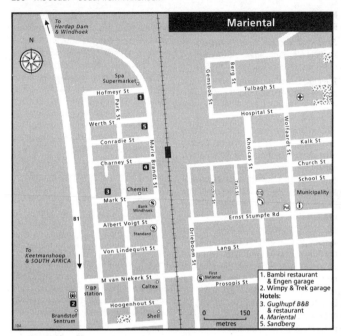

Mariental

1. Bambi restaurant
   & Engen garage
2. Wimpy & Trek garage
Hotels:
3. Guglhupf B&B
   & restaurant
4. Mariental
5. Sandberg

option with en suite rooms with a/c and phone, there is also an unremarkable restaurant and a bar; **D** *Guglhupf Café & Restaurant*, corner of Mark and Park sts, T 718, has modest, en suite rooms, with phone, some with a/c, bar and restaurant are popular with the local Afrikaans-speaking crowd and offer good steaks, schnitzel and ribs washed down by local draught beer.

● **Places to eat**
Mariental Hotel and *Guglhupf Café & Restaurant*, are both popular with locals, and offer tasty, filling, reasonably priced meals; *Sandberg Hotel* offer similar fare; *Bambi Restaurant* at the Engen Garage on Marie Brandt St offers fry-ups and steaks; *Wimpy Bar* is found at the trek Garage on the B1 just outside town. There are a number of takeaways at the garages in town.

● **Banks & money changers**
Bank Windhoek and Standard Bank are both found on Marie Brandt St; First National Bank is on Drieboom St. All three offer money changing facilities.

● **Hospital & medical services**
The State Hospital, T 2092.

● **Police**
T 10111, Ernest Stumpfe St.

● **Post & telecommunications**
Post Office: Khoicas Weg, Mon-Fri 0800-1630, Sat 0800-1130.

● **Transport**
264 km to Windhoek; 228 Keetmanshoop.

Train Windhoek (6 hrs), via Rehoboth, daily except Sat, 2350; **Keetmanshoop** (4½ hrs), daily except Sat, 0125.

Road Bus: *Starline*: **Walvis Bay** (12 hrs), via Maltahöhe, Mon 0730; **Gibeon** (1¼ hrs), Wed and Fri 0800; **Maltahöhe** (2 hrs), Wed and Fri. **Intercape**, T (061) 227847, coach picks up and drops off in front of Brandstof Sentrum: **Cape Town** (13 hrs), Mon, Wed, Fri, Sun, 2145; **Keetmanshoop** (2 hrs), Mon, Wed, Fri, Sun, 2145; **Upington** (7 hrs), Mon, Wed, Fri, Sun, 2145; **Windhoek** (3 hrs), Mon, Wed, Fri, Sat, 0345.

HARDAP DAM RECREATION RESORT AND GAME PARK

Approach Turn off the B1 at the sign 15 km N of Mariental. Follow the road 6 km to the resort entrance.

Background First proposed as the site for a dam in 1897 by German geologist Dr Theodor Rehbock, it took a number of surveys and until 1960 before construction began on Namibia's largest dam. The name Hardap derives from the Nama word meaning 'nipple' or 'wart', which is how the surrounding area of low conical-shaped hills appeared to the early inhabitants.

The dam has a surface area of 25 sq km and has a number of different functions. The original intention was for the dam to provide water for irrigation, and the Hardap Irrigation Scheme now covers an area of 2,500 ha. Here wheat, maize, lucerne, cotton, grapes and vegetables are cultivated on a series of small holdings. The dam also provides Mariental with its water and acts as a flood prevention mechanism, most recently at the beginning of 1997, when the first good rains for many years filled the dam.

As an added bonus the dam is an angler's paradise, being well-stocked with such fish as yellowfish, carp, mullet and catfish, and the resort is a popular weekend getaway for people living in the area. There are superb views of this artificial lake from the restaurant which has been built on the cliffs by the northern edge of the dam.

The **Game Park** attached to the dam is divided into two sections. A small section of 1,848 ha is located near the resort along the northern edge of the dam, and this is where the resident black rhinos live. The larger section of the park, consisting of some 23,000 ha lies to the S of the dam, and this is where the greatest concentration of game lives.

Upon proclamation as a game park, the area was restocked with antelopes, such as kudu, gemsbok, eland, red hartebeest and springbok, as well as with mountain zebra. Namibia's southernmost black rhinos are also found in the park, having been introduced from Damaraland in 1990. Leopards too have been spotted in the area of the Great Komatsas River.

Angling There are fishing spots at various points along the northern shore of

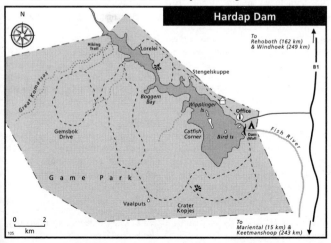

Hardap Dam

the lake. Permits, and a map of permitted fishing spots, are available from the resort office or from the magistrate's office in Mariental. Anglers are advised to watch out for one of the park's black rhinos living in this part of the resort when getting out of their vehicles.

Birdwatching A large number of birds can be observed around the dam, thanks to the diverse habitats on offer. Water birds, such as pelicans, cormorants, darters and spoonbill can be seen on the lake itself, as well as fish eagles and a small number of osprey. The reedbeds below the dam wall support large numbers of herons and between Apr and Oct are home to white dwarf bitterns.

Along the game drive there is a good chance of seeing ostriches, kori bustards and the ubiquitous Namaqua sandgrouse.

Hiking There is a 15-km hiking trail in the northwestern corner of the park, taking 4-5 hrs to complete, which can also be turned into a shorter 9-km walk. Vegetation along the route consists of dwarf shrub savannah such as shepherd's tree, stink-bush, wool bush and brittle thorn, with camel thorn and buffalo thorn found growing in the dry river-courses.

As the trail passes by the banks of the Great Komatsas River, the ruins of the country's first school for whites can be seen, and shortly after there is a spring surrounded by shady trees. This makes a good place to sit down, have a picnic and a break. As with all hiking in Namibia, it is important to take along a minimum of two litres of water per day.

Hikers should take care to watch out for black rhino along the route, especially when passing through the patches of dense vegetation.

Resort information The resort is open all year round but experiences very high (35°C+) daytime temperatures in summer (Dec-Mar) and very cold (0°C) nightime temperatures in winter (Jun

and Jul), so these may not be the best times to visit. Accommodation can be booked through Central Reservations in Windhoek. The resort has a restaurant, filling station, shop, kiosk and swimming pool. Day visitors entrance fee N\$10 adults, N\$2.50 children.

● **Accommodation D** *5 bed bungalow*, fully equipped apart from crockery and cutlery; **E** *2-bed bungalow*, field-kitchen cooking facilities; **F** *camping & caravan sites*, ablution blocks, shared cooking facilities, maximum 8 persons, 2 vehicles, 1 caravan/tent per site. Compared to other sites in Namibia, the camping here is expensive.

STAMPRIET AND GOCHAS

10 km N of Mariental the C20 heads E into the Kalahari Desert towards the small cattle town of Aranos. En route it passes Stampriet, a small settlement where thanks to artesian water flowing in from the Kalahari, fruit and vegetables are cultivated. At Stampriet, the C15 heads S towards Gochas, and along this route lie a number of battle sites and memorials dating back to the 1904-1907 war of resistance against the Germans.

20 km S of Stampriet along the C15 is the farm Gross Nabas, the sight of one of the bloodiest battles of the war. A small monument on the main road commemorates the battle of 2-4 January 1905, during which the Witbooi Nama inflicted heavy losses on the German forces. Another monument, a further 24 km on, indicates where a German patrol was ambushed and killed in Mar of that year.

GIBEON

Gibeon is a medium sized village lying some 70 km SW of Mariental and is perhaps best known nowadays as the source of the Gibeon meteorites displayed in the Post St Mall sculpture in Windhoek. Although the present name refers to the biblical character, the early Nama settlers called the area *Gorego-re-Abes* or 'drinking place of the zebras' after the stream found here.

Founded in 1863 by Kido Witbooi and the Rhenish Missionary Knauer, Gibeon is home of the Witbooi clan, which in the second half of the 19th century developed into a closely-knit, politically active community of Nama clans. Under the leadership of Hendrik Witbooi, Gibeon was a focal point of anti-German resistance in the S, which led to the establishment of a military post here in 1894. In the same year Gibeon was officially named a district and construction of a fort began.

In the 1890s after the discovery of kimberlite pipes, there were various unsuccessful attempts to mine diamonds in the area, however these were abandoned in 1910. In 1915, Gibeon was the site of a bloody battle between invading South African and German troops, during which 41 soldiers from both sides died and 96 were wounded. A graveyard where those who died are buried is found close to the station.

Although Gibeon has a long and interesting past, unfortunately none of the colonial buildings remain, and is not really worth the detour to visit.

MUKUROB

Close to the settlement of Asab, 100 km S of Mariental lies the site of one of Namibia's former best-known landmarks. A 34m high pinnacle of rock balanced precariously on a narrow neck and base of shale was known in English as the 'finger of God' and in Afrikaans as the *Vingerklip*. The rock was a survivor of the erosion of the Weissrand Plateau to the E and consisted partly of sandstone and partly of conglomerate. The rock tumbled from its perch in 1988 as a result of seismic tremors experienced after the Armenian earthquake of 7 Dec.

Legend has it that the Nama and Herero speaking peoples were constantly boasting that each had the best pastures. The Nama reputedly told the Herero that they could boast to their heart's content for they (the Nama) had a rock on their land that was unsurpassable. In response the Herero are supposed to have slaughtered 10 oxen and with the hides made ropes which were attached to the neck of the rock. The Nama jeered as the struggling Herero failed to pull down the rock saying *Mu-Kuro*, 'now you see', thereby giving the rock its Nama name.

Approach At Asab, 100 km S of Mariental on the B1, turn onto the D1066 and follow for 12 km. Turn right onto D620 and continue for a further 10 km.

● **Accommodation** **Guestfarms**: **C** *Anib Lodge*, T 0661 529, F 0661 516, located on the edge of the Kalahari close to Mariental, there are 6 en suite rooms next to the farmhouse by a swimming pool set in a small lush garden, friendly service and wholesome German home-cooking, game drives and birdviewing although not a stocked game farm, all inclusive. **Approach**: turn off B1 10 km N of Mariental onto C20. Follow for 24 km until sign-post indicates farm. **B** *Intu Afrika Game Lodge*, T 0661 652/329, F 0661 663, set amidst the red sand dunes of the Kalahari, the lodge offers 18 en suite rooms, swimming pool, restaurant, game drives, bird watching, all inc, a Khung bushman village is a particular attraction of this lodge with the opportunity to go on nature hikes with bushman guides. For those wishing to stay in the Kalahari, rec. **Approach**: turn off B1 at Kalkrand onto C21 and follow the signs for 54 km. Coming from the S, turn onto C20 10 km N of Mariental and follow the signs. **C** *Auob Lodge*, T 06662 (farmline) 39, only 6 km from Gochas, 16 en suite rooms, swimming pool, squash court, bar, restaurant, horse riding and game drives on stocked farm of antelope, giraffe and zebra. **Approach**: 6 km N of Gochas on the C15.

MALTAHÖHE

ROUTES Just S of Mariental on the B1, the tarred C19 passes over the Fish River, and heads W towards the small town of Maltahöhe, on the edge of the Namib Desert, 110 km away.

(*STD code* 0663) The small town of Maltahöhe, situated on the edge of the

Namib desert, was founded in 1900 and owes its name to Malta von Burgdorff, wife of the German commander of the Gibeon garrison. The town was once an important agricultural centre, the nearby farm Nomtsas was established as a sheep farm of some 100,00 ha by the turn of the century. Later Maltahöhe became the centre of the karakul trade, but years of drought and the collapse of karakul prices brought hard times to the town. Many of the white commercial farmers were forced to sell up and leave, and the resulting loss of revenue killed off many of the businesses in town. Today Maltahöhe is a pale reminder of its former self, run-down and faded, however with an excellent hotel it is a good base for journeys into the Namib and southern Namibia.

The area around the town is spectacular, encompassing as it does the Tsaris, Namgorab and Nubub mountain ranges situated on the edge of the central highland plateau. From Maltahöhe there is a choice of roads; W through the spectacular Tsarishoogte Pass before descending steeply into the Namib Desert and on to Sessriem and Sossusvlei; or S past Duwisib Castle, the Schwartzberge, through the hamlet of Helmeringhausen to Bethanie, Keetmanshoop and Lüderitz. The clear desert air and the absolute emptiness of the landscape make this part of southern Namibia well worth the effort of driving through for those with the time and inclination to prolong their journey.

● **Accommodation D** *Maltahöhe Hotel*, T 3013, is the only place to stay in town, voted 'Best Country Hotel' of 1995-96, this well-run and friendly hotel offers 24 simple en suite rooms with fans and phone, swimming pool. The restaurant serves good value, tasty home-cooked food and the bar is a pleasant place to sit and relax in the evening. The knowledgeable hotel owner arranges tours to Duwisib Castle, Sossusvlei and the spectacular surrounding countryside, rec.

● **Useful information** There is one main street in the town and all other services, post office, police station, garages and the two banks **First National** and **Standard Bank** are located on this street.

DUWISIB CASTLE

Approach Castle Duwisib is located on Route D826. Coming from either Maltahöhe or Helmeringhausen, take the C14, then D831 before turning onto the D826. The roads are rough, but manageable with an ordinary, sedan car.

Background Duwisib Castle is a unique reminder of Namibia's colonial past and is situated in an improbable location in the rugged, dry veld on the edge of the Namib desert SW of Maltahöhe.

Designed by the architect Willi Sander who was also responsible for Windhoek's three hill-top castles, Duwisib was commissioned in 1907 by Hansheinrich von Wolf and his wife Jayta, an American heiress. Von Wolf had arrived in Namibia in 1904 to serve in the Schutztruppe as a captain in command of a regiment. It was during this time that he became interested in the area around Maltahöhe. In 1906 he resigned his commission and returned to Germany where he met Jayta. The two were married in Apr 1907 after which they arrived to settle in Namibia, buying Farm Duwisib from the Treasury.

The castle took 2 years to build, a remarkably short time considering that many of the building materials were imported from Europe via Lüderitz, from where they were hauled by ox wagon across the Namib desert. Herero workers were employed to quarry stone from a site near to the castle, Italian stone masons were brought from Italy to finish off the stone and actually build the castle, and carpenters from Germany, Sweden and Belgium were responsible for the woodwork.

Von Wolf and his wife soon became known as the Baron and Baroness by the local German and Afrikaner farmers, in recognition of the lavish lifestyle they enjoyed. The Von Wolfs employed seven Europeans to assist in managing the castle and the business. 'Baron' von Wolf bred horses from imported Australian and British stock and some people believe that the wild horses of the Namib seen today in the Aus area are survivors of his original stud. He also imported Hereford bulls from England and wool sheep from the Cape with which to stock the farm.

In 1914, just before the outbreak of WW1, the Von Wolfs left for England to buy further stock for their stud. During the voyage war broke out and the boat they were travelling on was forced to seek shelter in Argentina where they were interned. Released a few months later, von Wolf was determined to join the German forces, which he succeeded in doing, only to fall at the Battle of the Somme in Sep 1916. Jayta never returned to Namibia to reclaim her property or to sell the farm, and died in New Jersey in 1946 at the age of 64. The farm itself was bought and sold twice before eventually, in 1979, the then colonial administration of South West Africa bought the castle with the intention of preserving it as a heritage site.

The castle is designed in neo-romantic style, with elements of both Gothic and Renaissance architecture present. In addition there is a fine collection of antique European furniture on display, as well as old armour, paintings, photographs and copperplate engravings. The courtyard at the rear of the castle has an ornamental fountain and a pair of large jacaranda trees which provide shade during the heat of the day and when in flower (Sep-Oct), fill the courtyard with their scent.

Castle information The castle is open all year round 0800-1700, admission N\$10 adults, N\$2.50 children.

● **Accommodation E** *Farm Duwisib Rest Camp*, next to the Castle, has 2 bed, 4 bed and 6 bed bungalows with self-catering facilities, swimming pool and landing strip; **F** *Duwisib Castle*, has a pleasant campsite with braai facilities, basic shared ablution facilities, maximum 8 people and 1 tent or caravan per site. **Guestfarms: A-D** *Namseb Rest Camp*, T 0663 3166, F 0663 3157, 5 fully equipped en suite chalets, 16 en suite double rooms, swimming pool, restaurant, game drives on this working ostrich farm. **Approach**: take D36 out of Maltahöhe and follow the signs. **C** *Daweb Guestfarm*, T 0663 3088, 6 en suite double rooms, restaurant, game drives, bird watching, walking trails, camping also possible. **Approach**: 2 km outside Maltahöhe on C14.

HELMERINGHAUSEN

(*STD code* 06362) This small settlement lies 120 km S of Maltahöhe on the gravel C14, en route for Bethanie, Aus and Lüderitz. There is a petrol station open Mon-Sat 0800-1800, a general store and small hotel.

Places of interest

The Agricultural Museum is worth a stop to look at the old farming implements, an old fire engine used at Lüderitz and one of the ox-wagons used to transfer building materials and furniture from the cast to Castle Duwisib. The key is available from the hotel next door.

Farm Mooifontein 19 km S of Helmeringhausen on C14 was the site of a German military station during the colonial period. The bodies of German soldiers who died whilst fighting the Nama lie in the graveyard, which contains a memorial in the form of a chapel. The iron gates were forged from the rims of ox-wagon wheels.

Local information
● **Accommodation**
D *Hemeringhausen Hotel*, T 06362 (farm line) 7, small, friendly country hotel with newly refurbished en suite rooms, dining room, bar and braai area, hotel owner arranges tours to places of interest around the area.

Guestfarms: C *Sinclair Guestfarm*, T 06362 (farmline) 6503, one of the oldest guestfarms in Namibia, 5 en suite double rooms, restaurant, game drives, hiking, landing strip, a nearby abandoned copper mine makes for an interesting excursion, all inclusive. **Approach**: take D407 NW out of Helmeringhausen for 50 km and follow the signs to the farm. **C** *Dabis Guestfarm*, T 06362 (farmline) 6820, 7 en suite rooms, fresh farm food on this working farm, hiking, game viewing, all inclusive. **Approach**: 10 km N of Helmeringhausen on C14. **C** *Farm Namtib*, T 06362 (farmline) 6640, a registered horse stud farm at the foot of the Great Tiras Mountains, accommodation consists of 5 en suite chalets, meals eaten with farm owners, game drives, hiking trails, horse riding. **Approach**: take C13 SW out of Helmeringhausen, then follow D707 NW to the farm.

KARAS

KEETMANSHOOP

ROUTES Keetmanshoop lies at the crossroads of southern Namibia and is therefore a transit point for people and goods to and from South Africa. From Keetmanshoop, the B4 heads W towards the Aus Mountains before descending to the desert floor, eventually arriving at the old German seaside town of Lüderitz 350 km away. The B1 from Windhoek continues for a further 165 km to Grünau where it branches into the B3 heading E to Karasburg and the border at Ariamsvlei. The B1 itself continues for a further 138 km to the South African border at Noordoewer.

Keetmanshoop is a convenient base from which to explore the 'deep' S, in particular the Fish River Canyon, the nearby Quiver Tree Forest and the volcano Brukkaros close to the old Nama settlement at Berseba.

(*STD code* 063, currently 0631 – changing sometime this year to 063) Keetmanshoop, sometimes referred to as the capital of the S, is one of the oldest established towns in Namibia. The original settlement, dating back to the late 18th century, was originally known as *Modderfontein* due to the presence of

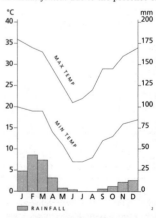

Climate: Keetmanshoop

a strong freshwater spring. Nama herders trekking N from the Cape settled here, calling the place *Swartmodder*, after the muddy river which ran through the settlement after good rains.

During the middle part of the 19th century, the Barmen Society gradually established a series of mission stations in the S of Namibia at places such as Bethanie, Warmbad and Berseba. In 1866, following a request by converted Namas living at Swartmodder, Johan Schröder was sent by Reverend Krönlein, the pastor at Berseba, to establish a mission station at Swartmodder. After struggling to build a church and home for himself and his family, Schröder appealed to the Barmen Society for funds to develop the station. Johan Keetman, a rich industrialist and Chairman of the Barmen Society, personally donated 2,000 marks to pay for the building of a church, and in appreciation Schröder renamed the settlement Keetmanshoop (Keetman's hope).

Like many other settlements in Namibia at the time, Keetmanshoop functioned both as a mission station and as a trading post. A successor to Schröder, Reverend Thomas Fenchel, came into conflict with the European traders who bartered liquor, usually brandy, with the Nama herders in exchange for livestock which was then sold in the Cape. Once the liquor was drunk the only source of food for the herders was the mission station.

In 1890 a freak flooding of the Swartmodder River washed away the original church, but Fenchel and his congregation had rebuilt it by 1895 from when it served a multiracial congregation until 1930. Abandoned for many years, the church was restored and declared a National Monument in 1978 and today houses the Keetmanshoop Museum.

The same year saw a wave of German immigration to the new colony, and in 1894 a fort was established in the town. In the following years as soldiers were discharged from the army, many bought farms or settled in the town which grew to support the surrounding farms. The growth of the town convinced the authorities of the necessity of improving communications and the railway to Lüderitz was completed in 1908. In the following year the military handed over the town to a civil authority and Keetmanshoop became the administrative centre for the S of the country.

Economically the town's prosperity was built upon the karakul sheep industry which reached its peak in the early 1970s; since the decline of the industry (see box) Keetmanshoop has earned its keep more mundanely as a transit point for goods and people between Namibia and South Africa. Efforts are currently underway to establish an ostrich processing plant which it is hoped will provide the town with badly needed jobs, and which it is also hoped will at the same time stimulate the ostrich farming industry in the S of the country.

Places of interest

The old Rhenish Mission Church on Kaiser St, now houses **Keetmanshoop Museum**, T 223316, open Mon-Fri 0730-1230 and 1400-1700, Sat 0900-1100. The displays focus on the history of the town, information on the surrounding area and a small art exhibition. Outside, by the rock garden of aloes, succulents and cacti, a traditional Nama hut stands cheek to jowl with early trekkers' wagons.

The stone church itself is a fine example of early colonial architecture, with its original corrugated iron roof and bell-tower with weather-vane, and inside there is an elegant pulpit and wooden balcony. The church looks particularly attractive at night when it is floodlit.

The former post and telegraph office, the **Kaiserliches Poststamp**, designed by government architect, Gottlieb Redecker, and built in 1910, is another of Keetmanshoop's fine early buildings.

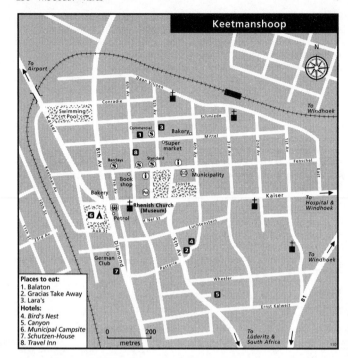

Keetmanshoop

Places to eat:
1. Balaton
2. Gracias Take Away
3. Lara's
Hotels:
4. Bird's Nest
5. Canyon
6. Municipal Campsite
7. Schutzen-House
8. Travel Inn

0   200
metres

The building now houses the **Southern Tourist Forum** and Air Namibia offices and is located on 5th Ave by Central Park.

Local information
● **Accommodation**

C *Bird's Nest B&B*, 16 Pastorie St, T 063 22906, newly established with 5 en suite a/c rooms with phone and secure parking, communal TV and braai area, pleasant decor with expansion work still underway; **C** *Canyon Hotel*, 5th Ave and Wheeler St, T 223361, F 223714, is a well-managed, friendly hotel with comfortable en suite rooms with a/c, TV, phone, the hotel has a new wing and recently renovated restaurant, coffee shop and bar, in the garden is a small swimming pool – a good place to escape from the intense summer heat of the S, rec.

D *Lafenis Rest Camp*, B1 2 km S of town, T 224316, F 222550, has adequate 4 bed en suite bungalows with TV, a/c and restaurant;

D *Travel Inn Hotel*, T 223344, F 222138, is the other choice in town, slightly shabby en suite rooms, some with a/c, TV, and phone, the restaurant offers reasonable food with game specialities although service is rather on the slow side, there is a bar and secure off-street parking.

E *Gessert's Bed & Breakfast*, 138 13th St, T/F 23892, is a small, friendly family-run guesthouse with en suite rooms and swimming pool, the owners also run *Gondwana Tours* which can arrange travel and tours around the S of Namibia.

Camping: **C-F** *Quivertree Forest Rest Camp*, 16 km from Keetmanshoop on the D29, T 222835, offers a variety of accommodation from en suite rooms with full board or B&B in the farmhouse, to rooms and self-catering igloos in the yard, and camping by the quivertree forest itself 1 km from the farmhouse; **F** *Municipal Campsite & Caravan Park*, T 223316, F 223818, is in the centre of town and has pleasant campsites, plug-in facilities for caravans, ablution blocks and laundry facilities.

● **Places to eat**
Canyon Hotel, has a good restaurant offering Namibian game dishes as well as fish, pasta and other European dishes, with a decent selection of wines to go with the food; *Travel Inn Hotel*, also offers tasty game dishes, steaks, ribs and fish, although service can be slow; *Lara's Restaurant*, 5th Ave and Schmiede St, is a good option for cheap and cheerful chicken and steak, and is open in the evenings; *Balaton Hungarian Restaurant*, Mittel St, offers such unlikely but tasty dishes as goulash and chicken paprika, as well as the usual light meals and takeaways; *Schutzen Haus*, 8th Ave, is a German club offering pub food, draught beer and right-wing jollity; *Trans-Namib Club*, Schmiede St, charges N$5 admission and is an Afrikaans-oriented club, also serving pub-grub, draught beer and right-wing humour.

Takeaways: all the garages on 5th Ave heading S towards the *Canyon Hotel* have takeaways.

● **Banks & money changers**
Bank Windhoek, **First National Bank** and **Standard Bank** are all situated on Fenschel St, and all change money. **Commercial Bank**, corner of Mittel St and 5th Ave, does not offer the swiftest of services.

● **Hospitals & medical services**
The State Hospital, T 23388, signposted just off B1 1 km N of town.

● **Post & telecommunications**
Post Office: 5th Ave, Mon-Fri 0800-1630, Sat 0800-1130.

● **Sports**
Swimming pool: excellent 50m municipal swimming pool, just off 8th Ave, open Sep-Apr.

● **Tourist offices**
Southern Tourist Forum, 5th Ave, T 22095, has a life-size replica of the collapsed 'finger of God' in the office, and also offers more mundane information on travel and accommodation in the S.

● **Useful addresses**
Police: 5th Ave, T 10111.

● **Transport**
500 km Windhoek; 350 km Lüderitz; 300 km Noordoewer (South Africa border).

Train Windhoek (11 hrs), via Mariental, daily except Sat, 1900; **Ariamsvlei** (9½ hrs), Wed and Sat, 0800.

Road Bus: Star Line, T (0631) 292202: **Lüderitz** via Aus (4 hrs): daily, 0800; **Bethanie** (2½ hrs): Mon, 0830, Thur, 0630; **Helmeringhausen** via Bethanie (6 hrs): Thur, 0630; **Lüderitz** via Goageb and Aus (5 hrs): daily, 0800, Fri, 1800, Sun, 1400.

Intercape, T (061) 227847, coach picks up and drops off in front of Du Toit Motors (BP Garage): **Cape Town** (11 hrs): Mon, Wed, Fri, Sun, 2400; **Upington** (5 hrs): Mon, Wed, Fri, Sun, 2400; **Windhoek** via Mariental and Rehoboth (5 hrs): Mon, Wed, Fri, Sat, 0145.

NAUTE DAM

Approach Drive 30 km W on the B4, then S on D545 for 20 km until you see the sign for the dam.

Background Located on the Löwen River surrounded by a series of small conical shaped hills, Naute is Namibia's third largest dam and provides Keetmanshoop with all its water, in addition to providing water for some small scale irrigation. At one time the dam was intended as a recreation area and nature park, but the plan never came to fruition and nowadays visitors are few and far between.

Bird watching Twitchers will find colonies of pelicans, cormorants, darters, Egyptian geese and other water birds on the reservoir.

Hiking There are no specific trails laid out, but it is quite possible to walk around the dam. There is a variety of game in the vicinity of the dam, as the animal spores on the sand dunes testify to, and kudu, springbok, ostrich and other animals may be spotted.

Camping There is no established campsite at the dam, however there are toilets and washing facilities and one can camp informally close to the entrance gate.

The gate to the dam is kept locked due to some petty vandalism in the recent past. However, the keys can easily be obtained from the staff at the water purification plant, 1 km before reaching the dam.

THE QUIVER TREE FOREST AND GIANT'S PLAYGROUND

Approach Follow B1 3 km N, take D29 for 13 km to sign for Farm Gariganus and Quiver Tree Forest.

Background The Quiver Tree Forest is one of the main attractions of southern Namibia. The 'trees' are in fact aloe plants or aloe dichotoma which usually only grow singly, but which in a few places grow in large groups, giving the impression of a small forest. The name quiver tree derives from the former practice of some of the San and Nama peoples of using the light, tough hollowed out branches of the plant as quivers for their arrows. The forest was declared a National Monument in 1955 and the quiver trees themselves are a protected species in Namibia. It is therefore forbidden to carry off any parts of the trees.

A good time to visit the forest is either early in the morning for sunrise, or late afternoon for sunset when the clear light offers good photographic opportunities. The view S over the veld to the Karas Mountains is especially beautiful at these times.

The Giant's Playground, 5 km further down the D29, is an area covered in huge, black, basalt rocks balanced precariously on top of each other. These strange formations were caused by the erosion of sedimentary overlying rocks 170 million years ago. The playground is a pleasantly eerie place to go for a gentle late afternoon walk before catching sunset at the Quiver Tree Forest.

● **Accommodation** See Keetmanshoop section above.

BRUKKAROS

Approach At Tses B1 80 km N of Keetmanshoop, follow C98 40 km towards Berseba, then take D3904 N for 18 km to Brukkaros.

Background This mountain, whose evolution started 80 million years ago, rises 650m above the surrounding plain, and dominates the skyline to the W of the main road between Mariental and Keetmanshoop. A climb to the top is well rewarded with superb views of the surrounding countryside. The name Brukkaros is the German version of the Nama name *Geitsigubeb*, referring to the mountain's supposed resemblance to the large leather apron traditionally worn by Nama women around their waist.

Brukkaros was formed when molten rocks intruded into rocks about 1 km below the earth's surface. These molten rocks must have encountered underground water, giving rise to steam which caused huge pressure, raising the overlying rocks into a 400m high, 10 km across, dome. The process was then repeated, but this time the cover of overlying rock was thin enough to allow the steam to blow out the centre of the cone in a vast explosion. Subsequent sedimentation over several hundred thousand years caused by rain washing the finely-shattered rock fragments into the crater and erosion created the crater floor.

In 1930 the Smithsonian Institute found the mountain the perfect site to establish a research station to study the surface of the sun, thanks to the incredibly clear desert air. This observation point on the northern edge of the crater is an ideal place to take in the view over the surrounding plains.

Hiking The road ends at the foot of the volcano and from here a footpath winds its way around the S side of the mountain for 3 km up to the crater lip. From here the path, such as it is, leads down into the crater and across a dried river bed, past a number of ancient quiver trees before starting the climb to the telecommunication tower on the northern edge of the crater.

There are still signs of the scientists'

Karakul Sheep

The use of Karakul sheep pelts to make high quality leather and fur clothes, formed the backbone of the farming industry in southern Namibia from the early 1920s to the mid 1970s. Often called Namibia's 'black gold' the karakul sheep originated in Bokhara in central Asia, from where they were imported to Germany in the early 1900s.

Experimental breeding started in Germany in 1903 and Paul Thorer, a prominent fur trader, started promoting the idea of exporting the sheep to German colonies. The then Governor of German South West Africa, Von Lindequist, supported the idea, and the first dozen sheep were brought into the country in 1907. In 1909 a further consignment of 22 rams and 252 ewes arrived, followed by smaller numbers of the animals in the years leading up to WW1. After the end of the war an experimental government karakul farm was set up at Neudam near Windhoek, in order to develop and improve the quality of the pelts. Breeders succeeded in developing pure white pelts in addition to the more normal black and grey ones, and although the former Soviet Union and Afghanistan produced larger numbers of the pelts, Namibian karakul fur was internationally recognized as being of the finest quality.

In 1919 the Karakul Breeders Association was founded to consolidate this new industry, and by 1923 thousands of the pelts were being exported to Germany. Over the next 50 years the numbers of pelts exported each year mushroomed to a peak of 3.2 million in 1973, earning millions of dollars for the farmers of the S. However, a combination of severe drought and changing views in Europe during the 1970s about the ethics of slaughtering millions of lambs only 24 hrs old for their pelts, sent the karakul fur industry into decline.

In response to this most farmers in the S switched to breeding dorbber sheep for their meat which guarantees a more reliable source of income, not affected by swings in the fashion industry. However, the recent extreme drought in Namibia has forced many farmers to sell all their livestock, creating a severe economic crisis in the farming industry of the S. Ironically however there has been a revival in the price of karakul pelts and demand for karakul wool in order to make carpets at present outstrips availability. Perhaps the hardy karakul sheep, well adapted to conditions of drought, will make a comeback to supply this new demand.

stay at the volcano – ancient rusting tins, a few old bottles and some graffiti etched into the trunks of the quiver trees. Maybe it's the American connection, but at any moment one expects a hungry creature from a 3rd rate Hollywood B-movie to come crawling over the lip of the volcano in hot pursuit.

Although the walk itself is not tough, there is no water and no shade on the mountain, so it is absolutely essential to take at least 2 litres of water per person. It is quite possible to camp on the volcano and well worth it for the fantastic

views of the night sky, but you will need to be completely self-sufficient.

The small Nama village of Berseba 18 km away is one of the oldest established settlements in southern Namibia, and dates back to 1850. As with other early 19th century settlements in Namibia, its establishment as a separate polity was directly linked to the acquisition of a missionary by the community. In 1851, Berseba was said to number 700 inhabitants and was lead by Paul Goliath, who had been the *onder-kaptein* or deputy chief at Bethanie during missionary

Schmelen's stay at the settlement.

Today the village numbers about 2,000 people and is rather a depressed community with little or no work for the adult population, who are dependent on their goats and sheep for survival.

● **Accommodation Guestfarms**: E-F *Kalahari Game Lodge*, T 06661 (farmline) 3112, F 06661 (farmline) 3103, 8 en suite 'A' frame chalets, restaurant, bar shop, swimming pool, petrol, situated on the Sandheuwel Game Ranch adjacent to the Kalahari Gemsbok Park, offers good game viewing, bird watching, horse riding and hiking trails. **Approach**: follow C15 towards South African border, or from Keetmanshoop take C17 past Koës to junction with C15, head SE to South African border and follow signs.

THE DEEP SOUTH

ROUTES Leaving Keetmanshoop the B1 heads S through the Karas Mountains towards the crossroads settlement of Grünau. From here the B1 itself continues a further 147 km to the border at Noordoewer, whilst the B3 heads towards Karasburg, 51 km away, before reaching the border at Ariamsvlei a further 108 km away.

The route through the Groot Karas Mountains is particularly beautiful, especially if the area has received good rains, when the bright light reflecting off the green veld contrasts the deep shadows cast by the rocky *kopjies*. For those with a sense of adventure the alternative route through the Klein Karas Mountains is well worth the extra hour or so it takes to get to Grünau. This gravel road twists and turns, climbs and falls like a roller coaster and must be approached with caution, however it takes you through breathtaking, pristine mountain scenery. Turn right onto the D608 6 km after leaving Keetmanshoop and continue for 125 km before turning left onto the C12 which leads you to Grünau.

The drive from Grünau to Noordoewer initially climbs steadily until a plateau is reached, thereafter it is all downhill to the Orange River, where summer temperatures can reach 50°C. It feels almost as if one is entering hell's kitchen, but the sight of the green irrigated banks of the Orange River soon dispels that notion. For those into canoeing this is the place to start an Orange River Canoe Safari.

FISH RIVER CANYON

Approach The two places to visit in the Canyon are the observation point and campsite at Hobas on the northeastern side of the canyon and Ai-Ais Hot Springs Resort at the southern end. From Grünau take the B1 S for 31 km, then turn onto the C10 which leads to Ai-Ais and the turn-off for Hobas. From Keetmanshoop take the B4 until the turn for the C12. Follow this for 77 km before the turn-off for the D601. This leads to Hobas and the D324 for Ai-Ais.

The route from Keetmanshoop is arguably the most desolate yet most impressive journey that can be taken in Namibia. If you ever have wondered what the surface of the moon looks like, albeit in blinding sunlight, then here is where to find out. Almost in defiance of the bareness of the landscape a host of desert plants, cacti, succulents and quiver trees survive and even prosper in this arid, rocky environment.

Background The history of the Fish River Canyon begins roughly 1,800 million years ago when sandstones, shales and lava were deposited along what are now the slopes of the canyon. Between 1,300 and 1,000 million years ago extreme heat caused these deposits to become folded and change into gneiss and granites. About 800 million years ago dolerite dykes intruded into these rocks and these are now visible inside the canyon.

Between 750 and 650 million years ago, the surface of these rocks was eroded to form the floor of a shallow sea which washed over southern Namibia. The two final pieces in the jigsaw took place about 500 million years ago when tectonic movement caused a series of fractures which lead to the formation of the Fish River Canyon. This early version of the canyon was deepened by the retreat southwards of glaciers during the Gondwana Ice Age some 300 million years ago.

However, this was not the end of the process. Within the main canyon a second or lower canyon was created by further movements of the earth's crust as it cooled. Initially a trough, this second canyon became the water-course which is now the Fish River. The Fish is the longest river in Namibia and plays an important role in both watering and

draining southern Namibia. In particular it feeds Hardap Dam, Namibia's largest artificial lake.

Early Bushman legends suggest an alternative origin to the canyon, altogether less scientific but equally fascinating. Hunters were chasing a serpent called *Kouteign Kooru* across the veld and in order to escape the snake slithered off into the desert, causing the massive gash that is the canyon. Archaeological evidence suggests that the Bushmen, or their ancestors, were here 50,000 years ago, so maybe there is something to their version of events.

With a supply of water even during the driest winter months and food in the form of fish and game birds, the canyon has attracted human beings for thousands of years. So far six Early and three Middle Stone Age sites have been identified in the canyon as well as the remains of a number of pre-colonial herders' camps.

Although all the tourist literature boasts that the Fish River Canyon is second in size only to the Grand Canyon in Arizona, this is not actually the case. Impressive though the canyon is, it is actually only Africa's second largest after the Blue Nile Gorge in Ethiopia.

HOBAS CAMPSITE AND OBSERVATION POINT

About half-way along the canyon at Hell's Bend are a series of tortuous curves in the Fish River where the canyon turns round and round on itself. Along this stretch, about 80 km N of Ai-Ais are a number of observation points perched on the edge of the canyon where its awe-inspiring splendour can be fully appreciated. As the viewpoint is westward facing, early morning rather than late afternoon, is probably the best time to come here.

● **Accommodation** F *The Hobas Campsite*, 10 sites, maximum 8 persons per site, communal toilets and washing facilities and braai sites for cooking, small kiosk, information centre and swimming pool, bookings must be

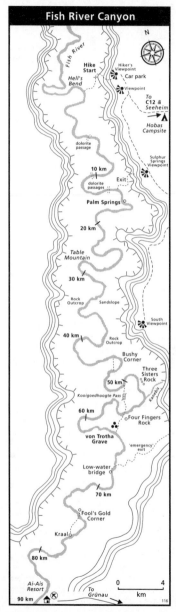

Fish River Canyon

Fish River

Hike Start

Hell's Bend

Hiker's Viewpoint

Car park

Viewpoint

To C12 & Seeheim

Hobas Campsite

dolorite passage

Sulphur Springs Viewpoint

10 km

Exit

dolorite passages

Palm Springs

20 km

Table Mountain

30 km

Rock Outcrop

Sandslope

South Viewpoint

40 km

Rock Outcrop

Bushy Corner

Three Sisters Rock

50 km

Kooigoedhoogte Pass

60 km

Four Fingers Rock

von Trotha Grave

'emergency' exit

Low-water bridge

70 km

Fool's Gold Corner

Kraal

80 km

Ai-Ais Resort

To Grünau

90 km

0   4

km

116

made in advance through Central Reservations in Windhoek, the campsite is 10 km from the viewpoint and is the starting point for the Fish River Canyon Hiking Trail.

About 20 km from the main viewpoint is a new lodge **B** *Cañon Lodge* T (061) 251863, an unusual design of 20 bungalows with natural rock walls, ensuite bathroom, wooden doors and a canvas roof. Meals will be available from a restaurant in a converted farmhouse dating from 1910. 60 km north is a further new development by the same group, a guesthouse **A-B** *Cañon House* T (061) 251863, 5 ensuite rooms, an ideal location for hikers. Further reports of both establishments would be welcome.

FISH RIVER CANYON HIKING TRAIL

This 85 km 4-day trail is reputed to be one of the toughest hiking trails in southern Africa, and is not for beginners or the unfit. Although the trail is more or less flat, loose sand and large boulders are tiring factors, which added to the fact that hikers have to carry all provisions with them, cause some to take the option of an early emergency 'escape' route from the Canyon. For those who are fit enough and determined enough to complete the trail the 4 days are a magical wilderness experience, offering opportunities for game and birdwatching as well as wondering at the scale and power of nature.

The route starts from the observation point nearest Hobas, but as no transport is provided, a 10 km walk from the campsite to the edge of the canyon is how most people start the walk. From the top of the canyon the path descends sharply to the canyon floor, losing 500m in altitude on the way. Parts of the descent are very steep and it is advisable to make use of the chains especially if you are carrying a rucksack. The route at the bottom follows the left hand side of the river over boulders and soft, loose sand – one of the worst stretches of the walk. 15 km downstream lie the wonderfully soothing waters of Sulphur Springs, also known as Palm Springs, the first overnight stop.

According to legend, during WW1 two German soldiers sought refuge from internment in the canyon. One of them was suffering from skin cancer and the other from asthma, however after bathing in the hot springs these ailments were miraculously cured. Whether true or not these springs, bubbling up from a depth of 2,000m at a rate of 30 litres per second offer much needed relief for sore feet and muscles after the long first day's trek.

Heading S of Palm Springs the shortest route criss-crosses the river as far as the Table Mountain landmark some 15 km on. This section of the trail is extremely tiring as it involves struggling one's way through deep sand and gravel – not much fun. Further on the canyon widens and the trail becomes firmer with more river crossings, more or less wet depending on the state of the river. 1997 trailists can expect a fair amount of water in the pools following excellent rains early in the year.

Close to the 30 km point is Table Mountain, one of the more easily recognisable natural landmarks along the trail. After a further 18 km you will reach the first of four possible short cuts. At this point the alternative path avoids an area of scrub vegetation known as Bushy Corner. Around the next corner of the canyon is the second short cut. Here the path climbs up to the Kooigoedhoote Pass. If you choose to take this short cut you will miss seeing the Three Sisters Rock and the point where the Kanebis river joins the Fish river. However from the pass you will enjoy an excellent view of Four Fingers Rock. Along the third short cut you will pass the grave of Lieutenant von Trotha, a German soldier killed in 1905 during the German-Nama war and buried where he fell. A couple of km beyond the grave, back in the main canyon is the second 'emergency' exit path. From here it is a further 20 km to

Kudu
Source: Steele, David (1972) *Game sanctuaries of Southern Africa* Howard Timmins: Cape Town. Illustrated by John Perry

Ai-Ais, a cold drink, soft bed and no more walking for a few days.

Equipment Hikers must take all their food with them – a camping stove is also suggested as wood for fires can be scarce. Water is available en route but will need to be purified or boiled. A fishing line is worth taking, provided the pools are deep enough, and freshly grilled fish is a great luxury after a hot day's hike.

A tent is not necessary but a sleeping bag is, as the temperature can fall dramatically at night. Tough walking boots, a hat, first aid kit and plasters for blisters are all an absolute must.

Bird and game viewing Small mammals such as rock dassies and ground squirrels are a common sight in the canyon and with luck larger mammals such as klipspringer, steenbok and springbok may also be spotted. Kudu, gemsbok and mountain zebra live in and around the canyon but are harder to spot and leopards the hardest of all. The rock pools and reeds attract a large number of water birds, including the African Fish Eagle, grey herons and hammerkops and other birds such as bee-eaters, wagtails and rock pigeons are all common.

Trail information Due to extreme temperatures and the risk of flash flooding in summer, the trail is open from May to the end of Sep. Groups must consist of 3 persons minimum, 40 maximum. Medical certificates of physical fitness issued within 40 days before the hike need to be shown to the ranger at Hobas before starting. All bookings must be made at Central Reservations in Windhoek, and it is advisable to book well in advance. There is no public transport to Hobas or Ai-Ais nor transport from the Hobas Campsite to the start of the trail. A final point to stress is to **remove all your rubbish**. In 1991 the Dorsland Hiking Club removed over 360 kg of rubbish from along the trail. Each year they conduct a similar cleanup walk and still manage to remove 35 kg, most of this material is paper: all of it has been left by hikers.

AI-AIS HOT SPRINGS RESORT

Approach See above.

Background Ai-Ais is a Nama name meaning 'fire-water', indicating the extreme heat of the hot springs here. Modern knowledge of the springs dates back to 1850 when a Nama herder discovered the springs whilst searching for lost sheep, however it is certain that Stone Age people inhabited the area thousands of years ago.

During the 1904-1907 German-Nama war the springs were used as a base camp by German forces. Following WW1 the site was partially developed but it was not until 1969 that the site was declared as a conservation area.

The present resort was first opened in 1971, but almost immediately destroyed by the Fish River coming down in flood. Since then flooding has occurred twice more, in 1974 and 1988 on each occasion forcing the closure of the resort for repairs.

The resort is very popular both with Namibians and South Africans as a place to come and relax and lounge around in the thermal baths and outdoor heated swimming pool. As with all thermal springs the water is supposed to have natural curative properties and is especially beneficial for sufferers of rheumatism.

For those feeling energetic there are some enjoyable walks into the Canyon, especially pleasant in the late afternoon when the shadows are long and the heat off the rocks contrasts with the cool sand. It is also possible to hire a horse and ride into the Canyon. On the other hand it is easy enough to allow the tranquility of the resort to lull you into a state of complete relaxation.

Resort information Open 2nd Fri in Mar to 31 Oct the resort offers thermal baths, tennis courts, restaurant, snack bar, shop, petrol, horse riding, hiking trails and bird watching in a beautiful and peaceful setting.

● **Accommodation C-F** *Luxury flat*, modern fully equipped en suite 2 bed flat; *flat*, fully equipped 4-bed en suite flat, rather cramped for 4; *hut*, simple accommodation with own cooking but shared ablution facilities; *camping*, attractive, grassy camp and caravan sites, maximum 8 people, 2 vehicles, one tent/caravan per site, shared cooking and ablution facilities. Entrance: N$10 adults N$1 children, thermal baths N$2 adults, N$1 children per session. **Guestfarms: C** *Canyon Nature Park*, T 061 226979, F 061 226999, situated on the western edge of the Fish River Canyon in 43,000 ha of land this Nature Park offers visitors the opportunity to take guide hikes into the canyon. Guides lead a 4-day hike through the canyon and back to the main camp, overnighting at basic shelters set up along the route. All bookings need to be made in advance.

KARASBURG

(*STD code* 06342 operator service) From the visitor's point of view, Karasburg is no more than a small settlement en route for other places. It has a number of garages and one reasonable hotel, but otherwise is devoid of attractions for the visitor.

Local information
● **Accommodation**

D *Kalkfontein Hotel*, Kalkfontein St, T/F 172/3, offers 17 rooms, 11 with en suite facilities, telephone and a/c, the hotel has a restaurant serving plain but acceptable meaty fare, a bar and lounge with TV, breakfast not included, off-street parking but not secure.

● **Places to eat**
Kalkfontein Hotel, has reasonably priced meals, but a better option is *Hansel Restaurant*, next to the Engen Garage which does tasty steaks, schnitzel, ribs with accompanying entertainment from an African grey parrot.

Takeaways: there are a few takeaways next to the garages.

● **Banks & money changers**
Bank Windhoek, First National Bank, both offer money changing facilities and auto tellers.

● **Hospital & medical services**
The State Hospital, T 167.

● **Post & telecommunications**
Post Office: Park St, Mon-Fri 0800-1630, Sat 0800-1130.

● **Useful addresses**
Police: T 10111.

● **Transport**
712 km to Windhoek; 110 km to the border at Ariamsvlei.

Train Windhoek (18½ hrs), via Keetmanshoop and Mariental, daily except Sat, 1125; **Ariamsvlei** (3 hrs), Wed and Sat, 1430.

Road Bus: Intercape, T (061) 227847, coach picks up and drops off in front of SP Motors: **Upington** (3 hrs), Mon, Tues, Thur, Sat, 0200; **Windhoek** via Keetmanshoop and Rehoboth (8 hrs), Tues, Thur, Fri, Sun, 2245.

Warmbad

Located 43 km S of Karasburg, Warmbad is the site of the oldest mission station in Namibia. In 1805 the Albrecht brothers Abraham and Christian started working with the semi-nomadic Nama people living in this area. Although Abraham died in 1810 Christian carried on to establish the mission station at Warmbad.

The village is also the site of a series of hot springs which give the place its name. The spring is surrounded by the

---

Canoeing on the Orange River

The canoe safaris start first thing in the morning so everyone pitches up the night beforehand and makes camp on the green lawns by the river bank. It's a good taste of what is to come as during the 4-day trip every night is spent sleeping under the stars by the banks of the river.

After some basic instructions in how the trip is going to be managed and a short environmental lecture, it's into the 2-person kayaks. Clothes and sleeping bags are squashed into water-proof plastic drums which fit neatly into the boats and then the trip starts.

The size of the group depends on pot luck and given that you spend 4 days in each other's company it is important to get on with the other people in the group. The guides take care of everything – navigating the river, choosing campsites and preparing all meals, as well as pointing out the different species of birds and animals living on and along the river.

The canoeing itself is not difficult and although the first day can be tiring if you are unused to this kind of exercise, by the fourth day it feels as if you could carry on for another 4 days. For the first 2 days the river is quite narrow and passes through a ravine. This is where the best rapids are – fun without being frightening – the highlight being the *sjambok* or 'whip' rapids which involve a fast descent through the rock-strewn river with an eddy at the bottom for added entertainment.

Later in the trip the river widens, the current slows and there's time to take in the lush vegetation on the banks, watch the monkeys swinging in the trees, or take a swim in the river. This is when one has a chance to appreciate the unspoiled beauty of this river wilderness. The trip ends with a minibus ride from the exit point back to Noordoewer.

ruins of the Old Fort and Mission Station and as with a number of such historical sites in Namibia, there are plans to establish a resort here. Until that happens Warmbad remains another tiny settlement stuck in the middle of the veld.

BORDER WITH SOUTH AFRICA

Ariamsvlei

The border at Ariamsvlei is open 24 hrs and consists of no more than a petrol station and the immigration offices. Apart from over-busy holiday periods it should not take too long to complete formalities here.

Noordoewer and the Orange River

Noordoewer is a small settlement on the banks of the Orange River and one of the hottest places in Namibia. Fortunately there is an abundance of water which is used to irrigate fruit trees – in particular grapes. The village consists of the border post, a couple of garages and minimarkets and one hotel, the **C** *Camel Lodge*. A few kilometres out of town along the banks of the Orange River are the base camps for a number of canoeing companies (see page 14, Introduction on canoeing in Namibia).

WEST FROM KEETMANSHOOP

ROUTES The B4 leaves Keetmanshoop and heads W over the high veld towards Goageb and the small mountain town of Aus 230 km away. After leaving Aus the road descends rapidly from the edge of the central highlands plateau to the desert floor, where it cuts a swathe through the sand dunes for a further 120 km until it reaches Lüderitz.

AUS

(*STD code* 063332) This small settlement perched high up in the Aus Mountains is famous in Namibia for the occasional snowfalls during cold winters. After summer rains the area is also known for the beauty of its wild flowers and is an appealing place to go for a hike. The village consists of a hotel, railway station, shop and garage, and a line of old cottages.

History Aus was established as a prisoner-of-war camp in 1915 following the surrender of the German colonial troops to the South African forces. The site was chosen for its strategic significance, situated as it is on the railway line between Keetmanshoop and the harbour at Lüderitz. This made it possible to ship food and equipment from Cape Town via Lüderitz to the camp.

By 15 August 1915, 22 POWs and 600 guards were stationed here, initially living in tents. The harsh climate however made life unbearable, and in the face of South African apathy to improve the situation, the inmates themselves set about making bricks which they used to build their own houses. By 1916 none of the prisoners were living in tents and they were even selling their surplus to the South African forces at 10 shillings per 1,000 bricks.

By 1916 the prisoners had built their own wood stoves on which to cook and the authorities had provided water for washing and laundry purposes. It seems as if the South African garrison was not so enterprising and continued living in tents until 1918 when barracks were finally constructed.

Following the signing of the Treaty of Versailles at the end of WW1, the prisoners were gradually released, the last group leaving on 13 May 1919 after which the camp was closed. Unfortunately little remains of the camp which is situated a few kilometres just outside of the town.

Places of interest The site of the old POW Camp can be visited and is indicated by a National Monuments plaque on a rock. Unfortunately, the only literature available is printed in Afrikaans.

Approach Turn off B4 into the village. Take the left fork at the T-junction and drive on for a further 3 km to the turn-off for Rosh Pinah. Ignore this and continue for a further 600m to the site of the camp.

● **Accommodation D-E** *Bahnhof Hotel*, T 44, this rather quaint hotel has adequate rooms with and without en suite facilities, a restaurant and the village's local bar, which can get very lively.

LÜDERITZ

(*STD code* 06331) The small coastal town of Lüderitz is one of Namibia's oddities, a faded, picturesque German colonial town lying between the inhospitable dunes of the Namib desert on the one side, and the vast iciness of the South Atlantic on the other. Ironically, both desert and ocean provide the resources necessary for Lüderitz's survival; diamonds from the desert and fish, rock lobster, seaweed and diamonds from the ocean.

20 years ago the town was as good as dead, but thanks to the reopening of the diamond mine at Elizabeth Bay and to the development of both tourism and fishing industries, Lüderitz is currently enjoying a mini-boom. A new harbour development scheme starts in 1997, both to cater for and attract more tourists and to increase the capacity of the

Wild horses of the Namib

The legendary wild horses of the Namib are probably the only wild desert-dwelling horses in the world, and their origins are a source of much speculation. Romantics suggest that they are the descendants of the stud kept by 'Baron' von Wolf at Duwisib Castle 160 km away. Other less fanciful suggestions are that they escaped from surrounding farms or that they originate from horses left behind by the German troops when they fled Aus in 1915.

These horses are uniquely adapted to survive in their desert environment. They move slowly, sweat less and drink as infrequently as once every 5 days, their only source of water coming from a bore-hole at Garub sunk especially for them. A blind here allows visitors to observe the horses from close up on the rare occasions when they do come to drink.

The numbers of horses are constantly fluctuating in response to the grazing conditions – only the toughest can survive the frequent droughts. However, during good rainy seasons grass grows on the dunes and the horses are able to fatten themselves in preparation for the lean years ahead. At one time a proposal was made to tame some of the horses and use them for patrols in the Etosha National Park, but nothing came of it.

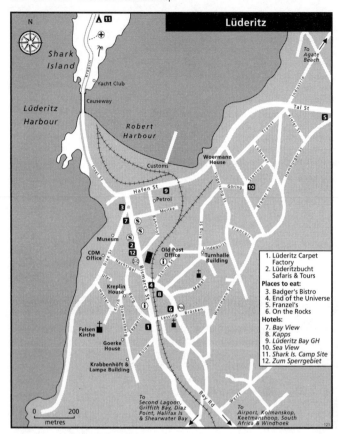

Lüderitz

1. Lüderitz Carpet Factory
2. Lüderitzbucht Safaris & Tours

Places to eat:
3. Badger's Bistro
4. End of the Universe
5. Franzel's
6. On the Rocks

Hotels:
7. Bay View
8. Kapps
9. Lüderitz Bay GH
10. Sea View
11. Shark Is. Camp Site
12. Zum Sperrgebiet

harbour itself. As a sign of Lüderitz's revival, 1996 staged the first traditional German carnival since 1960.

History

Stone implements and skeletons found arounde Lüderitz area testify that Khoisan people were visiting the area long before the first Europeans arrived. The Portuguese explorer Bartholomew Diaz was the first European to set eyes on Lüderitz Bay when he sought refuge from a South Atlantic storm on Christmas Day 1487. Upon his return from the Cape of Good Hope in Jul 1488 he erected a stone cross is accordance with Portuguese seafaring traditions of the time.

The next European to show up was Cornelius Wobma, an employee of the Dutch East India Company, who was sent to investigate the possibility of establishing trading links with the local Nama communities. However the attempt failed and although the Dutch authorities at the Cape annexed the bay and surrounding islands in 1793, it was to be a further 200 years after Wobma's visit before other European traders arrived.

From 1842 onwards European ships exploited the rich guano resources on the islands around the bay, and at times up to 450 ships lay anchored off the harbour. The cold seas of the South Atlantic also proved to be rich whaling grounds. Between 1842 and 1861 the British-ruled Cape Colony annexed all the islands along the coast.

In 1883 Heinrich Vogelsang negotiated a treaty with Nama chief Joseph Fredericks of Bethanie on behalf of the merchant Adolf Lüderitz. This treaty entitled Lüderitz to acquire all the land within a 5 mile radius of the harbour and cost £100 and 200 rifles. The following year Lüderitz successfully persuaded Chancellor Bismarck to offer German protection to the area, and this event signalled the beginning of the development of the town itself.

Unfortunately, Lüderitz himself did not live long enough to see the growth and development of his settlement, as he died in a boat accident whilst exploring the Orange River. The town was named in memory of him.

The main development of the town took place in the early years of the century during the period of German colonization, first as a base and supply point for the Shutztruppe during the 1904-1907 German-Nama war, and then as a wild west type boom town following the discovery of diamonds in the desert nearby in 1908. Lüderitz was officially declared a town the following year.

Lüderitz went into a period of long decline following the removal of the Consolidated Diamond Mining Headquarters (CDM) to Oranjemund in 1938. Ironically though the stagnation of the economy prevented the development of the town and thus ensured the preservation of the original buildings, giving the town its present day quaint turn-of-the-century feel. During the 1970s interest in Lüderitz as a tourist destination grew at the same time as the rock lobster, fishing and seaweed industries were starting to become successful.

The renaissance of the town is now in full swing with the harbour once again busy, hotels full and migrant workers arriving from the N of Namibia looking for work. 1997 sees the start of the construction of a new luxury hotel and conference centre and the first phase of water front development designed to boost the town's tourist appeal.

Places of interest

Lüderitz has a number of fine old colonial buildings which can easily be explored in a couple of hours walking around the town, as well as a small museum which is worth 30 mins.

A walk up Bismarck St, the main thoroughfare, will take you past the **Deutsche-Afrika Bank** building, built in 1907, on the corner of Diaz St. Further up the street is the **Station Building**, commissioned in 1912 and finished 2 years later in 1916. The railway line from Lüderitz to Aus was completed in 1906 and became important as a means of transporting troops into the interior during the 1904-1907 German-Nama war. Following the discovery of diamonds in 1908 and the subsequent extension of the railway line to Keetmanshoop, the existing station became too small and the German Colonial Administration authorized the building of the new station.

The **Old Post Office**, found on Shintz St was completed in 1908, and originally had a clock in its tower but this was removed in 1912 and transferred to the church. The building now functions as the headquarters of Nature Conservation. The **Turnhalle Building**, dating from 1912-13 on Lindequist St, was originally a gymnasium but now doubles as the town library and mini-theatre.

Two of the town's most impressive buildings, the **German Lutheran Church**, or Felsenkirche (Church on the Rocks), and **Goerke House** are situated

An early photo of Friederich Eberlanz's house,
now the Lüderitz Museum

on neighbouring hilltops in the old part of town and have excellent views of the town centre and harbour area. The foundation stone for the Church was laid in 1911 and the building was consecrated the following year. The building is notable for its fine stained glass windows and as with the Christuskirche in Windhoek, the altar window was donated by Kaiser Wilhelm II and the altar bible by his wife. The church is open daily from 1700-1800 in winter and between 1800-1900 in summer.

Goerke House, situated on Diamond Hill was named after its original owner Hans Goerke who had been a store inspector in the Shutztruppe and then became a successful local busi-

nessman. CDM/NAMDEB acquired the house in 1920, sold it to the government in 1944 when it became the town magistrate's official residence, and then repurchased the building in 1983. The house lay empty between 1980-83 after the magistrate was recalled to Keetmanshoop, there not being enough crime in Lüderitz to warrant his presence.

From the outside the house is an array of different architectural styles incorporating Roman and Egyptian, amongst others, and inside it is possible to imagine what many of the crumbling houses at nearby Kolmanskop must have looked like in their heyday. There is a fine stained glass window above the staircase depicting a flock of flamingoes on the beach, as well as an excellent view over the town and harbour from the balcony of the main bedroom. The house now functions as a guesthouse for NAMDEB visitors and as a local museum. It is open Mon-Fri 1400-1500 and Sat 1200-1300, admission N$5.

Lüderitz Museum, Diaz St, was founded by Friederich Eberlanz who arrived in Lüderitz in 1914. Fascinated by the local flora he started a private collection which soon incorporated ancient stone tools and other items he discovered. This private collection was soon attracting a wider interest and so the museum was established. Today the museum has displays of local history, the mining industry and an ethnology section displaying different tools and weapons from around Namibia. Open Mon-Fri 1530-1700, admission N$5.

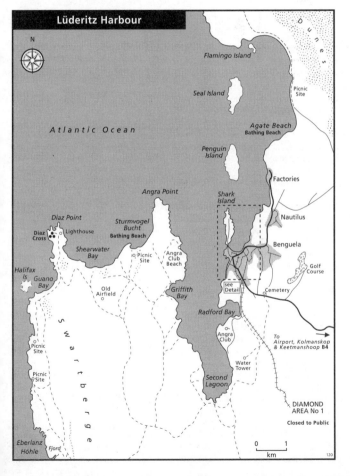

Excursions

A twisting gravel road heads S round the coast through a moonscape of rocky bays, beaches and small islands on the way to **Diaz Point**, 22 km away. A large cross stands there, a replica of the original erected by Portuguese explorer Bartholomew Diaz in 1486 on his way back to Portugal after sailing around the Cape of Good Hope. The nearby foghorn tower and lighthouse were built 1911-12 and can be visited by first making arrangements at the local tourist office.

A similar rocky drive N out of Lüderitz leads to **Agate Beach** (follow the signs from Hafen St), a fine, sandy stretch of coast suitable for surfing and swimming – for those brave enough for the cold sea. Small piles of stones and mini-trenches dot the beach, remnants from past diamond and agate diggings. In the late afternoon there is a good chance of seeing gemsbok and springbok which live in the desert beyond the beach.

All along this section of coast there is a profusion of wildlife; just off-shore from the Cross itself is a large seal colony and further down the coast on **Halifax Island** there are large numbers of jackass penguins and cormorants. Pink flamingoes flock in the bays and in small lakes on-shore also. The presence of so much wildlife is due to the strong, cold Benguela current which keeps the sea clean and also makes it an ideal place for catching rock lobster and cultivating oysters. The only drawback is the accompanying strong, cold SW wind which seems to constantly blow, making warm clothes essential.

A boat trip departs the harbour every morning at 0700 in summer and 0800 in winter, weather permitting. The trip takes about 2½ hrs down to Diaz Point and back and if the sea is calm may continue on to Halifax Island. Price N\$40 adults, N\$20 children with an extra N\$20 charged for the extended trip to Halifax Island.

Half day tours to **Elizabeth Bay** diamond mine, the **Atlas Bay Seal Colony** and all places mentioned above can be arranged through Lüderitzbucht Safaris & Tours, Bismarck St, T 2719.

Local information
● **Accommodation**

B *Sea View Hotel Zum Sperrgebiet*, corner of Woermann and Stettiner sts, T 3411, F 3414, the newest of the town's hotels situated on a hill overlooking the harbour, 22 en suite rooms, TV, phone, sauna, swimming pool, restaurant, rec.

C *Zum Sperrgebiet*, Bismarck St, T 2856, F 2976, the first of the two 'Sperrgebiet' hotels under the same ownership, 10 rooms, 5 en suite with phone, restaurant, a comfortable option in the middle of town.

D *Bay View*, corner of Bismarck and Diaz sts, T 2288, F 2402, 29 triple, double and single en suite rooms, phone, some with TV, built around two small courtyards, one with swimming pool, bar and snack bar downstairs, restaurant upstairs, friendly and clean, rec; **D** *Kapps Hotel*, Bay Road, T 2345/2995, F 2402, Lüderitz's oldest hotel dating back to the diamond boom days, now completely renovated, 21 en suite rooms with TV, restaurant, secure parking; **D** *Lüderitz Bay Guesthouse*, Hafen St, T 3347, F 3163, offers friendly German style B&B in an old colonial building, self-catering flat also available.

Camping: F *Shark Island Campsite*, at the northern end of Hafen St, has rocky campsites overlooking the harbour with communal facilities, great views but very exposed.

● **Places to eat**

There is a wide choice of restaurants in Lüderitz, all of which serve fresh seafood in addition to the customary Namibian fare. Any of the hotels above is a good option as are the restaurants listed below.

Franzel's Restaurant, Tal St, T 2292, is a popular place with locals and can get full so a booking is advisable, specializes in seafood and game dishes, rec; *On The Rocks*, Bay St, closed Wed, has friendly service and good seafood; *Badger's Bistro*, Diaz St, is a lively bar and serves good pub grub; *End Of The Universe*, Bay St, is a small bistro popular with the diamond divers, serves good seafood and vegetarian dishes in informal setting, rec; *Coffee Shop*, corner of Bismarck and Bay sts, is a good place for a coffee and lunchtime snacks.

● **Banks & money changers**
Commercial Bank, **First National Bank** and **Standard Bank**, all have their premises on Bismarck St and all have money changing facilities.

● **Hospitals & medical services**
State Hospital, T 2446.

● **Post & telecommunications**
Post Office: Bismarck St, Mon-Fri 0800-1630, Sat 0800-1100. Telephone boxes outside the PO, ask at the counter for international calls.

● **Shopping**
Crafts Centre, top of Bismarck St, sells a range of ostrich shell and other jewellery, as well as attractive karakul carpets from the next door carpet factory. There is also a small coffee bar. *Lüderitz Carpet Factory*, top of Bismarck St, produces high quality handwoven karakul rugs, visitors are welcome to watch the carpets being made and can place specific orders, excellent value for those interested in rugs as a souvenir.

● **Tourist offices**
Lüderitz Foundation, top end of Bismarck St, open Mon-Fri 0830-1200 and 1400-1600, Sat 0800-1200.

● **Tour companies & travel agents**
Lüderitzbucht Safaris & Tours, bottom end of Bismarck St, T 2719, F 2863, can arrange local tours as well as flights and bookings around Namibia.

● **Transport**
350 km to Keetmanshoop, 650 km to Noordoewer (South Africa border), 845 km to Windhoek.

Air: the stopping **Air Namibia** flight between Windhoek and Cape Town helps connect the town with the outside world. T (06331) 2850, F 2845. **Cape Town** (3 hrs): Tues, Thur, Sat, 1250, Sun, 1350; **Windhoek-Eros** via Swakopmund (2½ hrs): Mon, Wed, Fri, Sun, 1320.

Road Bus: Star Line, T (06331) 2875, service has replaced the passenger train between Lüderitz and **Keetmanshoop**. There is a daily bus at 1300; plus, Sat, 0600 and Sun, 1900. The journey takes between 4 and 5 hrs.

KOLMANSKOP GHOST TOWN

Approach Drive 10 km out of town on B4, then follow signs.

Background The former diamond boom town of Kolmanskop, finally deserted in 1956 is now a ghost town and lies crumbling in the desert 10 km inland of Lüderitz, gradually being eroded by the wind and buried by the sand. It is a fascinating place to visit, offering as it does a glimpse into an exciting part of Namibia's history.

History In Apr 1908, Zacharias Lewala, a worker on the Lüderitz-Aus railway line presented a shiny stone to his supervisor August Stauch, who was intelligent enough to obtain a prospecting license before handing over the stone to have it officially verified as a diamond. When this eventually did happen, a diamond rush exploded around the site of Kolmanskop, where in the early days men would crawl on their hands and knees in the full moonlight picking up the glittering stones in their paths.

In Sep 1908 the Colonial Government declared a 'Sperrgebiet' or forbidden zone extending from the Orange River in the S for 360 km northwards and 100 km inland in order to control the mining of the diamonds, and in Feb 1909 a central diamond market was established.

The WW1 effectively stopped diamond production and the recession which followed the war hit the diamond industry badly. However, Sir Ernest Oppenheimer, the Chairman of the Anglo-American Company, saw this as an opportunity to buy up all the small diamond companies operating in the Sperrgebiet, and combine them to form Consolidated Diamond Mines. CDM, as it became known, was to control all diamond mining in the area until entering into partnership with the Namibian government in 1995 under the new name of NAMDEB.

Kolmanskop enjoyed its heyday in

the 1920s when it grew rapidly to service the diamond miners and eventually the families which followed. A hospital, gymnasium and concert hall, school, butchery, bakery and a number of fine houses were built in the middle of the desert, and at its peak there were as many as 300 German and 800 Oshiwambo adults living in the town. The hospital was ultra-modern and was equipped with the first x-ray machine in southern Africa.

The sheer wealth generated at Kolmanskop is demonstrated by the way in which water was supplied to the town. Every month a ship left Cape Town carrying 1,000 tonnes of water, and each resident was supplied with 20 litres per day – free. Those requiring additional water had to pay for it, at half the price of beer! The lack of fresh water to power steam engines also forced the building of a power station which supplied electricity – very advanced technology at the time – to power the mining machinery.

However, the boom years ended in 1928 when diamond reserves six times the size of those at Kolmanskop were discovered at the mouth of the Orange River. The town of Oranjemund was built in 1936 to exploit these reserves and in 1938 most of the workers and equipment were relocated from Kolmanskop to this new headquarters. Following this the town went into steady decline, although the last people only left Kolmanskop in 1956, leaving this once flourishing town to the sand and the wind.

Kolmanskop was rescued from the desert in 1979 following a CDM commissioned report to assess the potential of this ghost town. In 1980 restoration began and the town was opened to tourism.

Information Guided tours take place every morning, at 1000 and 1100 starting at Kolmanskop. Admission N$10 per person, tickets must be purchased beforehand at Lüderitz Safaris and Tours on Bismarck St. If you have no transport you can arrange to be taken to the town.

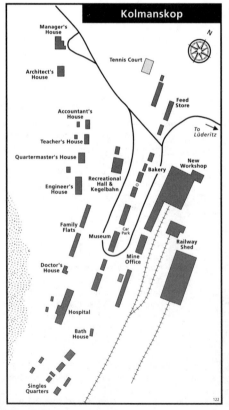

Kolmanskop

Manager's House
Tennis Court
Architect's House
Feed Store
Accountant's House
To Lüderitz
Teacher's House
Quartermaster's House
New Workshop
Recreational Hall & Kegelbahn
Bakery
Engineer's House
Car Park
Family Flats
Museum
Railway Shed
Doctor's House
Mine Office
Hospital
Bath House
Singles Quarters

NATIONAL DIAMOND AREA

Following the discovery of diamonds at Kolmanskop in 1908 and the ensuing diamond rush the German colonial authorities declared a *Sperrgebiet* or 'forbidden area' along the coast. This area extended from the Orange River in the S for 360 km northward to latitude 26S and inland for 100 km, and is known today as Diamond Area 1.

Exclusive mining rights for this area are held by NAMDEB owned jointly by the Namibian Government and De Beers, and it is forbidden to enter the area without permission. Even where the *Sperrgebiet* becomes part of the Namib-Naukluft Park, access is strictly controlled and visitors are required to remain on the road at all times.

In 1994 a British-Canadian company NAMCO obtained off-shore diamond mining concessions at Lüderitz, potentially breaking the current NAMDEB monopoly. Diamond divers, many from South Africa, Australia and New Zealand, suck up the sea bed with powerful vacuum pumps, after which the gravel is sorted for diamonds. It is difficult, unpleasant work which the divers can only carry out when sea conditions permit. The rewards however are potentially huge and consequently a small diver community lives in Lüderitz hoping to strike it rich.

A house in Kolmanskop abandoned to the sand

Information for travellers

BEFORE TRAVELLING

ENTRY REQUIREMENTS

All visitors must be in possession of a passport which is valid for a minimum of 6 months from their date of entry. In 1995 the visa requirements for many nationals were abolished. At present visitors from Angola, Austria, Belgium, Botswana, Canada, France, Germany, Ireland, Italy, Japan, Luxembourg, Netherlands, Moçambique, Russia, Singapore, South Africa, Switzerland, Tanzania, United Kingdom, United States of America and Zimbabwe can stay in the country for a period of 90 days with a permit issued at your point of entry. Extensions have to be applied for from the Ministry of Home Affairs in Windhoek, corner of Independence Ave and Kasino St in the centre of town, T 061 2929111. Tourist visas can also be obtained from Namibian Embassies overseas.

WHEN TO GO

There is no bad time to visit Namibia, but depending upon what you wish to see and do during your visit there are certain months which are better than others. Outside the winter months, Jun, Jul and Aug, excessively high temperatures can spoil a holiday for many visitors. This is not to say don't come in the summer, after all summer in Namibia coincides with winter in Europe and the United States. But it can get very hot in Windhoek. For the 2 weeks around Christmas and the New Year there is a mass exodus, for those who can afford it, to the coast where temperatures are significantly cooler. To the N around Etosha, the Kaokoland and Caprivi the average daytime temperatures are 34°C in summer. It is also worth noting the duration of local school holidays. Local families book all the good value National Parks accommodation 6-12 months in advance.

Namibia is essentially an arid country but during the rainy season many roads in rural areas can be closed to saloon cars for several days. If you are keen on game viewing then the dry winter months of May to Sep are the best months to visit. This is when most wild animals are forced to congregate around man-made waterholes. Bird watching is best after the rains when there are numerous flooded depressions which attract migrant species. Much of the countryside is totally unrecognizable after the rains, the landscape is green and many unusual flowering plants can be enjoyed. Hiking should not be attempted during the hot summer months, in fact the **Fish River Canyon trail** is **closed** between Oct and Apr, because of temperatures in excess of 45°C.

What to wear

Namibian fashions are basically exactly the same as Europe and the US. Day wear tends to be casual and most people on holiday wear shorts, sandals and a T-shirt. If you intend to do any game viewing clothes in green, muted browns and khaki colours are best. Most restaurants have dress codes where trainers, sandals, jeans and shorts are not appreciated. People are expected to sport more formal clothes in restaurants and bars. Long trousers, shirts and a good pair of leather shoes will do.

The weather in winter can get very cold at night especially if you are camping, and a fleece jacket or a thick sweater are essential. Sunstroke and sunburn can be a serious problem and a sun hat, long sleeved cotton shirts and sunglasses are vital for protection from the sun. It is a good idea to bring two basic sets of clothes, one set for formal evening wear and one set of sturdy outdoor action clothes made from light cottons.

Footwear should be as airy as possible for the hot weather, sandals or canvas trainers are ideal. European style leather walking boots can be too heavy for most walks except for the Fish River Canyon or the Waterberg Plateau. If you intend to hike for several days a good pair of comfortable boots are essential. Lightweight goretex boots are so popular that many travellers seem to wear them every day. In Windhoek and Swakopmund you can buy a good range of local hand made leather (kudu hide) desert boots. These are very good for local conditions but remember that they will need time to break in.

HEALTH

For your own peace of mind and so as not to encounter any delays, travel with medical insurance. Medical care is expensive in Namibia. There are two privately run hospitals in Windhoek each with fully equipped intensive care units. An important clause to look out for in any policy you take out is whether it will cover you for an emergency airlift. Most road accidents occur in remote regions where there is little traffic, the only way to get to a hospital quickly is by air, even if an individual was in a stable condition. **MedRescue International**, an emergency evacuation and intervention service for the region is on call 24 hrs a day. All forms of transport have ICU facilities. The Namibian company **Aeromed** has links with **Europassistance**, a large medical assistance network. **TourMed**, PO Box 31630, Windhoek, T (061) 235188, is another service, especially designed for tourists, which supplements normal travel medical insurance.

NB A very important consideration for most visitors to Namibia will be the taking of a malaria prophylactic, especially between Oct and Mar during the rainy season. See page 303 for further advice on health matters.

MONEY

There is no black market to speak of, the Namibian dollar is pegged one to one with the South African rand. Outside Namibia the local currency is not convertible, so remember to change any surplus Namibian dollars back into your own currency before your departure. This is a straightforward transaction which can be completed at any bank so long as you have a coupon proving your original purchase of Namibian dollars. There is a bank in the departure lounge of the international airport. The commissions charged vary slightly from bank to bank, averaging 1% for TCs with a minimum charge.

Warning Many of the soldiers fighting in Angola were paid off in US dollars. There has been a problem with forged US$100 notes for some time, do **not** accept any US currency, especially in the N, close to the Angola border. All the banks have equipment to detect forged notes. These machines were supplied by the US treasury to try and combat a worldwide problem.

ATMs

As long as you have the right type of card and sufficient funds, using an ATM (Automatic Teller Machine) is the most convenient and cheapest way of obtaining funds, assuming your own bank does not charge an excessive fee for foreign ATM transactions.

NB Currently the card system in Namibia does not handle Plus or Cirrus.

The ATMs have been installed in most banks, and are available 24 hrs a day. You can also use your credit card if you have applied for a PIN. Visa, Mastercard/Eurocard, American Express, Diners Club are all accepted. Occasionally the international computer links go down. The amount you can withdraw seems to vary between systems and cards, but you should be able to take out up to N$1,000 on each occasion; assuming the ATM is not faulty you can request a receipt with full details of the transaction.

Banks

The following high street banks offer foreign exchange services: **Bank Windhoek, First National, Nedbank, Standard**. Normal banking hours: Mon-Fri, 0900-1530; Sat, 0830/0900 to 1030/1100. Some small branches may close for an hour over lunch.

Exchange rates: April 1997	
Currency	**Namibian Dollar (N$)**
US $1	4.55
UK £1	7.83
DM 1	2.63
Dutch Guilder 1	2.33
Swiss Franc 1	3.09
French Franc 1	7.87
Aus $1	3.53
Yen 100	3.51
South Africa Rand 1	1
Botswana Pula 1	1.13
Malawi Kwatcha 10	1.87
Zimbabwe $10	4.00

Credit cards

Taking a credit card to Namibia is a sensible option, not only is it a convenient way to cover major expenses but they offer some of the most competitive exchange rates when withdrawing cash from an ATM, since the rate is based upon the wholesale rate set by major banks. The only drawback in Namibia is that all the authorizations have to be telephoned through to Pretoria in South Africa: at times this may mean a wait of 10-15 mins.

They are particularly useful when booking accommodation such as guest-farms, which by nature tend to be in isolated areas and when hiring a car. Some companies will only hire a car to foreign visitors if they have a credit card. If you fill out an open credit slip you will not be faced with the inconvenience of a large cash deposit of several thousand Namibian dollars. **NB** Credit cards are **not** accepted at petrol stations.

Credit card agencies: American Express, T (061) 249037, F (061) 224417; **Diners Club**, T (061) 2942143/4, F (061) 2942199; **Master Card**, contact the **Standard Bank of Namibia**, Head Office, Independence Ave, PO Box 3327, Windhoek, T (061) 2949111, F (061) 2942369; **Visa Card**, contact the **First National Bank of Namibia**, T (061) 229616, F (061) 223558, 24-hr service

T (011) 8339511, this is a Johannesburg number.

Currency

On 15 September 1993 Namibia issued its own set of bank notes, prior to this the South African Rand had been legal tender. At first only three notes were issued: N$10, N$50 and N$100. In Dec 1996 a N$20 note and N$200 note were introduced to complete the series of bank notes. The famous Nama chief, Hendrik Witbooi, features on all the notes. There are few forged Namibian notes in circulation.

Notes: N$10, N$20, N$50, N$100 and N$200. **Coins**: 5c, 10c, 50c, N$1 and N$5. Just to confuse matters the Rand is still legal tender, although you will see very few notes in circulation these days. Most have been withdrawn but your coin change can be a confusing mix of old and new Rand coins along with new Namibian cents.

Travellers' cheques

One advantage of TCs is that if you lose them there is a relatively efficient system of replacement which should not cost the customer anything. For this reason make sure you keep a full record of their numbers and value. The only drawback with this service is where you will have to go to collect replacement cheques. The chances are that only the banks in Windhoek will be able to issue replacement cheques.

The major disadvantage of TCs is the time it takes to cash them and the commission charged by the bank. Different branches of the same bank will alter commission depending on their distance from major banking centres. Small rural banks that exchange relatively few TCs will charge a higher commission than busy central banks. Bank charges range between 0.2% and 0.5% commission. The most widely recognized cheques are American Express, Citicorp, Thomas Cook and Visa. US$ and Sterling TCs can be exchanged at banks throughout the country. Eurocheques can be cashed at banks.

Wiring money

Western Union have a network of offices to which money can be transferred. Fees range between 4%-10% depending on the amount involved. Check with your bank before you depart, especially if you plan on being away for a long period, you may be able to leave specific instructions concerning your bank accounts. To transfer money to someone in Namibia, pay cash and give the receiver's passport number. The receiver will be able to collect from the international division in the Namibian bank 3 working days later.

GETTING THERE

AIR

International flights from Europe arrive at **Windhoek International Airport**. If you are already in the southern Africa region it is possible to fly into a small town on one of Air Namibia's regional flights before visiting Windhoek. For example there is a flight 3 times a week between Victoria Falls in Zimbabwe and Mpacha in the Caprivi Strip; or you could fly on the Cape Town to Windhoek flight but get out in either Lüderitz or Swakopmund before reaching the capital. The majority of charter, private and Air Namibia internal services fly from **Windhoek – Eros Airport**.

From Europe

Air Namibia and Lufthansa are the only scheduled airlines flying direct into Windhoek; they fly from London Heathrow and Frankfurt. There are charter flights from Germany, the most well known is **LTU** who fly between Düsseldorf/Münich and Windhoek / Johannesburg. Münich, T (089) 97591916;

Düsseldorf, T (0211) 941029; Windhoek, T (061) 238205, 141 Stuebel St. For residents of other European countries you would be best advised to look into flights to South Africa (Cape Town or Johannesburg), and then a connecting flight to Windhoek.

From North America

South African Airways and American Airlines run direct flights from New York to Johannesburg. South African Airways also fly direct from Miami to Cape Town. Once in South Africa there are regular connections between Johannesburg or Cape Town with Windhoek. For direct flights into Windhoek it will be necessary to fly to London Heathrow or Frankfurt airport in Germany. Discussions are underway for a direct flight between Namibia and the United States which may start operating before the end of 1997.

From Australia and New Zealand

Unless your travel agent can offer a particularly good deal, the best way to get to Namibia is to organize a flight to Johannesburg or Cape Town in South Africa and then make your own arrangements for an onward flight with South African Airways to Windhoek. A return ticket between Johannesburg and Windhoek should cost about US$400, and US$430 between Cape Town and Windhoek.

Quantas run flights from Auckland and Sydney to Johannesburg. MAS offer the cheapest flights to Johannesburg and Cape Town departing from Melbourne and Sydney, however they do involve a stopover in Kuala Lumpur. South African Airways (SAA) fly from Sydney via Perth to Johannesburg on Mon and Thur; from Johannesburg there are connecting (SAA) flights to Windhoek every day of the week except for Sat.

Intercape, one of the major South African coach companies runs a service linking Windhoek with Cape Town and Johannesburg (via Upington), but this journey is not much of a saving when you consider the time it takes and the transfer time from airport to bus station. If you want to spend a few days in Cape Town before entering Namibia then the coach journey up the West Coast is to be recommended, although it is a long day. The service runs 4 times a week in either direction and the journey takes 17 hrs.

From Southern Africa countries

South African Airways fly 9 times a week between Windhoek and Johannesburg and 3 times a week from Cape Town. Air Namibia operate 11 flights a week between Cape Town and Windhoek, as well as 10 flights to Johannesburg each week. There are also flights to Lusaka (Tues), Harare (Tues), Victoria Falls (Mon, Tues, Wed and Sun) and Maun (Tues and Wed). All of these are comparatively expensive routes, however South African Airways and Air Namibia offer a regional discount fare scheme for non-residents. With the Air Namibia 'Travel Pass' there are considerable savings to be made on flights between Namibia and Lusaka, Livingstone, Victoria Falls, Harare, Maun, Johannesburg and Cape Town (for details see Getting Around section below).

ROAD

From Angola

The principal road crossing is between **Oshikangi** and **Santa Clara**. See table below for border open times. It is possible to cross this border on a day trip, however we would strongly advise against travelling further into Angola at present.

From Botswana

The main border crossings between Botswana and Namibia are at **Buitepost** and **Ngoma Bridge**. Both of these border posts are in remote country, if you are crossing from Namibia into Botswana you will be faced with a lengthy journey on unsurfaced roads before

Border open times

Oranjemund-Alexander Bay	0600-2200
Noordoewer-Springbok	24 hrs
Velloorsdrif	0600-2200
Ariamsvlei	24 hrs
Gansvlei Suid	0600-1700
Hohlweg	0600-2200
Klein Menasse	0700-2100
Buitepos	0700-1700
Imapalili Island	0700-1700
Ngoma Bridge	0600-1900
Vanella	0600-1900
Mohembo	0600-1900
Rundu-Calais	0700-1700
Oshikango	0600-1900
Ruacana-Koaleck	0600-2200
Walvis Bay Harbour	24 hrs

reaching any settlement of note. Although each of these routes can be negotiated in a saloon car it is more sensible to use a 4WD vehicle along these roads.

From South Africa
The three main border posts between Namibia and South Africa are at **Rietfontein**, **Ariamsvlei**, and **Vioolsdrift**, each is open 24 hrs.

From Zambia
There is one common border post, Vanella, which involves a ferry across the Zambezi. However the road on the Zambian side of the border is notoriously bad; travellers wishing to travel between the two countries would be best advised to cross from Zambia to Zimbabwe at Victoria Falls and then cross into Botswana before entering Namibia via Ngoma Bridge.

CUSTOMS

Duty free shopping
There is a small shop at the international airport, but the choice is fairly limited. Since the only direct long distance international flights are from London and Frankfurt most visitors will have the chance to buy duty free goods before

leaving the UK or Germany.

Bona fide tourists to Namibia are exempt from paying sales duty or excise duty on luxury items such as jewellery or Swakara fur garments. The General Sales Tax (GST) is 8% on goods.

Export restrictions
CITES The CITES Convention was established to prevent trade in endangered species, attempts to smuggle controlled products in to countries which are signatories to the convention can result in confiscation, fines and even imprisonment. International trade in elephant ivory, sea turtle products and the skins of wild cats, such as the leopard is illegal. Restrictions have been imposed on the trade in reptile skins, coral, and certain plants and wild birds. Special import and export permits are available for some products but it is best to check before you buy. The animal products that tourists are most likely to encounter in Namibia are ivory, biltong made from protected species such as elephant and the African antelopes and wallets, shoes, and handbags made from kudu, crocodile or snake skins. Many of these products will be freely available for the domestic market, you would not be breaking any laws if you were to buy such an item as a gift for a local resident or someone in South Africa, but your conscience is your own issue.

ON ARRIVAL

Hours of business
Banks: Mon-Fri, 0900-1530; Sat, 0830/0900 to 1030/1100.

Businesses: Mon-Fri, 0800-1730; Sat, 0800-1300.

Government offices: Mon-Fri, 0830-1630. Most shut for lunch between 1300-1400.

Post Offices: weekdays 0830-1600; Sat, 0800-1200.

Shops and Supermarkets: Mon-Fri, 0800-1800; Sat, 0800-1300; Sun, 0900-1300.

Official time

Winter Time: GMT + 1 hr (6 Apr-7 Sep); Summer Time: GMT + 2 hrs (7 Sep-5 Apr).

SAFETY

Generally speaking Namibia is a safe country in which to travel, although there are of course some exceptions. It is important to stress that although Namibia is close to South Africa, conditions are not the same and there is nothing in Namibia to compare to Johannesburg for example.

Cities As with all larger towns and cities in the world, care should be taken with valuables such as wallets, expensive jewellery etc when walking in the streets. Obvious rules like putting money safely away before leaving the bank and not leaving purses or wallets on tables in outdoor restaurants/cafés apply in Namibia as with anywhere else. There have not been many incidents of tourists being mugged or robbed in the streets of Windhoek or Swakopmund, however the central shopping districts of all towns generally become deserted at night when a lone traveller might be unlucky. Overall, common sense precautions will be sufficient to ensure that your holiday is not spoiled by any unpleasant incidents.

Townships All central and southern Namibian towns have townships, the largest being Khomasdal and Katutura in Windhoek. Whilst by no means out of bounds to tourists, it would not be wise to wander into a township by yourself, as some people may not be inclined to be friendly to strangers. On the other hand, if you know a local or have friends living and working in Namibia who know their way around, a trip to a market or nightclub can be an interesting and rewarding experience. If you do have the chance to spend some time in a township, it will undoubtedly give you a very different picture of the way a very large number of urban Namibians live (see page 80 in Windhoek section.)

Women travelling alone Women, both local and foreign, do travel by themselves or in pairs around Namibia, and generally speaking Namibia is safe enough. However in the past couple of years, there has been an alarming increase in rapes and violence in general against women, albeit mostly confined to the townships. Therefore, women travellers unfamiliar with the area are advised to avoid walking around by themselves at night, although daytime is safe enough. For women hitchhikers see page 20, under hitchhiking.

Shopping

African art and curios are of widely varying quality and can be surprisingly expensive. Sculptures, baskets, ceramics and other souvenirs start as curios sold at roadside stalls but as the quality and craftsmanship improves these products are reclassified as art with prices to match. Animal products made from ivory and reptile skins are on sale in Namibia but if you take them back home you could well fall foul of CITES regulations. There are a number of excellent craft and curio shops in Windhoek, but don't expect any bargains when looking at the quality products.

Tipping

Waiters, hotel porters, stewards, chambermaids and tour guides, according to the service – 10% is an acceptable average. When leaving tips make sure it goes to who you intended, there is no guarantee that any kitty money gets to everyone.

Voltage

250 volts AC at 50 Hz. Most plugs and appliances are 3-point round-pin (one 10 mm and two 8 mm prongs), 15 amp plugs. Hotels usually have two round-pin sockets for razors and hairdryers, adaptors are not so easy to find. Travel with a battery razor as many of the small town hotels will not have a suitable socket.

Weights and measures

Metric system: speed limits are in kilometres per hour; food is weighed in kg and grams; petrol is sold in litres.

WHERE TO STAY

Until a few years ago accommodation in most Namibian towns was a choice between a couple of hotels and the municipal campsite. Visitors with their own transport could also make their own way to isolated Guestfarms and Game Farms. As more visitors arrive in the region local hoteliers have been forced to improve standards. Many of the major hotels have been refurbished recently and a number of new three and four star hotels have opened in the last 3 years. At the other end of the price range there has been a steady growth in cheap accommodation for the backpacker. Many of the regional centres now have some form of backpacker hostel as well as a campsite.

Backpacker hostels

For anyone who has just come from South Africa they will instantly recognize the set up. Many of the managers spent time in Johannesburg and Cape Town gathering information on how best to set up and run such an establishment. Apart from camping these hostels are the cheapest form of accommodation in Namibia. A bed in a dormitory will cost between N$20-30 a night, a double room costs N$80 and a tent in the garden or backyard costs as little as N$15.

The facilities offered at backpackers

hostels vary widely from houses that look like chaotic student squats to clean well run hostels. There are usually cooking facilities for travellers and some hostels offer breakfast and the occasional barbecue. Many hostels are a good source of information for budget safari tours, car hire, local restaurants, entertainment and other hostels throughout southern Africa. There is sometimes a problem leaving valuables at reception as they do not always have safes and your property will simply be stored in a locked cupboard. On the whole security is not a problem, especially when compared to the problems faced in South Africa.

Bed and breakfast

Outside Windhoek the notion of a B&B has not yet really caught on in a big way, although some guesthouses could be classified as B&B. There are a number in Windhoek (see page 93) which offer reasonably priced comfortable accommodation, particularly suitable for budget travellers. Some of these place will provide a full cooked breakfast, whilst others will have small kitchens where you can make your own. As with all B&Bs you will be staying in someone's home, which can be a good way to meet local people and gain some insight into people's everyday lives.

Camping and caravan parks

For the visitor on a limited budget, but who wishes to see as much of the country as possible, staying in campsites and using the money saved towards a hired car can lead to a most enjoyable holiday. Camping is not a neglected end of the market, a sizeable number of domestic tourists will spend their annual family holidays in caravans or large tents. In the most popular Game Reserves and National Parks even the sites for a tent or a caravan can be booked up to a year in advance, so if you are in Namibia during the school holidays (see page 295 for school holiday dates) don't always assume there will be space at a campsite.

Since many people camp every year the facilities at most sites are excellent. Even the most basic site will have a clean washblock with electric points and lighting along with plenty of hot water. For a small extra fee you can have access to electricity with your site. This is meant for caravans, but the points are suitable for most electric appliances, you may need to buy a special adaptor from the camp shop.

Camping equipment is available to buy in Windhoek and Swakopmund, some items are rather dated and can seem heavy and cumbersome when compared to the latest hi-tech products from the USA and Europe. We would recommend you bring at least your own light-weight tent and sleeping bags. A bit of advance reading about the areas you plan to visit will help in deciding what further items to bring. The cooking side of camping is the most awkward for the overseas visitor. Many sites do have a kitchen block so your only major concern is keeping food fresh. For this reason we would recommend buying a cool box or 'eskie' for your trip and try to sell it on to a fellow traveller when you leave. The major car rental companies stock 4WD vehicles fully equipped for camping – if cost is of no concern you can hire a vehicle with a built-in refrigerator, built-in water tank, solar-heated portable shower, roof tents, long-range fuel tanks and all the smaller items necessary for a successful and safe journey into the bush. To save time **do not** leave the hire of a vehicle and camping equipment until you arrive in Namibia, you could easily have to wait for several days at the busiest time of year. If you manage to fix everything in advance you could even collect your car at the airport on your arrival, ready to head off into the desert!

The last point worth mentioning about caravan sites is that many of the municipal sites also have self catering rooms. These vary in quality and facilities, at their most basic they are a single room with just a couple of beds, but you may find chalets with several rooms and fully equipped kitchens.

Costs will vary slightly between camps but in government controlled game parks and resorts you should expect to pay N\$30-40 per tent/caravan site and then N\$5 per adult.

Camping equipment hire: Camping Hire Namibia, PO Box 80029, 12 Louis Raymond St, Windhoek, T (061) 251592, F 252995; **Gav's Camping Hire**, PO Box 80157, 76 Sam Nujoma Drive, Windhoek, T (061) 220604, F 220605; **Le Trip**, PO Box 5408, Wernhil Park, Windhoek, T/F (061) 233499.

Car Hire with camping equipment: **Bush-Veld**, PO Box 80240, 34 Daphne Hasenjäger St, Windhoek, T (061) 251710, F 263320; **Champion 4WD**, PO Box 6221, 165 Diaz St, Windhoek, T (061) 251306, F 251620; **Inshore**, PO Box 1769, Kaiser Wilhelm St, Swakopmund, T (064) 405223, F 405228; **Kalahari**, PO Box 1525, 109 Daan Bekker St, Windhoek, T (061) 252690, F 253083.

Game farms and guestfarms

Until independence when most of the visitors to Namibia originated from South Africa, visiting a working farm or game ranch was largely confined to those who knew the owner in some way or another. There are a number of guestfarms which have been operating for many years, however these are the exception rather than the rule, and the vast majority of guestfarms have sprung up in the few years since independence.

After independence, with the rapid increase in the number of foreign visitors arriving each year, the existing accommodation supply proved insufficient. Some farmers noted the gap in the market and set themselves up in business as guest-farms, offering riding, hiking, good food and relaxation in a bush setting. Inevitably, other farmers and entrepreneurs jumped on the bandwagon, seeing the possibilities of making some easy money from the passing tourist trade. Still others, hard hit by the drought saw the possibility of alleviating their situation with some tourist dollars.

Having said that, there are a number of excellent guest/gamefarms which, although not cheap, offer a superb opportunity to experience the bush first-hand, with guides who know their land and everything that lives on it intimately. Coming from Europe it is easy to be misled by the word farm. In fact most Namibian farms are ranches, vast tracts of land often as large as 10,000 ha used predominantly for livestock farming.

The basic difference between a guest-farm and a game farm is that a guestfarm will usually be a working commercial farm offering visitors the chance to experience this at first hand. There may be hiking or horse-riding trails, there will usually be a swimming pool, and often the opportunity for a tour around the farm. Although most guestfarms will usually have some game such as springbok, gemsbok, warthogs etc. they are not the places to visit for a real wild game experience.

A game farm or ranch on the other hand will have been especially stocked with wild game such as giraffe, zebra, wildebeest, elephants, lions, leopards, cheetah and the many varieties of antelope on which these predators feed. Here the emphasis will be on game viewing drives and possibly guided hikes in the bush to get a first hand view of the animals on foot. A stay at a good game ranch does not come cheap but is well worth the expense for the unique experience it offers to visitors; a few such ranches are *Ovita Game Lodge*, *Epako*

Game Lodge and *Mount Etjo Safari Lodge*.

There are also a small number of hunting farms where licensed trophy hunted is carried out, strictly regulated by the government. Whatever your views about hunting, most Namibians see it as normal and acceptable; the meat is used to make biltong or eaten fresh and hunting is seen as part of the process of wildlife conservation and game management.

Most guestfarms cater for a limited number of visitors and therefore by their very nature offer a personnel service. Generally your hosts will be very friendly, and will be happy to discuss any and everything about Namibia with you; on the other hand it is worth noting that a small number of farms are predominantly German speaking and not really geared for the non-German speaking visitor. If you fall in the latter category you may prefer to avoid such places.

Whilst it has not been possible to visit all guest and game farms in the country, each section of the book has a list of the main farms in that specific area, with recommendations where possible.

Guesthouses

These tend to be a cross between a hotel and a bed and breakfast and are generally found in Windhoek, Swakopmund and the towns of the central and southern regions. Guesthouses generally offer en-suite twin rooms sometimes with phone and TV, there is also usually a small swimming pool for guest to cool off in. A hearty cooked breakfast is usually included in the price which will range from N$100 per person up to as much as N$250 per person.

Guesthouse usually do not have bars or restaurants, although there may be a drinks fridge in your room and it may also be possible to arrange an evening meal. Smaller than your average hotel, guesthouses tend to offer a more per-

Accommodation prices for National Parks and Resorts

Admission fees
General:
Adults N$10; Children (6-16) N$1; Cars N$10

Etosha, Skeleton Coast and Sossusvlei:
Adults N$20; Children (6-16) N$2; Cars N$10

Ais Ais Hot Springs
Luxury Flat (2 bed)	N$200
Flat (4 bed)	N$180
Hut (4 bed)	N$120
Camping	N$ 40

Daan Viljoen
Bungalow (2 bed) (inc breakfast)	N$150
Camping	N$ 40

Etosha National Park:
Okaukuejo
Luxury Bungalow (4 bed)	N$230
Bungalow (4 bed)	N$200
Bungalow (3 bed)	N$170
Bungalow (2 bed)	N$120
De Luxe Room (2 bed)	N$170
Camping	N$ 40

Halali
Bungalow (4 bed)	N$200
De Luxe Room (2 bed)	N$160
Camping	N$ 40

Namutoni
Bungalow (4 bed)	N$200
Flat (4 bed)	N$160
Room (2 bed)	N$100
De Luxe Room (2 bed)	N$170
Camping	N$ 40

Gross Barmen Hot Springs
Bungalow (5 bed)	N$190
Bungalow (2 bed)	N$100
Room (2 bed)	N$ 90
Camping	N$40

Hardap Dam Recreational Resort
Bungalow (5 bed)	N$180
Bungalow (2 bed)	N$ 90
Camping	N$ 40

Hobas & Fish River Canyons
Camping	N$ 40

Lüderitz (Shark Island)
Camping	N$ 40

Kaudom Game Reserve
Hut (4 bed)	N$ 60
Camping	N$ 30

Namib-Naukluft Park:
Sossusvlei/Sesriem
Camping	N$ 40

Naukluft
Camping	N$ 30

Namib desert sites
Camping	N$ 10

Popa Falls Rest Camp
Hut (4 bed)	N$120
Camping	N$ 30

Reho Spa Recreational Resort
Bungalow (6 bed)	N$170
Bungalow (5 bed)	N$130
Bungalow (4 bed)	N$110
Camping	N$ 30

Skeleton Coast Park:
(N of Ugab River – permit holders only)

Terrace Bay
(all inc 3 meals per day)
Single	N$290
Double (pp)	N$195

Torra Bay
Camping	N$ 20

West Coast Recreational Area:
Mile 14 & Jakkalsputz
Camping	N$ 20

Mile 72 & Mile 108
Camping	N$ 10

Von Bach Recreational Resort
Hut (2 bed)	N$ 50
Camping	N$ 30

Waterberg Plateau Park
Bungalow (4 bed)	N$220
Bungalow (3 bed)	N$160
De Luxe Room (2 bed)	N$160
Camping	N$ 40

sonal service which some people enjoy; others prefer the relative anonymity of a hotel where they can come and go unnoticed.

Hotels

Every medium sized town has at least one small hotel, in many cases the hotel will also be the only comfortable bar and restaurant in town. Many of these hotels are family run and have been so since they were built. Under these circumstances the owners are not always that susceptible to any form of criticism about the ways things operate. As more visitors from overseas stay in Namibia so many of the small hotels are improving their facilities and image.

All hotels in Namibia are classified under a star rating of one to four. Whilst one star hotels must offer en-suite bathrooms with a quarter of their rooms, to obtain a four star rating, a hotel must cater for the international traveller demanding a/c, valet service and other such luxuries.

The vast majority of Namibian hotels fall into the two star category, offering basic, clean rooms, a restaurant serving three meals a day and a bar. Prices will generally range from between N$100 to N$200 per person and usually include a full cooked breakfast. For such places it is usually not necessary to book in advance, although during school holidays it is possible that places en-route for Etosha and in Swakopmund will get crowded.

National Parks accommodation

The Ministry of the Environment and Tourism (MET) is responsible for 20 different sites across Namibia, these range from the totally untouched Mamili National Park to the fully developed Gross-Barmen Hot Springs Resort, complete with accommodation, restaurant and conference facilities. Most of the parks and resorts have some form of accommodation which can be booked up to 18 months in advance. The accommo-

dation is a mix of self catering bungalows with 2-6 beds, campsites with full facilities and a few simple camps with overnight huts. Payments must be made in full if the accommodation is to be taken up less than 25 days from the date of the reservation. Visitors from overseas can organize their accommodation by fax and pay in advance by credit card. This is worth considering for Etosha National Park if you are going to be in Namibia close to Christmas.

Some of the accommodation is in need of minor repair but overall they represent excellent value and in most cases the camps have been located in beautiful positions. Full details of the facilities and the actual costs are included under the separate entries for the parks and reserves.

The reservations office is in the fine Kaiserliche Landesvermessung building on the corner of John Meinert and Moltests, more or less opposite the Kudu Statue in Independence Ave. Open for information: Mon-Fri, 0800-1700; for reservations and payments: Mon-Fri, 0800-1500.

FOOD AND DRINK

The braai

One of the first local terms you are likely to learn will be the 'braai', quite simply cooking food by a barbecue. The braai is incredibly popular, every campsite, picnic spot, layby will have at least one permanent grate. Learning how to cook good food on a braai is an art that needs to be mastered quickly and is part of the fun of eating in Namibia.

Drink

The standard shop selling alcohol is known as the '**bottle store**'. NB Open daily, 0900-1800. You cannot buy drink from shops in the evening. At the end of each month you will see queues of Namibians withdrawing their wages from

ATMs and then going straight to the bottle store. Alcohol abuse is a serious problem in the country. Drink driving is also a major problem.

Food
Overall the choice of food can be disappointing, in small towns the only restaurants are likely to be attached to hotels. Vegetarians will find their choice greatly limited, you will be better off catering for yourself. Only Windhoek and Swakopmund have a choice of restaurants.

GETTING AROUND

AIR

Internal flights
Internal flights within Namibia are the quickest way to get around the country. Most destinations are within 2 hrs flying time of each other. **Air Namibia** serves all the regional centres, while private operators and tour companies will fly visitors into remote regions, game parks as well as private guestfarms. All internal flights arrive/depart from **Eros Airport**, which is next to the *Safari Court Hotel* complex. Eros is no more than a 10-min drive from the city centre.

Visitors who flew with Air Namibia from Europe can take advantage of a special coupon scheme for regional flights. You must **book within 7 days** of your arrival within Namibia to take advantage of this scheme known as the Air Namibia **Travel Pass**. If you plan this carefully it can represent a considerable saving as well as being very convenient for getting around the region quickly. The pass works on the basis of coupons which you purchase for each leg of your route up to a maximum of 5. The price for the coupons is fixed no matter what your selected route is. For example 2 flight coupons cost US$146; this could be used for a return flight between Windhoek and Harare or a return flight

between Windhoek and Swakopmund. Clearly it would be cheaper to pay the normal fare for the flight to Swakopmund, but for Harare this represents very good value. The coupons are valid for up to 3 months and you are not permitted to travel any same direction twice.

The following towns are a complete list of **travel pass destinations** (note the towns outside of Namibia): Cape Town, Harare, Johannesburg, Katima Mulilo, Keetmanshoop, Livingstone, Lüderitz, Lusaka, Maun, Mokuti Lodge, Ondangwa, Ongava, Oranjemund, Rundu, Swakopmund, Tsumeb, Walvis Bay, Victoria Falls. **Coupon prices**: 2 coupons, US$146; 3 coupons, US$253; 4 coupons, US$362; 5 coupons, US$471. There is a US$66 surcharge for Victoria Falls in Zimbabwe. Check with the Air Namibia office close to the *Kalahari Sands Hotel* for the latest details and prices of the scheme.

TRAIN
Few tourists use the Namibian railway service because it is so slow and only serves a few centres which are of interest to the overseas visitor. Once you have done one journey by train you are likely to choose a bus for your next journey.

Luxury trains: in an effort to tap into the luxury market that has recently been expanded in neighbouring Zimbabwe and South Africa a new luxury train service between Windhoek and Swakopmund is due to start running in Apr 1997. At the time of writing this service had not yet started to run so we were unable to comment on the quality of this service. The train will be known as the **Desert Express**. It will run 3 times a week in either direction. The train will stop at various places enabling the passengers to transfer to microbuses (carried on the train) and explore areas of the desert.

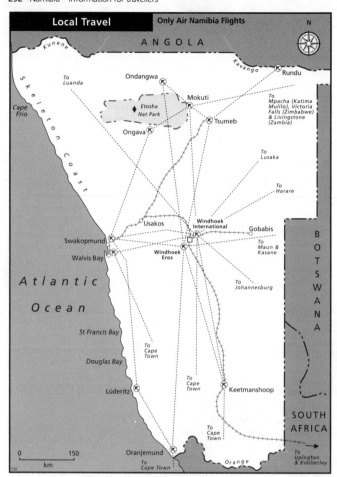

Local Travel   Only Air Namibia Flights

ANGOLA

Kunene

Kavango

Skeleton Coast

Cape Frio

To Luanda

Ondangwa

Mokuti

Rundu

Etosha Nat Park

Tsumeb

Ongava

To Mpacha (Katima Mulilo), Victoria Falls (Zimbabwe) & Livingstone (Zambia)

To Lusaka

To Harare

Usakos

Windhoek International

Gobabis

Swakopmund

Windhoek Eros

To Maun & Kasane

Walvis Bay

Atlantic

Ocean

To Johannesburg

St Francis Bay

Douglas Bay

To Cape Town

Lüderitz

To Cape Town

Keetmanshoop

SOUTH AFRICA

B O T S W A N A

To Cape Town

Oranjemund

To Cape Town

Orange

To Upington & Kimberley

0   150
km

BUS

Intercape, T (021) 3864400, runs luxury buses between Namibia and South Africa. For the budget traveller this service is only of value for the long journey. The coaches are air conditioned, have toilets, some show videos and the crew will serve tea and biscuits.

There are a whole variety of local firms which run coaches on limited routes. These are far less expensive but they do not run to a timetable and the risk of an accident or a breakdown is quite high.

CAR HIRE

Third-party insurance is included in the price of petrol. We would strongly advise all visitors to take out Collision Damage and Loss Waiver.

Driving is on the left side of the road and

speeds range from 60 km/h in town and built up areas to 120 km/h on the main highways. The police are very strict on drink driving and speed traps with on the spot fines are employed. **Automobile Association of Namibia**, T 224201; 24 hr medical hotline, T 4034400. Offices are at the corner of Independence Ave and Peter Muller St.

OTHER LAND TRANSPORT

Hitchhiking

If you choose to hitch it is a good idea to take public transport out of towns and then start hitching once you've passed the townships. Namibia is generally not a place where you could recommend hitchhiking. The major problem facing most travellers is the lack of transport rather than the willingness of Namibians to give lifts or a problem of security. In rural areas where there is no public transport this is the only way to get around.

You may well be asked to contribute for a lift in remote areas where private transport can often end up as a taxi service as well.

COMMUNICATIONS

Language

Although English is the official language, Afrikaans is still the *lingua franca* in the central and southern parts of the country. In the N, the majority of people are Oshiwambo speakers with English as second choice. Afrikaans is spoken in the Kavango with English most common in the Caprivi Strip. Visitors who speak German will find this is one of the few countries in the world where German is widely understood.

Postage

Post Offices are open weekdays 0830-1600, Sat 0800-1200. Internal mail can be very slow – up to 3 weeks. But there

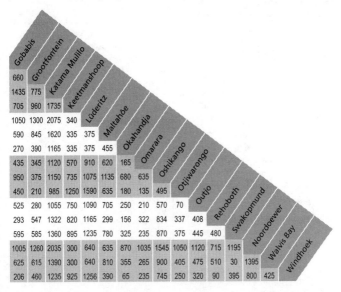

	Gobabis	Grootfontein	Katama Muilo	Keetmanshoop	Lüderitz	Maltahöe	Okahandja	Omarara	Oshikango	Otjiwarongo	Outjo	Rehoboth	Swakopmund	Noordoewer	Walvis Bay	Windhoek
	660															
	1435	775														
	705	960	1735													
	1050	1300	2075	340												
	590	845	1620	335	375											
	270	390	1165	335	375	455										
	435	345	1120	570	910	620	165									
	950	375	1150	735	1075	1135	680	635								
	450	210	985	1250	1590	635	180	135	495							
	525	280	1055	750	1090	705	250	210	570	70						
	293	547	1322	820	1165	299	156	322	834	337	408					
	595	585	1360	895	1235	780	325	235	870	375	445	480				
	1005	1260	2035	300	640	635	870	1035	1545	1050	1120	715	1195			
	625	615	1390	300	640	810	355	265	900	405	475	510	30	1395		
	206	460	1235	925	1256	390	65	235	745	250	320	90	395	800	425	

are efficient overnight parcel services – Fast Lane and DHL. Postcards cost 85 cents. Expect letters to take a minimum of 10 days to get to Europe.

Telephones

Country code: 264. When dialling a number in Namibia from abroad drop the first 0 in the area code.

Namibia has a very efficient service which was installed originally by the South Africans. Be on the lookout for number changes in rural areas as more computerized exchanges are installed (most of the new numbers have 6 digits). Take note that hotels rates are very high, even a short international call can become very expensive.

Telecards are sold for N$10, N$20 and N$50, divided into 20 cent units. They are obtainable at post offices, dealers and teleshops.

Major dialling codes: Windhoek, (061); Swakopmund, (064); Walvis Bay, (0642); Lüderitz, (06331); Keetmanshoop, (0631); Katima Mulilo (0); Tsumeb, (067); Otjiwarongo, (0651); Omaruru, (064). (Local codes in rural areas have been included with the listed telephone number since it is not always obvious which exchange a remote guestfarm or game reserve may be connected to.) Watch out for code changes as the system is being upgraded.

International enquiries: T 1025. IDD is available. International calls are expensive, there is one price band no matter what time of day you make the call.

Local enquiries: T 1023.

Cellular phones: Namibia uses the GSM system for cellular phones and overseas visitors are able to use their cellular phones in the country. Check on arrival with local cellular companies how the billing system will work, you could be in for a shock.

ENTERTAINMENT

Cinema

Only Windhoek and Swakopmund have comfortable cinemas which show International releases and South African films. The main cinema in Windhoek, *Ster-Kinekor* (3 screens), is located in the relatively new Maerua Park complex, the cinema in Swakopmund is called the *Atlanta* (1 screen), Roon St.

Newspapers

Namibian (daily), *Advertiser* (daily), *Observer* (Sat) – are the three main newspapers in English. Also *Tempo* (multilingual) on Sun; *Republikain* (daily Afrikaans); *Mail* and *Guardian* (weekly South African and International news).

Radio

Local FM Radio: Windhoek has two commercial radio stations: Radio 99 and Radio Energy.

Television

The state broadcaster is the **Namibian Broadcasting Corporation (NBC)** which broadcasts in English. The corporation produces 8 radio services and 1 television channel. The South African paying channel, M-Net, is available in most hotels and backpacker hostels. Most subscribers tend to take this service for the films and the sport. Football fans will have no trouble keeping in touch with events back in Europe – there is a weekly summary of Italian, German and Spanish football and an overall look at European football. To top it all you can watch three live Premier League football matches from England each week. It is not surprising to find that Namibian children are well informed on all the results and stories back in Europe. To make room for all the American sports such as basketball and baseball there are 2 dedicated sports channels – Supersports 1 and 2. A digital satellite service has just been introduced, but it will have to take off in South Africa before it can be afforded in Namibia.

HOLIDAYS AND FESTIVALS

Festivals

Apr: *Namibian International Trade Fair*.

Apr/May: *Windhoek Carnival* (last week of Apr and first week of May). *Oktoberfest*.

Oct: *Agricultural and Industrial Show* (first week of Oct).

Nov: *Enjando Street Festival* (a Sat in Nov).

Public holidays – 1997/98

There are 12 public holidays. Cassinga Day and Africa Day fall on a Sun so the next day, Mon, will be a public holiday.

1 Jan:	New Year's Day
21 Mar:	Independence Day
28 Mar:	Good Friday
31 Mar:	Easter Monday
1 May:	Workers' Day
4 May:	Cassinga Day
8 May:	Ascension Day
25 May:	Africa Day
26 Aug:	Heroes' Day
10 Dec:	Human Rights Day
25 Dec:	Christmas Day
26 Dec:	Family Day

School holidays

It may seem trivial as you plan your visit but the dates of local school holidays can have a significant bearing on your visit. During local holidays the price of some accommodation is put up and most of the popular destinations become fully booked. In Swakopmund over Christmas there simply won't be anywhere to stay if you have not made an advance reservation. This also applies to the National Parks accommodation, in particular the 3 camps in Etosha National Park. The dates below are for the School Holidays, 1997, not terms.

Namibian Government Schools: 26 Apr-19 May; 16 Aug-8 Sep; 6 Dec-12 Jan 1998.

Rounding up

ACKNOWLEDGEMENTS

Assimilating all the information necessary for such a book is only possible with the help of many people. We would like to extend a special thanks to the following people and organisations and hope that you will all continue to help and correct us in the future. Vigilance on all sides will help create a better book which in turn will help travellers get the most out of Namibia, and have a holiday to remember.

Roy & Audrey Bradford, Rugat, Spain; Marcus Burrow, London; Mark Easterbrook, Australia; David Elek, Dusseldorf, Germany; Lawrence Santcross, London; the staff of the Sam Cohen Library, Swakopmund; Peter Hothershall, London; Justina Linton, Cirencester; Chris McIntyre, London; Rosemarie & Colin, Bulawayo, Zimbabwe; Jacko, Pretoria, South Africa; Grant & Marie, Lianshulu Lodge, Namibia; and all the staff of the Swakopmund Hotel & Entertainment Centre.

READING

Heywood, Annemarie; *The Cassinga event*, National Archives of Namibia. Detailed investigation into the Cassinga massacre.

Jafta, M; *et al An Investigation of the shooting at the Old Location on 10 December 1959*, Discourse/Msorp. Investigation of forced removals of black population to townships.

Katjavivi, Peter; *A History of Resistance In Namibia*, UNESCO. Concise history of Namibia.

Lau, Brigitte; *Hendrik Witbooi Papers*, National Archives of Namibia. Personal letters and papers of influential 19th century Namibian leader.

Lau, Brigitte; *History and Historiography*, Discourse/Msorp. Four essays on Namibian history.

Lau, Brigitte; *Namibia in Jonker Afrikaner's Time*, Windhoek Archives. Detailed account of central and southern 19th century Namibian history.

Lau, Brigitte; *Trade & Politics in Central Namibia 1860-64* (Charles John Andersson Papers Vol 2), Windhoek Archives. Personal diary of 19th century hunter, trader and explorer.

Lush, David; *Last Steps to Uhuru*. English journalist's personal account of the years immediately preceding Independence.

Amukugo, Elizabeth Magano; *Education & Politics in Namibia*, Gamsberg McMillan. Historical account of development of education in Namibia.

Malan, JS; *Peoples of Namibia*, Rhino Publishers. Concise anthropology of Namibian people.

Martin, Henno; *The Sheltering Desert*, Creda Press. Adventures of German geologists hiding in Namib during Second World War.

Mossolow, Dr N; *Otjikango or Gross Barmen*, John Meinnert. History of first Rhenish Mission Station in Namibia.

Olivier, Willie and Sandra; *A Guide to Namibian Game Parks*, Longman Namibia. Concise guide to Namibian Game Parks.

Pool, Gerhard; *Samuel Maherero*, Gamsberg McMillan. Biography of late 19th and early 20th century Herero leader — covers 1904-1907 Namibia-German war.

Schnieder, Ilme; *Waterberg Plateau Park*, Shell Guide. Detailed guide to history, flora and fauna of Waterberg Plateau Park.

Seely, Mary; *The Namib*, Shell Guide. Detailed natural history of the Namib desert.

Sylvester, Jeremy; *My Heart Tells Me That I Have Done Nothing Wrong*, Discourse/Msorp. The Fall of Owambo King Mandume Ndemufayo.

SHORT WAVE RADIO

If you are not familiar with short wave radio read the notes in the manual about reception; a simple attachment can greatly enhance the quality of your signal. Signal strength varies throughout the day, with lower frequencies generally better at night. For programme listings contact BBC, PO Box 76, Bush House, London.

British Broadcasting Corporation (BBC, London). These bands cover the whole region from Namibia to Moçambique, as well as different times of the day. 90m band: 3255 kHz; 49m band: 6005 kHz, 6190 kHz; 25m band: 11860 kHz, 11940 kHz; 19m band: 15400 kHz; 16m band: 17885 kHz; 13m band: 21470 kHz, 21660 kHz.

Voice of America (VoA). "This is the Voice of America". 25m band: 11920 kHz; 22m band: 13680 kHz; 19m band: 15580 kHz; 16m band: 17895 kHz; 13m band: 21485 kHz.

Useful addresses

Belgium
Avenue de Tavuren 454, B-1150, Brussels, T 7711410, F 7719689.

France
80 Avenue Foch 17, Square de l'Avenue Foch, Paris, T 173265, F 173273.

Germany
Mainzer Strasse 47, Bonn 53179, T 346021, F 346025.

South Africa
Tulbach Park, Eikendal Flat Suite 2, 1234 Church Street, Colbyn, Pretoria 0132, T 3423520, F 3423565.

Sweden
Luntmakargatan 86-88, 11122, PO Box 26042, S 100 31, Stockholm, T 6127788, F 6126655.

United Kingdom
6 Chandos Street, London W1M 0LQ, T (0171) 6366244, F (0171) 6375694.

United States
1605 New Hampshire Avenue, NW, Washington DC 20009, T 9860540, F 9860443.

Zimbabwe
31A Lincoln Road, Avondale, Harare, T 304856, F 304855.

NAMIBIA TOURISM OFFICES

HEAD OFFICE
Namibia Tourism, Private Bag 13346, Windhoek, T (+264 61) 2842366, F (+264 61) 221930.

REGIONAL OFFICES

Gobabis
Kalahari-i, Eastern Tourism Forum, PO Box 33, T (0681) 2551, F 3012.

Keetmanshoop
Southern Tourist Forum (STF), 5th Avenue, T (631) 22095, F (631) 23818.

Lüderitz
Lüderitz Foundation, Bismarck Street.

Omaruru
Namib-i, Main Street, T (064) 570261.

Swakopmund
Namib-i, corner Roon & Kaiser Wilhelm Street, PO Box 1236, T (064) 402224, F 405101.

Tsumeb
Etosha-i, 24 4th Road, PO Box 779, T (067) 220720, F 220916.

Windhoek
7 Post Street Mall (close to the Gibeon Meteorites), T 220640; Continental Building, Independence Avenue, T 2842111.

OVERSEAS OFFICES

Germany
Namibia Verkehrsbüro, Postfach 2041, 61290, BAD HOMBURG; Im Atzelnest 3, 61352 Bad Homburg, T (6172) 406650/4, F (6172) 406690.

South Africa
Main Towing, Standard Bank Centre, Adderley Street, PO Box 739, Cape Town 8000, T (21) 4193190, F (21) 215840;

Shop 258, Level 200, Carlton Shopping Centre, PO Box 11405, Johannesburg 2000, T (11) 3317055/6, F (11) 3312037.

UK
6 Chandos Street, London, WIM OLQ, T (171) 6362924, F (171) 6372969.

SPECIALIST TOUR OPERATORS

EUROPE

Abercrombie & Kent Travel
Sloane Square House, Holbein Place, London, SW1W 8NS, England, T (0171) 7309600, F (0171) 7309376.

Africa Exclusive
Hamilton House, 68 Palmerston Rd, Northampton, NN1 5EX, England, T (01604) 28979, F (01604) 31628.

Bayenthaler Reiseburo
Cologne, Germany, web address: http://www.bayenthaler.de.

Explore Worldwide Ltd
1 Frederick Street, Aldershot, Hants, GU11 1LQ, England, T (01252) 319448, F (01252) 343170.

Footprints
19 Johan Albrecht St, T/F 249190, specializes in eco-tourism activities, rec.

HoGaTourS GmbH Reisebüro
76646 Bruchsal, Germany, T (07251) 55011, F (07251) 55045, e-mail: hgts@ilk.de, web address: http://www.ilk.de/hgts/index.html; specialise in southern Africa, their Namibian offerings are with **Jacana Tours** for general adventure travel and **Pinder Reisen** who organize golf trips to Namibia.

Iwanowski's Individuelles Reisen GmbH
Büchnerstraße 11, 41540 Dormagen, Germany, T (02133) 260300, F (02133) 260333, e-mail: lwanowski@german-business.de, web address: http://www.afrika.de/iwannami.htm; tailor made holidays in Namibia, everything from chauffeur driven safaris, 4WD trips, guestfarms, wilderness trips, 2 weeks in the desert, all types of adventure holidays.

Kumuka Expeditions
40 Earls Court Rd, London, W8 6EJ, England, T (0171) 9378855, F (0171) 9376664; group tours to all major tourist destinations, including neigbouring countries.

Namibia Safaris & Spezialreisen
Schottenstr 75, 78462 Konstanz, Germany, web address: http://home.t-on-line.de/home/namibia.travel.

Southern Africa Travel
7 Buckingham Gate, London, SW1E 6JX, England, T (0171) 6300100, F (0171) 6309900.

Sunvil Discovery
T (0181) 2329777, wed address: http://www.itsnet.co.uk/si/sunvil.htm; your first call should be to this company if you are planning on a self drive tour of Namibia, you will receive useful up-to-date advice and plenty of guidance when planning a route.

Tim Best Travel
68 Old Brompton Road, London, SW7 3LQ, England, T (0171) 5910300, F (0171) 5910301.

Travel Worldwide
Hermelijnlaan 23, B-2900 Schoten, Belgium, T (03) 6583702, F (03) 6850636.

Union-Castle Travel
86/87 Campden Street, London, W8 7EN, England, T (0171) 2291411, F (0171) 2291511.

Windrose Fernreisen GmbH
Neue Grünstraße 28, 10179 Berlin, Germany, T (030) 2017210, F (030) 20172117, wed address: http://www.windrose.de; good deals for organized luxury tours.

World Wide Adventures
Valkyrigaten 15, 0166 Oslo, Norway, T (022) 609920, F (022) 569766.

USA

Himalayan Travel
112 Prospect Street, Stamford, Ct 06901, USA, T (203) 3593711, F (203) 3593669.

CANADA

Travel Cuts
187 College St, Toronto, Ontario M5T 1P7, Canada, T (416) 9798608, F (416) 9798167.

AUSTRALIA & NEW ZEALAND

Jet-Age Marketing
Travel House, 6 Walls Road, Penrose, Auckland, New Zealand, T (09) 5252360, F (09) 5252227.

Top Deck Travel
Wholesale Pty Ltd, 8th floor, 350 Kent Street, Sydney, NSW 2000, Australia, T (02) 2998844, F (02) 2998841.

Glossary

bakkie
 pickup truck.

berg
 a mountain.

boma
 a traditional enclosure for cattle, nowadays frequently used at safari lodges to refer to a sheltered area where guests sit outside.

braai
 South African equivalent of a barbecue.

burg
 a term referring to a borough.

dorp
 a small country settlement

drift
 where a road crosses a dry river bed, or a ford.

kloof
 gorge or a ravine.

koppie
 flat-topped hillock, often used to describe outcrops of granite boulders.

veld
 open grasslands.

vlei
 shallow lake or swamp

Health

WITH the following advice and precautions, you should keep as healthy as you do at home. However, the range of health problems in Namibia is different from that in other sub-Saharan areas of the Continent. This is because much of the country is not tropical, the cities in particular are cleaner and more sophisticated than in other parts of Africa and the standard of medical facilities is much higher. There are under developed areas of course and infectious diseases predominate there in the same way as they did in the West some decades ago. It is quite possible however, for a tourist or business traveller who is only visiting major cities to be no more at risk from infectious disease, etc than at home.

Medical care

Medical facilities in rural areas and in the ex-homelands are frequently not up to a good standard. In rural areas and game parks infectious diseases and insect borne diseases still occur and they are no respecters of persons. Diseases such as River Blindness and Schistosomiasis (Bilharzia) still occur, HIV infection is very much on the increase and Tuberculosis is still widespread.

Medical facilities vary. You will only find a fully equipped hospital in Windhoek. Drugs and medicines are generally of high quality. Remember that the shelf life of vaccines and antibiotics in particular is reduced in hot condidtions.

With the following precautions and advice you should keep as healthy as usual. Make local enquiries about health risks if you are apprehensive and take the general advice of families who have lived in or are living in the area.

BEFORE TRAVELLING

Take out medical insurance including the possibility of medical evacuation by air ambulance to your own country. You should have a dental check up, obtain a spare glasses prescription and, if you suffer from a longstanding condition such as diabetes, high blood pressure, heart/lung disease or a nervous disorder, arrange for a check up with your doctor who can at the same time provide you with a letter explaining details of your disability. Check the current practice for malaria prophylaxis (prevention) for the areas you intend to visit.

For a simple list of 'Health Kit' to take with you, see page 16.

Vaccination and immunization

Smallpox vaccination is no longer required. Neither is cholera vaccination. Namibia requires yellow fever vaccination certificates from travellers who have entered from other, (especially Central and West) African, countries. Even though cholera vaccination is not officially required, nor recommended by the WHO because its effectiveness is limited, travellers are occasionally asked to produce vaccination certificates if they have been in cholera endemic areas such as parts of Asia or South America. If you are concerned this may be a problem but do not want to be given an ineffective vaccine, ask your own doctor for a cholera vaccination exemption certificate. The following vaccinations are recommended:

Typhoid (monovalent): one dose followed by a booster in one month's time. Immunity from this course lasts 2-3 years. Other injectable types are now available as are oral preparations marketed in some countries.

Poliomyelitis: this is a live vaccine, generally given orally and the full course consists of three doses with a booster in under-developed regions every 3-5 years.

Tetanus: one dose should be given with a booster in 6 weeks and another at 6 months and 10 yearly boosters thereafter are recommended.

Children should in addition be properly protected against diphtheria, whooping cough, mumps and measles. Teenage girls, if they have not yet had the disease, should be given rubella (german measles) vaccination. Consult your doctor's advice on BCG inoculation against tuberculosis.

Infectious hepatitis (jaundice): this is fairly common in rural areas. It seems to be frequently caught by travellers probably because, coming from countries with higher standards of hygiene, they have not contracted the disease in childhood and are therefore not immune like the majority of adults in developing countries. The main symptoms are stomach pains, lack of appetite, nausea, lassitude and yellowness of the eyes and skin. Medically speaking, there are two main types: the less serious but more common is *hepatitis A* for which the best protection is careful preparation of food, the avoidance of contaminated drinking water and scrupulous attention to toilet hygiene. Human normal immunoglobulin (gamma globulin) confers considerable protection against the disease and is particularly useful in epidemics. It should be obtained from a reputable source and is certainly recommended for travellers who intend to live rough. The injection should be given as close as possible to your departure and, as the dose depends on the likely time you are to spend in potentially infective areas, the manufacturer's instructions should be followed. Vaccination against hepatitis A is now generally available and provides good immunity for many years but is expensive.

The other more serious version is *hepatitis B* which is acquired as a sexually transmitted disease, from a blood transfusion or injection with an unclean needle or possibly by insect bites. The symptoms are the same as hepatitis A but the incubation period is much longer, (up to 6 months) and there are more likely to be complications.

You may have had jaundice before or you may have had hepatitis of either type before without becoming jaundiced in which case it is possible that you could be immune to either hepatitis A or B already. Immunity can be tested before you travel with a blood test. If you are not immune to hepatitis B already, a vaccine is available (3 shots over 6 months) and if you are not immune to hepatitis A already then you should consider vaccination (or gamma globulin if you are not going to be exposed for long).

There are other kinds of viral hepatitis (C, E etc) which are fairly similar to A and B but no vaccinations are available as yet.

AIDS

In Namibia it is mainly spread by heterosexual intercourse. Men and women are about equally affected. Some transmission occurs through infected blood transfusions. Screening for the HIV virus in blood for transfusion is performed or should be in all hospitals. The main risk to travellers is from casual sex, heterosexual or homosexual. The same precautions should be taken as when encountering any sexually transmitted disease. Female prostitution is common in Namibia and an alarmingly high proportion of the prostitute population is HIV positive. There may in addition be transmission, especially in the big cities and holiday areas, via intravenous drug abuse. The AIDS virus (HIV) can be passed via unsterile needles which have been previously used to inject an HIV positive patient but the risk of this is very small indeed. It would however be sensible to check that needles have been properly sterilized or disposable needles used. Hepatitis B is a much greater risk. Be wary of carrying disposable needles as Customs officials may find them suspicious, not so much in Africa but in Europe and North America.

Catching the AIDS virus (HIV) does not necessarily produce an illness in itself (although it may do). The only way to be sure if you feel you have been put at risk is to have a blood test for HIV antibodies on your return to a place where there are reliable laboratory facilities. The test does not become positive for many weeks and during those weeks the person who has caught the virus is likely to be extremely infectious.

MALARIA

Malaria occurs in Northeast Namibia with the highest risk area being along the Caprivi Strip. There is a much lower risk around Etosha National Park but the risk is still there. It increases markedly after heavy rains. Malaria remains a serious disease and you are advised to protect yourself against mosquito bites as described above and to take prophylactic (preventive) drugs where and when there is a risk. Start taking the tablets a few days before exposure and continue to take them 6 weeks after leaving the malarial zone. Remember to give the drugs to babies and children and pregnant women also.

There are various different kinds of malaria of which the most important is that due to plasmodium falciparum – important because it is fatal if treatment is delayed. Even the other kinds of malaria, though not usually fatal, cause serious disease.

The subject of malaria prevention is becoming more complex as the malaria parasite becomes immune to some of the more well known prophylactic drugs. This immunity on the part of the falciparum malaria parasite is commonly termed Chloroquine resistance and the phenomenon is now widespread.

No presently used regime of malaria prophylaxis is one hundred percent effective – it is still possible to catch malaria when on prophylactic drugs but you will not catch it if you are not bitten by malaria carrying mosquitoes. These usually only bite in the evening and early morning so you should redouble your precautions at these times. Taking prophylactic drugs will reduce your chances of contracting malaria if you are exposed and may make the disease less serious. There is great controversy in the medical world at the present time as to the best drugs to use for prevention. European and North American opinions often vary and frequently clash with local African opinion. Be prepared for this. Seek expert advice before you travel and stick to it religiously. No drug regime, however complicated, will work if you do not take the tablets as prescribed. Two commonly used regimes are to take either Chloroquine plus Paludrine or to take Mefloquine which may be more effective and suitable for short journeys but has side effects and is not recommended if you are likely to be pregnant.

If you do develop symptoms of malaria (high fever, shivering, severe headache, sometimes diarrhoea) seek medical advice immediately. If this is not available, then self treatment of Chloroquine resistant malaria can be tricky. Halofantrin is the drug most easily carried and self administered but serious side effects can occur and it must be taken with advice from a knowledgeable doctor in the right dosage.

COMMON PROBLEMS

HEAT AND COLD

Full acclimatization to high temperatures takes about 2 weeks and during this period it is normal to feel a degree of apathy, especially if the relative humidity is high. Drink plenty of water (up to 15 litres a day are required when working physically hard in hot, dry conditions), use salt on your food and avoid extreme exertion. Tepid showers are more cooling than hot or cold ones. Large hats do not cool you down but do prevent sunburn. Remember that, especially in the mountains, there can be a large and sudden drop in temperature between sun and shade and between night and day so dress accordingly. Clear desert nights can prove astoundingly cold with a rapid drop in temperature as the sun goes down. Loose fitting cotton clothes are still the best for hot weather, warm jackets and woollens are essential after dark in some desert areas, and especially at high altitude.

INTESTINAL UPSETS

Most of the time intestinal upsets are due to the insanitary preparation of food. Do not eat uncooked fish or vegetables or meat (especially pork), fruit with the skin on (always peel your fruit yourself) or food that is exposed to flies. Tap water is generally held to be safe throughout Namibia. Filtered or bottled water is generally available. Really dirty stream water should first be strained through a filter bag (available through camping shops) and then boiled or treated. Bringing the water to a rolling boil at sea level is sufficient but at high altitudes you have to boil the water for longer to ensure that all the microbes are killed. Various sterilizing methods can be used and there are preparatory preparations available containing chlorine or iodine compounds. Alternatively you can use one of the portable anti-microbial water filters or pump action sterilizers.

Pasteurized or heat treated milk is widely available as is ice cream or yoghurt produced by the same methods. Unpasteurized milk products, including cheese, are sources of tuberculosis, brucellosis, listeria and food poisoning germs.

Diarrhoea

Diarrhoea is usually caused by eating food which is contaminated by food poisoning germs. Drinking water is rarely the culprit. Seawater or river water is more likely to be contaminated by sewage and so swimming in such dilute effluent can also be a cause. Infection with various organisms diarrhoea can be due to viruses, bacteria (e.g. Escherichia coli, probably the most common cause), protozoa (amoeba), salmonella and cholera. The diarrhoea may come on suddenly or rather slowly. It may or may not be accompanied by vomiting or by severe abdominal pain and the passage of blood or mucus when it is called dysentery. How do you know which type you have and how to treat it?

If you can time the onset of the diarrhoea to the minute (acute) then it is probably due to a virus or a bacterium and/or the onset of dysentery. The treatment, in addition to rehydration, is Ciprofloxacin 500 mgs every 12 hrs. The drug is now widely available as are various similar ones.

If the diarrhoea comes on slowly or intermittently (sub-acute) then it is more likely to be protozoal i.e. caused by an amoeba or giardia and antibiotics will have little effect. These cases are best treated by a doctor as is any outbreak of diarrhoea continuing for more than 3 days. Sometimes blood is passed in sub-acute amoebic dysentery and for this you should certainly seek medical help. If this is not available then the best treatment is probably Tinidazole (Fasigyn) 1 tablet 4 times a day for 3 days. If there are severe stomach cramps, the following drugs may help but are not very useful in the management of acute diarrhoea: Loperamide (Imodium, Arret) and Diphenoxylate with Atropine (Lomotil).

Any kind of diarrhoea whether or not accompanied by vomiting responds well to the replacement of water and salts taken as frequent small sips of some kind of rehydration solution. There are proprietary preparations consisting of sachets of powder which you dissolve in boiled water or you can make your own by adding half a teaspoonful of salt (3.5 grams) and 4 tablespoonfuls of sugar (40 grams) to a litre of boiled water.

Thus the lynchpins of treatment for diarrhoea are rest, fluid and salt replacement, antibiotics such as Ciprofloxacin for the bacterial types and special diagnostic tests and medical treatment for the amoeba and giardia infections. Salmonella infections and cholera can be devastating diseases and it would be wise to get to a hospital as soon as possible if these were suspected. Fasting, peculiar diets and the consumption of large quantities of yoghurt have not been found useful in calming travellers diarrhoea or in rehabilitating inflamed

bowels. Oral rehydration has on the other hand, especially in children, been a lifesaving technique and it should always be practised whatever other treatment you use. As there is some evidence that alcohol and milk might prolong diarrhoea they should probably be avoided during and immediately after an attack. Diarrhoea occurring day after day for long periods of time (chronic diarrhoea) is notoriously resistant to amateur attempts at treatment and again warrants proper diagnostic tests. There are ways of preventing travellers diarrhoea for short periods of time by taking antibiotics but this is not a foolproof technique and should not be used other than in exceptional circumstances. Doxycycline is possibly the best drug. Some preventatives such as Enterovioform can have serious side effects if taken for long periods.

INSECTS

These can be a great nuisance. Some, of course, are carriers of serious disease – not just malaria but dengue, river blindness (onchocerciasis), leishmaniasis (Kala-azar) and sleeping sickness. The best way of keeping insects away at night is to sleep off the ground under a mosquito net and to burn mosquito coils containing Pyrethrum. Aerosol sprays or a 'flit' gun may be effective but best of all are insecticidal tablets which are heated on a small mat which is plugged into the wall socket (if taking your own check the voltage of the area you are visiting so that you can take an appliance that will work). Similarly check that your electrical adaptor is suitable for the insecticide bearing plug.

You can use personal insect repellent, the best of which contain high concentrations of Diethyltoluamide. Liquid may be best for arms and face (take care around eyes and make sure you do not dissolve the plastic of your spectacles, watch strap etc.). Aerosol spray on clothes, ankles and hair deters mites and ticks as well as flying insects. Liquid DET suspended in water can be used to impregnate cotton clothes and mosquito nets. Wide mesh mosquito nets are now available impregnated with an insecticide called Permethrin and are generally more effective, lighter to carry and comfortable to sleep in than the traditional variety. Permethrin is now being incorporated into some repellent sprays. If you are badly affected by insect bites try cool baths or showers and anti-histamine tablets (take care with alcohol or driving). Local anaesthetics and anti-histamine creams do not have a very good reputation. Weak corticosteroid creams may help but do not use if there is any hint of sepsis. You may find that careful scratching of all your bites in a controlled fashion once a day may help. Calamine lotion and cream have limited effectiveness.

Bites which become infected (commonly in dirty and dusty places) should be treated with a local antiseptic or antibiotic cream such as Cetrimide as should infected scratches. Skin infestations with body lice, crabs and scabies are unfortunately easy to pick up. Use Gamma benzene hexachloride for lice and Benzyl benzoate for scabies. Crotamiton cream (Eurax) alleviates itching and also kills a number of skin parasites. Malathion lotion 5% is good for lice but avoid the highly toxic full strength Malathion used as an agricultural insecticide. In grassland areas where animals graze, ticks are common and if you walk in such areas, get somebody else to examine your legs and body for these small spider-like insects after you have finished walking. Ticks can be removed with tweezers or by pinching them out carefully with fingers, doing it gently so that the head end disengages and is extracted with the body.

In some parts of Africa the jigger flea commonly burrows its way into people's feet causing a painful itchy swelling which finally bursts in a rather disgusting fashion. Avoid these by not going barefoot or wearing sandals and if they do become established have someone ex-perienced winkle them out with a sterile needle.

SUNBURN AND HEAT STROKE

The burning power of the sun in Namibia is phenomenal especially at altitude. Always wear a wide brimmed hat and use some form of suncream or lotion on un-tanned skin. Normal temperate zone suntan lotions (protection factor up to 7) are not much good. You need to use the types designed specifically for the tropics or for mountaineers or skiers with a protection factor (against UVA) between 7 and 15. Certain creams also protect against UVB and you should use these if you have a skin prone to burning. Glare from the sun can cause conjunctivitis so wear sunglasses, especially on beaches or on snow.

There are several varieties of heat stroke. The most common cause is severe dehydration. Avoid this by drinking lots of non alcoholic fluid, adding some salt.

SNAKE BITE AND OTHER BITES AND STINGS

If you are unlucky enough to be bitten by a venomous snake, spider, scorpion, lizard, centipede or sea creature, try (within limits) to identify the animal. In general the reactions to be expected are fright, swelling, pain and bruising around the bite, soreness of the regional lymph glands, nausea, vomiting and fever. If in addition any of the following symptoms supervene, get the victim to a doctor without delay: numbness, tingling of the face, muscular spasms, convulsions, shortness of breath or haemorrhage.

Commercial snake bite or scorpion sting kits may be available but are only useful for the specific type of snake or scorpion for which they are designed. The serum has to be given intravenously so is not much good unless you have had some practice in making injections into veins. If the bite is on a limb immobilize it and apply a tight bandage between the bite and body releasing it for 90 secs every 15 mins. Reassurance of the bitten person is very important because death by snake bite (or any other kind of bite) is in fact very rare. Do not slash the bite area and try and suck out the poison because this kind of heroism does more harm than good. Hospitals usually hold stocks of snake bite serum appropriate to the local area. Do not walk in snake territory with bare feet, sandals or shorts and if you are confronted by a snake, keep still until it slithers away.

If swimming in an area where there are poisonous fish such as stone or scorpion fish (also called by a variety of local names) or sea urchins on rocky coasts, use footwear. The sting of such fish is intensely painful and this can be helped by immersing the stung part in water as hot as you can bear for as long as it remains painful. This is not always very practical and you must take care not to scald yourself but it does work. Avoid spiders and scorpions by keeping your bed away from the wall and look under lavoratory seats and inside your shoes in the morning.

WATCH OUT FOR

Remember that **rabies** is endemic throughout Africa. If you are bitten by a domestic or wild animal, don't leave things to chance. Scrub the wound with soap and water and/or disinfactant, try to have the animal captured (within limits) or at least determine its ownership where possible and seek medical assistance at once. The course of treatment depends on whether you have already been satisfactorily vaccinated against rabies. If you have (and this is worthwhile if you are spending lengths of time in developing countries) then some further doses of vaccine are all that is required. Human diploid cell vaccine is the best, but expensive: other, older kinds of vaccine such as that derived from duck embryos may be the only types available. These are effective, much cheaper and interchangeable generally with the human derived types.

If not already vaccinated then anti-rabies serum (immunoglobulin) may be required in addition. It is wise to finish the course of treatment whether the animal survives or not.

Dengue Fever is a growing problem in Namibia is transmitted by the bite of mosquitoes and causes a severe headache, fever and body pains. There is no treatment. You must just avoid mosquito bites.

Intestinal worms are difficult to avoid but on the whole fairly easy to treat and usually you can leave this until you come home. The more serious ones such as hook-worm can be contracted by walking bare foot on earth or beaches.

Filariasis causing such diseases as elephantiasis occurs in Namibia. It is also transmitted by mosquitoes.

Leishmaniasis causing a skin ulcer which will not heal occurs in Namibia. It is transmitted by sand flies.

Schistosomiasis (Bilharzia) is a parasite harboured by snails which live in fresh water lakes. The parasites enter through the skin and are responsible for serious, ongoing disease in the gastrointestinal tract or bladder. Do not swim in freshwater lakes which are known to harbour the disease.

Trypanosomiasis (sleeping sickness). This disease, essentially a brain infection causing drowsiness, is transmitted by a large, tenacious insect – the tsetse fly. This is a fly not always repelled by DET but very susceptible to Pyrethroid fly spray and Permethrin. The main risk is in game parks where these rather aggressive flies are common.

Prickly heat is a common itchy rash which can be avoided by frequent washing of clothes and body and by wearing non restrictive clothing. The regular use of talcum powder also helps. A bad attack of prickly heat can be most distressing. The best treatment is probably a couple of nights in an air conditioned hotel.

Athlete's foot and other fungal infections of the skin, especially the groin area, are best treated by exposure to sunshine and fresh air and the use of a preparatory preparation such as Tolnaftate. Regular dusting of the feet, armpits and groin is worthwhile.

WHEN YOU RETURN HOME

Remember to take your anti-malarial tablets for 6 weeks. If you have had attacks of diarrhoea, it is worth having a stool specimen tested in case you have picked up amoebic dysentery. If you have been living rough, a blood test may be worthwhile to detect worms and other parasites. If you have been exposed to bilharzia by swimming in rivers. check by means of a blood test when you get home but leave it for 6 weeks because the test is slow to become positive. Report any untoward symptoms to your doctor and tell the doctor exactly where you have been and, if you know, what the likelihood of diseases to which you were exposed is.

FURTHER HEALTH INFORMATION

Further information on health risks abroad, vaccinations etc, may be available from a local travel clinic. If you wish to take specific drugs with you such as antibiotics, these are best prescibed by your own doctor. Beware however that not all doctors can be experts on the health problems of tropical countries. More detailed or more up to date information than local doctors can provide are available from various sources.

In the UK there are hospital departments specializing in tropical diseases in London, Liverpool, Birmingham and Glasgow and the Malaria Reference Laboratory at the London School of Hygiene and Tropical Medicine provides free advice about malaria, T 0171 636 7921. In the USA the local public health services can give such information and information is available centrally from the Centres for Disease Control in Atlanta, T (404) 332 4559.

There are in addition computerized databases which can be accessed for specific destination, up to the minute information. In the UK there is MASTA (Medical Advisory Service to Travellers Abroad) T 0171 631 4408, Tx 895 3474, F 0171 436 5389 and Travax (Glasgow, T 0141 946 7120, extension 247).

Further information on medical problems overseas can be obtained from the book by Richard Dawood (Editor) – Travellers Health, How to Stay Healthy Abroad, Oxford University Press, 1992, £7.99. This revised and updated edition is recommended, especially to the intrepid traveller heading for the more out of the way places. General advice is also available in the UK in 'Health Advice for Travellers' published jointly by the Department of Health and the Central Office of Information available free from your UK Travel Agent.

The above information has been compiled by Dr David Snashall, Senior Lecturer in Occupational Health, United Medical Schools of Guy's and St Thomas' Hospitals and Chief Medical Adviser, Foreign and Commonwealth Office, London.

Tinted boxes

Illustrations

Index

Maps

Map Symbols

Administration

International Border

Neighbouring country

Neighbouring province

Capital/Major Towns

Other Towns

Roads and travel

Main Roads

Other Roads

Minor gravel roads

Railways with station

Water features

River   *Orange River*

Seasonal Rivers

Lakes and Dams

Seasonal delta and flood plains

Beaches, sand dunes, dry river bed

Ocean

Waterfall

Ship wreck

Topographical features

Contours (approx),
Rock Outcrops

Mountains

Mountain Pass

Gorge/Canyon

Escarpment

Palm trees

Cities and towns

Built Up Areas

Main through routes
Main streets
Minor Streets
Pedestrianized Streets
One Way Street
Sorts grounds. ornamental gardens

Airport

Banks

Bus Stations (named in key)

Hospitals

Market

Police station

Post Office

Public telephones

Tourist Office

Key Numbers

Bridges

Cathedral, church,
mission station

Guided routes

National parks, trekking areas

National Parks, Game Reserves
and Recreational Areas

Hotel, Guestfarm, Luxury Lodge

Hiking hut and self catering
accommodation

Campsite
Hide

Park Gates

Naltional Park &
Game Reserves
Motorable track

Hiking trail

Other symbols

Archaeological Sites

Places of Interest

Viewing point

Historical Battlefied

000

Footprint Handbooks

All of us at Footprint Handbooks hope you have enjoyed reading and travelling with this Handbook, one of the first published in the new Footprint series. Many of you will be familiar with us as Trade & Travel, a name that has served us well for years. For you and for those who have only just discovered the Handbooks, we thought it would be interesting to chronicle the story of our development from the early 1920's.

It all started 75 years ago in 1921, with the publication of the Anglo-South American Handbook. In 1924 the South American Handbook was created. This has been published each year for the last 73 years and is the longest running guidebook in the English language, immortalised by Graham Greene as "the best travel guide in existence".

One of the key strengths of the South American Handbook over the years, has been the extraordinary contact we have had with our readers through their hundreds of letters to us in Bath. From these letters we learnt that you wanted more Handbooks of the same quality to other parts of the world.

In 1989 my brother Patrick and I set about developing a series modelled on the South American Handbook. Our aim was to create the ultimate practical guidebook series for all travellers, providing expert knowledge of far flung places, explaining culture, places and people in a balanced, lively and clear way. The whole idea hinged, of course, on finding writers who were in tune with our thinking. Serendipity stepped in at exactly the right moment: we were able to bring together a talented group of people who know the countries we cover inside out and whose enthusiasm for travelling in them needed to be communicated.

The series started to grow. We felt that the time was right to look again at the identity that had brought us all this way. After much searching we commissioned London designers Newell & Sorrell to look at all the issues. Their solution was a new identity for the Handbooks representing the books in all their aspects, looking after all the good things already achieved and taking us into the new millennium.

The result is Footprint Handbooks: a new name and mark, simple yet assertive, bold, stylish and instantly recognisable. The images we use conjure up the essence of real travel and communicate the qualities of the Handbooks in a straightforward and evocative way.

For us here in Bath, it has been an exciting exercise working through this dramatic change. Already the 'new us' fits like our favourite travelling clothes and we cannot wait to get more and more Footprint Handbooks onto the book shelves and out onto the road.

The Footprint list

Mail Order

Footprint Handbooks are available worldwide in good bookstores. They can also be ordered directly from us in Bath (see below for address). Please contact us if you have difficulty finding a title.

The Footprint Handbook website will be coming to keep you up to date with all the latest news from us (http://www.footprint-handbooks.co.uk). For the most up-to-date information and to join our mailing list please contact us at:

Footprint Handbooks
6 Riverside Court
Lower Bristol Road
Bath BA2 3DZ, England
T +44(0)1225 469141
F +44(0)1225 469461
E Mail handbooks@footprint.cix.co.uk